Transnational Labour Regulation

A Case Study of Temporary Agency Work

P.I.E. Peter Lang

Bruxelles · Bern · Berlin · Frankfurt am Main · New York · Oxford · Wien

SALTSA

A Joint Programme for Working Life Research in Europe

SALTSA was a programme of partnership in European working life research run by the Swedish Confederations of Trade Unions (LO), Professional Employees (TCO) and Professional Associations (SACO). SALTSA was a cooperation venture of these three confederations and Swedish National Institute for Working Life until the Swedish government closed NIWL in 2006. The SALTSA programme continues in new forms at Uppsala University.

The aim of SALTSA is to generate applicable research results of a high academic standard and relevance. Research is largely project-based.

Chairman of the SALTSA Programme is Professor Lars Magnusson and programme secretary for this project was Torbjörn Strandberg.

Kerstin Ahlberg, Brian Bercusson,
Niklas Bruun, Haris Kountouros,
Christophe Vigneau & Loredana Zappalà

Transnational Labour Regulation

A Case Study of Temporary Agency Work

Arbetslivsinstitutet
LO TCO SACO
SALTSA — JOINT PROGRAMME
FOR WORKING LIFE RESEARCH IN EUROPE
The National Institute for Working Life and The Swedish Trade Unions in Co-operation

"Work & Society"
No. 60

© P.I.E. PETER LANG S.A.
Éditions scientifiques internationales
Brussels, 2008
1 avenue Maurice, 1050 Brussels, Belgium
info@peterlang.com; www.peterlang.com

ISSN 1376-0955
ISBN 978-90-5201-417-3
D/2008/5678/16

Bibliographic information published by "Die Deutsche Bibliothek"
"Die Deutsche Bibliothek" lists this publication in the "Deutsche Nationalbibliografie"; detailed bibliographic data is available on the Internet at <http://dnb.ddb.de>.

CIP available from the British Library, GB and the Library of Congress, USA.

Contents

Part III
Failure or Success? EU Regulation of Temporary Agency Work and the Transnational Provision of Services

Part IV
The EU and Transnational Labour Regulation

Appendices

Preface

This book is the result of a project within SALTSA, which was a programme for research on working life in Europe organised by the Swedish National Institute for Working Life (Arbetslivsinstitutet) and the three Swedish trade union confederations, LO, TCO and Saco.

The research was undertaken by an international group of scholars: Dr Kerstin Ahlberg, Arbetslivsinstitutet, Professor Brian Bercusson, King's College London, Professor Niklas Bruun, University of Helsinki and Arbetslivsinstitutet, Dr Haris Kountouros, King's College London, Professor Christophe Vigneau, Université de Paris 1 (Panthéon-Sorbonne) and Dr Loredana Zappalà, Università degli Studi di Catania.

In addition to this research group many individuals contributed to the project, including trade union representatives, employers' representatives and government officials whom I interviewed for the chapter on the social dialogue on temporary agency work and the subsequent negotiations in the Council of Ministers. As most of these sources wished to remain anonymous, none will be mentioned by name. However, we owe them many thanks. Our research could not have been completed without their help.

We also are very grateful to the national correspondents of the European Industrial Relations Observatory (EIRO) who contributed to a survey on temporary agency work in the new Member States in October 2004. They were Inga Blaziene, Institute of Labour and Social Research, Lithuania; Ludovit Cziria, Bratislava Center for Work and Family Studies, Slovakia; Manwel Debono, Malta Workers' Participation Development Centre, Malta; Raita Karnite, Institute of Economics, Latvian Academy of Sciences, Latvia; László Neumann, National Employment Office, Research Unit, Hungary; Kaia Philips, Institute of Economics, University of Tartu, Estonia; Stefan Skledar, Institute of Macroeconomic Analysis and Development, Slovenia; Piotr Sula, Institute for Public Affairs, Poland; and Renáta Vasková, Research Institute for Labour and Social Affairs, Czech Republic.

Before the final manuscript was forwarded to the publisher, a seminar was held in Stockholm at which a number of prominent scholars and representatives of the social partners commented on our papers and helped us improve the text. They were Jon Erik Dølvik, Research Manager at Fafo, Oslo, Professor Ronnie Eklund, Stockholm University, Sverker Rudeberg, Senior Adviser for Social Affairs at the Confederation of processes of formulation of transnational labour regulation which, until now, have been largely invisible. Knowledge of the operation of the European social dialogue between employers and trade unions at EU level is confined to the very small number of those actively engaged in the process, while the legislative processes of the EU, particularly the proceedings in the Council of Ministers and the Committee of Permanent Representatives (COREPER), are notoriously lacking in transparency.[4] In other words, these processes of the formulation of European transnational labour regulation are effectively unknown. Readers interested primarily in learning about these vital dimensions of the construction of Social Europe may choose to start with the chapter by Kerstin Ahlberg.

The earlier research on the Directive on Fixed-term Work included a chapter exploring the substantive content of the fixed-term work agreement against the background of Member State experience of regulation of this form of temporary work. It was decided that this research project would expand this approach to provide detailed accounts of the regulation of temporary agency work in the national context of a number of Member States: Germany, France, Italy, the UK, the Nordic countries and the new Member States.[5]

The purpose of these chapters on national experiences, however, was emphatically not to replicate existing descriptive accounts of the position in the EU Member States. Rather the objective was to highlight distinctive features of national regulation of temporary agency work as they interacted with the debates on EU transnational labour regulation. Thus, for example, Niklas Bruun and Kerstin Ahlberg point to the insistence on regulation by collective agreement in the Nordic countries. Loredana Zappalà demonstrates the instrumental use of EU regulation to liberalise the labour market in Italy. Haris Kountouros describes the regime of liberalisation of temporary agency businesses in the UK without the cushion of collective bargaining. Kerstin Ahlberg reports on Germany's experimenting with the anticipated content of EU regulation. Christophe Vigneau notes the studied indifference towards EU regulation in France.

---

4 The necessity of cross-national collaboration for research on transnational labour regulation was recognised by the Swedish National Institute for Working Life (Arbetslivsinstitutet). The many advantages of cross-national collaboration revealed by this research project, also useful to others, may be illustrated by Kerstin Ahlberg's use of the principle of public access to official records enshrined in the Swedish Constitution. As she notes, this enabled her to gain access to the positions adopted by the Swedish Government in the EU Council of Ministers and thereby to identify, to some extent, the positions of other EU Member States.

5 The ten new Member States joining the EU in May 2004: Cyprus, the Czech Republic, Estonia, Hungary, Lithuania, Latvia, Poland, Slovakia, Slovenia and Malta.

Kerstin Ahlberg describes the new Member States' attitude to what is taken to be the imminent *acquis communautaire*. It may be that readers will prefer to absorb these distinctive features in the chapters on national systems of regulation before proceeding to read the chapter on the processes of EU transnational regulation.

The failure of both the EU social dialogue and the EU legislative process to produce their expected outcomes in the form of a framework agreement or directive led us to explore other aspects of transnational labour regulation. Thus, the failure of the EU social dialogue and of the EU legislative process did not lead to the conclusion that there was a vacuum in transnational labour regulation of temporary agency work. In two chapters, Loredana Zappalà reviews the historical background of legislation on atypical work, refers to judicial activism in the European Court of Justice and explores the alternative path of transnational labour regulation through the "open method of coordination".

At a time when the debates over temporary agency work had cooled and heated discussion was confined to relatively obscure corners of EU deliberation during 2003, the atmosphere suddenly became incandescent with the Commission's proposal for liberalisation of trade in services: the so-called "Bolkestein" draft directive of January 2004.[6] The extraordinarily heated debates over this proposal during the run-up to the referenda on the proposed Treaty establishing a Constitution for Europe[7] re-ignited the issue of temporary agency work due to its overlap with the transnational trade in services. The same issues of labour standards (the "country of origin" principle) and regulatory mechanisms (the role of collective agreements) came to the fore in the debate over the draft Services Directive. For this reason, the chapter by Brian Bercusson and Niklas Bruun explores the overlap between transnational regulation of temporary agency work and transnational trade in services.

Finally, in a concluding chapter, the contributors have collaborated in an attempt to draw lessons from the experience of regulation of temporary agency work at national and European levels for transnational labour regulation in general. Of course, the theme of transnational labour regulation is of central importance to the now 27 Member States of the EU.

---

6 Proposal for a Directive on Services in the Internal Market, COM (2004) 2/3 final, adopted 13.1.2004. Now Directive 2006/123/EC of the European Parliament and of the Council of 12 December 2006 on services in the internal market, OJ L376/26 of 27 December 2006.

7 Treaty establishing a Constitution for Europe adopted by the Member States at the Intergovernmental Conference meeting in Brussels, 17–18 June 2004, OJ C 310/1 of 16 December 2004.

But it is also of potential interest to the rest of the world because transnational labour regulation is a central feature of the European social model.[8] The final chapter of this book aims to provide a basis for reflection on the potential of the European experience for transnational labour regulation on a global scale.

This outline of the structure of our book should assist the reader to identify those chapters which will be of particular interest: features of national regulation of temporary agency work; the processes and substance of attempts at transnational labour regulation of temporary agency work; other forms of such regulation through soft law and judicial processes; the overlap with regulation of the transnational provision of services; and finally, general lessons for transnational labour regulation drawn from this case study. The remainder of this introductory chapter is intended to provide a wider context for the book's detailed case studies.

2. National, International and Transnational Labour Regulation

The regulation of temporary agency work at *national* level has been the subject of extensive research and study.[9] Similarly, temporary agency work was the subject of a recent initiative in *international* labour law: ILO Convention 181 on Private Employment Agencies was adopted in 1997 via the processes of the International Labour

8 Particularly when compared with that of the USA. While there may be no or little military competition in a unipolar world dominated by the USA, the economic and political stature of the EU (the largest single unit in the world economy, the EU-15 in 1997 had a nominal GNP of about $6 trillion, compared with $5 trillion for the US and $3 trillion for Japan and a population approaching that of the USA and Japan combined) makes the European economic and social model the subject of considerable attention elsewhere. For the Japanese interest in the European social model see the three-page headlined dossier in *Le Monde Economie* of 28 May 2002, entitled "*Le Japon en crise s'intéresse au modèle social européen*".

9 The European Foundation for the Improvement of Living and Working Conditions undertook a major survey of temporary agency work in the European Union in 2000. The results were published in 2002. General Report: *Temporary agency work in the European Union* http://www.eurofound.eu.int/publications/files/EF0202EN.pdf. Summary of the Report: http://www.eurofound.eu.int/publications/files/EF0247EN.pdf. There are also national reports on Austria, Belgium, Denmark, Finland, France, Germany, Greece, Ireland, Italy, Luxembourg, the Netherlands, Portugal, Spain, Sweden and the UK. A more recent report, which revisits the study of 2002, is Arrowsmith (2006). See also European Trade Union Institute (2000) and Blanpain and Graham (2004). For a comparative table covering also countries in North America, South America, Asia and Oceania, the Middle East and Africa, see Table B.3 in Florkowski (2006), pp. 211–13.

Organisation.[10] *Transnational* labour regulation raises issues distinct from either national or international labour law.

In the EU context, transnational regulation of temporary agency work may be understood in at least two senses. First, transnational labour regulation may refer to the harmonisation of different national labour standards governing temporary agency work in the EU Member States. The objective may be to eliminate unfair competition among the employers of temporary agency workers, the older common market objective of the European Community (EC), and/or to secure decent terms and conditions of employment for temporary agency workers, the newer social policy objective of the European Union. Secondly, transnational labour regulation may target the international operations of temporary agency businesses, often multinational enterprises, or be concerned with the labour standards applicable when there is transnational movement of temporary agency workers between EU Member States. This book aims to draw lessons from the European experience of attempts at transnational regulation of temporary agency work in both these senses.

The EU is the foremost example of a system of transnational labour regulation. The European Economic Community was created by the Treaty of Rome of 1957. The law of the EC was famously declared by the European Court of Justice in *Van Gend en Loos* to be:[11]

> a new legal order of international law for the benefit of which the states have limited their sovereign rights, albeit within limited fields, and the subjects of which comprise not only Member States but also their nationals.

This new legal order may also be said to have a labour law, European labour law, a rare example of transnational labour regulation.

The impact of European labour law on labour standards in the Single European Market has led to growing awareness of the potential of transnational labour standards at the international level. There has been a burgeoning of the literature concerned with labour standards in international trade and the labour practices of multinational corporations.[12]

10 It has been noted that "Temporary Work Agencies are in many cases examples of powerful multinationals which possess substantial and effective lobbying capabilities. Indeed, this is the case to such an extent that ILO Convention 181 on Private Employment Agencies is regarded by trade unions as an employers' initiative", Jones (2002), p. 189.

11 Case 26/62, N.V. Algemene Transport- en Expeditie Onderneming van Gend & Loos v. Nederlandse administratie der belastingen (Netherlands Inland Revenue Administration) [1963] ECR 1, at p. 12.

12 Hepple (1997), Herzfeld Olsson *et al.* (1998), Bercusson (1999), Hepple (2001), Hepple (2005a and 2005b), Bercusson and Estlund (2007).

The evolution of a transnational labour law on the European continent has potential significance for the development of international labour standards beyond the geographical limits of Europe. The role of regional integration in the process of economic globalisation is a well-known theme: "The basic issue is the relationship between forces of globalisation and forces of regionalisation. Regionalism is one possible approach to 'a new multilateralism'", and "Europe represents the most advanced regional arrangement the world has seen".[13] It has been said of the supranational political entity which is the European Union that it "continues to occupy a central position as a catalyst and a precursor of global institutional developments".[14] The view of the EU as a catalyst and precursor in the field of global labour regulation may be either an optimistic aspiration or a fearful threat; the reality arguably still falls somewhat short of fulfilling such a role.

The experience of the EU highlights many of the problems identified when international systems involve competing national regulatory authorities in the sphere of labour regulation and efforts are made to coordinate them.[15] The freedom of enterprises to move throughout the single European market shifted the balance of economic power towards employers. This is manifest in the overwhelming economic power of multinational enterprises, the magnitude of global capital mobility, the social dumping impact of global trade, delocalisation, unemployment, de-skilling, and so on. The changing balance of economic power threatens European integration. There are ominous signs of strain: rejection of the proposed Constitutional Treaty, the contested Services Directive, resistance to further enlargement for fear of migration of labour from new Member States.

From the beginning of the European Community, improvement of living and working conditions was stipulated as a social policy objective. Protection of labour standards was not an obstacle to free movement, it was a *condition* of free movement.[16] There is now a substantial body of transnational labour regulation in EU law (ranging from directives to European Employment Guidelines) and policy (including, for example, soft law on restructuring). This imposes both substantive obligations and procedural constraints (for example, information and consultation). Taken together: the *acquis communautaire social*.

13 Hettne (2000), pp. 359, 362.

14 Bratton, McCahery, Picciotto and Scott (1996), p. 4.

15 See Bercusson (2000).

16 For the argument that collective action protecting labour standards is not a restriction, but rather is consistent with market integration and the effective functioning of the common market, see Maduro (1999).

In an era of economic globalisation, unfettered free movement of services across borders potentially could have a major impact on labour standards. The imbalance of economic power consequent on employer mobility in the EU makes collective industrial action much less able to redress the balance. One solution is through transnational labour regulation: the *acquis communautaire social*. Transnational economic activities are to be regulated consistently with the evolution of the EU from a purely economic Community establishing a common market to a European Union with a social policy. EU social and labour policy is aimed at protecting workers employed in the common market who are also citizens of the Union: "*ordre communautaire social*". Labour is not a commodity like others (goods, capital). Transnational labour regulation pursues the objective of improved working conditions, respects the fundamental rights of workers as human beings, acknowledges the central role of social dialogue and social partnership at EU and national levels, and adheres to the strict principle of equal treatment without regard to nationality.[17]

European labour law offers many practical illustrations of the concerns in the debate over regulatory competition in the EU context, specifically the potential competition between EU labour law and national labour laws. Three examples will suffice.

2.1 Free Movement of Goods and Transnational Industrial Action

Obstructions to free movement of agricultural produce from other countries caused by protesting farmers led to a complaint by the Commission against France for failing to take appropriate measures to guarantee free movement of goods.[18] At the same time, the Commission was considering a proposal emanating from DG XV (Internal Market), headed by Commissioner Mario Monti. This proposal sought to put pressure on Member States to take measures removing obstacles when required to by the Commission.

Both these developments aroused considerable anxiety in trade unions, particularly in the transport sector, where industrial action could have similar effects on the free movement of goods. The outcome of lengthy consultations was a Regulation which includes the following provision:[19]

> This Regulation may not be interpreted as affecting in any way the exercise of fundamental rights as recognised in Member States, including the right or freedom to

17 See Bercusson and Bruun (2005a), especially pp. 4–11.

18 Case C-265/95, *Commission v. France*, [1997] ECR I-6959.

19 Council Regulation (EC) No. 2679/98 of 7 December 1998 on the functioning of the internal market in relation to the free movement of goods among the Member States. OJ L337/8 of 12 December 1998, Article 2.

> strike. These rights may also include the right or freedom to take other actions covered by the specific industrial relations systems in Member States.

The EU drew back from asserting that its regulatory power over the free movement of goods prevailed over national regulation of collective industrial action, at least insofar as this took the form of the exercise of fundamental rights.[20]

2.2 Member State Improvements on EU Minimum Safety Standards

In an Opinion of 28 April 1998 in the *Borsana* case,[21] Advocate General Mischo applied the principle of proportionality so as to annul Member State legislation imposing stricter rules than those required by health and safety directives. This Opinion aroused considerable disquiet among trade unions at EU and national levels.

In its decision in the *Borsana* case, handed down on 17 December 1998, the European Court rejected Advocate General Mischo's Opinion. The key paragraph of the judgment reads:[22]

> Since the legislation at issue is a more stringent measure for the protection of working conditions compatible with the Treaty and results from the exercise by a Member State of the powers it has retained pursuant to Article 118a(3) [now Article 137(4) EC] of the Treaty, it is not for the Court to rule on whether such legislation and the penalties imposed therein are compatible with the principle of proportionality.

Contrary to the Advocate General, the Court was unwilling to allow EC law to interfere with the discretion of the Member States to improve upon EC regulatory standards in the field of health and safety.

---

20 At the time of writing, two references to the European Court of Justice, by the Swedish Labour Court in Case C-341/05, *Laval un Partneri Ltd v. Svenska Byggnadsarbetareförbundet, Svenska Byggnadsarbetareförbundet, Avdelning 1, Svenska Elektrikerförbundet*, and by the English Court of Appeal in Case C-438/05, *Viking Line Abp OU Viking Line Eesti v. The International Transport Workers' Federation, The Finnish Seamen's Union*, highlight this issue of the limits to free movement: specifically, whether EC Treaty provisions on free movement may be limited by collective action which is lawful under national law. On *Laval/Vaxholm* see Ahlberg, Bruun and Malmberg (2006); on *Viking* see Bercusson (2007).

21 *Società italiana petroli SpA (IP) v. Borsana Srl*, Case C-2/97 [1998] ECR I-8597.

22 *Ibid.* paragraph 40.

2.3 Effective Implementation of EU Rights

The Working Time Directive of 1993[23] was implemented in the UK by the Working Time Regulations 1998. These Regulations implemented Articles 3 and 5 of the Directive which provided that an adult worker is entitled to daily and weekly rest periods.[24] The UK's Department of Trade and Industry published a set of guidelines which included the following statement: "employers must make sure that workers can take their rest, but are not required to make sure that they do take their rest". There had long been complaints about the UK's implementation of these provisions in the form of mere "entitlements", with no effective means of securing that workers could avail themselves of the mandatory rest periods deemed minimum requirements for their health and safety. The Court upheld a Commission complaint against the UK, based on the third paragraph of Article 249 EC,[25] that these guidelines were "national measures likely to encourage a practice of non-compliance with [the Directive's] provisions relating to the daily and weekly rest rights of workers".[26] The Court stated that Articles 3 and 5 meant "that workers must actually benefit from the daily and weekly periods of rest provided for by the directive [...] Member States are under an obligation to guarantee that each of the minimum requirements laid down by the directive is observed, including the right to benefit from effective rest."[27]

2.4 The Purpose of this Book

The purpose of this book is to explore the dynamic evolution of transnational European labour law through a detailed case study of the regulation of temporary agency work. The book charts the EU's attempt to regulate temporary agency work in order to provide insights into the problems and potential of this new form of labour law, both as to its processes of formulation and its substantive content.

---

23 Council Directive 93/104/EC of 23 November 1993 concerning certain aspects of the organisation of working time; OJ L307/18 of 13 December 1993, as amended by Directive 2000/34 of 22 June 2000, OJ L195/41. Consolidated in Directive 2003/88/EC of 4 November 2003 concerning certain aspects of the organisation of working time; OJ L299/9 of 18 November 2003.

24 The Working Time Regulations 1998. S.I. 1833.

25 "A directive shall be binding, as to the result to be achieved, upon each Member State to which it is addressed, but shall leave to the national authorities the choice of form and methods."

26 *Commission of the European Communities v. United Kingdom*, Case C-484/04, decided 7 September 2006, paragraph 29.

27 *Ibid.*, paragraphs 39–40.

3. The Substantive Content of Transnational Labour Regulation

3.1 The Influence of National Labour Laws

The evolution of transnational labour regulation in the EU is inevitably influenced by the national labour laws of the Member States and prevailing international labour standards. A major premise in understanding transnational labour regulation in the EU is the need to avoid thinking about it *exclusively* in terms of EU institutions and legal provisions. Accounts of EU labour law must, of course, incorporate an understanding of these supranational institutions and the basic legal framework of the EU. But equally, if not more, necessary is an appreciation of the relationship between EU labour law and national labour laws and international labour standards.

For instance, it is easy to demonstrate that national labour law systems have been subject to mutual influence.[28] It would seem likely, therefore, that EU labour law also is not wholly autonomous and independent. It is easy to point to many developments in EU labour law which are due to the influence of highly developed and technically sophisticated national labour law systems.[29] Not surprisingly, in formulating EU labour law, the law- and policy-making institutions of the EU have to come to terms with these systems and are influenced by them.

This book includes accounts of the regulation of temporary agency work in the national context of a number of Member States (Germany,[30] France,[31] Italy,[32] the UK,[33] the Nordic countries[34] and the new Member States[35]). This is intended to illuminate three crucial features of the EU system of transnational labour regulation.

First, it thereby becomes possible to better understand the positions adopted in the social dialogue by the EU social partners, comprising affiliated trade unions and employers' organisations from the Member States whose experience of temporary agency work is specific to their national context. Secondly, the substantive proposals emanating from the

---

28 See Edlund (1986).

29 See Bercusson (1996), pp. 9–11.

30 Kerstin Ahlberg, Chapter 5.

31 Christophe Vigneau, Chapter 3.

32 Loredana Zappalà , Chapter 4.

33 Haris Kountouros, Chapter 2.

34 Kerstin Ahlberg and Niklas Bruun, Chapter 1.

35 Kerstin Ahlberg, Chapter 6.

Commission are recognisably drawn from the spectrum of national experience of regulating temporary agency work. Finally, the positions adopted by Member States in the Council debates on these proposals reflect that national experience.

In sum, the *transnational* regulation of temporary agency work in the EU is powerfully influenced by *national* policies, *national* labour law traditions and *national* industrial relations structures.

But although regulation at national level is determined by, and strictly confined to, the operations of temporary work agencies and the protection or otherwise of temporary agency workers in a national context, the EU regulation of temporary agency work engages quite different policies, labour laws and industrial relations structures in a transnational context. The relatively narrow concerns of national supervision of the operations of temporary work agencies and enforcement of laws protecting temporary agency workers are transformed when these operations extend beyond national borders and the workers concerned originate outside the national territory.[36] This dramatic change in context was apparent long before the subject of temporary agency workers came onto the agenda of the EU social dialogue in 1999, to be followed, after the breakdown of the social dialogue in May 2001, by the Commission's proposal of a draft directive on working conditions for temporary workers in March 2002.

3.2 The Presently Applicable **Acquis Communautaire Social**

Transnational movement of workers, including temporary agency workers, was part of the original concerns of the Treaty of Rome of 1957 to create a common market for goods, services, capital and, of course, labour. Temporary agency workers were among the workers migrating from one Member State to another, or engaged in the temporary provision of services from one Member State to another. Principles were laid down to govern migrant workers in the common labour market.

In the aftermath of the approval of the Charter of the Fundamental Social Rights of Workers in December 1989, as the exigencies of protecting a fragmented workforce required a regulatory framework appropriate to its particular circumstances, initiatives took the form of proposals for legislation: Council Directives on certain employment relationships.[37]

---

36 See the Explanatory Memorandum to the Proposal for a Council Directive concerning the posting of workers in the framework of the provision of services, COM(91) 230 final – SYN 346, Brussels, 1 August 1991F. Now Directive 96/71/EC concerning the posting of workers in the framework of the provision of services. OJ 196, L 18/1.

37 Proposal for a Council Directive on certain employment relationships with regard to working conditions; Proposal for a Council Directive on certain employment relation

The proposals were accompanied by a lengthy Explanatory Memorandum which pointed out differences between Member States in the numbers and proportion of the workforce employed in such relationships. It was estimated that the workers concerned by the Directives accounted for some 20% of total employment.[38]

Eight main issues were considered to call for particular attention: access to training; taking into account such employees in calculating numbers or persons employed with a view to setting up representative bodies for workers; information for workers' representative bodies in the event of recourse to the workers concerned; grounds for recourse to temporary employment; information for the temporary workers employed where the employer intended to recruit full-time employees for an indefinite period; rules concerning access to social assistance; access to the social services of undertakings; and the specific situations of workers employed through temporary employment businesses.[39]

---

ships with regard to distortions of competition. COM(90) 228 final – SYN 280, Brussels, 13 August 1990. Another proposal introduced at the same time (Proposal for a Council Directive supplementing the measures to encourage improvements in the safety and health at work of temporary workers, COM(90) 228 final – SYN 281, Brussels, 13 August 1990) was eventually approved and became Council Directive 91/533 of 25 June 1991 supplementing the measures to encourage improvement in the safety and health at work of workers with a fixed-duration employment relationship or a temporary employment relationship. OJ 1991 L 206/19.

38 Explanatory Memorandum, paragraph 20. As regards *part-timers*, in 1988 these made up over 30% of the working population in the Netherlands, and more than 20% in Denmark (23.7%) and the UK (21.9%), some 13.2% in the Germany, but around 5% in Spain (5.4%), Italy (5.6%), Greece (5.5%) and Portugal (6.5%) (8% in Ireland) (*A Social Portrait of Europe*, Luxembourg, 1991, p. 62, Table 5.6; and Explanatory Memorandum, paragraph 15). The Community average was 13.6%, more than 14 million part-time employees. As regards *temporary employment*, in 1988, employees with a temporary contract were 22.4% in Spain, 18.5% in Portugal and 17.6% in Greece, but fell from just over 11% in Germany and Denmark, to 8.7% in the Netherlands, 7.8% in France and 5.9% in the UK (*A Social Portrait of Europe*, p. 64, Table 5.13). A 1989 survey showed that 30% of employment relationships in Spain were limited in time, but the figure was around 10% in Italy, Greece, Ireland and Portugal and below 10% in all other Member States (Explanatory Memorandum, paragraph 16). A Commission Green Paper of 2006 reports that "The share of total employment taken up by those engaged on working arrangements differing from the standard contractual model as well as those in self-employment has increased since 2001 from over 36% in 2001 to almost 40% of the EU-25 workforce in 2005". "Modernising labour law to meet the challenges of the 21st century", COM(2006) 708 final, Brussels, 22 November 2006, p. 7.

39 Explanatory Memorandum, paragraph 48.

Instead of being incorporated into one Directive, however, these issues were divided among three different draft Directives, each ostensibly concerned with a different theme: (1) working conditions, (2) distortions of competition, and (3) health and safety, and each with a different legal basis. The significance of the legal basis lay in the capacity of the Council of Ministers to approve proposed Directives either by qualified majority voting or by unanimity. The working conditions draft Directive was based on Article 100 (now Article 94) of the Treaty of Rome, requiring unanimity.[40] The draft Directive on distortions of competition[41] was based on Article 100A (now Article 95), and that on health and safety[42] on Article 118A (now Article 137(1)(a)), both of which required only qualified majority voting.[43]

---

40 The working conditions draft Directive (Article 100) applied to temporary and part-time workers and covered access to training, services and social assistance/social security schemes (Articles 2.1, 3 and 4); calculation of employee numbers relating to employee representative bodies (Article 2.2); information and consultation of employee representatives (Article2.3); informing about full-time open-ended vacancies (Article 5); contents of temporary employment contracts (Article 2.4); temporary work agencies and user companies (Article 6); and obligations of temporary employment agencies (Article 7).

41 The distortions of competition draft Directive (Article 100A) also applied to temporary and part-time workers and dealt with entitlement to social protection under statutory and occupational social security schemes (Article 2); holidays, dismissal payments and seniority allowances (Article 3); and termination of a temporary contract before term (Article 4(b)).

42 The health and safety draft Directive (Article 118A) applied only to temporary workers and concerned the contents of the contract between the user company and the temporary work agency (Article 3); the user company's responsibilities (Article 4); information and training of temporary workers (Article 5); and work requiring special medical supervision (Article 6).

43 Prior to their presentation, there was an intense debate on which Articles of the Treaty of Rome should constitute their legal basis. The two proposed Directives on certain employment relationships were based respectively on Article 100 and Article 100A of the Treaty. Article 100 required unanimous approval in the Council of Ministers. This was not forthcoming. Article 100A allowed for qualified majority voting, but not, according to Article 100A(2), if it related to "the rights and interests of employed persons". The interpretation of this phrase would have been stringently tested by an attempt to extend qualified majority voting to the second proposal. The third proposal, however, was based on Article 118A of the Treaty, inserted by the Single European Act 1986, which allowed for qualified majority voting on proposals concerning "the working environment, as regards the health and safety of workers". The draft Directives were accompanied by considerable dispute as they progressed through the legislative procedure. Within the Commission, the Legal Service and Directorate-General V (Social Affairs) had differences over the appropriate legal bases for the draft Directives. Parliament and the Economic and Social Committee objected to the divi-

Only the third proposal, relating to the health and safety of temporary workers, was approved by the Council of Ministers.[44] This required attention being paid to the specific risks to health and safety entailed in the triangular relationship between agency, worker and the user employer.

Towards the completion of the Single European Market Programme in 1992, the Commission noted that this would bring about a considerable number of employment relationships which would be only temporarily performed in a Member State other than the State in which they are habitually performed. The Commission anticipated that:[45]

> Thus, a new intra-Community mobility of workers within their jobs, different from the traditional mobility in search of new employment, is growing within the European Community in the framework of the economic freedoms, in particular, of the freedom to provide services.

The Commission highlighted the potential of the services industry, which then accounted for half the Community's production and 40% of jobs, in a wide range of activities. In particular, transnational subcontracting was developing in the construction sector and public works:[46]

> There are more and more instances of firms based in one Member State moving with their staff to another State to provide a service, or of firms sending their workers from their country of origin to another Member State to work for a legally distinct undertaking.

Free movement of workers in the Community had focussed on the right to seek and take up permanent employment. *Conditions* of employment for migrant workers had not heretofore been regulated – subject to the

---

sion of issues among different drafts with different legal bases. In the case of ECOSOC, a tripartite body, the employer members approved the substantive content of the draft Directives on atypical work, but objected to the legal basis allowing for qualified majority voting. In contrast, Parliament objected to the draft Directives where approval required unanimity in the Council of Ministers. Parliament put forward amendments inserting the content of the working conditions draft directive (based on Article 100) into the other two.

44 Council Directive 91/383 of 25 June 1991 supplementing the measures to encourage improvements in the safety and health of workers with a fixed-duration employment relationship or a temporary employment relationship, OJ 1991 L206/19.

45 Explanatory Memorandum to the Proposal for a Council Directive concerning the posting of workers in the framework of the provision of services, COM(91) 230 final – SYN 346, Brussels, 1 August 1991, paragraph 1.

46 *Ibid.*, paragraph 5. The increase in the number of transnational acquisitions by top European industrial enterprises was noted as liable to stimulate the temporary expatriation of workers within groups of companies or within companies with multiple operations throughout Europe. Paragraph 8.

overriding requirement of non-discrimination on grounds of nationality. The principle of equal treatment of migrant workers received a further impulse, however, as a result of a further initiative of the Commission which was identified as part of its plan to "encourage high labour standards as part of a competitive Europe": the Directive concerning the posting of workers in the framework of the provision of services.[47] The Directive confronted the crucial issue of how to balance the economic dimension of the internal market (free movement of workers) with the social dimension (protection of employees, but also of national industrial relations models). The implementation, application and enforcement of this directive was under review at the same time as the subject of temporary agency workers was on the EU social dialogue and legislative agendas.[48]

In 1999, the European social dialogue produced a framework agreement and a Directive on fixed-term workers which clearly overlapped with workers temporarily engaged through an employment agency.[49] The framework agreement acknowledged this and proposed that the social partners address the concerns regarding temporary agency workers along lines analogous to those agreed for fixed-term workers.[50] Negotiations were expected to reflect the principles common to the two previous framework agreements concluded on other forms of so-called "atypical" work: part-time[51] and fixed-term work, later added to by the framework agreement of July 2002 on telework.

The revision in the year 2004 of the EU directives concerning transnational public procurement has also focussed attention on the protection of labour standards of workers temporarily moving from one Member State to another in order to engage in the performance of these public con-

47 Directive 96/71/EC concerning the posting of workers in the framework of the provision of services. OJ 1996, L18/1.

48 Commission of the EC, Communication from the Commission, *The implementation of Directive 96/71/EC in the Member States*, COM(2003) 458 final, Brussels, 15 July 2003.

49 Council Directive 1999/70/EC of 28 June 1999 concerning the framework agreement on fixed-term work concluded by ETUC, UNICE and CEEP. OJ L175/43 of 10 July 1999.

50 The Preamble to the Framework Agreement on fixed-term work had declared "the intention of the parties to consider the need for a similar agreement relating to temporary agency work".

51 Council Directive 97/81/EC of 15 December 1997 concerning the framework agreement on part-time work concluded by UNICE, CEEP and the ETUC, OJ L14/9 of 20 January 1998.

tracts.[52] The public procurement directives, subject to recent revision, were the subject of considerable controversy regarding their provisions on the labour standards applicable to workers employed by contractors seeking to obtain, and then carrying out public contracts in other Member States.[53]

Finally, the Commission's proposal for a draft directive liberalising the market in services was the subject of fierce debate specifically regarding the labour standards of workers engaged in transnational provision of services.[54] The proposed "country of origin" principle was hotly contested both as to its merits in principle and its proposed application in practice.

In sum, EU transnational regulation of agency workers is not a *tabula rasa*. Nor is it driven exclusively by the sometimes conflicting Member State labour law and policy traditions regarding temporary agency work. As the long list elaborated above illustrates, the regulation of migrant workers, the specific health and safety risks to agency workers, "posted" workers, workers engaged in public contracts, other categories of "atypical work" and labour standards applicable to the transnational provision of services, all reveal a complex and detailed body of principles, standards and mechanisms already embodied in EU law. The *acquis communautaire social* already provides a foundation for the transnational regulation of temporary agency work.

Finally, it should also be noted that, as *EU* labour and social law norms develop, they begin to influence *national* labour laws. Two processes are thus linked in a specific symbiosis. Just as EU transnational regulation is influenced by national labour regulations, the labour law of the Member States of the EU is increasingly influenced by EU labour law. The dynamic of national labour laws is no longer determined solely or even mainly by domestic developments. It is not merely that national labour laws are required to incorporate EU norms. EU norms are themselves the reflection of the national labour laws of Member States. In this indirect

52 Directive 2004/17/EC of the European Parliament and of the Council of 31 March 2004 coordinating the procurement procedures of entities operating in the water, energy, transport and postal services sectors, OJ L134/1 of 30 April 2004; Directive 2004/18/EC of the European Parliament and of the Council of 31 March 2004 on the coordination of procedures for the award of public works contracts, public supplies contracts and public service contracts, OJ L134/114 of 30 April 2004.

53 See Bercusson and Bruun (2005a).

54 Proposal for a Directive on Services in the Internal Market, COM (2004) 2/3 final, adopted 13 January 2004. Now Directive 2006/123/EC of the European Parliament and of the Council of 12 December 2006 on services in the internal market, OJ L376/26 of 27 December 2006.

way, national labour laws are influential in the development of each other and national labour laws become more European.

The labour law of the EU Member States is, and will increasingly become, more truly European than appears from the formal imprint of EU labour law. It is European rather as reflecting the cumulative experience of national labour laws, filtered through the prism of the EU institutions and refined in the crucible of the developing European polity. The tendency towards convergence of the labour laws of EU Member States is driven in the main by the institutional pressures of EU membership, and is to a lesser extent the consequence of the workings of an international economy and, though less significant, a single European labour market. The dynamic of this convergence process is complex and its results are far from complete. But European labour lawyers must come to terms with this new dynamic of labour law evolution and its results.

In sum, the symbiosis of national labour law systems and EU labour law is of major importance in understanding both EU law and national labour laws. The nature of their relationship, however, is complex, with major dissonances between them at certain periods, and variation between Member States in terms of their interaction with EU labour law. Comparison of very different systems of national regulation, some of which are described in this book, provides insight into the substantive choices open to instruments of transnational regulation of temporary agency work.

4. The Processes of Transnational Labour Regulation

The *process* of EU transnational labour regulation of temporary agency work was notable as engaging *both* transnational private actors – trade unions and employers' organisations – at EU level in the *European social dialogue*, aimed at concluding an agreement between the European social partners, *and* the EU institutions in the *EU's legislative process* aimed at producing a Directive binding the Member States.[55] The regulation of temporary agency work is an excellent case study of transnational labour regulation precisely because it engaged both regulatory mechanisms: first, the social dialogue process, and then the legislative process.

A brief explanation may be necessary of how the transnational context of labour regulation in Europe came to engage *both* the legislative institutions of the European Union (Commission, Council and Parliament),

55 Commission of the European Communities, *Proposal for a Directive of the European Parliament and the Council on working conditions for temporary workers*, COM(2002) 149 final, Brussels, 20 March 2002; *Amended Proposal*, COM(2002) 701 final, Brussels, 28 November 2002.

and the European actors engaged in social dialogue (ETUC, UNICE/UEAPME and CEEP).[56]

The election of Mrs Thatcher, Prime Minister of the UK from 1979, halted the programme of EU social legislation emerging from the Social Action Programme of 1974. The then EC Treaty requirement of unanimous voting in the Council (Article 100, now Article 94 EC) enabled the UK to veto the Commission's social policy proposals. It was the Commission's inability to launch a social dimension of the Single European Market through the legislative channel which stimulated the effort by Jacques Delors, the incoming President of the Commission in January 1985, to find an alternative regulatory mechanism. In the EU Member States, there was a well-known alternative: social dialogue. The irony of history is that Mrs Thatcher, the most determined opponent of collective bargaining at national level in the UK, was responsible for the launch by the Commission of the initiative to create a dialogue between the social partners at EU level. The social dialogue was institutionalised as a process of transnational labour regulation by the Protocol and Agreement on Social Policy of the Maastricht Treaty on European Union in December 1991.

The dynamic of development of transnational labour regulation in the EU may be identified from the first experience of EU social dialogue after the adoption of the Protocol on Social Policy of the Maastricht Treaty. The EU social partners engaged in social dialogue on European works councils (EWCs). Their inability to reach agreement over European works councils led a then dynamic Commission to propose, and eleven Member States (excluding the UK) to adopt, the EWC directive in 1994.[57]

The catalyst for the European social dialogue which led eventually to the EWC directive was the Hoover affair of January 1993, involving the closure of a factory in Dijon and its transfer to the UK.[58] But the impact of catalysing events, though important, is subordinate to another, longer-term dynamic: "bargaining in the shadow of the law".

56 See Bercusson (1996), Chapter 6, "The Strategy of European Social Dialogue", pp. 72–78. For detailed studies, Dolvik (1997), Chapter 8, pp. 189–239; Kare F.V. Petersen (1995), pp. 89–96.

57 Council Directive 94/45/EC of 22 September 1994 on the establishment of a European Works Council or a procedure in Community-scale undertakings and Community-scale groups of undertakings for the purposes of informing and consulting employees, OJ L 254/64 of 30 September 1994. Council Directive 97/74/EC of 15 December 1997 extending to the United Kingdom Directive 94/45/EC, OJ L 10/22 of 16 January 1998.

58 "The Hoover affair and social dumping", *European Industrial Relations Review*, No. 230, March 1993, pp. 14–20.

It has become clear that the willingness of the social partners to engage in social dialogue is dependent on the political balance of power in the EU institutions. If the Commission takes initiatives, if the Member States mobilise in Council and if Parliament is supportive, the social partners are confronted with the likelihood of regulation. A logical calculus of self-interest points to incentives to self-regulate via social dialogue.

This explains the 31 October 1991 agreement which led to the Maastricht Protocol and is now in Articles 138–39 EC. Then, faced with the Dutch Presidency's draft of the Maastricht Treaty proposing expansion of social and labour competences exercised through qualified majority voting, employers and unions at EU level agreed on the alternative of labour regulation through social dialogue.

But this dynamic is fragile. It is contingent on the political balance of power in the EU institutions. If the Commission does not push for social policy initiatives, if there are blocking minorities of Member States in the Council of Ministers, if the Parliament is not supportive, then the likelihood of legislative regulation recedes. In these circumstances, employers, in particular, are unlikely voluntarily to look to alternative forms of regulation, unless they can be offered incentives.[59]

There is a major difference between transnational labour regulation in the form of European social dialogue and national labour regulation through collective bargaining in the Member States. Unlike trade unions in the Member States, the European Trade Union Confederation (ETUC) lacks the power to force employers to come to the bargaining table. This has become ever more evident. EU employers' organisations will not agree to engage in social dialogue, or, if they do, only on marginal issues, and then only if the results do not take the form of binding obligations.

This book's detailed account of the attempt to regulate temporary agency work through the EU social dialogue, and the subsequent legislative proposal of a Directive on temporary agency work, illustrates this dynamic of transnational labour regulation in Europe. Though the European social dialogue failed to produce an agreement on temporary agency work, the detailed research and analysis of these processes pro-

59 Thus, the Renault affair of February 1997 led to a fresh Commission initiative on information and consultation of workers' representatives (see Moreau 1997 and *European Industrial Relations Review* 1998). However, this time there was no social dialogue. The European employers' organisations, calculating that a Commission initiative, even if forthcoming, could be blocked in the Council, refused to engage. The eventual framework Directive 2002/14 on information and consultation only emerged in March 2002 after long and painful negotiations among the institutions. Council Directive No. 2002/14 establishing a framework for informing and consulting employees in the European Community, OJ 2002, L80/29.

vided in Kerstin Ahlberg's chapter in this book is essential to understanding its potential for transnational labour regulation.[60] Her account of the interaction of the EU institutions and the Member States engaged in the legislative process provides many insights into the problems of achieving transnational labour regulation engaging fifteen sovereign States with very different starting points in terms of national regulation and, consequently, different agendas for transnational regulation. Loredana Zappalà's exploration of judicial activism and soft law mechanisms of the "open method of coordination" offers alternatives to social dialogue and legislation as forms of transnational regulation of temporary agency work in the EU.

This research highlights many questions. For example, do different and competing ideologies and motivations for transnational labour regulation – for example, liberalisation of market forces vs social protection and cohesion – make transnational labour regulation a zero sum game, with inevitable winners and losers among workers, employers, Member States and the EU institutions? Is transnational labour regulation, with multiple players[61] and processes[62] impossibly complex and lacking in transparency? Do different topics of labour law encounter varying degrees of national diversity which render transnational labour regulation more or less difficult? Are there generally accepted principles of labour regulation which can provide a basis or at least a starting point for agreement, or are there specific legal obstacles or differences in the understanding of basic concepts which prevent it? In a concluding chapter we attempt to draw lessons from this research which will suggest answers to some of these questions.

4.1 A Potential Catalyst: The Proposed Services Directive

On 13 January 2004, the Commission adopted a proposal for a Directive on Services in the Internal Market.[63] Services account for over two-thirds

60 Comparison with an earlier successful social dialogue which produced the Agreement on Fixed-term Work provides further illumination of the internal dynamics of the actors engaged in social dialogue. See Bercusson (2002); see also Vigneau, Ahlberg, Bercusson and Bruun (1999).

61 Social partners: national, sub- and supranational, and internal divisions within them, at sectoral and intersectoral levels; competing EU institutions: Commission, Council, Parliament; Member States and their coalitions; multinational enterprises; international organisations, and so on.

62 Social dialogue, legislation, soft law, administrative coordination, judicial activism, and so forth.

63 Proposal for a Directive on Services in the Internal Market, COM (2004) 2/3 final, adopted 13 January 2004.

of employment in the EU.[64] The proposed liberalisation of the provision of services in the EU may potentially have a huge impact. A central feature of the freedom to provide services in the internal market is that the provision of services usually involves *employees* of the service provider crossing borders to perform the services.

But the Commission's proposal for a draft directive liberalising the market in services aroused a fierce debate specifically on the labour standards of workers engaged in transnational provision of services. The "country of origin" principle at the heart of that proposal raised the prospect of regression from established EU labour standards. The substantive issues involved in regulation of temporary agency work became the focus of unusual public concern following enlargement to an additional ten Member States in May 2004. These raised fears of "social dumping" and regression from national labour standards due to migration of workers from the new Member States providing services in the old Member States.[65] The resulting conflicts among and within the EU institutions, between different parties within the European Parliament and different Member States in the Council of Ministers, did finally produce agreement on and adoption of a Directive on services in the internal market. However, the disputed reference to "country of origin" was deleted and particular formulations were adopted in an attempt to remove employment standards from the scope of the directive. The implications for temporary agency work of the principles proposed in the draft Services Directive, and the outcome in the formulations of the final directive, are the subject of analysis in a separate chapter by Niklas Bruun and Brian Bercusson. Insofar as the Services Directive reflects a principle fundamental to transnational labour regulation of temporary agency work it is the substantive principle of non-regression from established labour standards at national and transnational level.

5. The Current Position and This Study

Following the breakdown of the European social dialogue on temporary agency work in May 2001, a blocking minority of Member States in the Council (Denmark, Germany, Ireland and the UK) initially prevented adoption of the Commission's proposal of a directive on temporary agency work in March 2002 and its amended version in November

64 *Ibid.* Explanatory Memorandum to the Services Directive, Section 1: "Necessity and objective", p. 5: "Services are omnipresent in today's economy, generating almost 70 per cent of GNP and jobs".

65 Indeed, these developments have been cited as one reason for the rejection of the European Constitutional Treaty in referenda in France and the Netherlands in 2005.

2002.[66] It was decided to delay publication of the research project's results as changes in Member States' positions on the proposed temporary agency work directive occasionally raised the prospect of progress. However, on 27 September 2005 President of the Commission José Antonio Barroso stated that the Commission would attempt to abolish pending legislative proposals and would reconsider that on temporary agency work in light of future discussions. The European Parliament has resisted this, but present indications are that there is no immediate prospect of a directive being adopted.[67]

Meanwhile, the proposed Services Directive, the subject of heated contestation in the EU institutions, with the social partners actively involved in the debates, has finally been adopted. It was felt, therefore, that the research had produced sufficiently rich material to warrant proceeding to publication even in the absence of a directive or agreement on temporary agency work.

This book explores the dynamic evolution of transnational labour law and temporary agency work in the European Union. European labour law provides a reservoir of experience of key issues facing transnational labour regulation. Although confined to the European continent, with a relatively limited variation of economic, political and social arrangements among Member States, European transnational labour law nonetheless has had to confront questions which are also on the agenda of efforts to achieve global transnational labour regulation. The experience of European labour law has much to teach about regulatory competition and coordination between national and international levels. It is hoped this study will contribute to addressing some of the challenges of transnational labour regulation.

Bibliography

Ahlberg, K., N. Bruun, and J. Malmberg (2006), "The *Vaxholm* case from a Swedish and European perspective", *Transfer: European Review of Labour and Research*, 12 (2): 155–66.

Arrowsmith, J. (2006), "Temporary Agency Work in an Enlarged European Union": (http://www.eurofound.europa.eu/publications/htmlfiles/ef05139.htm).

Bercusson, B. (1996), *European Labour Law*, London: Butterworths.

66 Commission of the European Communities, *Proposal for a Directive of the European Parliament and the Council on working conditions for temporary workers*, COM(2002) 149 final, Brussels, 20.3.2002; *Amended Proposal*, COM(2002) 701 final, Brussels, 28 November 2002.

67 *European Industrial Relations Review*, No. 381 (October 2005), p. 2.

Bercusson, B. (1999), "Labour Regulation in a Transnational Economy", *Maastricht Journal of European and Comparative Law*, 6: 244–70.

Bercusson, B. (2000), "Regulatory Competition in the EU System: Labour", in D. Esty and D. Geradin (eds.), *Regulatory Competition and Economic Integration: Comparative Perspectives*, Oxford: Oxford University Press.

Bercusson, B. (2002), *The Role of the Social Partners in the Member States in Labour Regulation through the EU Social Dialogue*, Brussels: ETUI.

Bercusson, B. (2007), "The Trade Union Movement and the European Union: Judgment Day", *European Law Journal* 13 (3): 279–308.

Bercusson, B., and N. Bruun (2005a), Overview to the *European Industrial Relations Dictionary*, published by the European Foundation for the Improvement of Living and Working Conditions, Luxembourg: Office for Official Publications of the European Communities, pp. 2–50.

Bercusson, B., and N. Bruun (2005b), "Labour Law Aspects of Public Procurement in the EU", in R. Nielsen and S. Treumer (eds.), *The New EU Public Procurement Directives*, Copenhagen: Djøf, pp. 97–116.

Bercusson, B., and C. Estlund (eds.) (2007), *Regulating Labour in the Wake of Globalisation: New Challenges, New Institutions*, Columbia-London Law Series, vol. 2, Oxford: Hart.

Blanpain, R., and R. Graham (2004), *Temporary Agency Work and the Information Society*, Bulletin of Comparative Labour Relations No. 50, Kluwer Law International, The Hague.

Bratton, W., J. McCahery, S. Picciotto and C. Scott (eds.) (1996), *International Regulatory Competition and Coordination: Perspectives on Economic Regulation in Europe and the United States*, Oxford: Clarendon Press.

Dølvik, Jon Erik (1997), *Redrawing Boundaries of Solidarity? ETUC, Social Dialogue and the Europeanisation of Trade Unions in the 1990s*, ARENA Report No 5/97, Fafo Report No. 238, Oslo.

Edlund, S. (ed.) (1986), *Labour Law Research in Twelve Countries*, Stockholm.

European Industrial Relations Review (1998), "The Repercussions of the Vilvoorde Closure", *European Industrial Relations Review*, No. 289 (February): 22–25.

European Trade Union Institute (2000), *Survey of Legislation on Temporary Agency Work*, Report No. 65.

Florkowski, G.W. (2006), *Managing Global Legal Systems,* London: Routledge.

Hepple, B.A. (1997), "New Approaches to International Labour Regulation", *Industrial Law Journal*, 26 (40): 353–55.

Hepple, B.A. (ed.) (2001), *Social and Labour Rights in a Global Context: International and Comparative Perspectives*, Cambridge: Cambridge University Press.

Hepple, B.A. (2005a), *Labour Laws and Global Trade*, Oxford: Hart.

Hepple, B.A. (2005b), *Rights at Work: Global, European and British Perspectives*, London: Sweet & Maxwell.

Herzfeld Olsson, P., B. Bercusson and N. Bruun (eds.) (1998), *Transnational Trade Union Rights in the European Union*, Arbetslivsrapport No. 36, Swedish National Institute for Working Life.

Hettne, B. (2000), "Global Market versus the New Regionalism", in David Held and Anthony McGrew (eds.), *The Global Transformations Reader*, 2nd ed., Cambridge: Polity Press, pp. 359–69.

Jones, E.L. (2002), "Temporary Agency Labour: Back to Square One?", *Industrial Law Journal*, 31 (2): 183–90.

Maduro, M. (1999), "Striking the Elusive Balance Between Economic Freedom and Social Rights in the EU", in Philip Alston (ed.), *The EU and Human Rights*, Oxford: Oxford University Press, pp. 449–72.

Moreau, M.-A. (1997), "A propos de l'affaire Renault…", *Droit Social*, No. 5: 493–509.

Petersen, Kare F.V. (1995), *Step-by-Step into the Future: Three Decades of Social Dialogue*, Research Report for the Swedish Centre for Working Life, mimeo, Stockholm.

Vigneau, C., K. Ahlberg, B. Bercusson and N. Bruun (1999), *Fixed-term Work in the EU. A European Agreement against Discrimination and Abuse*, SALTSA, Stockholm, National Institute for Working Life.

Part I

The National Context

Denmark, Finland and Sweden: Temporary Agency Work Integrated in the Collective Bargaining System

Kerstin AHLBERG and Niklas BRUUN

1. Introduction

The regulatory development of temporary agency work in Denmark, Finland and Sweden has several common features. In all three countries a very restrictive approach to the hiring of manpower prevailed until the 1980s.

In the early 1990s a significant liberalisation of the regulation of temporary agency work took place: in all three countries the former state monopoly on job placement was abolished. In Finland and Sweden this led to the renunciation of ILO Convention 96 of 1949 on Fee-charging Employment Agencies; Denmark had never ratified the Convention, only ILO Convention 88 of 1948 on Employment Services. Temporary agency work became a legitimate and accepted form of labour utilisation and was no longer regarded as employment exchange, but as a specific, flexible form of employment. Since then, temporary agency work has increased significantly and at the same time has become integrated into the labour market mechanisms of the three countries.

In all three countries the integration of temporary agency work into the collective bargaining system has been the crucial issue. In Denmark and Sweden this development has taken place through autonomous collective bargaining without any intervention from the legislator. In Finland, however, where the collective bargaining system has distinct features due to the fact that sectoral collective agreements are made generally applicable (*erga omnes*) by force of law, the legislator too has been involved in the process.

In the following we describe the characteristics of the present way of regulating temporary agency work in each of the three countries in order to show that the working conditions of temporary agency workers can be successfully regulated by collective agreements, even where substantive legislation is lacking. It goes without saying that a precondition of this is that there is a strong collective bargaining system covering the "traditional" part of the labour market.

In Finland and Sweden the fundamental rule for the legal assessment of temporary agency work is very clear and uncontested: The temporary work agency is regarded as the employer and the worker as its employee who, within the framework of his or her employment relationship, performs work for a third party (the user company). In Denmark the situation seems to be more complicated, especially regarding white-collar workers.[1] However, developments seem to be going in the same direction as those in Finland and Sweden. For example, collective agreements, which cover most agency workers, define the agency as employer and the worker as its employee.[2]

A distinctive feature of developments in Finland is that the transnational, cross-border aspects of temporary agency work have been important since the 1970s. In this respect, the Finnish situation differs from that of the other two countries.

2. Historical Background

2.1 Denmark

Until 1990 temporary agency work in the strict sense was regulated in *Denmark* by the Act on the Placing of Workers and Insurance against Unemployment, and in an administrative decree by the Ministry of Labour of 1970, which regulated temporary work arranged by firms in the retail and office sectors. In other sectors temporary agency work was prohibited, but if the hired-out manpower was employed on an open-ended contract by the employer, such an arrangement was regarded as regular job contracting.[3] Since 1990, the only statutory restrictions that remain are that agencies employing nurses have to have a licence, and that drivers/chauffeurs have to be certified if they are to work as temporary agency workers.[4]

2.2 Finland

Finland ratified ILO Convention 96 in 1951 and the post-war legal regime was quite restrictive: all private manpower agencies were banned. The relationship between banned placement (manpower) services and temporary agency work was contested, however, and some temporary agencies were active in the market. In 1985 a liberalisation of the legislation took place.[5]

However, as early as 1969 the trade union confederations and employers' organisations concluded an agreement on the principles for using

1 See Nielsen (2005), Koldby Dalager (2005) and case law referred to by these authors.
2 Jørgensen (2005).
3 See Eklund (2002). p. 317.
4 Jørgensen (2005).
5 See the argumentation for the relevant Government Bill, No. 125/1984, p. 4.

"outside labour". The background was a number of examples of misuse of agency work in the building and construction sector.

The issue of temporary agency work and similar atypical ways of using labour became even more topical in Finland in the 1970s. Unlike Finland, Sweden and Norway had a labour shortage, and Finnish workers were hired by more or less unofficial temporary agencies to work in the neighbouring countries. At that time Finnish legislation and also many collective agreements were conceptually clarified so that the criteria for the following activities were defined:

1. *pure intermediary agency activities:* no employment relationship between employee and agency;
2. *temporary agency work* (hiring out of workers): partly shared employer responsibility between the user enterprise and the agency;
3. *subcontracting:* the contracting party delivering services bears full responsibility for the performance of the work by its employees but the work is often performed on the premises of the buyer of the services.

Since this period there has existed a common understanding in Finland on what is meant by temporary agency work. Earlier the different categories were often mixed up and there was a grey zone in which the borderline between legal and illegal was unclear. This partly explains the fact that cross-border hiring out of workers took place although the legislation was quite restrictive.

According to the 1985 reform, setting up a temporary work agency required authorisation from the state. The control also encompassed the terms and conditions of employment for the workers, and a condition for authorisation was that the agency fulfilled a legitimate need for manpower for a limited period. The legislator wanted to limit the agencies' activities to providing temporary staff for companies with special needs, while open-ended contracts between employer and employee were promoted as the regular form of employment. The hiring out of workers without authorisation was prohibited by criminal law.

At the beginning of the 1990s the authorisation system was abolished and Finland also renounced its ratification of ILO Convention 96. Instead, agencies had to notify the competent occupational safety and health authority when starting up, but in essence the system was totally liberalised. On the other hand, Finland later ratified ILO Convention 188, which led to some amendments to the legislation in 1999. Thus, a labour provider may be requested to supply certain information, for example.

With the new Employment Contracts Act adopted in 2001 temporary agency work was regulated and its relation to the Finnish collective bargaining system was clarified.

2.3 Sweden

In *Sweden* the Act of 1935 on the Ban of Private Employment Exchange, amended in 1942, regarded the hiring out of manpower as constituting employment exchange. Consequently, the Act prohibited all temporary agency work. But the prohibition was not fully implemented in practice, and was finally lifted in 1991. With the 1993 Private Job Placement and Hiring-out of Labour Act almost all restrictions were abolished. Today Sweden has one of the most liberal legislations on agency work in the EU. Only three restrictions specific to temporary agency work remain:

1. Although the ban on profit-oriented private employment services was abolished, the agency may not charge the worker – only the user enterprise – for offering or referring work to him or her. To do so is a criminal offence.
2. The agency may not hinder the worker from accepting an offer to enter into a direct employment relation with the user company.
3. A worker who has terminated his/her employment with one enterprise and taken up employment with a temporary work agency must not be hired out to his/her former employer until six months have elapsed from the termination of his/her former employment.

3. Nature and Extent of Temporary Agency Work

3.1 Denmark

In *Denmark*, the use of temporary agency work has been increasing steadily for a number of years. In 1992, there were 73 registered temporary work agencies, growing to 673 agencies by 2005.[6] In 1992 agencies employed around 3,000 workers, but by November 2003, 22,238 persons had agency work as their primary employment.[7] In 2003 the proportion of agency workers in the total workforce amounted to 1.2%, or 0.3% in full-time equivalents.[8] In 2004, agencies' turnover was EUR 440 million – a more than tenfold increase over a decade.[9]

The major employers' organisation for temporary work agencies in Denmark is Danish Commerce & Services (Dansk Handel & Service, DHS). Their market share is estimated to be 80–90%. The trade association, the Association of Temporary Work Agencies in Denmark (Foreningen af vikarbureauer i Danmark, FVD), is a member of DHS.

The temporary work agencies in Denmark cover a wide range of economic sectors. Three sectors are dominant: welfare and health-care work,

6 Kudsk-Iversen & Andersen (2006), p. 7.

7 Jørgensen (2005).

8 Jørgensen (2005).

9 Arrowsmith (2006), p. 6.

clerical work and storage work. The vast majority of the agencies affiliated to DHS operate within these three main sectors.

The most important group of users of agency work are companies in the private sector. In 2004 they accounted for 61% of temporary agency work assignments. The public sector was the second biggest user with 37% of assignments.[10]

There are clearly flexibility aspects behind the use of temporary agency work in Denmark; the labour force is usually not cheaper (see below). On the contrary, especially in the health sector nurses and doctors employed by temporary work agencies are paid better than colleagues employed directly by the users in order to compensate for the greater insecurity of employment.

A group of researchers in 2004 drew the following general conclusion concerning temporary agency work in Denmark:[11]

> In a few segments, where there is a high demand for skilled workers, temps can achieve relatively favourable wages and working conditions and have often chosen to be "temps" because of the attractiveness of agency work compared to standard employment. In other segments, people choose to work for a temping agency as an alternative to low paid jobs or unemployment. Wages and other conditions are often less attractive than conditions in mainstream employment and often the flexibility "choice" is a take-it-or-leave-it option.

3.2 Finland

In *Finland* the temporary agency work sector has never been large. According to statistics from early 2000, about 0.4% of the workforce was employed on this kind of contract. Although a sharp increase in the number of employees in this sector has been reported lately, their relative numbers are still comparatively small. In 2005 the share of the total workforce amounted to approximately 0.7% counted in full-time equivalents over a 12-month period.[12]

As already pointed out, temporary agency work has long had a transnational dimension in Finland. During the 1970s and 1980s Finnish workers went abroad, hired by temporary work agencies, and the general policy in Finland was to try to get the foreign user companies to take employer responsibility for these workers.

Since the enlargement of the European Union in 2004 a significant number of workers have been posted to Finland from the Baltic States

10 Arrowsmith (2006), p. 7.

11 Rasmussen, Visser and Lind (2004), p. 87.

12 These figures are the official statistics given by the Labour Ministry.

(especially Estonia), mainly by temporary work agencies. Since then, several hundred Finnish-owned companies have been registered only in Estonia in order to do business in temporary agency work or the construction sector, with the aim of providing workers for Finnish user companies in different fields such as construction, cleaning, and so on. Although many of these companies may not conduct any real business, it is obvious that there has been a dramatic increase in the cross-border hiring out of workers to Finland in the wake of Estonian EU membership. One of the reasons for this boom was the restriction on free movement of workers that Finland introduced for a transitional period. In light of this development there is – at least almost – consensus in Finland that these transitional restrictions were misplaced, and early in 2006 they were lifted.

The growth of temporary agency work has been marked, especially in the construction sector, as a result of transnational or cross-border supply of temporary agency workers. By the end of 2004 the share of temporary agency workers in the construction sector corresponded to 7.8% of the user companies' own personnel and 27% of the companies in the sector used temporary agency workers.

In Finland temporary agency workers are usually employed for a fixed term. In some cases even workers on longer assignments are given successive contracts of two weeks' duration, which are prolonged every second week, a practice that has been criticised by the trade unions.[13]

There are two generally binding (erga omnes) collective agreements applicable specifically to temporary agency work. Party on the employers' side to both agreements is the Private Employment Agencies Association (HPL), with approximately 150 member companies. Party on the trade union side to the collective agreement for clerical work, book keeping and IT work is the Federation of Special Service and Clerical Employees (Erityisalojen toimihenkilöliitto, ERTO), while the Finnish Musicians Union (Suomen muusikkojen liitto) is party to the one regulating the work of restaurant musicians.

3.3 Sweden

In *Sweden* temporary agency work expanded very quickly after liberalisation in the 1990s. In 1994 temporary work agencies employed 5,000 persons; six years later 42,300 persons worked for agencies. After a substantial decline in the first years of the new century, growth was again evident in 2004. That year 35,000 persons were employed as temporary agency workers in Sweden. Irrespective of the growth of the sector it still accounts for a small proportion – only 1% – of the labour market. A study

13 See Viitala and Mäkipelkola (2005), p. 212.

from 2004 concludes that persons who are less established on the labour market – women, young people and immigrants – are overrepresented among agency workers in Sweden.[14]

Initially, temporary agency work was almost synonymous with office work. In Sweden today, occupations in warehouse/industry account for the largest share (25%) of the turnover of the agency work sector, followed by office (20%) and finance work (15%).[15]

The structure of temporary agency business in Sweden is characterised by a few, mainly multinational players which dominate the market (Proffice, Manpower, Adecco and Poolia), but also many small companies. For example, between 2000 and 2002 nurses and doctors in particular left their permanent positions in the health care sector,[16] and some of them set up their own temporary work agencies. This enabled them to take up employment as temporary agency workers with their former employers on considerably higher pay. In 2004 there were 550 temporary work agencies in Sweden; the total turnover of these companies was EUR 929 million.[17]

4. Working Conditions for Temporary Agency Workers

4.1 Denmark

In *Denmark* there is a tradition of integrating temporary agency work into the collective bargaining system. In his Nordic Council study on contract labour in 1993 Ronnie Eklund found examples from Denmark in which the affected workers had been thoroughly integrated into the terms of the user employer's collective agreement, and whose conditions had been tailored by the local trade union of the user employer.[18]

More recently there have been two models for regulating the working conditions of temporary agency workers by collective agreements in Denmark. Both models are based on negotiations between employers' associations and trade unions and not between individual companies and trade unions.[19]

The first alternative is to make special collective agreements covering temporary agency workers. This type of agreement has been concluded between the employers' organisation DHS and a number of trade unions,

14 Andersson and Wadensjö (2004), p. 32.

15 http://www.almega.se

16 Andersson and Wadensjö (2004), p. 6.

17 Arrowsmith (2006), p. 6.

18 See Eklund, *JT* (1995–96), No. 3, p. 653.

19 The following description is based on Jørgensen and Minkes (2004) and Kudsk-Iversen and Andersen (2006).

such as the United Federation of Danish Workers (3F), the Danish Trade Union of Public Employees (FOA) and the Danish Nurses Organisation (DSR). They cover very different sectors of the labour market where there is a significant amount of temporary agency work: the agreement with 3F covers drivers and warehouse functions, the agreement with the Danish Trade Union of Public Employees covers welfare work and the agreement with the Danish Nurses Organisation covers nurses.

The other alternative is to apply the traditional collective agreements to temporary agency work. These are typically collective agreements between DHS and a trade union covering work within a certain sector (for example, office and warehouse functions) or work carried out by employees who are members of the trade union in question. The temporary work agencies can use these agreements, but they are often not applicable in the situations specific to temporary agency work. Therefore, the parties have added protocols with a specific focus on temporary agency work to some of these general collective agreements.

The technique of adding a special protocol to general collective agreements has also been used by employers' association the Confederation of Danish Industries (Dansk Industri) and the Central Organisation of Industrial Employees in Denmark (CO-industri). It is also used by some other Danish organisations.

Basically, the collective agreements emphasise that wages and working conditions follow the conditions of the user company as a minimum, whereas social issues (pensions, and so on) are provided for by the temporary work agency, which is to be regarded as the employer.

The need for special collective agreements for temporary agency workers is to some extent due to the character of traditional collective agreements, which often contain provisions requiring seniority in employment for a worker to acquire certain rights, such as employer contributions to pension schemes, extra holidays, paid leave on a child's first day of sickness, term of notice and paid vocational training. These rights are typically acquired after six to nine months of service in the company. In some collective agreements the wage is also in some way linked to seniority in employment.

The collective agreement between DHS and 3F covering temporary agency workers has a special focus on some of the issues mentioned above, for example contributions to pension schemes, extra holidays and paid leave on a child's first day of sickness. However, these rights are not acquired from the beginning of the employment, but after 1,443–1,924 hours of work (varying with the type of rights) for the agency or different agencies. Seniority must be achieved within a limited time, however, and seniority lapses after twelve months without employment at the agency.

The protocols on temporary agency work added to the general agreements between the Union of Commercial and Clerical Employees in Denmark (HK) and DHS and between CO-industri and the Confederation of Danish Industries contain no special provisions concerning seniority in relation to pension schemes, extra holidays, terms of notice and paid leave on a child's first day of sickness. This means de facto that the temporary agency worker is in a disadvantaged position compared to workers directly employed by the user company concerning rights based on seniority, although formally the same rules apply.

Collective bargaining plays a dominant role in relation to temporary agency work in the health sector. The Danish Nurses Organisation (DSR) cooperates with the National Health Service, which automatically informs the trade union when it approves a new agency. On the basis of this information the trade union contacts the agency and demands that it enters into a collective agreement. DSR has threatened to blacklist agencies not covered by collective agreements, advising nurses not to work for them. Also, trade unions can exclude members who take up work with agencies with no collective agreement. The overall impact of this has been significant and consequently over 90% of temporary agency workers are covered by collective agreements. In 2004, DSR had collective agreements with 74 active temporary agencies that send out nurses and are approved by the health authorities.

The nurses are normally hired on an hourly basis. The collective agreements for these nurses regulate issues such as wages, working time and special payments for overtime and work on nights and weekends. However, the agencies have no obligation to pay contributions to pension schemes, sickness benefits or payment during maternity leave for nurses hired on an hourly basis

In Denmark temporary agency workers are usually employed on fixed-term contracts for the duration of an assignment. The worker might still be registered by the temporary work agency between assignments, but is usually not entitled to wages or any other compensation during periods when no actual work is being performed.

Several cases in Danish courts (and arbitration procedures) have cleared the ground concerning temporary agency work. The Labour Court has decided that trade unions are entitled to use industrial action in support of demands concerning temporary agency work.[20] In a judgment of 11 January 2006 the Court confirmed not only that the general collective agreement regulating the work of electricians had to be applied also to electricians performing their work as temporary agency workers, but

20 See AT 1999/66 (99.342) and Christiansen (2004), p. 252.

also that a user company that is bound by this collective agreement and hires electricians from a temporary work agency has to make sure that this agency fulfils the provisions in the collective agreement in relation to its employees.[21]

4.2 Finland

Unlike Denmark and Sweden, *Finland* has quite a comprehensive body of legislation specifically regulating temporary agency work. Temporary agency work, or "hiring out of workers", is defined in the Employment Contracts Act as a tripartite relationship between the agency, the user company and the worker/employee. The relationship between the agency and the user company is a contractual business relation; the relationship between the agency and the employee is an employment relationship governed by labour law. There is no contractual relation between the worker and the user company.

In accordance with the Employment Contracts Act and the Occupational Health and Safety Act, the employer's obligations with respect to the hired employee become the responsibility of both the agency as his or her actual employer, and the user enterprise. The agency is responsible for the obligations laid down by labour legislation and employment contracts, whereas the employer's obligations which directly concern the right to direct and supervise the work are the responsibility of the user enterprise.

The employer and the user company bear joint responsibility for health and safety issues.[22] The user enterprise has to ensure that working conditions are in order so that the hired employees will be able to perform their work as safely as other employees in the workplace. Also, the user enterprise, which exercises the employer's competence to direct and supervise the work, is responsible for meeting the requirements of the working time regulation, for example concerning rest periods. The user enterprise is also responsible for ensuring that the hired employee's working hour documents are properly filled in.

The most important responsibility of the agency is the obligation concerning wages. The agency is obliged to pay employees the pay determined by the employment contract or collective agreement, including all annual holiday compensation and additional benefits provided by law and contract. In addition, the agency's obligations include providing occupational health care and fulfilling the obligations laid down in the Act on Cooperation within Undertakings. Temporary agency workers have the same rights to information and consultation in relation to their

---

21 See Danish Labour Court (Arbejdsretten) case A2004.229.

22 See EC Directive 91/383.

employer, the agency, as other workers have. According to the Act on Equality (sex discrimination), the user company bears the responsibility of an employer in relation to the agency worker regarding his own decisions, for instance, concerning the supervision of work.

The Employment Contracts Act lays down the minimum terms of employment applicable to the employment relationship. The minimum terms of employment of the hired employee are primarily determined on the basis of the so-called normally applicable collective agreement which is binding on the temporary work agency by virtue of the Act on Collective Agreements; that means a collective agreement entered into especially for regulating certain types of work in the temporary agency work sector. If there is no such collective agreement, the terms of employment of the hired employee are determined either on the basis of the collective agreement applicable to the user enterprise as provided in the Collective Agreements Act or, secondarily, on the basis of a generally binding collective agreement applied to the sector of the user enterprise. Thus in cases where there is no collective agreement specifically regulating temporary agency work, the agency must always apply a collective agreement for the sector in which the employee works at the moment.

As already indicated there are some nationwide collective agreements regulating work typically performed by temporary agency workers, such as the agreement regulating clerical work, book keeping and IT work. This collective agreement is quite comprehensive, a document containing 40 pages. There are also some company-specific collective agreements entered into by the largest agency in the country and some unions, such as the United Service Sector Union and the Chemical Workers Union.

If neither the agency nor the user enterprise is bound by either a specific or a generally binding collective agreement, the terms and conditions of employment for the temporary worker are determined by the individual employment contract. If there is no explicit contract the employee is entitled to receive reasonable and normal pay for the work performed.

In practice, temporary agency workers in Finland are usually paid only for the period of assignment in the user company. According to some collective agreements a certain wage might also be due for the period between assignments.

The main problems for temporary agency workers in Finland are due to the fact that almost all of them are employed on a fixed-term contract. This means that in practice neither the agency nor the user company is responsible for offering the workers special benefits, such as different types of family leave.

4.3 Sweden

In *Sweden* there are very few statutory provisions specifically regulating temporary agency work, besides the three remaining restrictions mentioned earlier.

The Work Environment Act stipulates that a person hiring rented labour to work in his operations shall take the safety measures needed for that work. This means that the user company and the agency have a joint responsibility for the health and safety of the agency worker. The agency's responsibility follows from the fact that the worker is an employee of the agency, and as such is covered by all acts of Swedish labour legislation.

A few of the provisions of anti-discrimination legislation are applicable between the agency worker and the user company. In a report presented early in 2006, a Government committee proposed a completely new Prohibition and Other Measures against Discrimination Act that would replace the existing legislation. The new Act would provide temporary agency workers with enhanced protection against discrimination by user companies.

The absence of specific legislation on temporary agency work has not led to a lack of protection. On the contrary, as we see it, here is an example of the Swedish tradition of trade unions and employers' associations regulating their affairs autonomously through collective agreements working at its best. An important driving force is without doubt the will of the temporary work agencies to be accepted as "normal" employers – and in Sweden normal employers conclude collective agreements.

The first trade union to conclude a collective agreement for agency workers was the Salaried Employees' Union (Tjänstemannaförbundet, HTF) affiliated to the confederation for white-collar workers, TCO, in 1988. The collective agreement guaranteed agency workers at least half the minimum wage (stipulated in the collective agreement itself) each month, irrespective of whether the agency could find work for them. With the conclusion of this agreement agencies started to employ their workers on open-ended contracts, which is now the general rule in the sector.

The current successor to this agreement does not stipulate any minimum wage. The members of HTF and of the trade unions affiliated to the Swedish Federation of Professional Associations (academics and graduate professionals) that joined the agreement in 1998 have individual wages. However, the agreement guarantees them a monthly salary corresponding to work of at least 133 hours (calculated on their personal wage) irrespective of the extent to which they are hired out. After 18 months of employment the guaranteed monthly salary is based on an estimation of work corresponding to 150 hours.

Since October 2000 there has also been a collective agreement between the Swedish Association for Staff Agencies (Bemanningsföretagen) and the confederation for blue-collar workers, LO, for the sixteen trade unions affiliated to the latter. The basic principle of this "staffing agreement" is that when agencies hire out workers to perform work covered by any of the LO unions' "normal" sectoral collective agreements, the agency must apply to the worker the provisions on wages and other terms and conditions of employment of this sectoral agreement. However, the wage is to be calculated according to specific rules in the staffing agreement.

The staffing agreement also contains provisions on issues that require special solutions for the sector (such as forms of employment, the employee's "availability" and duty to work and the duty (!) of the agency worker not to perform work where industrial action is taking place), issues in respect of which the parties find it reasonable that the employer apply only one set of rules (such as public holiday allowance, paid time off, sick pay and maternity pay) plus rules on work environment responsibility, labour market insurance, skills development and rules of procedure in case of disputes.

As regards employment forms, the staffing agreement is stricter than the Employment Protection Act. The main rule is that the agency worker has a full-time, open-ended contract. The exceptions to this rule are few and the local trade union branch has mechanisms to monitor whether these opportunities are being abused.

In the employment contract, the agency and the worker shall agree on a personal monthly or hourly wage, which must be at least that stated in the staffing agreement (for 2006 between SEK 14,445 and 16,585 per month or between SEK 83.02 and 95.32 per hour). However, this is merely the worker's minimum wage. For assignments of more than ten days the agency worker shall be paid the average wage for comparable groups of workers employed directly by the user company. If the assignment is of shorter duration, the worker will be paid according to his or her own average earnings for the last three months, but never less than his or her personal wage plus any extra benefit that the applicable sectoral agreement may provide for.

When workers are not posted to a user enterprise but do some work at the agency or participate in training, they will be paid their personal wage.

Even for periods when the worker works at neither a user enterprise nor the agency nor participates in training, he or she is guaranteed pay of 90% of his/her average earnings during the last three months.

Another important step was taken in 2004. From time to time trade unions have argued that temporary work agencies should have to have some form of license from the authorities. So far, the government has not heeded this demand. As a result, the LO, HTF and Bemanningsföretagen, which now has some 400 affiliates, agreed on voluntary authorisation for temporary work agencies. Authorisation will be decided by a committee with representatives of the parties to the agreement and given for one year at a time, which means that it is revised every year. In order to be authorised, the agency must:

- follow the Association of Staff Agencies' ethical guidelines;
- be a member of the Association of Staff Agencies and the Confederation of Swedish Enterprise;
- be bound by collective agreements (possibility of exemption where there is no collective agreement for a certain kind of work);
- apply the general terms of delivery of the Association of Staff Agencies as a minimum;
- have liability insurance;
- have been in business for at least twelve months;
- have an equality plan;
- operate the business as a limited company;
- emphasise that it is authorised when it advertises its services;
- pay the authorisation fee.

According to a survey that Bemanningsföretagen made a couple of months later, 79% of user companies regard it as important or very important that the agency they engage is authorised.

What – apart from their wish to obtain recognition as employers like all other employers – made the Swedish agencies accept collective agreements according to which full-time, open-ended contracts are the rule and workers are paid between assignments? Part of the explanation may perhaps be found in how unemployment insurance is implemented for agency workers. In order to prevent undependable agencies from using unemployment insurance as a cushion between assignments, agency workers are to some extent treated differently from other workers. An agency worker who has recurrent fixed-term contracts with the same agency is presumed to be at the employer's disposition for work also between assignments, which means that he or she is not entitled to unemployment benefits. Likewise, agency workers can never receive benefits as part-time unemployed, since it is presumed that they are at the agencies' disposal for full-time work. Thus, offering open-ended, full-time contracts where the workers are paid between assignments may have been unavoidable for the agencies if they were to attract qualified staff.

Even in the days when temporary agency work was prohibited in Sweden it was allowed to use contract work and subcontracting,[23] and

23 See Nyström (2004), p. 197.

with the Codetermination Act of 1976 a right to trade union veto in such situations was introduced. Today, this provision indirectly promotes the interests of reliable agencies and their employees. Thus, before an employer decides to have work performed for him by someone who is not his employee – for example, a temporary agency worker – the employer is obliged to initiate negotiations with the trade union with which he is bound by a collective agreement covering the work in question. The employer must postpone the decision until the negotiations have been concluded. If the hiring of temporary agency workers seems likely to involve setting aside legislation or a collective agreement for the work or otherwise to run contrary to generally accepted practice in the industry, the union has the right to veto the decision. In practice this happens very seldom. The veto is not to be used to protect the employment of the user's own employees, only to counteract unlawful practices. The significance of the rule lies in the fact that the employer has to inform the trade union of his plans and initiate negotiations, which gives the trade union an opportunity to influence the employer's decision-making.

The legitimacy that temporary agency work has acquired in Sweden is illustrated by the Labour Court's judgment in the Abu Garcia case (AD 2003 No. 4). The background to the case was that some employees had been dismissed due to economic reasons. In such situations former employees have a preferential right according to the Employment Protection Act to be re-employed within nine months of the termination of their employment. However, instead of re-employing its former employees, Abu Garcia hired temporary agency workers. According to the trade union, this was a breach of the Employment Protection Act, but the Labour Court did not agree. Although there may be situations in which such action would be inappropriate, this was not the case here, due to the circumstances.

One remaining statutory restriction on temporary agency work is highly contested, the provision that prevents an agency worker from being hired to his or her former employer until six months have elapsed. According to a communication from the Swedish Government to the Parliament, the primary objective of this provision is to prevent "blackmail" on the part of employees attempting to raise their wage for the same job by moving to a temporary work agency when there is a shortage of labour in a certain profession.[24] The temporary work agencies call for its deletion, arguing that workers in professions where there is only one big employer within a reasonable distance are like serfs, as they cannot change jobs. Not surprisingly, the municipalities and county councils – very big employers that employ doctors and nurses – want to keep this provision.

24 Regeringens skrivelse 2005/06:91 Anställningsvillkor i bemanningsföretag.

5. Conclusions

In Sweden in particular, the evolution of collectively agreed frameworks regulating temporary agency work has taken place in parallel with European-level social dialogue on temporary agency work and the subsequent negotiations between the Member States on the Commission's proposal for a Directive. Supported by Denmark and Finland, Sweden fought hard in the Council to guarantee the freedom of trade unions and employers' organisations to conclude autonomous collective agreements on the terms and conditions of employment for temporary agency workers. At least some of the other delegations seemed to suspect that this would be a means of avoiding the application of the principle of equal treatment – especially as regards pay – between agency workers and workers employed directly by the user company.

In contrast, we have demonstrated that in all three countries the terms and conditions in the collective agreements covering agency work are to a large extent the same as or comparable with those of the user companies' own employees. Thus, legislation may not necessarily be a better option than regulation by means of collective agreements.

But again we stress that a precondition of this development in the Nordic countries is that there was already a strong collective bargaining system in place covering the "traditional" part of the labour market.

Bibliography

Andersson, P., and E. Wadensjö (2004) *Hur fungerar bemanningsbranschen?* Rapport 2004:15, Institutet för Arbetsmarknadspolitisk Utvärdering.

Arrowsmith, J. (2006) *Temporary Agency Work in an Enlarged European Union*, European Foundation for the Improvement of Living and Working Conditions.

Christiansen, J. (2004) *Grundlaeggende arbejdsret*, Jurist- og Økonomforbundets forlag.

Eklund, R. (1995/96) "A Look at Contract Labour in the Nordic Countries", *Juridisk Tidskrift*, No. 3: 625 –54.

Eklund, R. (2002) "Temporary Employment Agencies in the Nordic Countries", in *Stability and Change in Nordic Labour Law*, Scandinavian Studies in Law, Vol. 43, Stockholm Institute for Scandinavian Law, pp. 311–33.

Jørgensen, C. (2005) "Temporary Agency Work in an Enlarged European Union", EIRO thematic feature, www.eiro.eurofound.eu.int dk0506104t

Koldby Dalager, L. (2005) "Vikarbureauansatte vikarer Udvalgte arbejdsretlige problemstillinger", *Justitia*, No. 1 (February): 49–97.

Kudsk-Iversen, S., and S.K. Andersen (2006) *I krydsfeltet mellem fleksibilitet og sikkerhed. Om overenstkomstreguleringen af bureauvikarers løn- og ansættelsesvilkår*, Faos 071 at http://faos.sociology.ku.dk

Nielsen, R. (2005) *Laerebog i Arbejdsret*, 9. reviderede udg. Jurist- og Økonomforbundets Forlag.

Nyström, B. (2004) "Sweden", in R. Blanpain and R. Graham (eds) *Temporary Agency Work and the Information Society*, Bulletin of Comparative Labour Relations 50, Kluwer Law International.

Rasmussen, E., J. Visser and J. Lind (2004) "New Employment Patterns: Agencies and Agency Workers in the Netherlands and Denmark", in J. Burgess and J. Connell (eds), *International Perspectives on Temporary Agency Work*, Routledge, pp. 72–90.

Regeringens skrivelse 2005/06:91 Anställningsvillkor i bemanningsföretag.

Viitala, R., and J. Mäkipelkola (2005) *Työntekijä vuokrattuna. Vuokratyövoiman käytön vaikutuksia työyhteisöissä*, Publication of Labour Administration 283, Ministry of Labour, Helsinki.

The UK: Responding to the Need for Protection in a System Preoccupied with Flexibility

Haris KOUNTOUROS

"Pick out very light ones, if you please, young man", interposed a genteel female in shepherd's-plaid boots, who appeared to be the client.

"'Mrs Marker,'" said Tom, reading, "'Russell Place, Russell Square; offers eighteen guineas, tea and sugar found. Two in family, and see very little company. Five servants kept. No man. No followers.'"
"O Lor!" tittered the client. "That won't do. Read another, young man, will you?"
"'Mrs Wrymug,'" said Tom. "'Pleasant Place, Finsbury. Wages, twelve guineas. No tea, no sugar. Serious family –'"
"Ah! you needn't mind reading that", interrupted the client.

Charles Dickens: *Nicholas Nickelby*, first published 31 March 1839.

The temping agency readily agreed to my job preferences (no sales work or call centres), thought my £7 minimum hourly rate sensible and stated that, given my skills and experience, they would ensure a suitably challenging role. Naturally I was thrilled when they stuck me in the call centre of a double glazing company, paying me £5.50 an hour as a filing clerk.

Mark Roberts, "The Invisible Temp", *The Guardian*, 9 May 2005.

This chapter looks at the characteristics of temporary agency work in the UK and the domestic approach to its regulation, and examines the case for a Directive on temporary agency work from a UK perspective. The aim is to draw some conclusions that can illuminate the discussion on the interplay between transnational labour regulation and the domestic – UK – approach to regulation, focusing on temporary agency work. The UK policy on temporary agency work has mainly been one of liberalisation, reflecting successive governments' preoccupation with flexibility. On the other hand, recent years have witnessed some (re)regulatory measures, coupled with judicial decisions elaborating on the employment status of agency workers – a huge problem in the UK – which are rooted in the practical need to protect agency workers from exploitation. These developments may in practice indicate greater receptiveness on the part of the

UK system to labour law concerns than what is instantly apparent. The chapter is structured in three sections, followed by a conclusion.

1. Main Characteristics of Temporary Agency Work in the UK

A first characteristic of the temporary agency work sector in the UK is its long tradition; a second is its high degree of fragmentation. It is estimated that there are about 17,000 to 20,000 firms in the area of personnel recruitment, which includes the supply of workers to user undertakings.[1] More than two thirds are micro-enterprises staffed by fewer than ten people. Firms with more than 250 employees make up just 2.3% of the industry, while the country's top five companies in terms of turnover comprise a mere 16% of the domestic industry share. This compares with a share in excess of 75% in Sweden, France, Belgium and the Netherlands.

The number of agencies in the UK rose significantly during the mid-1990s, partly as a result of deregulatory measures introduced by the Conservative administration in 1994, against a backdrop of widespread outsourcing and high unemployment.[2] The agency industry has also grown in economic size. In 2004/2005 the industry had an annual turnover of £23.5 million, representing a 2.6% increase from 2000/2001, though this sum is lower than the peak reached in the previous year (£24.5 million).[3] The vast majority of revenue came from the supply of agency workers.

During the 1990s the number of agency workers also rose significantly, although there is a significant lack of consistency between available data, which makes it difficult to obtain a precise idea of the extent and distribution of agency work in the UK. On the basis of data produced by the Labour Force Survey, agency work increased throughout the 1990s at an average annual rate of 18.6%, compared to 10% for the EU-15, but since 2000 there has been a halt in the increase and even a small decrease in the overall numbers.[4] However, recent anecdotal evidence suggests that the numbers may be on the rise again, due to the increase of migrant workers following EU enlargement in 2004.[5]

According to the UK Department of Trade and Industry (DTI), the number of temporary agency workers is estimated to be between 600,000 and 700,000.[6] This represents 2.6% of the working population and com-

1 DTI (2002) p. 23 and fn 60 therein.

2 In 1994 more than 2.5 million people were unemployed in the UK. The unemployment rate then was 9.3%, compared to 4.7% in 2004.

3 REC (2006a); LRD (2002a).

4 *Cf.* TUC (2003a) p. 9.

5 See Tripathi (2005); Whewell (2006).

pares with an average of 2% in the EU-15. Agency work appears to be equally divided between men and women; however, non-white groups are significantly overrepresented: almost 87% of agency workers come from a non-white background.[7] In terms of age, agency workers are typically at the younger end of the spectrum. About 35% of all agency workers are under 25 years old; 65% are under 35 years old.[8] On the other hand, only 15% of agency workers are over 50 years old.[9]

Agency work in the UK is concentrated in services, in particular health care, transport, finance and business services, which together make up almost half of all temporary agency workers. Manufacturing provides a source of employment for a fifth of agency workers. The remaining (sub-)sectors comprise mainly education, public administration and defence, energy and water, and construction. In contrast to the size of agency firms, user undertakings are typically of a larger size.[10] Temporary agency workers are concentrated in low-skilled occupations, such as administrative and secretarial jobs and, to a lesser extent, in elementary occupations and plant operative categories. Professional and managerial jobs are rare amongst agency workers.[11]

A much higher number of agency workers is estimated by the largest employers' association in the area, the Recruitment and Employment Confederation (REC). This puts the number of agency workers at 1.3 million, double the official DTI estimate.[12] On the other hand, the Labour Force Survey, which is based on workers' self-assessment of their status, estimates the figure at around 275,000.[13] It is widely accepted, however, that this figure is a major underestimate because the LFS considers only those who are classed as employees of an agency and therefore does not account for many agency workers who believe that they are employed by the user undertaking, or those who are classed as self-employed.[14]

To add to the confusion, a report on temporary workers in agriculture and horticulture, prepared for Defra and published in August 2005, estimates that, on average, 100,000 temporary workers in agriculture are currently being supplied to farms by labour providers (gangmas-

6 Figures relate to 2002. See DTI (2003b) p. 7.

7 LFS 2002. See DTI (2003b) p. 12.

8 LFS 2002. See TUC (2003a) p. 5.

9 *Ibid.*

10 DTI (2002) p. 20.

11 LFS 2002. See DTI (2003b) p. 11 and TUC (2003a) pp. 7-9.

12 REC (2004a).

13 See DTI (2003b) p. 7.

14 *Ibid.*, and see TUC (2003a).

ters).[15] According to the report, gangmasters work with a pool of between 300,000 to 450,000 temporary workers, made up of approximately 35% women and 65% men.[16] Overall, gangmasters supply three quarters of all temporary workers in agriculture.[17] Non-UK nationals are significantly overrepresented in this group. There are twice as many non-UK temporary workers supplied by gangmasters as there are British ones, making up almost half of all temporary workers in agriculture, horticulture and co-located pack-houses.[18] These figures suggest that the extent of temporary agency work in the UK may be considerably underestimated. The physiognomy of the sector also changes in light of this report. While the DTI estimates that agriculture makes up only 1% of the total number of agency workers, the report's estimate would put this closer to 12.5%. As already pointed out, these discrepancies make it difficult to establish trends in temporary agency work with precision.

The increasing use of agency workers in the 1990s is partly linked to the rising importance of numerical flexibility over that period.[19] But according to surveys of user undertakings, the main reasons for such use are, first, the need for short-term cover for staff absence (including maternity leave and annual leave) and, second, to meet variations in demand (seasonal fluctuations or unexpected peaks).[20] While labour cost reduction does feature as a reason for opting for agency workers in some instances,[21] agency work is not always a cheap option for user undertakings, in particular where this is used due to inability to fill vacancies directly. A prominent example is the National Health Service (NHS) where, according to reports, agencies charge the health service up to 20% in commission for providing nursing staff. In 2003 the total cost to the NHS from private recruits was estimated to have exceeded £600 million.[22]

---

15 Precision Prospecting (2005), p. 15. "Defra" stands for the Department of Environment, Food and Rural Affairs.

16 Precision Prospecting primary research conducted for Defra, Spring 2004, *ibid.*, p. 16.

17 *Ibid.*, p. 17.

18 *Ibid.* On the other hand, almost three times more UK nationals than non-UK ones are recruited directly by farm enterprises as temporary workers.

19 See Storrie (2002) p. 36; Gray (2004) pp. 3-4.

20 See Cully *et al.* (1999) pp. 8-9 and Figure 3 therein.

21 Only about 1-2% of user undertakings state that they use temporary agency work as a means to cut costs. However, cost savings has been a dominant factor in some sectors, in particular education and construction. See EFILWC (2002) pp. 5. and 18 and NATFHE (2002).

22 Revill (2003). By mid-2006 a round of cost-cutting, involving staff reduction, was underway in NHS trusts across the country. Initial reports and commentary seem to indicate that agency nurses are amongst the most severely affected. See BBC1 News Broadcast, 28 June 2006.

From the workers' perspective, agency work is often, though not always, an option of last resort. An LFS survey in autumn 2002 reported that more than half of men (52%) and almost a third of women (32%) chose this form of work because they could not find a permanent job (making an overall average of 42%).[23] On the other hand, almost two in five female agency workers (37%) and a quarter of men (24%) opted for temporary agency work because they did not want a permanent job. This general picture masks some gender and age differences. Men between the ages of 50 and 64 were even more likely to say they took agency work because no permanent jobs were available (59%). This compares with 50% of younger men under 25. However, the reverse was true for women. Only 14% of female temporary agency workers between 50 and 59 said they could not find permanent work, compared to 43% of female temporary agency workers under 25.

Agency workers are commonly engaged on short assignments. The Labour Force Survey reports that, in cumulative terms, a third of all agency workers are on assignments of less than three months. About one in five agency workers works on an assignment of less than six weeks. The level of unionisation of temporary agency workers (8%) is lower than the average for the labour force as a whole (28%).[24]

2. Regulation of Temporary Agency Work in the UK

One of the striking features of temporary agency work in the UK is its very light regulation. Legal regulation consists mainly of an Act of Parliament, the Employment Agencies Act 1973,[25] and a set of Regulations,[26] which set out a number of rules that have to be satisfied before and during a contract between an agency and the worker. These rules do not create directly enforceable rights for workers and are aimed instead at ensuring the proper operation of the agency industry. Collective regulation, especially at sectoral level, is almost non-existent.

Hepple and Napier have remarked that the 1973 Act, which was promoted by a private Member and received all-party support, "was

23 LFS 2002. See TUC (2003) pp. 5–6.

24 Rates for unionisation levels relate to 1999. See Storrie (2002) p. 21.

25 Employment Agencies Act 1973 (c. 35), as amended by the Employment Protection Act 1975, the Deregulation and Contracting Out Act 1994 and the Employment Relations Act 1999.

26 The Conduct of Employment Agencies and Employment Businesses Regulations 2003 (SI 2003/3319). These Regulations replaced the 1976 Regulations and a number of other Regulatory instruments governing specific occupations. See Reg. 4(2) of the 2003 Regulations.

nothing less than a legitimation of fee-charging services at a time when their fiercest critics, notably the TUC, were demanding their abolition".[27] At best, it was "a tardy (and partial) implementation of a promise made in 1951 by the then Labour Government to bring Britain into line with the recommendations of ILO Convention No. 96 of 1949".[28] Notably, however, the UK has not ratified any of the ILO conventions in the area of agency work.[29] Later amendments to the Act removed the system of licensing which operated under the 1973 regime and, together with amendments to the accompanying Regulations, portray a clear predilection for a liberal framework, pursuant to the orthodoxy of flexibility prevailing in the United Kingdom.[30]

Both the Act and the Regulations apply in general to both profit-making and non-profit-making employment agencies, employment businesses and their clients in all sectors.[31] It is important to follow the distinction between employment agencies and employment businesses.[32] Section 13 of the EAA provides that:

> Employment agency means the business (whether or not carried on with a view to profit and whether or not carried on in conjunction with any other business) of providing services (whether by the provision of information or otherwise) for the purpose of finding persons employment with employers or of supplying employers with persons for employment by them.[33]
>
> Employment business means the business (whether or not carried on with a view to profit and whether or not carried on in conjunction with any other business) of supplying persons in the employment of the person carrying on

27 Hepple and Napier (1978) pp. 96–97.

28 *Ibid.*, p. 90.

29 These are C34: Fee-Charging Employment Agencies Convention, 1933; C96: Fee-Charging Employment Agencies Convention (Revised), 1949; and C181: Private Employment Agencies Convention, 1997.

30 *Cf.* Collins (2001).

31 There are a number of exceptions, including for services provided by university appointments boards and certain other educational institutions, by local authorities, by trade unions, employers' organisations and certain professional bodies for their members or by charitable organisations and certain services provided exclusively for ex-members of HM Forces, or for persons released from prisons or from other institutions. Services provided in respect of the supply of qualified nurses and certified midwives are also excluded but these are subject to licensing and control under the Nurses Agencies Act 1957 (in England and Wales) and the Nurses (Scotland) Act 1951. Licensing and enforcement are carried out by local authorities.

32 The distinction between "employment business" and "employment agency" is followed in this section which examines the provisions of legislation. Other sections use the term "agency" to refer to what the Act deems an "employment business".

33 EAA, s. 13(2). This section was prospectively amended by the Employment Relations Act 1999, Schedule 7, paragraphs 1 and 7. See also EAA, s. 13(1).

the business, to act for, and under the control of, other persons in any capacity.[34]

In plainer language, an employment agency introduces workers to clients for direct employment by those clients (either on a temporary or a permanent basis), while an employment business places workers with user undertakings to work, but retains the contractual relationship with the worker.[35] The distinction is significant. In the case of an employment agency the contract is with the hirer and not with the agency. Therefore, it is the hirer who is responsible for pay and all other duties normally associated with an employer. It is, in fact, unlawful for an employment agency to pay a worker directly or indirectly on behalf of the host employer where the contract is made directly between the worker and the host employer.[36] On the other hand, in the case of an employment business it is this (the business) which is responsible for the worker's pay, though supervision and control over the actual performance of the work is left to the hirer. It follows that the proposed Directive on temporary work would apply only in respect of employment businesses.

A "hirer" is defined as "a person (including an employment business) to whom an agency or employment business introduces or supplies or holds itself out as being capable of introducing or supplying a work-seeker".[37] Therefore, the term "hirer" is used to refer to clients of employment agencies, as well as user undertakings which are supplied with agency workers by employment businesses.[38] What we commonly refer to as an "agency worker" is referred to in the Regulations as a "work-seeker". This is "a person to whom an agency or employment business provides or holds itself out as being capable of providing work-finding services".[39] The use of the term "work-seeker" throughout the Regulations, in particular in those provisions where reference is made to work that has actually been performed, is rather misleading. The terminology does not fit easily with the case law of the European Court of Justice, pursuant to which what the Regulations call "work-seekers" would arguably be classed as

34 EAA, s. 13(3). See also EAA, s. 13(1).

35 The terms "hirer", "user undertaking" and "host employer" are used throughout the chapter interchangeably.

36 Reg. 8. Though there is an exception for agencies supplying work-seekers in the entertainment industry, as well as for agencies which are connected to the hirer within the meaning of Reg. 3. An example in this respect would be an in-house employment business. See Regs. 25(2)-(5), 26 and Schedule 3.

37 Reg. 2.

38 Other domestic measures, such as those on equality, use the term "principal" rather than "hirer".

39 Reg. 2.

"workers", implying more rights (especially of a Community dimension and particularly relevant to migrant workers) than what the Regulations allow for at face value.[40]

The principle of non-discrimination/equal treatment in respect of agency workers is not protected under UK legislation. However, agencies and employment businesses (as well as user undertakings) have to comply with other relevant legislation, statutory codes and official guidance relating to, for example, equal opportunities, equal pay, health and safety, immigration, national minimum wage, working time and trade union membership. Relevant legislation includes the Minimum Wage Act 1998,[41] the Sex Discrimination Act 1975,[42] the Race Relations Act 1976,[43] the Disability Discrimination Act 1995,[44] the Employment Equality (Sexual Orientation) Regulations 2003[45] and the Employment Equality (Religion or Belief) Regulations 2003.[46] As underlined in the Guidance on the Regulations, "the Government expects employment agencies and employment businesses, and hirers, to follow high standards as regards equality of opportunity".[47] One cannot but feel a sense of irony on the face of the Government's position with respect to the proposed Directive on temporary work, but at least it underlines the point that agencies and user undertakings must not ignore the wider legislative standards which apply in the area of temporary agency work.

Contrary to some other Member States' rules, UK legislation does not place any restrictions on temporary agency work, be that in terms of nature of use, duration or sector of activity. There is, however, one exception in that it is unlawful for an employment business to knowingly supply workers to provide direct or indirect cover for employees taking part in official industrial action, including strikes.[48]

---

40 See Case 66/85, *Lawrie-Blum* [1986] ECR 2121; Case C-292/89, *Antonissen* [1991] ECR I-745.

41 Minimum Wage Act 1998, sections 1 and 34.

42 Sex Discrimination Act 1975, sections 9 and 15.

43 Race Relations Act 1976, sections 7 and 14. Note that section 14 was amended by the Race Relations Act 1976 (Amendment) Regulations 2003, Reg. 16(a).

44 Disability Discrimination Act 1995, section 12.

45 Employment Equality (Sexual Orientation) Regulations 2003 (SI 2003/1661), Reg. 18.

46 Employment Equality (Religion or Belief) Regulations 2003 (SI 2003/1660), Reg. 18.

47 DTI (2004a) p. 1.

48 See Reg. 7(1). By implication, it is an excuse for an employment business which supplies a work-seeker in such situations that it "does not know and has no reasonable grounds for knowing that the first worker is taking part in a strike or other industrial dispute" (Reg. 7(1)). Note that the prohibition applies only in respect of an official strike or any other industrial action. See Reg. 7(2).

2.1 Restrictions on the Charging of Fees

With some exceptions in entertainment and modelling, employment agencies and businesses are not allowed to charge the worker a fee for finding either temporary or permanent work.[49] Given that certain services and goods can be legitimately charged (for example, advice on drafting CVs, provision of tools, cleaning materials or uniforms for sale or hiring), the Regulations specify further that employment businesses and agencies cannot render the provision of work-finding services to a work-seeker conditional upon purchasing or hiring these fee-incurring services and goods.[50] The work-seeker must receive prior notification of the services or goods for which a fee may be charged, together with details of any such fee.[51] Subsequent variations of fees must be notified to the work-seeker in advance.[52]

2.2 Requirements to Be Met before Services Are Provided

The work-seeker and the employment agency or business must agree upon terms and conditions before the provision of work-finding services begins.[53] These must normally be recorded in a single contract and given to the work-seeker before the start of the relationship.[54] The agency or business is not allowed to unilaterally alter these terms.[55] Terms and conditions must state whether the service provider will act as an agency or as an employment business, as well as the type of work that it will find, or try to find, for the work-seeker.[56]

In the case of an employment business, the contract must also state:[57]

(a) whether this is a contract of service or apprenticeship, or a contract for services and, in either case, the terms and conditions that apply, or will apply;

(b) an undertaking that the employment business will pay the work-seeker in respect of work done by him, whether or not it is paid by the hirer in respect of that work;

---

49 EAA 1976, s. 6 and *cf.* Schedule 3 of the Regulations. However, the new regulations (Reg. 26) make it illegal for agencies to charge upfront fees before finding work to work-seekers belonging to these groups.

50 Reg. 5.

51 Reg. 13(1).

52 Reg. 13(3).

53 Reg. 14(1).

54 Reg. 14(2), but *cf.* Reg. 14(3).

55 Reg. 14(4) and see Reg. 14(5).

56 Reg. 14(1)(a)-(b).

57 Regs. 14(1)(c) and 15.

(c) the length of notice of termination which the work-seeker will be required to give the employment business, and which he will be entitled to receive from the employment business, in respect of particular assignments with hirers;
(d) the rate of remuneration payable to the work-seeker, or the minimum rate of remuneration the employment business reasonably expects to achieve for the work-seeker;
(e) details of the intervals at which remuneration will be paid; and
(f) details of any entitlement to paid annual holidays.

2.3 The Employment Status of Agency Workers

The requirement to specify whether the contract is one of service, or is for services seeks to clarify from the outset the nature of the employment relationship and the employment status of the work-seeker. For employment law purposes individuals are either employed or self-employed. An employee is a person who "has entered into or who works under … a contract of employment",[58] defined as "a contract of service or apprenticeship, whether express or implied and (if it is express) whether oral or in writing".[59] The self-employed can be divided into two groups: workers and independent contractors. A worker is a person who works either under a contract of employment or under a contract for personal services other than on the basis of conducting a profession or a business activity.[60] If the individual is neither a worker nor an employee then he is an independent contractor.

Accordingly, if the contract between the parties is one of service then the individual is considered to be an employee; if it is for services then the individual is self-employed. The distinction is very important because employees have a greater range of statutory rights than workers who, in turn, have a greater range of rights than independent contractors. Employees, for example, have the right not to be unfairly dismissed, as well as redundancy rights (including the right to consultation), protection under TUPE, the right to statutory notice periods, statutory maternity pay and paid paternity leave. Workers benefit from such rights as the minimum wage, from working time Regulations, including on paid holiday and maximum working hours, and the right to be accompanied at disciplinary and grievance hearings. Those who are neither employees nor workers may benefit from rights deriving from rules safeguarding the principle of non-discrimination in a number of areas (for example, race, ethnicity, sexual orientation), as well as from a number of obligations on

58 Employment Relations Act 1996, s. 230(1).
59 *Ibid.*, s. 230(2).
60 See ERA 1996, s. 230(3).

health and safety that companies owe to a broad category of people. Acts and regulations on these issues use the term "persons" rather than "workers" or "employees".

Many standard contracts which are prepared and used by employment businesses are stated to be for services in order to avoid the more onerous legal obligations applying to employees. A written contract is not, however, determinative of the true nature of the relationship between the parties. Accordingly, in a legal dispute, employment tribunals will look at a range of issues before deciding the nature of the relationship and the status of the worker. When considering whether an individual is an employee, the courts must first decide whether there is a contractual relationship between the individual and the alleged employer. If there is, they go on to decide whether it is an employment contract. The two essential tenets of an employment contract are (1) mutuality of obligation[61] and (2) control. Mutuality of obligation exists where the company is obliged to provide work and the individual is obliged to accept it (though the extent of this obligation is a matter ultimately to be decided by the courts).[62] Control exists where the company controls sufficiently what the individual does and how he/she does it, although it need not actually supervise the work. The existence of mutuality of obligation and control does not, in itself, mean that there is a contract of employment and there is typically a need to look at other factors.[63] The two are, however, typically considered as "the irreducible minim[a]" of an employment contract.[64]

Traditionally, agency workers have had great difficulty in establishing that they are employees of either the agency (in the terms of the 1973 Act "employment business") or the hirer. This is because there is no direct contractual relationship with the hirer, while the employment business – with which the worker has a contract – does not normally exercise sufficient control over the work once he or she is posted to a hirer. The fact that the employment business is responsible for payment of wages renders it more unlikely that the worker can establish a contractual relation-

---

61 Note that a growing number of cases have held that "mutuality of obligation" is a prerequisite for any contract to exist, that is for both the "employee" and "worker" definitions. See *Stephenson v Delphi Siesel Systems Ltd* [2003] ICR 471 EAT; *Cotswald Developments Construction Ltd v Williams* [2006] IRLR 181 EAT.

62 In *Cotswald Developments Construction Ltd v Williams* the EAT held that for there to be "mutuality of obligation" there only needed to be a commitment to pay for work done and a minimum, or at least some reasonable amount, of work that a person was obligated to do.

63 See *Lane v Shire Roofing Company (Oxford) Ltd* [1995] IRLR 493 (CA).

64 *Carmichael v National Power plc* [1999] ICR 1226 HL, at 1230g, *per* Lord Irvine of Lairg and 1235c, *per* Lord Hoffmann.

ship with the hirer, but it is not sufficient to establish employee status with the employment business.[65] Needless to say, in a legal dispute between the worker and the hirer, the latter will, as a matter of course, dispute "mutuality of obligation". Over a period spanning no less than thirty years courts have struggled with this issue. The majority of reported cases depict a conservative stance on the part of the courts and employment tribunals, reflected in a formalistic application of the tests which need to be satisfied in order to determine the existence and nature of a contractual relationship. The result has been that agency workers are often denied basic legal rights.[66]

It should, however, be noted that a series of recent decisions of the Court of Appeal have challenged the notion that agency workers can be denied basic legal protection on account of their triangular relationship. In *Dacas* the Court of Appeal decided by a two-to-one majority that, in the normal course of events, the user undertaking should typically be considered to be the employer, given that it will be the one exercising control over the worker.[67] It was further held that employment tribunals should examine the possibility of an implied contract of employment, in the absence of an express contract and even where there is a contract but this is stated to be one for services, rather than of services.[68] This examination should take into account in particular the factual circumstances surrounding the case. The *Dacas* ruling was confirmed more recently in *Cable & Wireless plc v Muscat*, reflecting a welcome acknowledgement by the judges of the realities of today's complex employment relationships and of the need for legal protection for agency workers.[69]

2.4 Temp-to-perm Fees

A typical practice in the area of agency work is for employment businesses to charge hirers when the latter decide to offer direct employment to the worker. This transfer charge is commonly known as a "temp-to-perm fee" and has led to concerns that high fees can inhibit the promotion of more stable forms of employment and limit market flexibility because they discourage hirers from offering direct employment to agency work-

65 *Costain Building & Civil Engineering v Smith* [2000] I.C.R. 215; *Construction Industry Training Board v Labour Force Ltd* [1970] 3 All E.R. 220.

66 See, for instance, *Wickens v Champion Employment* [1984] ICR 365; *Ironmonger v Movefield* [1988] IRLR 461; *Stephenson v Delphi Diesel Systems Ltd* [2003] ICR 471; *Montgomery v Johnson Underwood Ltd* [2001] IRLR 269.

67 *Dacas v Brook Street Bureau (UK) Ltd* [2004 IRLR 358 CA. In his opinion, Mummery LJ considered the possibility of concurrent, or joint employers (par. 19). Sedley LJ called this "a trilateral contract of service" (par. 78).

68 See also Franks *v Reuters Ltd* [2003] IRLR 423 CA.

69 *Cable & Wireless plc v Muscat* [2006] All E.R. (D) 127 CA.

ers.[70] On the other hand, agencies and employment businesses are entitled to protect their legitimate business interests.[71]

Regulation 10 seeks to strike a balance between these two concerns. The regulation applies to three situations. The first is where an employment business introduces but does not actually supply a work-seeker to a hirer. Second, there has been a supply and the temporary worker is engaged directly by the client (on a temporary or permanent basis), or through another employment business. The latter occurs when the client puts the work out to tender and requires workers currently supplied by one employment business to transfer to the books of another employment business whose tender was accepted. Finally, there has been a supply to a client and the client has introduced the work-seeker to a third party.

In the first situation an employment business must offer the hirer (client) the opportunity to either pay a fee, or give notice that the work-seeker will continue working in that capacity for a negotiated period of time, in which case no fee may be charged.[72] In the second situation the rules are broadly the same but the Regulations provide for a fixed period of time and lay down a system of calculation for that period.[73] In the third situation the rules state that the employment business is allowed to charge a fee, provided the transfer takes place within a fixed period of time, specified by the Regulations.[74] Where a hirer pays money pursuant to a contractual term which is unenforceable under Regulation 10, the hirer is entitled to recover that money.[75]

2.5 Protection against Detrimental Clauses and Action

The regulations offer protection from detrimental action taken against work-seekers. An employment agency or employment business must not take, or threaten to take, any detrimental action, or include restrictions in contracts which would prevent work-seekers from either terminating their contract with the employment agency or employment business, or working for others, such as for the client, directly or through a competing employment agency or employment business.[76] Nor can an employment agency or employment business require the work-seeker to notify

---

70 See TUC (1999) par. 5.2.

71 DTI (2004a) p. 8.

72 Reg. 10(1)-(3).

73 Reg. 10(4)-(6).

74 Reg. 10(1), 10(4)-(6). Temp-to-third party fees where there has been no supply are not covered by this Regulation and fees in this regard can be charged without restriction.

75 Reg. 31.

76 Reg. 6(1)(a).

them of the identity of any future employer.[77] Moreover, an employment agency or employment business cannot subject, or threaten to subject, a work-seeker who has lawfully terminated any contract with it, or given notice to do so, to any detrimental action.[78] In addition, a work-seeker cannot be subjected to detrimental treatment because he or she does not agree to a variation of the terms and conditions of his or her contract.[79]

2.6 Prohibition of Withholding of Pay

Regulation 12, which was introduced in 2003, makes it unlawful for an employment business to withhold, or threaten to withhold, the whole or part of any payment to a temporary worker in respect of any work he or she has done on the basis that:

a) the employment business has not received payment from the hirer;
b) the worker has not produced a signed timesheet confirming that he or she has worked during a particular period of time;
c) the worker has not worked during any period in addition to the period he or she is claiming payment for; or
d) in relation to any other matter which is within the control of the employment business.

2.7 Enforcement and Sanctions

The enforcement of the Act and the Regulations is the responsibility of the DTI's Employment Agency Standards Inspectorate. Following abolition of the licensing system that had existed up to 1994, observance of standards is scrutinised in accordance with a system of inspection provided under the Act. Employment agencies and employment businesses must keep detailed records, including contracts made, names and addresses of work-seekers and hirers, fees, dates of commencement and termination of assignments and details of work-seekers' qualifications.[80] Inspectors may enter the premises of an employment agency or employment business and request to inspect records,[81] and to be furnished with information relevant to compliance with the rules by any person on the premises.[82]

---

77 Reg. 6(1)(b).

78 Reg. 6(1)(a). Note, however, that "a requirement in a contract with the agency or employment business for the work-seeker to give a period of notice which is reasonable to terminate the contract" does not constitute a detriment – Reg. 6(2)(c).

79 Reg. 14(6).

80 See Reg. 29 and Schedules 4-6.

81 EAA 1973, s. 9(1)(a)-(b).

82 EAA 1973, s. 9(1)(c).

In cases of gross misconduct the Act empowers the Secretary of State to apply to an employment tribunal for a prohibition order against a particular person.[83] Such orders ban a person from carrying on, or being concerned with the carrying on of, any employment agency or employment business for up to a maximum of ten years.[84] Prior to issuing any such order a tribunal must be satisfied that the person in question "is, on account of his misconduct or for any other sufficient reason, unsuitable to do what the order prohibits".[85] Provided the same applies to a director, secretary, manager or similar official of a body corporate, a tribunal may also issue a prohibition order in relation to a body corporate.[86] Appeals on a question of law may be made to the Employment Appeal Tribunal.[87] More minor breaches of the Act or the Regulations are liable to a summary conviction and a fine (currently not exceeding £5,000).[88] An agency worker who believes that he or she has been the victim of an action by an employment agency or employment business in breach of the Act or the Regulations may contact the DTI's Inspectorate. This receives around 10,000 enquiries a year. Between 1999 and 2004 it prosecuted 24 agencies, resulting in seven banning orders.[89]

2.8 Collective Regulation

Sectoral collective agreements covering temporary agency work are almost unknown in the UK. One reason for this is that the REC, the largest confederation of recruitment companies, does not have a negotiating mandate. Some informal links have begun to be developed with the TUC, especially on issues such as training, health and safety and promotion of good practice.[90] The exception to this general rule is the agreement between BECTU and PACT on the conditions of employment of freelance workers.[91] The agreement, which affects 6,500 workers in the sector, dates back to the early 1970s and it was renewed most recently on 1 November 2004.[92] It regulates the basic wage rates (as well as the basic

83 EAA 1973, s. 3A(1)-(3).

84 EAA 1973, s. 3A(1)-(3).

85 EAA 1973, s. 3A(4).

86 EAA 1973, s. 3A(5)-(6).

87 EAA 1973, s. 3D(1).

88 EAA 1973, ss. 3B, 5(2), 6(2), 9(3), 10(3).

89 House of Commons Hansard Written Answers for 11 February 2004.

90 EFILWC (2002) p. 21.

91 "BECTU" stands for Broadcasting, Entertainment, Cinematograph and Theatre Union. "PACT" stands for Producers Alliance for Cinema and Television.

92 The basic details of the agreement may be found in the depository of the Labour Research Department. Visit www.lrd.org.uk

pay for holiday leave) of freelance workers and provides for a 40-hour guaranteed minimum week. However, while PACT negotiate on behalf of their members, they do not enforce compliance with the agreement.[93] According to the UK Report for the European Foundation's survey on temporary agency work in 2002, "this is a major cause of grievance between BECTU and PACT. BECTU nonetheless believes that the agreement is useful in terms of setting minimum terms and conditions; it has also in the past served as a legal reference point in disputes with employers".[94]

A somewhat larger number of agreements exists at company level. Manpower has been the leading agency in this respect; Adecco also has a number of agreements. Manpower has agreements with several unions, including the T&G – its main partner – at national level, dating back to 1983.[95] This agreement provides that pay rates for agency workers must be at the same level as the rate for the job they are supplied to fill. Where no reference exists, the agreement regulates basic pay rates for a number of grades at local level. It also provides for rights to individual representation, for the provision of information about the union in the induction pack for new workers and for check-off facilities. There are also some provisions on training.[96] There are few other known examples of company-level agreements with unions. Typically, these include provisions broadly similar to those in the Manpower/T&G agreement.[97] One of the unions actively involved in the area is the AEEU,[98] whose sample agreement contains a clause allowing agency workers to choose their employment status.[99] For its part, the GMB makes it a condition of their dealing with agencies that these are members of the REC and are signatories of the REC's Code of Practice.[100]

Nonetheless, the fact remains that temporary agency work in the UK is largely outside collective regulation. The fact that the REC does not have a negotiating mandate, coupled with the unwillingness of many of the smaller agencies to engage with trade unions, can be cited as the main

93 EFILWC (2002) p. 21.

94 *Ibid.*

95 EFILWC (2002) p. 22 and visit www.lrg.org.uk. "T&G" (formerly "TGWU") stands for Transport and General Workers' Union.

96 EFILWC (2002), *ibid.*

97 *Ibid.*

98 "AEEU" stands for Amalgamated Engineering and Electrical Union. Following its merger with MSF in 2001, the union was renamed as Amicus.

99 EFILWC (2002) p. 22.

100 *Ibid.* "GMB" stands for General, Municipal, Boilermakers and Allied Trade Union. REC's Code of Practice may be accessed at http://217.118.140.148/rec/about-the-rec/code-of-practice-2006.pdf

reasons for this. This seems to confirm Gray's observation that oligopoly in the recruitment industry may "paradoxically ... work to the agency temp's advantage".[101] This is because small agencies, like those dominating the UK market, are more likely to engage in cut-throat competition in their local market, while larger, national or multi-national agencies "are more likely to compete on "quality" (of matching and training, for which they are better resourced than small agencies) and show some willingness to engage in union agreements".[102] But it should also be noted that the relatively small number of agency workers within the total working population has – perhaps understandably – meant that unions have traditionally focused their priorities elsewhere (for example, union recognition, outsourcing and working time).[103] Having said that, the TUC has been actively campaigning for the adoption of the proposed Directive on temporary agency work since the launch of the procedure by the Commission.

2.9 *Gangmasters' Act*

As noted earlier, the general licensing system which was set up in 1973 was abolished in 1994. The old licensing system was generally held to be rather weak,[104] although this was not the main reason for its demise. This was mainly driven by the government's wish to deregulate the agency market in order to expand it. Trade unions have since been demanding the re-introduction of a licensing system, arguing that the fragmented nature of the agency industry in the UK makes it very difficult to spot and prevent abuses.[105] More recently, this concern has been shared by agencies themselves. An REC survey in 2003 showed that 70% of the industry wanted a return to licensing.[106] While the DTI has no plans to re-introduce a general licensing system, an Act of Parliament passed in 2004 introduced a licensing system for labour providers in agriculture. The Gangmasters Licensing Act 2004 was prompted by the drowning of up to 23 Chinese cockle pickers (two bodies were never recovered) earlier that year whilst working in Morecambe Bay. The incident exposed the appalling conditions under which many temporary workers in agriculture work (many of whom are foreign nationals, often in a desperate financial situation, with little command of English and no knowledge of the law).

Within the framework of the Act, a Gangmasters' Licensing Authority has been set up with the responsibility of issuing licenses to gangmasters

101 Gray (2004) p. 6.
102 *Ibid.*
103 EFILWC (2002) p. 26.
104 EFILWC (2002) p. 2.
105 TUC (1999).
106 REC (2006b).

who meet a set of standards following inspection.[107] Licenses are required for the supply of workers to agriculture, horticulture and processing and packaging of any produce derived from agriculture, fish or shellfish. The first license was issued on 2 May 2006 and it is expected that about 1,000 gangmasters will be licensed within the first year of the system.[108] From 1 October 2006 it is an offence, carrying a maximum penalty of 10 years' imprisonment and/or a fine of up to £5,000, to operate as a labour provider without a license.[109] Further compliance inspections by the Authority can result in the revocation of licenses or the imposition of requirements which then have to be met by the gangmasters concerned. It is also an offence, liable to up to 51 weeks' imprisonment (6 months in Scotland and Northern Ireland) and/or a fine, for a labour user to knowingly employ an unlicensed labour provider.

The standards which need to be observed by gangmasters are, as stated in the GLA Guide to the Licensing Standards, "no more than current legal requirements",[110] consisting broadly of the rules operating under the Employment Agencies Regulations and a range of other relevant legal provisions (such as VAT registration and health and safety obligations). During consultations prior to their adoption, unions had criticised the standards for not going far enough, while labour providers' organisations took the view that they were too onerous.[111] The new system should serve to emphasise the importance of complying with minimum legal requirements and ensure that labour providers and users know what these requirements are. In turn, this should bring some order and transparency into a sector which has traditionally been beset by problems. In the longer run, the success of the system obviously depends vitally on its enforcement, and in particular on the effectiveness of compliance inspections and sanctions.[112]

---

107 See also The Gangmasters (Licensing Authority) Regulations 2005.

108 GLA (2006a).

109 In the shellfish gathering sector licensing begins on 1st October 2006. Offences for this sector will be introduced in April 2007. *Ibid.*

110 GLA (2006b).

111 See REC (2006b).

112 A system of categories and points, ranging from "critical" (incurring automatic revocation of a license, or refusal to provide a license) to "correctable" (incurring just 2 out of a maximum 30 points) determines the severity of non-compliance with the standards. For instance, evidence of physical or mental mistreatment of a worker is classed as a "critical" (30 points) breach of standards, while supplying workers to a user to cover for workers on strike is classed as a "reportable" breach of standards, incurring 4 points. Preventing workers from taking trade union membership or penalising them from doing so is a "major" breach of the standards and incurs 8 points.

3. Prospects of the Adoption of a Directive on Temporary Agency Work from a UK Perspective

The launch of the procedure for adopting a Directive on temporary agency work has ignited a heated debate on the need for such a measure.[113] The main parties' positions differ: unions favour the prospect of adoption, while employers oppose the Directive, particularly as currently drafted. The REC has lobbied extensively to ensure (a) that pay would be excluded from the scope of the Directive; (b) that Member States can choose between an agency or user comparator; (c) that the six-week derogation would be extended to a minimum of 12 months; and (d) that it would be clarified that temp-to-perm fees are not banned.[114] Its lobbying has not been limited to the UK government, which during the negotiations in the Council of Ministers effectively sided with the employers' position, but has been extended to the governments of the new Member States and the EU institutions.[115] A press release issued in 2004 states that "the Directive was successfully blocked in 2003 following a pro-active lobbying campaign by the REC and a strong line taken by the UK Government".[116] The CBI has taken an equally hard line and has also campaigned powerfully against the Directive.[117] This is clearly shown by the impact the CBI had on UNICE's position during the negotiations between the European social partners.[118]

Employers and Government are concerned that the proposed Directive would increase operating costs and lead to job losses.[119] In addition, it is argued that the Directive would be "hugely detrimental to the flexibility of the UK labour market".[120] Furthermore, on the basis of research it commissioned, the REC claims that the majority of temporary workers are satisfied with the degree of independence and control that temporary agency work gives them.[121] For the REC, moreover, agency work pro-

113 The discussion in this section is based on the amended proposal for a Directive on temporary work. See European Commission, "Amended Proposal for a Directive of the European Parliament and the Council on working conditions for temporary work ers", COM(2002) 701 final, 28 November 2002.

114 REC (2002).

115 REC (2004b), (2004c) and (2004d).

116 REC (2004e).

117 Hall (2002b).

118 See Ahlberg, Chapter 9 in this volume.

119 See REC(2002); Hall (2002a); House of Commons European Standing Committee C (2002), columns 4-20; House of Commons Trade and Industry Committee (2005), paras. 42 and 45.

120 REC (2005b). See also Hall (2002a).

121 REC (2005a).

vides a stepping stone to permanent employment, especially for younger workers. The last two claims may be true, although one should not necessarily assume that temporary agency workers would have been unemployed had they not been agency workers; they may well have been permanent workers from the start. In fact, evidence does not lend strong support to the hypothesis that temporary agency work leads to permanent employment, especially in the long run.[122] On the other hand, it should be acknowledged that, in spite of the liberal legal regime, the degree of temporary agency work in the UK is broadly similar to that of many other EU countries.[123]

Implementation of the Directive would not be a panacea for problems in the area of temporary agency work in the UK. The legal uncertainty regarding the employment status of agency workers – a major problem in this area – would not be resolved even after implementation of the Directive. Nor would the Directive solve continuing problems in enforcing the Regulations and protecting agency workers from rogue agencies. Serious difficulties in ensuring effective enforcement, largely due to a lack of sufficient resources for the DTI's Inspectorate, have been noted by both the TUC and the REC.[124] A particularly problematic area has been ensuring compliance with Regulation 12. As noted earlier, this Regulation was introduced in 2003 and aims to prevent abuses in respect of workers' pay, in particular where a worker omits to produce a timesheet confirming the hours he or she has worked. A TUC report published in February 2005 argues that, in practice, the new Regulations have had little impact on curbing incidents of exploitative deductions from workers' pay by their agencies.[125] According to the report there is:

> an apparently widespread continuing abuse of agency workers, in particular migrant workers, by some employment businesses or "temp agencies". The TUC is particularly concerned at the practices of some agencies which routinely make deductions for items such as cashing a pay cheque; for transport; and for providing equipment and/or uniforms, with the result that the worker's pay then falls below the national minimum wage. In some cases these deductions can swallow up most or all of a week's wages. Migrant agency workers are especially vulnerable to this type of exploitation because of language difficulties and a lack of knowledge about UK employment law.[126]

122 See Kvasnicka (2005); TUC (2003a) pp. 11-12; TUC (2005) p. 11.

123 See TUC (2005c) p. 10

124 See TUC (2003a); REC (2005c).

125 TUC (2005b). See also TUC (2005a).

126 TUC (2005b).

In many cases such practices remain unreported because, as the TUC states, "many workers remain unaware of their rights and are terrified of losing their jobs and their accommodation".[127] Another area likely to remain problematic is that of pensions, especially if these are excluded from the scope of the Directive. A TUC survey of workplace representatives in 2002 found that 70% of agency workers did not have access to a pension scheme.[128] Many of these were denied pension rights because of their status; others faced serious problems due to the fact that they moved from one user undertaking to another. The ruling of the European Court of Justice in *Allonby* in 2004 has the potential to address at least some of the problems in this area.[129] In its decision the Court held that it is discriminatory, contrary to Article 141 EC, to maintain rules which exclude workers who are notionally self-employed from pension schemes just because of their status. Yet these issues portray some of the practical limitations of a prospective transnational regulation of temporary agency work by means of the proposed Community Directive.

These limitations, however, do not lessen the need for adoption and implementation of the proposed Directive in the UK.[130] This is so for three reasons in particular. First, there is a need to end discrimination against agency workers. Research on the working conditions of agency workers has found that temporary agency work is typically accompanied by inferior working conditions in terms of pay, holiday entitlement, training (including on health and safety issues) and career development opportunities.[131] This is mainly due to the lack of legal protection for the principle of equal treatment in temporary agency work. On closer examination, these findings are not called into question even by the REC's own research.[132] In some cases the gap in earnings can reach 20 percentage points (this was even higher before the introduction of the minimum wage in 1998).[133]

127 TUC (2005a).

128 TUC Workplace Representatives Survey 2002, cited in NATFHE (2002) p. 3.

129 Case C-256/01, *Debra Allonby v Accrington & Rosendale College and Others* [2004] ECR I-873. For a commentary see Fredman (2004).

130 COM(2002) 701 final.

131 DTI (2003b) esp. 18-25; Wiseman and Gilbert (2000) esp. 44-47; NATFHE (2002) p. 3; EFILWC (2002) p. 8;

132 See REC (2005a). The REC research states that "over 50% of agency workers *feel* they receive at least the same pay as permanent workers. A substantial number (24%) *believe* that they actually get paid more." (Emphasis added.)

133 This is especially the case with workers in process, plant and machine operatives and skilled trades. See DTI (2003b) p. 18. Agency nurses constitute the only specific category that earns a higher rate of pay.

A second reason supporting the case for adopting and implementing a Directive on temporary agency work is the need for a statutory minimum floor of rights to address the pervasive lack of collective regulation of this area. Voluntary codes of practice, though important, do not seem sufficiently effective in addressing the problems of agency workers.[134] A third reason relates to the need for improving the quality of temporary agency work in line with the strategic goal set by the European Council in Lisbon, to improve economic growth and competitiveness, promote job creation and quality in work and increase social cohesion.[135] The principles laid down in the draft Directive, such as the protection of the principle of equal treatment and the promotion of social dialogue, not least in order to improve temporary workers' access to training,[136] are vital elements of a policy aiming at improving the quality of temporary work and meeting the Lisbon objectives.[137]

According to the DTI's own regulatory impact assessment (RIA), implementation of the principle of equal treatment in the UK is expected to enhance working conditions and improve training and therewith career development and job security for temporary agency workers.[138] Despite this, as stated above, both government and employers' associations have obstructed the adoption of the Directive, demanding a long qualifying period in respect of the principle of equal treatment. Otherwise, they claim, business flexibility could be damaged, leading to loss of employment.[139] But if the Directive was implemented with a six-month qualifying period, half the agency workers in the UK would not have access to the right to equal treatment; if this was raised to 12 months, a staggering 71% of all UK agency workers would be left without protection.[140] Remarking on the issue, the House of Commons Trade and Industry Committee states:

> The business organisations and the Government, by focussing on the six week derogation period, are missing the more important issue which is the scope of the directive. We fully support the principle that temporary agency workers should, in most respects, enjoy the same working conditions as the permanent staff. Whilst the agency worker is in place, he or she should be entitled to the same hours and have access to the same facilities, for example, as directly

134 TUC (2003a) at 15.

135 European Council, "Presidency Conclusions of the Meeting in Lisbon", 23–24 March 2000, par. 5.

136 COM(2002) 701, draft Articles 5 and 6(5).

137 *Cf.* European Commission, "Employment and Social Policies: A Framework for Investing in Quality", COM(2001) 313 final, 20 June 2001.

138 See DTI (2003b) for a detailed assessment of benefits.

139 See REC (2002), (2004d) and (2004e); Hall (2002a) and (2002b).

140 DTI (2003b) pp. 9-10.

> employed colleagues. This should be the case from the day that the assignment starts and should not be subject to any derogation period whatsoever. If the intention of the directive is to ensure that agency workers enjoy adequate conditions in their temporary posts, we can see no reason why they should have to wait six weeks before enjoying this "privilege".[141]

One can only speculate on what the Committee would have to say had it been informed that the Government was actually arguing for a six-, and preferably a 12-month qualifying period. It is unlikely that this is the result of a deliberate confusion, but one gets the impression that the Parliament has not been following very closely the Government's activities in the Council of Ministers and that the Government itself has been rather vague with its information to the Parliamentary committees responsible for scrutinising progress on the negotiations.[142] It is also worth noting that in its "Warwick agreement" with the trade unions (done to secure the latter's support for the former in the (then) forthcoming elections), in July 2004, the Government pledged "to support the EU Agency Workers Directive and to engage with the Commission with a view to reaching an early agreement on the proposed Directive".[143] From Kerstin Ahlberg's exposition of the negotiations within the Council in this volume, it appears that the Government maintained its position as regards the qualifying period and other issues (like the scope of exclusions) at the same time as it promised unions a constructive position on adoption of the Directive.[144] This is remarkable.

Yet there is a deeper issue here. Is it really the case that the prospect of implementation of the proposed Directive, in particular as regards the principle of equal treatment, implies a trade-off with competitiveness and employment? Are the Government's concerns, and those who support it, justified? The DTI's own regulatory impact assessment (RIA) does not provide evidence to support the claim that the Directive will compromise competitiveness or that it will lead to a loss of employment, even if the principle of equal treatment applied from day one.[145] On the contrary, the RIA explicitly states that "more people may enter the labour market as agency workers, due to improved employment conditions".[146] At worst, the RIA notes, there is a possibility of a reduction in the demand for temporary agency workers, which cannot, however, be quantified.[147] Yet, as

141 House of Commons Trade and Industry Committee (2005) par. 50.

142 See, in particular, House of Lords European Union Committee (2003).

143 Visit http://www.amicustheunion.org/Default.aspx?page=3002

144 See Ahlberg in this book, pp. 191–262.

145 DTI (2003b) pp. 30–31.

146 DTI (2003b) p. 1.

147 *Ibid.*, at 30.

already noted, employers make use of agency workers principally in order to provide short-term cover and meet short-term fluctuations in demand.[148] Given the nature of these reasons, there is very little, if any, scope for a change in the demand for agency workers due to a relative increase in the labour costs of agency work.[149]

More likely, implementation of the Directive would make it less attractive for employers to recruit agency workers instead of directly recruiting permanent or fixed-term employees (or replacing permanent staff with temporary agency workers), where the reason for doing so is simply labour cost reduction. This type of cost advantage for user undertakings is indeed likely to diminish somewhat after the implementation of the principle of equal treatment. However, in terms of employment quantity objectives, this will only cause a problem if companies do not replace temporary agency workers with directly-recruited temporary or permanent staff.[150] Judging from the experience relating to the implementation of the Fixed-term work Directive (which seems to have contributed to a modest reversal in the expansion of temporary work but not in the overall number of jobs in general), we may expect that any losses in temporary agency work would be compensated by gains in permanent work and/or direct recruitment, without a loss in the overall rate of employment.[151] Benefits in terms of increased income (largely from the implementation of the principle of equal treatment) would also constitute a small, but significant, contribution to the effort to combat in-work poverty and promote social inclusion, especially as many agency workers are at the low end of the income scale.

Additionally, the very small number of agency workers means that the overall impact on labour costs would not be significant. The vast majority of implementation costs are expected to be passed on to user undertakings and accordingly the agency market would not be substantially affected.[152] Nor is there any appreciable risk of harming the general economy, even assuming the worst case scenario in which some small agency companies close. At most, "it is possible that the Directive may affect

148 See Cully *et al.* (1999).

149 In fact, if one takes into account developments in relation to the extension of paternity leave there is every reason to assume that the need for cover for permanent staff absence will increase even further.

150 *Cf.* DTI (2003b) p. 30.

151 See TUC (2005b). A recent REC study has found that, in 2005, demand for TA workers diminished as a result of greater direct recruitment, reflecting tighter labour market conditions. See REC (2006). The fact that in such conditions especially, employers appear to give greater emphasis on ensuring appropriate skills, reinforces the need for enhancing the quality of temporary agency work, not least in terms of training.

152 DTI (2003b) pp. 24-27.

smaller agencies to a relatively greater extent than larger agencies. However, small agencies only make up about 1.5% of small businesses in the UK, therefore the effect on the small business sector as a whole will not be large".[153] The start-up of agency businesses is also unlikely to be affected, since agencies will not face additional set-up costs.[154] The DTI concludes unreservedly that "competition in the labour market should remain. Consumers will not be adversely affected".[155]

User undertakings, while likely to incur some costs from implementation of the principle of equal treatment, also stand to benefit, not least from efficiency and productivity gains. These are expected to flow mainly from improvements in workers' skills, provided the Directive's provisions on training are respected in practice.[156] In addition, "implementation of the non-discrimination provisions of the Directive, for example in terms of enhanced pay and holiday entitlement, will also serve to increase the motivation and commitment of temporary agency workers", which are important factors in productivity.[157] Agency workers' integration and retention could also be improved by implementing the Directive's provisions requiring the supply of information about vacancies in user undertakings.[158]

4. Conclusions

A first conclusion is that the UK approach to the regulation of temporary agency work is not a labour-law approach. Instead, temporary agency work regulation has been used as an instrument to ensure the proper operation of the agency industry, establishing a number of basic standards for both employment businesses/agencies and users. Yet remarkably little concern has been given to agency workers themselves. This holds true even taking into account the reforms that took place in 2003 and which primarily sought to consolidate and simplify the regulatory framework. While some of the changes were partly aimed at offering some protection to agency workers (for example, the prohibition of withholding of pay),[159] it is also the case that the reformed regulatory framework has remained far away from traditional labour law concerns, most notably perhaps the need to vest agency workers with rights to equal treatment and to clarify their employment status. Consequently, equal rights for

153 *Ibid.* p. 37.

154 *Ibid.* p. 29.

155 *Ibid.*

156 *Ibid.* p. 22.

157 *Ibid.*

158 *Ibid.*

159 SI 2003/3319, Reg. 12.

agency workers are still, by and large, alien to the domestic context. To understand the UK approach better, it is useful to remember also that regulation and associated rights for atypical workers in general have been purely EU-driven developments. It is also worth pointing out that the UK's implementation of legislation in respect of part-time and fixed-term workers has a conspicuously minimalist flavour and never goes beyond the minimum requirements of the relevant Framework Agreements.[160] In this environment it is not too difficult to appreciate the opposition to the prospect of an EU Directive on temporary agency work by business circles in the UK, even if one does not agree with them.

Another conclusion relates to the Government's position. At best, this can be described as inconsistent. It may be that the Government has been anxious to appease both employers and trade unions for its own political benefit. The 2004 "Warwick agreement" between the Government and trade unions, in particular, indicates that temporary agency work was an important issue for the relationship between the parties in the run-up to the general election of 2005. Yet, in the end, lobbying by employers' associations proved more successful than trade union pressure, as the Government's actual position in the Council of Ministers reveals. However, attributing the Government's position solely to stakeholders' lobbying conceals another factor which should be considered. This is the Government's own ideological preoccupation with "competitiveness" and "flexible markets";[161] a trail which has continued from the previous (Conservative) administration. However, while competitiveness and flexibility are not in themselves objectionable, they can lead to serious problems for workers and the economy if no measures exist to protect workers and channel restructuring towards a path of lasting competitiveness and sustainable growth, rather than one based on social dumping and short-term solutions.[162] According to the (Labour) Government's own rhetoric, flexible markets need to be accompanied by "fairness".[163] This arguably includes measures to ensure access to training and rules prohibiting discrimination against workers engaged in flexible forms of work, in particular agency workers. The Government's position in respect of the proposed Directive on temporary work amounts to a serious failure to make good its own promises with implications which far exceed the domestic context, given the devastating impact it has had on

160 What is more, there are serious concerns that, on certain issues, the UK regulations fail to meet even the minimum requirements. For instance, the implementing regulations on fixed-term work apply only in relation to "employees", while the Agreement explicitly extends to "workers".

161 See Collins (2001) and cf. Kilpatrick (2003).

162 Cf. Deakin and Wilkinson (1994); Deakin (1996); Sengenberger (1990).

163 Cm 3968, White Paper: Fairness at Work, 1998.

the prospect of adopting this measure. More broadly, the Government's stance may be said to reflect a more general reluctance towards the prospect of further development of transnational labour regulation.

Notwithstanding the above, a further conclusion emerges relating in particular to the adoption of the Gangmasters' Act and more recent court judgments on the employment status of agency workers. Both these developments are important in the context of the interplay between domestic and transnational regulation because their underlying rationale belongs to the more traditional labour-law approach to regulation of agency work. That is, protection of workers and improvement of employment conditions. This labour law approach also inspires the proposed Directive on temporary agency work.

It is possible to view these national developments simply as reactions to domestic concerns or incidents, uninfluenced by transnational considerations. On this view, these developments have nothing significant to add to the discussion on the interplay between domestic and transnational regulation. But it is also possible to venture another interpretation. While recognising the domestic particularities giving rise to them, it is possible to view domestic developments as reflective of a slowly increasing willingness on the part of some regulatory actors in the UK, namely the courts and Parliament, to embrace the EU aim of setting some minimal standard of protection for temporary agency workers. If this interpretation is accepted, we can speak of an evolutionary domestic process involving an expanded range of regulatory players that may even be in tension with each other. Taken in its totality, this evolutionary system indicates a greater receptiveness on the part of the UK system to labour-law concerns (familiar in transnational regulatory approaches) than appears at first sight.

Bibliography

Allen, S., and C. Wolkowitz (1987), *Homeworking: Myths and Realities*, London: Macmillan Education.

Broad, D. (2000), "The Periodic Casualization of Work. The Informal Economy, Casual Labor, and the Longue Durée", in F. Tabak and M.A. Crichlow (2000), pp. 23–46.

Collins, H. (2001), "Regulating the Employment Relation for Competitiveness", 30 *Industrial Law Journal* 17.

Cully, M., A. O' Reilly, N. Millward, J. Forth, S. Woodland, G. Dix and J. Bryson (1999), *The 1998 Workplace Employee Relations Survey. First Findings*, London: Routledge.

Deakin, S. (1996), "Labour Law as Market Regulation: the Economic Foundations of European Social Policy", in P. Davies *et al* (eds), *European Community Labour Law: Principles and Perspectives*, Liber Amicorum Lord Wedderburn of Charlton, Oxford: Clarendon Press, pp. 63–93.

Deakin, S., and F. Wilkinson (1994), "Rights vs Efficiency? The Economic Case for Transnational Labour Standards", 23 *Industrial Law Journal* 289.

Department of Trade and Industry (DTI) (2002), *Proposal for a Directive of the European Parliament and of the Council on Working Conditions for Temporary Agency Workers – Regulatory Impact Assessment*, London: DTI.

Department of Trade and Industry (DTI) (2003a), *Employment Agencies Act 1973 and Regulations – General Guidance*, London: DTI (http://www.dti.gov.uk/er/agency/regs-pl971.htm).

Department of Trade and Industry (DTI) (2003b), *Proposal for a Directive of the European Parliament and of the Council on Working Conditions for Temporary Agency Workers – Regulatory Impact Assessment* (revised), London: DTI.

Department of Trade and Industry (DTI) (2004a), *Guidance on the Conduct of Employment Agencies and Employment Businesses Regulations 2003*, London: DTI.

Department of Trade and Industry (DTI) (2004b), *The 1998 Workplace Employee Relations Survey*, London: DTI (http://www.dti.gov.uk/er/emar/1998wers.htm).

European Commission (2001), "Employment and Social Policies: A Framework for Investing in Quality", COM(2001) 313 final, 20 June.

European Commission (2002), "Amended Proposal for a Directive of the European Parliament and the Council on working conditions for temporary workers", COM(2002) 701 final, 28 November.

European Council (2000), "Presidency Conclusions of the Meeting in Lisbon", 23–24 March.

European Foundation for the Improvement of Living and Working Conditions (EFILWC) (2002), "Temporary Agency Work: National Reports: United Kingdom" (http://www.eurofound.eu.int/publications/files/EF0236EN.pdf).

Fredman, S. (2004), "Marginalising Equal Pay Laws", 33 *Industrial Law Journal* 281.

Gangmasters Licensing Authority (GLA) (2006a), Press Release: "Traditional Gangmaster Gets First License", 2 May.

Gangmasters Licensing Authority (GLA) (2006b), Licensing Standards. Agriculture, Horticulture and Processing and Packaging for Food, Fish or Shellfish (www.gla.gov.uk/ documents/GLA%20Standards.pdf).

Gray, A. (2004), "Dilemmas in the Regulation of Temporary Work: Some European Comparisons". Research paper, at http://www2.umist.ac.uk/management/ewerc/ wes2004/papers/gray.pdf

Hall, M. (2002a), "Directive on Temporary Agency Work Could Damage Flexibility, Warn CBI and Government", EIRO: UK0203101N.

Hall, M. (2002b), "CBI Renews Attack on Draft Temporary Agency Workers Directive", EIRO: UK0212101N.

Hemming, J. (2003), "A Question of Status", *New Law Journal* 1213.

Hepple, B.A., and B.W. Napier (1978), "Temporary Workers and the Law", 7 *Industrial Law Journal* 84.

House of Commons European Standing Committee C (2002), "Working Conditions for Temporary Workers", Minutes of procedure, 10 July.

House of Commons Trade and Industry Committee (2005), UK Employment Regulation, Seventh Report of Session 2004-05, 08 March, HC 90-I.

House of Lords European Union Committee (2003), Forty-ninth Report, Session 2002-03, 18 November.

Kilpatrick C. (2003), "Has New Labour Reconfigured Employment Legislation?", 32 *Industrial Law Journal* 135.

Kvasnicka, M. (2005), "Does Temporary Agency Work Provide a Stepping Stone to Regular Employment?", Discussion Paper 31/2005, Collaborative Research Center 649 (http://econwpa.wustl.edu/eps/lab/papers/0510/0510005.pdf).

Labour Research Department (LRD) (1999), "Equality Near for Agency Workers", *Labour Research* (June).

Labour Research Department (LRD) (2002a), "Employers Exploit Agency Work Boom", *Labour Research* (August).

Labour Research Department (LRD) (2002b), "Selecting Employees for Redundancy", in *Redundancy Law – A Trade Unionist's Guide* (LRD Booklets, February).

Maguire, K. (2003), "BT Strike Over Indian Call Centres", *The Guardian* (3 June).

NATFHE (2002), *Working Conditions of Temporary (Agency) Workers. Response to DTI Consultation on Proposed European Commission Directive* (London).

Precision Prospecting (2005), *Temporary Workers in UK Agriculture and Horticulture. A Study of Employment Practices in the Agriculture and Horticulture Industry Co-Located Packhouse and Primary Food Processing Sectors*. Report prepared for Defra, 05 August.

Recruitment and Employment Confederation (REC) (2002), "Response to the Consultation on the Proposed Agency Workers Directive" (http://www.rec.uk.com/rec/lobbying/ AWDresponseOct2002.pdf)

Recruitment and Employment Confederation (REC) (2004a), "Annual Recruitment Industry Survey Summary" (29 October).

Recruitment and Employment Confederation (REC) (2004b), Press Release: "AWD Update – REC in Hungary and Slovakia" (21 October) (http://www.rec.uk.com/rec/press-centre/RECinHungaryandSlovakia_-1004.aspx).

Recruitment and Employment Confederation (REC) (2004c), Press Release: "AWD Update – REC visit to Estonia and Lithuania" (19 November) (http://www.rec.uk.com/rec/press-centre/Estonia-lithunania.aspx).

Recruitment and Employment Confederation (REC) (2004d), "AWD Update – Feedback from October 4 Council of Ministers Meeting" (http://www.rec.uk.com/rec/ lobbying/agency-workers-directive.aspx).

Recruitment and Employment Confederation (REC) (2004e), "Agency Workers' Directive Back in the Agenda" (http://www.rec.uk.com/rec/lobbying/agency-workers-directive.aspx)

Recruitment and Employment Confederation (REC) (2005a), Press Release: "REC Counters TUC Attack" (14 October) (http://www.rec.uk.com/rec/press centre/2005-10-tucattack. aspx).

Recruitment and Employment Confederation (REC) (2005b), "EU Agency Workers Directive" (http://www.rec.uk.com/rec/lobbying/policy-agencyWorkers.aspx).

Recruitment and Employment Confederation (REC) (2005c), Press Release: "The REC Urges Local Businesses to Stand Strong in Fight Against Red Tape" (http:// www.rec.uk.com/rec/press-centre/2005-08-redtape.aspx).

Recruitment and Employment Confederation (REC) (2006a), "Annual Recruitment Industry Survey Summary" (11 January) (http://www.rec.uk.com/rec/research/industry-survey-summary.aspx).

Recruitment and Employment Confederation (REC) (2006b), "Licensing Starts for Agencies Again in April 2006 – What Does This Mean for the Industry?" (http://www.rec.uk.com/ rec/gangmaster/gangmasters.aspx, accessed 15 February 2006).

Sengenberger, W. (1990), *The Role of Labour Standards in Industrial Restructuring: Participation, Protection and Promotion*, DP/19/1990 (rev.91), ILO, Geneva.

Storrie, D. (2002), *Temporary Agency Work in the European Union. A Study for the European Foundation for the Improvement of Living and Working Conditions*, Luxembourg: OOPEC.

Tabak, F., and M.A. Crichlow (eds) (2000), *Informalization: Process and Structure*, London: Johns Hopkins University Press.

Trades Union Congress (TUC) (1999), Regulation of the Private Recruitment Industry – TUC Response, 30 September, http://www.tuc.org.uk/law/tuc-360-f0.cfm

Trades Union Congress (TUC) (2003a), "Agency Work in Britain Today", 23 May, http://www.tuc.org.uk/law/tuc-6676-f0.cfm

Trades Union Congress (TUC) (2003b), Press Release: "Agency Temps Get Some Protection But Not Enough", 27 November, http://www.tuc.org.uk/work_life/tuc-7364-f0.cfm

Trades Union Congress (TUC) (2005a), Press Release: "Illegal Deductions Mean Many Agency Workers Fail to Earn the Minimum Wage", 22 February, http://www. tuc.org.uk/law/tuc-9424-f0.cfm

Trades Union Congress (TUC) (2005b), "Below the Minimum: Agency Workers and the Minimum Wage", http://www.tuc.org.uk/law/tuc-9440-f0.cfm

Trades Union Congress (TUC) (2005c), "The EU Temp Trade: Temporary Agency Work Across the European Union", 17 June, http://www.tuc.org.uk/extras/eu_agency.pdf

Tripathi S. (2005), "Catering for Globalisation", *The Guardian* (24 August).

Whewell T. (2006), "Poles Come to Crewe", BBC Newsnight, 20 January, http://news. bbc.co.uk/1/hi/programmes/newsnight/4631802.stm

Wiseman, J., and F. Gilbert (2000), *Survey of the Recruitment Agencies Industry*, prepared by the Bostock Marketing Group for the Health and Safety Executive, Norwich: HSE.

Wong, G. (2004), "Whose Employee Am I Anyway?", *New Law Journal* 610.

France: Another Approach to Flexicurity

Christophe VIGNEAU

1. Introduction

Temporary work refers in French labour law to the triangular form of employment whereby a company, called a temporary work firm, assigns a worker to a customer company, called a user. This emerged in France in its modern form between the two world wars, but the temporary employment service industry has experienced substantial growth during the second half of the twentieth century. From 1988 to 2006, the percentage of agency workers within the total workforce increased from 0.7% to 2.1%.[1] The profile of temporary workers also changed during the 1970s. During the 1950s and 1960s the temporary employment sector had a majority female workforce, mainly in secretarial work and services. This situation changed from the end of the 1970s due to the growth of temporary agency work in industry. In 2005, the population of temporary workers comprised 27.7% females and 72.3% males.[2] Males are predominantly employed in building and industry, which represent respectively 20.6% and 45.8% of temporary agency employment. However, it is worth noticing that temporary agency work is growing within the service sector. From 1999 to 2005, the proportion of agency workers employed in this sector rose from 29.4% to 32.9%. In contrast, within industry the proportion decreased during the same period, from 51.9% to 32.9%. Agency work in France also tends to be predominantly for young workers. The average age of agency workers was 29 in 2005; 33% of agency workers were under 25. These figures demonstrate that agency work is a way of getting one's first work experience for a significant proportion of workers. The fact that a lot of students temp during their studies explains the high rate of young people amongst agency workers. Finally, statistics show that agency workers tend to be lower qualified than average. In 2000, the rate of unqualified workers rose by 20% amongst temporary agency workers. All these data confirm that temporary agency work is mainly a transitory form of employment.

1 This proportion reaches 3.5% in the private sector.

2 The statistics come from the annual report of the *Syndicat des Entreprises de Travail Temporaire*, the organisation representing employment agency firms.

This form of work was legalised and regulated in France by Act No. 72-1 of 3 January 1972. However, agency work had been growing for 20 years without regulation. Due to the lack of legislation, various dubious practices had emerged. This form of work was highly controversial, even amongst legal scholars, because it was considered a form of exploitation and was assimilated to the unlawful practice of "*marchandage*", whereby a person employs workers on behalf of another person or company. Over the past 50 years a number of important factors have modified the economic, social and legal context of the development of temporary agency work. During the 1950s and 1960s, the growth in temporary agency work took place in a context of full employment. Therefore, workers found temporary agency work an easy way of better capitalising on their abilities or qualifications. Workers tended to choose temporary agency work and enjoyed, in terms of pay in particular, a comparatively better situation than workers in a bilateral employment relationship. However, from the middle of the 1970s onward, the increase in unemployment changed the context of temporary agency work. Temporary agency work became an alternative form of employment for the unemployed or those who could not find a permanent position.

After regulation of fixed-term contracts in 1979, the agency work contract is considered an atypical form of employment in contrast to the open-ended contract. The main characteristic of these forms of employment is their precarious nature. To the employers' demands for more flexibility, the French legislator has responded with the introduction of new categories of contracts concluded for a limited period. Besides the open-ended contract protected by the legislation on dismissal, new types of contracts have appeared allowing employers to hire employees on a fixed-term basis. Like fixed-term contracts, agency work contracts will be considered the first elements of precariousness in labour law. Workers employed on such contracts will be considered precarious workers. Inherently precarious, these contracts are concluded for a definite duration. The French legislator tried to achieve a compromise between the employers' desire for more flexibility and the workers' need for security. This flexicurity "à la française" has been achieved by restricting the use of these forms of contract, mainly by requiring an objective basis for the use of agency workers and by limiting the duration of the contract. It has also made it more difficult to breach the fixed-term contract before its term, requiring a serious misdemeanour. The open-ended employment contract remains the most common way of hiring workers, fixed-term contracts being exceptional. From an historical perspective, it is interesting to observe that agency work does not give rise to as much criticism as before. This might be explained by the growing precariousness of employment in general. In fact, the French legislator recently provided new employers with more flexibility. Instead of expanding the number of situations in which employers may use fixed-term contracts or agency work, the French legislator decided to make it easier to breach the open-ended contract. This was the idea behind the "*contrat nouvelle embauche*" adopted in August 2005 and the "*contrat première embauche*" withdrawn after the protest demonstrations of spring 2006. These contracts establish a probationary period of two years during which the employer does not have to provide an objective ground ("*cause réelle et sérieuse*") to dismiss a worker. In other words, the open-ended contract cannot be considered the most secure form of employment, at least during the first two years. Consequently, a two-year fixed-term contract might appear more secure for a worker than a "*contrat nouvelle embauche*", even if it is open-ended.

Therefore, while temporary agency work is on the EU's agenda, this form of work is no longer a preoccupation in France. In 1953, France ratified the ILO's Fee-Charging Employment Agencies Convention 96 of 1949. However, France has not ratified the Convention 181 on private employment agencies of 1997. In fact, temporary agency work is no longer an issue in France. The content of the French regulations is very close to the directives proposed by the European Commission during the 1980s.[3] The main idea was to reach a balance between flexibility for enterprises and security for workers. In this sense, the most recent proposals of the Commission[4] appear very liberal in comparison with the French regulations. The equilibrium found in French law is based on three aspects: (i) a restricted use of agency work, (ii) a more secure employment contract and (iii) legal status for temporary agency workers.

2. Restricted Use of Agency Work

2.1 The Regulation of Temporary Work Firms

Under French law, hiring temporary workers is not without restrictions. On the contrary, companies who want to specialise into this activity must meet a number of legal conditions, aimed at guaranteeing the reliability of the temporary help service sector. First of all, hiring temporary agency workers must be the company's exclusive activity. According to this principle, a temporary work firm is not allowed to engage in anything other than leasing workers. Job placement is consequently excluded from the

3 Proposal for a Directive of the Council on temporary work, OJ, C 128/2, 19 May 1982; Amended proposal for a council directive concerning the supply of workers by temporary employment businesses and fixed-duration contracts of employment, OJ, C 133/1, 21 May 1984.

4 Proposal for a Directive of the European Parliament and the Council on working conditions for temporary workers, OJ, C 203 E, 27 August 2002.

activities of temporary work firms. On the other hand, only temporary work firms may engage in the activity of leasing temporary agency workers. In other words, temporary work firms enjoy a private monopoly on supplying temporary workers. It is a criminal offence to violate these requirements.

In addition, the founder of the company must provide financial guarantees. The 1972 Act did not foresee any mechanism to guarantee the payment of wages in case of the insolvency of the temporary work agency. In order to prevent such problems an act of 2 January 1979 imposed on temporary work firms the obligation to deposit funds in a bank or other financial body. This provision aims at ensuring the payment of wages to workers and tax contributions to the state in case of the insolvency of the temporary work agency. The level of the guarantee depends on the company's annual turnover and must not be lower than a sum fixed by decree.

Finally, the company must be registered with the labour administration. In addition to the requirement of exclusive activity and a financial guarantee, temporary work firms are subject under French law to a procedure of declaration. The declaration must be made to the labour inspector of the place where the temporary work firm is located. The procedure of declaration is less rigorous than that of licensing. Furthermore, a system of authorisation, in contrast to a system of declaration, often gives rise to a significant number of legal disputes if license applications are rejected. The mechanism of declaration only requires the communication to the labour administration of certain information concerning the temporary work company.

2.2 Limited Grounds for the Assignment of Agency Workers

French law restricts the use of agency work. Only an objective and temporary need for workers justifies recourse to temporary workers. These restrictions also apply to the use of fixed-term contracts. In this sense, no distinction is made between agency work and fixed-term work. A double legal requirement is imposed by Art. L. 124-2 of the Labour Code. First, this article establishes the general principle according to which "whatever the ground, the temporary contract of employment can have neither as an aim nor as its effect to permanently fill a job related to the normal and permanent activity of a company". The second paragraph of this article specifies that only a "precise and temporary task called a 'mission'" may justify the use of temporary agency workers. The legal terminology, which retains the concepts of "task" and "mission", expresses this specific and objective character of the assignment of the temporary agency workers. The main preoccupation of the legislator is to avoid the use of agency workers to fill permanent jobs within companies. Only jobs of a temporary character within the user company may justify recourse to agency work or fixed-term work.[5] In practice, many infringements of this rule occur. In particular, these contracts are often used in lieu of a probationary period which is not permitted for hiring agencies or fixed-term workers.

Secondly, French law lays down a number of situations in which the use of temporary agency workers is authorised. Assignments are classified under three headings: (i) the replacement of workers on leave, (ii) the temporary increase of activities and seasonal jobs, or (iii) jobs for which, in some sectors, it is usual not to hire workers on an open-ended contract. The first category of recourse encompasses all situations involving workers on leave. Any employee on leave may be replaced by a temporary agency worker, whatever the nature of their contract of employment (open-ended or fixed-term, full-time or part-time). The leasing of temporary agency workers is prohibited only for the replacement of striking workers. With the exception of the latter, all forms of leave may justify recourse to temporary agency workers (holiday, illness, accident, disciplinary action, national service, and transformation of a full-time job into a part-time one).

Employers enjoy a certain flexibility concerning the replacement of employees on leave by temporary agency workers. The courts have accepted that an agency worker does not have to be posted in the job performed by the employee on leave. The company is entitled to substitute the employee on leave by another company employee and to post the agency worker in the latter's job. The courts also consider the successive replacement of several employees by the same temporary agency worker as lawful. But in this situation, a new employment contract must be concluded for the replacement of each successive employee on leave.

The second category enabling recourse to a temporary work agency concerns increases in company activity. This category covers a large number of forms of recourse to temporary workers. All increases in usual activity justify recourse to temporary agency workers. But this category also includes situations of exceptional increases in workload not related to the company's normal activity. The only condition is the temporary character of the increase of workload. Examples of exceptional increases in workload not related to the usual activity of the company may be training, computerisation or a company audit. The installation of safety equipment may also furnish a lawful reason to employ agency workers.

The third category of recourse comprises all seasonal activities and activities for which, in certain sectors, it is usual not to resort to perma-

---

5 The French *Cour de cassation* often recalls this rule and turns an agency contract into an open-ended contract between the user and the worker. For an example: Soc., 21/01/2004, *Droit social*, obs. C. Roy-Loustanau.

nent workers. Seasonal sectors are mainly agriculture, food and tourism. Seasonal work is defined as any activity that is repeated each year, at approximately fixed dates, according to a seasonal rhythm or collective ways of life. Concerning jobs for which it is not usual to resort to open-ended contracts, the employer has to comply with two legal requirements: (i) the company must be in a sector included on a list drawn up by the labour administration, although inclusion on the list does not imply that the company may use agency workers; (ii) the job for which an agency worker is employed should be one for which workers are generally not employed on a permanent basis. However, in a case of 2003 this second requirement was set aside by the French *Cour de cassation.*[6] This case has been criticised mainly because it contradicts Articles L.122-1 and L.124-2 of the Labour Code. Indeed, these texts have general scope and exclude the hiring of fixed-term and agency workers for employment of permanent character in the company. This rule applies whatever the ground for the assignment.

The requirement of an objective ground for bringing in agency workers constitutes the restriction on agency work under French law. Any use of agency workers in violation of the provisions on objective grounds renders the user liable under civil and criminal law. The second restriction consists of limiting the duration of the assignment period.

2.3 Limited Duration of Assignments

In terms of the duration of assignments, French law presents a rather complex character mainly because the maximum duration of an assignment depends on its grounds. For most situations, the total duration of an assignment must not exceed 18 months, renewal included. This maximum duration is reduced to 9 months when the assignment occurs on specific grounds (recruitment of a worker for indefinite duration, urgent work). On the other hand, the maximum legal duration is extended to 24 months in case of assignments carried out in a foreign country, for the replacement of a worker who left the company because his or her job no longer exists or to meet an exceptional export order.

An important feature of the French regulations is the strict link between the duration of the employment contract and the duration of the assignment. The end of the assignment contract dictates the termination of the employment contract. Article L.124-2-2 of the French Labour Code lays down that "*the temporary mission must have a precisely determined end from the signing of the contract*". Therefore the assignment contract must determine a time limit and it is on this basis that the employment contract is established. Some provisions, however, aim at

---

6 Soc., 26/11/2003, *Droit social*, 2004, p. 629, note C. Roy-Loustanau.

giving employers some flexibility in adapting the end of the assignment contract. First, the contract's expiry date may be brought forward or postponed to a limited extent determined by the law. For assignments of less than 10 days, the law allows a margin of two days. For longer assignments, the duration may be postponed or put forward by a day for every five working days. In any case, on the one hand the termination date may not be brought forward by more than ten days and, on the other, postponement must not go beyond the maximum laid down in the legislation.

Second, French law envisages, under the three grounds of recourse, the possibility for an employer to set an indefinite term to the contract of assignment. The replacement of an employee on leave constitutes the first situation in which the fixing of a definite term is not required; in this case, only a minimum duration need be mentioned in the contract and the termination of the contract may be postponed until the person on leave returns to work, without consideration of maximum legal periods. Here the necessarily unknown return of the employee on leave explains the flexibility given to the employer. The second exemption concerns assignments related to seasonal work or to sectors in which it is not usual to employ permanent workers. This hypothesis covers all tasks the duration of whose execution is uncertain. Again, a minimum duration must be specified in the contract. The third situation in which no definite term is required concerns how long a worker recruited on a permanent contract has to wait to take up his post. The contract has to be concluded for a minimum duration and must not exceed nine months, a period which constitutes the legal limit envisaged in this case of recourse. In contrast to the previous cases of derogation, a maximum period is therefore applicable.

French law only admits one renewal of the assignment contract. In addition, this renewal is subject to strict conditions. First, the renewal must not go beyond the maximum legal duration. Second, the grounds of the renewal must be similar to the initial contract. Third, the renewal is forbidden in situations in which an indefinite term is allowed. Another preoccupation of the French legislator has been to prevent employers from engaging agency workers on a long-term basis by successive assignments. Specific provisions are therefore established to avoid abuses. Paragraph 3, Article L.124-7 foresees that, at the end of an assignment contract, a period of one-third of the duration of the contract must be allowed to lapse before hiring a worker under fixed-term contract or bringing in an agency worker for the same position. The important element is not the worker but the position when it comes to deciding whether the successive assignment contracts are lawful. An employer may lawfully sign successive assignment contracts with the same agency worker if his occupation varies from one assignment to another. In any case the employer will have to provide a specific ground for each assignment. Similarly, an employer is not allowed to conclude successive assignment contracts for the same position, even though the worker is different.

The regulation of successive missions is intended to prevent improper use of temporary agency work. Article L.124-7 al.3 of the Labour Code rules that an employer may not use an agency or fixed-term worker for a position previously occupied by the same type of worker. At the end of an agency worker's assignment contract, the employer may not have recourse to an agency worker or contract a fixed-term worker before a period equal to at least one-third of the duration of the previous contract. With this provision, the French legislator aims to prevent companies from using on a same workstation workers supplied by a temporary agency firm and subsequently employed under a bilateral fixed-term contract. The break period is not required in cases where the use of agency workers is due to unforeseeable circumstances: a new absence of a permanent employee on leave, urgent work needed for safety purposes, jobs for which it is not common to resort to workers on open-ended contracts, and seasonal employment. However, if an agency worker refuses to renew his mission or terminates the contract before its expiry date, the user is entitled to have recourse to another agency worker without respecting the waiting period.

For any infringement of the rules regarding the duration, renewal or successive number of assignments the user company may incur criminal or civil liability. French law also establishes an open-ended contract between the user and the agency worker each time the assignment goes beyond the maximum legal duration or the term of the contract. This sanction strongly deters companies from violating the provisions related to the duration of assignments. Special provisions cover the premature ending of the assignment contract. If the temporary work firm breaches the contract, the worker must be offered a new contract of temporary employment within three working days. The new contract must last as long as the previous one. Agency workers who are not offered a new assignment must be paid what they would have received if the broken contract had lasted to its end.

3. A More Secure Employment Contract

3.1 Contractual Formalism

Temporary agency work constitutes a tripartite form of employment articulated around two distinct contracts: a contract of assignment and a contract of employment. Under French law, the contract of employment must coincide in time with the assignment contract. Consequently, the assignment contract between the user company and the temporary work firm dictates the length of the employment contract. Therefore the commercial contract pre-empts the labour contract. In order to facilitate control of the coincidence between the two contracts, the French legislator imposes a strict contractual formalism. This contractual formalism requires that the contracts be written, in contrast to the common rule which does not require the written form. This applies to both the contract of assignment and the contract of employment.

3.2 A "Grave Misdemeanour" Required for a Breach of Contract

Fixed-term contracts and agency work contracts are commonly considered to be precarious employment. This interpretation is based on the fact that such contracts are concluded for a limited duration. To a certain extent, the open-ended contract is linked to stable employment, whereas fixed-term contracts and agency work contracts are related to precarious employment. If this last proposition seems correct considering French law, the former appears more debatable. Fixed-term contracts and agency work contracts have a less precarious character than open-ended contracts in terms of legal regime. It is indeed more difficult for an employer to break an agency work contract or a fixed-term contract than an open-ended contract. This situation was heightened by the recent reform which introduced the "*contrat nouvelle embauche*" whereby during the first two years the employer may dismiss an employee with an open-ended contract without any justification. In contrast, in order to end a fixed-term contract before its term, French law requires that the employer prove a grave misdemeanour on the part of the employee or a situation of "*force majeure*". The French Cour de cassation applies this rule very strictly, denying the employer any other way of ending the contract before its term. No other ground is admitted apart from an agreement between the parties to put an end to the fixed-term contract before its due term. The employer cannot claim non-performance of the contract on the part of the employee (*exceptio non adimpleti contractus*). Any contractual clause organising premature ending is void. The employer must prove a "grave misdemeanour"[7] on the part of the worker if he wants to end the contract. In this sense, these contracts are more secure than an open-ended contract which can be broken merely on the basis of a "real and serious cause". Therefore, on the scale of faults in French labour law, the one required for breaking a fixed-term contract or an agency work contract is stricter than the one imposed to justify a dismissal of a worker under an open-ended contract.

French law compensates the limited duration of the contract by providing the worker with some guarantees that the contract will last until its

7 A 'grave misdemeanour' is defined as an act which constitutes a breach of the labour contract that makes it impossible to keep the employee within the company during the notice period.

term. First, if the user company breaks the assignment contract with the agency it does not entail a breach of the employment contract between the agency and the worker.[8] Second, this rigorous position is expressed by the sanction imposed in case of a breach of contract before term by the agency. In this situation, the agency must find another assignment for the worker of the same duration. If not, the agency must pay the worker the wages he would have received until the end of the contract. In this way, the French legislation wants to deter employers from breaking the contract before term, making it more secure for the worker. The idea behind the French legislation is to protect the worker against any premature breach of the agency contract. The aim is to give the worker some security in the employment relationship, unless he commits a grave misdemeanour. One should not increase the precariousness of contracts of definite duration by making it easier to breach them before term. A breach of contract before term by the worker is not sanctioned so rigorously: the worker only has to pay damages according to the losses suffered by the employer. Since 2002, the worker has not had to pay any damages if he was recruited by the user company on an open-ended contract.

4. Legal Status for Temporary Agency Workers

Temporary agency work creates for the worker a dualistic relationship: with the temporary work firm on one side, and with the user company on the other. The first company takes on the legal status of employer, while the second constitutes only the user of the worker's labour power. Therefore, agency work constitutes a new kind of legal position, the user of the worker. Distinct from the familiar status of employer, the status of user appears more singular in terms of labour law structures. Nevertheless, the distinction between the one who employs and the one who uses the worker is fundamental to the legal machinery of temporary agency work. To an employer a worker is subordinated; to a user a worker is at their disposal. As one author has pointed out, agency work allows "the direct use of labour power without subordination".[9] While in the past the criterion of subordination assimilated the employer to the user, it is not necessarily the case nowadays.

The tripartite relationship inherent in agency work defines the legal rights given to agency workers under French law. The rights of temporary agency workers are determined according to different factors: their legal status as employees, their integration within a working community and the precarious character of their employment.

8 Soc., 9/07/2003, *Bulletin civil de la Cour de cassation*, V, No. 203.

9 Gaudu (1986), p. 151.

4.1 Rights Related to the Presence of the Agency Worker on the User Company's Premises

Two main consequences may be drawn from the performance of the job on the premises of the user company. First, agency workers must enjoy similar treatment to that given to the user's employees. Therefore, permanent workers at the user company serve as comparators for determining most of the employment rights of agency workers. Consequently, the French legislator gives priority to the working community over legal status in determining the rights of agency workers. Equality applies to pay and all working conditions in the broad sense.

Secondly, the user may be found liable for any damages suffered by the agency worker during the assignment. Regardless of the contractual link between the temporary agency worker and the user company, some rights and obligations exist between the two. The mere fact that the agency worker performs his work within the user undertaking imposes some legal obligations on the company. The French labour code foresees that during the assignment the user is responsible for all working conditions. Therefore, the user has a general obligation of protection in relation to the agency worker. Any harm caused to the agency worker during the assignment may lead to criminal or civil liability on the part of the user. The user is also liable for all damages caused by the temporary agency worker to third parties. In particular, the user has a duty to ensure the safety of temporary agency workers.

4.2 Rights Related to Employee Status within the Agency Work Firm

Like any other employees, agency workers are entitled to collective and individual employment rights. However, the precariousness of the employment relation sometimes hampers the full exercise of these rights. Most employment rights have been developed according to a model of open-ended contract. Nevertheless, the French legislator has in some cases tried to adjust employment rights to the peculiar situation of agency workers. These particular provisions aim at allowing temporary workers the possibility to exercise some basic employment rights. In other words, they try to make these rights effective. Among the employment rights adapted to the specific situation of agency workers, it is worth studying more carefully access to vocational training, collective rights and social protection. The access of temporary agency workers to vocational training requires adjusting common rules to the characteristics of this form of employment. In 1983 a collective agreement was concluded at national level by the national federation of temporary agency work and trade unions. This agreement organises vocational training for agency workers. A training insurance fund was to subsidise vocational training for agency workers. In 1990, the contribution of temporary work firms to the development of vocational training was raised to 2% of the total wage bill, while in other sectors the rate is generally fixed at 1.5%. This measure shows the significance accorded to training by the social partners in the temporary work industry. In order to provide access to training for agency workers, the collective agreement created a specific regime. First, seniority conditions are calculated on the basis of the number of hours performed as agency workers. Therefore seniority is not calculated on a company basis, as is usually the case, but on a sectoral basis. Any assignment counts, whatever the temporary work firm. However, the collective agreement requires that at least half of these hours are performed within the temporary work firm where the training leave is granted. Another adjustment of the common legal provisions relates to the calculation of the temporary worker's remuneration during his leave for training. Remuneration during the leave is calculated on the basis of the wages being received during the mission at the time the leave was requested. These collective agreements facilitate agency workers exercising their right to vocational training.

The collective rights of temporary workers constitute a very sensitive issue. The precarious character of agency work prevents agency workers from exercising their right to collective representation. Most agency workers hesitate to join a trade union or to stand for professional elections mainly because they fear reprisals from the temporary agency firm. To be more precise, they fear not being offered further assignments. In a sense one might wonder whether this form of employment is compatible with collective rights. The performance of the assignment within the user company, the short duration of the assignment and the permanent change of employer make it particularly difficult for agency workers to exercise collective rights. In order to give agency workers such a possibility, a specific regime has been established. The first problem was to determine on what basis agency workers should be counted within the workforce of the user company for all matters related to collective rights. The law includes agency workers in the calculation of the workforce in order to decide whether the number of employees of the temporary work agency goes beyond the threshold established for a trade union representative or elected works committee. The total workforce of the temporary agency firm must include not only the permanent employees but also the temporary workers employed for at least three months during the last calendar year. The second problem relates to the rights of agency workers to vote and stand for election. French law has laid down rules to permit agency workers to exercise these collective rights. Agency workers may vote in elections at the temporary work agency when they have three months' seniority during the last twelve months preceding the drawing up of the lists. In order to stand for election they must have been employed by the temporary agency firm for at least six months out of the last eighteen before the election. Workers must also have been employees of the temporary agency firm at the time the lists were drawn up.

Two others aspects of the collective rights of agency workers are worth mentioning because they reflect the specificity of this form of employment. One interesting development of French law concerns the crediting of hours to agency workers acting as trade union representatives or workers' representatives. French law gives these categories of workers a number of hours for performing their tasks. However, the nature of the agency work relationship required that a specific regime be established for this category of workers. A sectoral collective agreement foresees that agency workers with a mandate of representation enjoy the full monthly credit of hours without consideration for the duration of the assignment month. Moreover, a period between two assignments of less than a month does not interrupt the mandate. Therefore, an agency worker with a mandate of representation will be able to perform his tasks even if he has no assignment if this period is less than a month. The hours granted representatives so they can perform their tasks can be taken during or apart from the periods of the assignment.

Another interesting development of French law relates to the protection of agency workers who are trade union representatives or elected workers' representatives. Collective agreements lay down that these agency workers should not suffer any discrimination in assignment offers. Besides, it is assumed that these workers will seek a new assignment when the existing one comes to an end. A presumption of extinction of the mandate is made when the agency worker trade union representative has not performed any assignment for at least three months. This period is extended to six months in the case of agency workers who are members of the works committee. Finally, the dismissal of these categories of agency workers is subject to the special rules concerning trade union representatives and workers' representatives. The authorisation of the labour administration is therefore necessary. Despite these innovative provisions, the collective representation of agency workers remains very low.

4.3 Rights Related to the Precarious Character of Temporary Agency Employment

Statutory provisions and collective agreements grant agency workers specific employment rights in order to compensate for the precarious character of their employment. For example, these rights provide agency workers with some compensatory allowances. Agency workers receive wage supplements to compensate the precarious character of their employment. The first compensatory mechanism is a 10% indemnity allowance based on the total remuneration received by the worker at the end of his contract. This indemnity allowance is not given when, at the end of the assignment, the user company hires the agency worker on an open-ended contract. The second indemnity allowance concerns agency workers' right to paid holidays. The short duration of the contract prevents agency workers from exercising their rights to paid holidays. Under French law, employees gain two days of paid holidays for every month of work. This way of calculating appeared inadequate for agency workers. Therefore the French legislation concedes to agency workers another indemnity allowance of at least 10% of their remuneration.

There are also rights regarding social assistance for agency workers. As we have seen, collective bargaining has been a significant means of improving the situation of agency workers: many collective agreements have adapted common rules to their specific circumstances. In particular, collective bargaining has provided interesting and often innovative solutions with respect to the training and social protection of agency workers. These collective agreements reduce the most harmful effects of this precarious form of employment, such as the difficulty of exercising individual or collective rights. But collective agreements also try to improve the social life of agency workers. Being an agency worker often makes it very difficult to rent an apartment or get a mortgage. Lessors and bankers are often reluctant to accept a lease or a loan from workers with a precarious job. In order to find a solution to this problem, a collective agreement set up a social action fund for agency workers. This fund is financed by contributions paid by temporary work firms and is responsible for developing a range of social initiatives. First, it informs agency workers concerning their employment and social rights. Second, the fund may act as guarantor for agency workers who would like to rent an apartment or to take out a loan. To benefit from this assistance, the agency worker must have completed a certain number of hours of employment within the temporary work agency sector. The social fund offers other social services, such as the payment of school or university fees for the children of agency workers, the organisation of a medical mutual insurance company and the housing of young temporary workers.

Bibliography

Gaudu, F. (1986), "L'emploi dans l'entreprise privée", PhD dissertation, University of Paris I.

Italy: From Prohibition to Introduction of Temporary Agency Work as a Measure to Promote Employment

Loredana ZAPPALÀ

1. Legalisation of Temporary Work in the Italian System

Temporary agency work in Italy is a relatively recent phenomenon. Until the 1990s there was no room in the Italian system for this type of work for historical reasons: on the one hand, Law 1369/1960 prohibited any form of intermediation in the hiring of employees, as well as labour-only subcontracting, in order to prevent abuse and fraud; on the other hand, Law 264/1949, on the assumption that weaker parties needed to be assisted by objective criteria, regulated access to the labour market by providing a public placement service *(collocamento),* the main rule of which was that mediation in concluding a labour contract was necessarily a public function. These two laws combined made any type of temporary work illegal. It was prohibited by law for an employer simply put an employee in contact with another employer, or to hire an employee himself and lend him (for use) to other entrepreneurs.[1]

A first attempt to introduce temporary work was made in 1993. However, because of strong opposition by the trade unions, the attempt failed. A second and more successful attempt was made in 1996 when the government, the trade unions and the employers' confederation signed the *Patto per il Lavoro* (work pact) that was intended to promote employment and support Italy's economic development.[2] The pact was subsequently transposed into Law 196/1997 (the so-called "Treu Law") introducing temporary agency work into Italy for the first time.[3]

Brief mention must be made of the fact that, from the early 1980s onwards, the idea of combating widespread unemployment in Italy by

1 See Treu (1993).

2 The three main trade union confederations, CGIL, CISL and UIL, have acknowledged this form of atypical work and have created branches in their organisations that deal specifically with these kinds of workers.

3 It is useful to recall that the introduction of temporary work was also possible thanks to the gradual reform of the placement system under the threat of an ECJ decision

favouring a spontaneous balance in the labour market through the introduction of greater flexibility in types of work contract started to gain favour even with the trade unions. The trade unions were, in fact, persuaded to accept the new forms of flexibility by the fact that the relevant legislation did not adopt the technique of cut-and-dried deregulation. Flexibility was, in contrast, a result of various strategies of negotiated legislation, most of them converging on the common aim of involving trade unions in the process of making laws previously considered to be mandatory more flexible by means of recourse to collective agreements, and also regulating new types of contract.[4] As regards fixed-term contracts, for example, from the 1980s onwards the trade unions progressively acquired a significant regulatory role: the law gave collective bargaining stipulated by national or local trade unions belonging to the most representative confederations the possibility of contemplating further reasons for which an employer could use fixed-term contracts under the rigid regulation of Law 230/1962. Collective bargaining was also entitled to lay down the percentage of the total workforce that could be hired via fixed-term contracts.

In this phase of *negotiated flexibility* temporary agency work was introduced within a broader framework of measures to promote employment. Although it injected greater flexibility into the system, Law 196/1997 confirmed the regulatory model used for fixed-term contracts, introducing into the Italian system the regulation of temporary agency work, with rather strong characteristics of rigidity, compared with other European countries.

On the one hand, Italian legislation regulated this type of contract by assigning private agencies a significant role in making the labour market more dynamic; on the other hand, it ensured the workers involved a series of norms aimed at guaranteeing the stability and reliability of private agencies, as well as an array of provisions safeguarding temporary workers against the possibility – arising from the nature of their employment contract – of discrimination or a reduction in the economic and legal pro-

---

in *Job Center II* (C-55/96 Job Centre Coop [1997] ECR I-7119). Following a preliminary ruling procedure, the Court had been asked to evaluate whether the public nature of placement offices in Italy would exempt them from competition rules. The Courtfound that such offices did not satisfy market demands. Furthermore, it added that statutes prohibiting the placement of workers by private companies made it impossible to perform placement within or outside the state. Also in the spectrum of the ECJ ruling was the introduction in the Italian system of legislation on temporary work which, combined with the reform of the placement system in 1997, represented a historic landmark in the abolition of the state monopoly in the hiring system. On this evolution see Sciarra (2004).

4 On this topic see Caruso (2004).

tection enjoyed by standard workers. The "Treu Law" thus ensured that Italy had no difficulty in ratifying, on 1 February 2000, the ILO C181 Private Employment Agencies Convention of 1997 (which came into full force in May 2000), thereby recognising "the role which private employment agencies may play in a well functioning labour market".[5]

In this perspective, which aimed to preserve the central role of the permanent work contract as the *normal* type of employment relationship, Law 196/1997 also established typical legal circumstances in which it was possible to have recourse to temporary work (in cases of temporary use for tasks not forming part of the company's normal production arrangements; to replace absent employees; and in the circumstances permitted under the national agreement for the industry to which the user enterprise belongs, concluded by the comparatively most representative unions). At the same time, it entrusted collective bargaining with identifying further circumstances and establishing the maximum number of temporary workers companies could employ. The social partners were also given further important tasks in making flexibility more acceptable: trade unions were required to regulate extensions of temporary labour supply contracts (the maximum number of extensions and/or the maximum duration of temporary employment relationships), as well as the provision of training for temporary workers financed by a special fund to which agencies are obliged by law to contribute.

Having said that, this model of *negotiated or selective flexibility* has in the last few years guaranteed trade union monitoring of the real need for flexibility in companies and at the same time respect for certain rules conditioning recourse to fixed-term contracts and temporary agency work that are both transparent and judicially verifiable.

2. The Liberal Reform of the 2003 "Biagi Law"

At the beginning of the new century a lack of faith in *negotiated flexibility* began to take root among entrepreneurs, certain political milieus and even labour law experts. This lack of confidence did not correspond, at least at the beginning of 2000, to a common strategy. Such a strategy was obviously not easy to find and the possible directions to take – deregulation or re-regulation of certain fundamental labour law institutions – became an issue of heated debate at political and trade union levels.

In 2001 the new centre-right government came to power and, in order to implement EU Directive No. 99/70/EC on fixed-term contracts,

5 On the effects of the ILO C181 Private Employment Agencies Convention of 1997 in certain national contexts, see Peck *et al.* (2005).

launched new regulations governing this type of contract – re-baptised in the policy statement of the Government's "first 100 days" as a "European work contract". The result was approval of Legislative Decree 368/01, which implements directive 99/70/EC, abrogating the previous restrictive regulation laid down by Law 230/1962. Legislative Decree 368 was, without doubt, the first step in a broader design by the current centre-right government to reform the labour market, employment relationships and the model of trade union relations consolidated in the Italian tradition. The new regulations signalled a departure from a model which detailed a limited number of legal and contractual types considered to be exceptions to the general rule. The new model provided general grounds legitimising the stipulation of fixed-term contracts for "reasons of a technical, production, organisational or substitutive nature". In this way, the fixed-term contract became a "normal" tool in determining the makeup of company workforces, juxtaposed with, but not countering, permanent contracts. Although the new regulations confirm certain forms of standard protection for workers on fixed-term contracts (such as the principle of equal treatment), as provided for by the 1962 law, they significantly redimension the monitoring role of collective bargaining, signalling a significant break with the model of negotiated flexibility applied hitherto. However, despite the fact that the government's aim was purportedly to introduce a "more simple and controllable system" of fixed-term contracts, the new regulations, above all on account of the extremely generic nature of their general grounds, would appear to have led to a framework of rules which employers themselves find hard to apply, thus increasing the margins for discretionary rulings by judges assessing their legitimacy.[6] In connection with this, brief mention should be made of the fact that implementation in the Italian system of EU Directive No. 99/70/EC, containing a soft regulation that was much less restrictive than previous legislation, was a "pretext" for the partial liberalisation of fixed-term contracts, although this was not allowed by the "non-regression clause" (clause 8, par. 3) of the European agreement.[7]

Community regulation of fixed-term contracts thus does not appear to be referable to the notion of "EU framing policy", that is, a European policy which, unlike both positive and negative integration, is "highly

---

6 On this topic see Zappalà (2004).

7 According to which "implementation of this agreement shall not constitute valid grounds for reducing the general level of protection afforded to workers in the field of the agreement". For a first interpretation of this clause, see the Opinion of Advocate General Tizzano of 30 June 2005, Case C-144/04, *Mangold v. Rüdiger Helm* and the judgment of 22 November 2005.

dependant on the specific conditions which shape policy making at national level" and therefore "may provide additional legitimisation for domestic leaders to justify the content and implementation of national reform policies".[8] Directive No. 99/70/EC constituted an opportunity and some sort of legitimisation for the centre-left government of 2001 to complete a process of demarginalisation of fixed-term work, which was certainly not one of the aims of the EC legislation.

Although in the case of temporary agency work, the centre-right government could not take its cue and legitimation from any inputs from the European Union to start a reform process, temporary work regulation happened to be influenced by the above-mentioned vicissitude concerning the implementation of Directive No. 99/70/EC.

A month after approval of the new regulations governing fixed-term contracts – in October 2001 – the centre-right government issued a *White Paper on the Labour Market in Italy*[9] in which it expressed its satisfaction with Legislative Decree 368. On the basis of the White Paper, the government also announced its intention to coordinate temporary agency work and fixed-term contract regulations, increasing the level of flexibility "so that temporary work through agencies is not unjustly penalised by this *jus superveniens*". The plans for reform were outlined in greater detail in the White Paper and ultimately led to approval of Legislative Decree 276/2003, the so-called "Biagi Law". As promised, Legislative Decree 276/03 (Articles 20–28), which establishes a broad range of regulations in various areas of the labour market and employment relationships,[10] abrogated Law 196/1997 and rewrote the rules applying to temporary work through agencies, now called "*somministrazione di lavoro*" ("administration of labour").

It should be pointed out that Legislative Decree 276/03 did not introduce deregulation *tout court*, but rather neo-liberal reregulation of this type of contract, inspired by a labour policy aiming at providing incentives for the supply of labour by reducing the excessive constraints and costs involved.[11] As we shall see, on the one hand the new regulations confirm the guarantees affecting working conditions provided by Law 196/1997,[12] while on the other hand they substantially liberalise the circumstances in which it is possible to use fixed-term contracts, thus under-

8 See Knill and Lehmkuhl (1999); see also Lo Faro (2004).

9 See Lo Faro (2002).

10 For an overview of the reforms introduced by Legislative Decree 276/03 see Tiraboschi (2005).

11 See, in particular, De Luca Tamajo (2004).

12 With the exception of certain derogations from the principle of equal treatment; see Section 6 below.

mining some of the main principles on which Italian labour law is based: more specifically, the principle whereby an employment contract is *normally* a permanent one, and the principle, based on Art. 2094 of the Italian Civil Code, which establishes that the employer in a work relationship and the party using the worker's services should be one and the same.

As already mentioned, the drive towards change in certain aspects of temporary work regulations was due to the recent reform of fixed-term contracts and the desire to make both forms of contract available to employers in search of flexibility. Therefore in Italy an unusual and almost paradoxical form of influence of Community law on the evolution of national law has occurred. Directive No. 99/70/EC, having the aim of introducing a series of minimal prescriptions in defence of fixed-term workers, had the effect of producing a partial deregulation of the matter, as well as to influence the fate of temporary agency work, which has been the object of a similar, if anything more radical, liberalisation process.

In the debate preceding the 2003 reform there was, on the contrary, no echo of the almost parallel debate at European level following the Commission's presentation of a draft directive regarding working conditions for temporary workers.[13] In line with a trend typical of the current centre-right government, aimed at using EU law as a "crowbar" to unhinge some of the rigidity of the Italian labour market in the name of Europe and its employment policy, some of those behind the 2003 reform pointed out that the "suppression of all norms exclusively aiming at stiffening the regulations regarding the use of labour, even where there are no instances of worker protection" was perfectly consistent with the provisions laid down by Art. 4 of the 2002 draft for an EU directive[14] on the review of restrictions or prohibitions.[15]

---

13 European Commission, Com (2002) 149 final of 20 March 2002 and the subsequent proposal for a modified Directive, COM (2002) 701 of 28 November 2002. On this proposal see Zappalà (2003).

14 According to which "1. Prohibitions or restrictions on the use of temporary work are justified only on grounds of general interest relating in particular to the protection of temporary workers, the requirements of health and safety at work and the need to ensure that the labour market functions properly and abuses are prevented. 2. The Member States, after consulting the social partners in accordance with national legislation, collective agreements and practices, shall review any restrictions or prohibitions mentioned above in order to verify whether they are justified on the grounds given in paragraph 1. If not, the Member States shall discontinue them. The Member States shall inform the Commission of the results of that review. 3. Paragraphs 1 and 2 are without prejudice to national requirements with regard to registration, licensing, certification, financial guarantees or monitoring of temporary agencies."

15 Tiraboschi (2003).

3. Characteristics of the Italian Temporary Work Market

Following the "Treu Law", temporary work rapidly expanded. According to recent investigations, temporary workers number about 157,000,[16] that is 0.7% of total employment and 1% of subordinate occupation,[17] below the average in other European countries (circa 1.8%), although this contractual instrument was introduced earlier there than in Italy. The low incidence of temporary work in Italy can undoubtedly be linked to the presence and competition of atypical contractual formulas which are more economically convenient for enterprises.

In recent years, temporary work agencies have mainly invested their resources in northern Italy, in a limited number of regions. At the moment no updated data about the branches' territorial distribution are available, but it has to be taken into account that of the 2,230 branches referring to 69 temporary work agencies authorised in 2003, 73.4% were located in northern Italy, 30.4% in Lombardy alone, whereas in central and southern Italy the figures were only 15.6% and 11.0% respectively.[18] Thus in Italy the spread of temporary work has taken place according to a kind of *filtering down* process, since initially temporary work agencies mainly invested in the north – that is, where the market is more dynamic – and only subsequently have opened branches in the south. The south of Italy remains an area where the presence of agencies is small; in fact, many of them deem that in the south there is no market to justify investment.

Most temporary workers live in northern Italy: 56.7%, of whom 25.5% live in Lombardy. Some temporary work agencies, in order to address the lack of labour in some northern areas, have developed programmes to boost workers' mobility from the south to the north. In the south, agencies have not only opened so-called "offerer" (*offertiste*) branches[19] in order to recruit workers to send north, but have also offered "aid" to workers to facilitate their transfer to other regions. As confirmed by the

16 See Istat, *Rilevazione delle Forze di lavoro* (IV trimestre 2004).

17 However, often the missions' shortness makes it difficult to "capture" the temporary workers' occupational position, so that the incidence of employment could be underestimated. Undoubtedly, in flow terms the volume of temporary workers within the period of a year is definitely higher than the figure given by Istat. For instance, the Minister of Labour estimated that in July 2003 alone the number of workers involved was 91,000, which was 127,000 in terms of equivalent workers. According to statistics developed by one of the most important employers' associations, in 2004 workers employed on this type of contract in fact numbered 502,000.

18 See IRES, *Dal lavoro interinale alla somministrazione di manodopera: primo monitoraggio su cosa cambia per le Agenzie per il lavoro e per le imprese utilizzatrici*, July 2005.

19 See Altieri and Oteri (2004).

agencies' operators, this has not solved the northern firms' problems in recruiting labour, in relation to some professional profiles in particular.

As for the socio-anagraphic features of temporary workers, it has to be pointed out that women account for 50.2% of temporary workers. Unlike what some initial empirical researches revealed, temporary work is not exceptional compared to other forms of atypical work. It is a contractual formula that, like the others, involves a larger number of women.[20]

A recent study based on a national data set compiled by Manpower – one of the personnel leading companies also in Italy – showed that over 44% of temporary workers are aged between 25 and 34, almost 17% are younger than 25, while more than a quarter are older than 40.

The vast majority of workers are Italian; 8% are of other nationalities.[21]

From recent data supplied by the Italian Ministry of Labour,[22] it emerges that most temporary workers are factory operatives or apprentices (57.6%), followed by clerical workers (38%) and a small proportion of executives and managerial staff (2.7% and 1.6% respectively). The sectors most frequently employing temporary workers are the service sector (44.2% – excluding trade, which accounts for 10%) and industry in the strict sense (40.4%).

As regards qualifications, almost 40% of temporary workers only possess a "*licenza media*", or middle school qualification; almost half possess a high school diploma, and 14% are university graduates.

The data also show that in many cases the workers involved are "involuntary" temporary workers (that is, they agree to work on a fixed-term basis only because they cannot find a permanent job). In fact, 21.6% of temporary workers state that they are in search of another job, either a new one (20.4%) or a second job (1.2%). In most cases they attribute the search to the precarious nature of their current job (57%); this is more common amongst women, younger workers (62% of 25/34 year-olds), and in north-west Italy.

In addition, a number of studies have investigated the reasons why Italian enterprises make use of temporary labour, under the influence of

20 See IRES (2005), in which territorial differences are emphasised: while in the North women make up 52.5% of temporary workers, in the South they make up only 35.6%. The highest percentages for women are reported in central Italy, where 35.6% of temporary workers are women. Undoubtedly, these data reflect the economic differences between the three parts of the country. The north, where there is a greater concentration of industry also reveals a highest presence of men in industry; in contrast, in central Italy, where tertiary activities are widespread, there is a higher presence of women amongst temporary workers.

21 See Nannicini (2004).

22 Ministero del Lavoro e delle Politiche Sociali (2005).

the institutional rules governing the Italian system. In short, these include short-term requirements for which – given the absence of efficient public employment services or significant alternative sources of labour supply – temporary work saves companies money on the fixed costs of worker selection. Temporary work is also used when firms need to meet specific requirements (which remain temporary, although they may be of quite long duration) and thus avail themselves of skilled professionals who are particularly difficult to find on the labour market and for whom the direct costs of selection would be too high for firms to bear. This form of contract is also used as a tool for pre-selecting staff: given the restrictions on the trial period during which an employer can freely terminate the work relationship, temporary work allows a worker to be effectively tested before being hired directly.[23] In this framework, temporary work has contributed significantly to improving the functioning of the labour market in Italy, in relation not only to meeting short-term flexibility requirements but also to promoting the growth of professional mediation mechanisms, as well as covering more permanent job vacancies.

Finally, firms also use temporary work in order to take advantage of greater flexibility in working hours and shift organisation. In fact, temporary workers show greater flexibility than other workers: the percentage of temporary workers working shifts, at night, or on Saturdays and Sundays is significantly higher than that of employees with contracts of indeterminate duration.[24]

4. The Triangular Relationship between Agency, User and Worker

According to the new regulations, the so-called "*somministrazione di lavoro*"[25] envisages two kinds of contract:

a) A labour supply contract, which is a commercial contract between a temporary work agency and a user firm. In the Italian system, this contract can be either a fixed-term contract, which is the case of real temporary agency work, or an open-ended contract, which entails staff leasing. Art. 20 of Legislative Decree 276/2003 establishes that "labour supply contracts" can only be signed with agencies authorised by the Ministry for Employment and Social Policy and therefore registered with the Ministry as such. In order to guarantee fair-

23 See, for example, Montanino and Sestito (2003) who point out that temporary work in fact provides a loophole in Italian legislation restricting the use of a trial period in the most common types of contract.

24 See ISTAT, *Rilevazione delle Forze di lavoro*, IV trimestre 2004.

25 On the new regulation see Ichino (2004), Bonardi (2004), Chieco (2004) and Speziale (2004).

ness in the labour market agencies seeking authorisation for labour supply activities must meet certain legal and financial requirements (they must be "società di capitali" or cooperatives or a consortium of cooperatives; they are required to have their head office, or at least a branch office, in Italy or another EU country; they must provide suitable premises and meet adequate professional standards; they are not allowed to have any individuals at management level who have ever been convicted of a criminal offence; they must guarantee paid-up capital of no less than EUR 600,000, and so on.).

b) A "subordinate" employment contract between a temporary work agency and a worker. Here the agency is the employer and the employee has an employment contract which may be a fixed-term contract or an open-ended one. If the contract is of unlimited duration, the agency must provide an income guarantee for those periods when no assignments are available.

In this connection it should be pointed out that the recent reform is not an attempt to deconstruct from the inside a regulatory model founded on the Civil Code definition of "subordinate worker" (Art. 2094 Civil Code) and the series of protective regulations that have since been introduced, but rather to neutralise it and transform it into just one of a number of models, regulating an ever-decreasing proportion of the overall workforce. Subordinate employment as the main beneficiary of a whole series of juridical effects has not, that is, disappeared but its paradigmatic regulatory status has been diluted.

A particular feature of this type of contract, however, is that although the agency is the actual employer, the work is carried out for the duration of the contract in the interest and under the control of the user enterprise.

There is a very clear separation of typical managerial prerogatives from the concrete control exercised by the user. It is, for example, specified that recourse to disciplinary powers is an agency's prerogative, following the user's communication of the reasons why disciplinary measures should be taken. The managerial prerogative to move workers from one job to another appears similarly split and implies the user's obligation to inform the agency in case of changes in the content of the job.

The temporary work agency is under an obligation to inform the worker of the contents of his or her contract and the foreseeable duration of the assignment with the user enterprise. This obligation must be fulfilled in writing and the worker is to be notified on signing the contract, or when he is sent to work for the user enterprise.

If the contract is a fixed-term one, the regulations laid down by Legislative Decree 368/01 will apply with some exceptions. In particular, no limits are set on the succession of contracts. In addition, as regards the extension of contracts, the 2003 regulations differentiate between temporary work through agencies and the provisions set forth in Legislative Decree 368, giving collective bargaining the power to regulate the cases and length of extensions differently and with greater flexibility than is allowed for fixed-term contracts. Sanctions in the event of continuation of the employment relationship beyond the term agreed on will apply to temporary work through agencies but – taking into account the important work placement role played by employment agencies – no limit is set on the possibility of renewing the contract between workers and these agencies, even without interruptions, thus allowing workers to be sent to either the same or another user.

The rationale that lies behind this differentiation seems to be quite clear and can be said to have been inspired in part by the draft temporary agency workers directive presented in 2002, in which Member States were asked to eliminate constraints and obstacles to the spread of temporary work in an attempt to boost employment rates.

There are also some important exceptions to the normal regulations governing work contracts. Temporary workers, for example, are not counted amongst the staff of the user enterprise for the purpose of applying general legal or collective bargaining regulations, with the exception of those referring to health and safety in the workplace. This provision, which was also present in Law 196/1997, appears to be a natural consequence of the fact that as temporary workers do not sign a contract with the user firm they do not – with the exception of health and safety provisions – increase the number of staff regularly employed by the user.

c) Finally, there is a relationship between the user and the worker through which the worker performs work assignments at the user firm. No contract regulates this relationship, where the user manages the work and exercises control over the details. But Italian law regulates several aspects of this relationship, such as the user firm's responsibility for agency workers' wages and health and safety, and agency workers' rights within the user firm.

5. Grounds Enabling a User Firm to Have Recourse to Temporary Work

Under the new regulations (Art. 20), an agency authorised by the Ministry of Labour and a company called the "user" are allowed to stipulate a fixed-term labour supply contract "for reasons of a technical, production, organisational or substitutive nature".

In this way the new regulations provide a general clause that legitimises the recourse to temporary work, "borrowed" from the recent law on fixed-term contracts (Legislative Decree 368/2001). As well as the new regulation regarding fixed-term contracts, the technique used in Legislative Decree 276/2003 to regulate flexibility thus takes control of a broad area of the labour market away from the trade unions. The adoption of this general clause allowing temporary work contracts to be stipulated for technical, production, organisational or substitutive reasons thus presupposes abandoning the criterion of *negotiated flexibility* to strengthen a regime of individual agreements. The only remaining form of trade union control lies in the fact that collective bargaining is assigned the task of identifying the quantitative, possibly not always uniform, limits to the use of temporary work, that is, the proportion of workers who can be hired on this kind of contract as compared to the number of permanent employees working for a firm.

It should first of all be stated that interpretation of this general clause has led to heated debate among Italian labour law experts. One particular topic of discussion has been the identification of the technical, production and organisational reasons that justify the stipulation of a temporary work contract instead of a permanent one. One authoritative line of thought is that the only element that makes it objectively possible to distinguish between the reasons for stipulating temporary work contracts and those which make a permanent contract necessary is the *temporary nature* of the reasons themselves: *only* the existence of temporary technical, production, organisational or substitutive reasons legitimises setting a term on a work contract. It is, however, true that even when it is considered necessary for employers' requirements to be temporary, the concept of *temporariness* still remains essentially vague. Perhaps aware of the debate regarding interpretation of the technical, production, and so on, reasons specified in Legislative Decree 368/01, the 2003 legislation tries to limit the possibility of legal dispute by establishing that these reasons may also "refer to the ordinary activity of the user". The new regulations also establish that "in order to evaluate the reasons that justify recourse to temporary work, control by labour courts is limited, in accordance with the general principles of the system, to ascertaining the existence of the reasons that justify it and cannot be extended to controlling the merits of technical, organisational and production evaluations and choices, which remain the concern of the user".

There are also circumstances in which employers are not allowed to make use of temporary work. These include the need to replace striking employees; when the employer has implemented collective dismissals during the previous six months or has introduced shorter working hours affecting employees performing the tasks for which temporary work is being requested; and when the employer does not comply with legal requirements relating to health and safety in the workplace.

The commercial contract between the agency and the user enterprise must also provide information, in writing, regarding the reasons for recourse to temporary work; the official registration of the agency; the number of workers requested; the tasks involved and the relevant job classification; the location, working hours and financial and regulatory terms and conditions for the work envisaged; the starting and finishing dates of the contract; and so on. It must also expressly contain the obligation on the part of the agency or, in the event of default, on the part of the user enterprise, to pay the worker directly.

6. Working Conditions of Temporary Workers: The Principle of Equal Treatment

Regarding the working conditions of agency workers, the most important aspect of Italian legislation on agency work is the principle of equal treatment for agency workers and workers directly employed by the user firm. Art. 23, clause 1 of Legislative Decree 276/2003 establishes that agency workers are entitled to "financial and regulatory treatment that is in no way inferior to that afforded to comparable workers employed by the user firm". This principle means that the agency has to apply to agency workers the same conditions fixed by the collective agreement of the user firm, with regard to equal pay and working conditions, such as working hours, holidays, dismissal and so on; and equal social services. The "comparable worker" to whom the equal treatment provisions refer is thus a comparable worker within the user company. Some problems may arise if, in actual fact, the user firm does not employ a comparable worker (in these cases the comparison can be made with a hypothetical comparable worker within the user firm).

This issue, which is considered of central importance by the trade unions, means that a firm cannot use agency work to cut labour costs. The minimum wage for temporary workers does not, therefore, depend on the financial agreement between the agency and the user firm, but is legally established as depending on the wages and working conditions applied within the user firm which, at a technical and judicial level, determine whether a contract is legal or not. In other words, it is not the temporary, occasional labour market but the permanent one that establishes the treatment temporary workers are to be ensured, obviously according to ordinary variations between the various sectors of production and professional categories.

However, as individual conditions – such as special wage arrangements – are excluded from this equality, the existence of this principle in the Italian regulations does not mean that agency worker conditions are the same as those applied to workers directly employed by the user firm. There are, in fact, several forms of remuneration related to being directly employed by a company, such as wages based on seniority, social insurance and other fringe benefits. These forms of remuneration may represent a considerable element of a worker's total wage and be a significant part of a firm's personnel policy. Moreover, it is possible that firms, in consideration of this equal treatment condition affecting the costs of agency work, will implement personnel policies based on individual arrangements and benefits. For the part of a worker's wage that is connected to achieving results, Italian law gives an important role to the collective agreement: collective bargaining will decide how it will be distributed among all workers.

The presence since the 1997 regulations of the principle of equal treatment between temporary workers and those employed directly by companies thus ensures that Italian legislation complies with one of the most controversial principles contained in the 2002 draft directive, thus including Italy amongst those member states in favour of introducing supranational regulations to guarantee the spread of "quality" temporary work in Europe.[26]

Although it confirms the principle of equal treatment, the Italian legislation parallels Art. 5, par. 2, of the draft directive,[27] with specific regulations applying when a worker is hired by an agency on an open-ended contract, alternating periods during which he is assigned to a user firm with others, at which he remains "at the disposal" of the agency, waiting for an assignment. In such cases, the worker is entitled to a "retainer", at a rate established by the collective contract applicable to the administrator – given that there is, in such cases, no comparable worker to whom reference can be made – but in any case no lower than the rate established and periodically updated by ministerial decree. The purpose of this fee is to compensate the worker for his availability to work, that is, curtailment of the individual's freedom to plan his working and private life. When the worker is sent back to work with the user or with another firm, however, the equal treatment principle comes into full force again.

---

26 See Article 2 of the proposal which declares that one of the aims of the directive is "to ensure the protection of temporary workers and to improve the quality of temporary work by ensuring that the principle of non-discrimination is applied to temporary workers".

27 The draft directive establishes that "as regards pay, Member States may, after consulting the social partners, provide that an exemption be made to the principle established in paragraph 1 when temporary workers who have a permanent contract of employment with a temporary agency continue to be paid in the time between postings".

Finally, unlike the 1997 regulations, the new law contains a provision which has been harshly criticised by Italian labour law experts. Art. 13 of Legislative Decree 276/2003 does not guarantee equal treatment for certain categories of workers it defines as "disadvantaged",[28] for whom an individual scheme of insertion or re-insertion into the labour market is provided "with suitable training and the involvement of a tutor with adequate competence and professional qualifications, and when the worker is hired by an authorised agency with a contract lasting no less than six months". It is claimed that this is merely a "promotional" measure aiming to insert weaker groups of workers in the labour market on a "fair treatment" basis. However, the provision has invoked charges of the illegitimacy of derogations introducing substandard terms with a view to ensuring disadvantaged workers of greater job opportunities. The provision of an "attenuated equality" regime for certain categories of workers seems in part to have been inspired by the exemption from the principle of equality established by Art. 5, par. 3 of the 2002 draft directive,[29] even though Italian legislators – unlike the proposal – identified the workers to whom these exemptions may be applied *a priori*, without involving the social partners, who potentially would have been more competent to evaluate the social acceptability of any derogation on a case-by-case basis.

Labour law experts are divided between those who justify substandard treatment for disadvantaged workers by the need to guarantee the right to work, and therefore consider it to be constitutionally legitimate as the disparity introduced depends on the different situation affecting the workers involved, and those who, on the basis of the principle of substantial equality enshrined in Art. 3, clause 2 of the Italian Constitution, maintain that the principle, intended to remove any obstacle to the full development of the individual, can never justify the setting of lower standards.

---

28 As in Art. 2, letter f of the Commission Regulations 2204/2002, to which Legislative Decree 276/2003 refers, a "disadvantaged worker" is taken to mean "a person belonging to a category which has difficulty entering the labour market without assistance", such as those under 25 years of age, migrant workers or those belonging to an ethnic minority, a single parent with one or more children, any person with no secondary school or equivalent qualifications or over 50 years of age without a job or about to lose one, the long-term unemployed, that is, those out of work for 12 of the previous 16 months, or 6 out of the previous 8 months in the case of workers under the age of 25, and so on.

29 "Member States may, after consulting with social partners at the appropriate level, give them the option of upholding or concluding collective agreements which derogate from the principle established in paragraph 1 as long as an adequate level of protection is provided for temporary workers."

7. Other Forms of Protection for Temporary Workers

Besides the principle of equal treatment, the Italian regulations also contain a series of further provisions to protect temporary workers.

First, a remedy provided by Italian law against the possible negative consequences of agency work is the provision of a principle of solidarity between the agency and the user firm for wages and social security contributions. This means that workers and the social security authorities are able to sue both the agency and the user firm for wages and social security contributions. Both firms are obliged to pay the entire amount owed to the workers. Solidarity in obligation was introduced to induce firms to use agencies that provide solid financial guarantees. The law requires that the commercial contract between the agency and the user state explicitly a number of obligations on their part: the agency is required to pay the worker's wages and social security contributions: in the event of default by the agency the user takes on this obligation, but is entitled to sue the agency for compensation. This second provision relies on company action and assigns statutory rules the role of an incentive: the more trustworthy the agency is, the smaller the risk of the user having to assume responsibility for its employment obligations. Users will therefore be encouraged to seek out solid, reliable agencies.

Another form of protection for temporary workers is the provision that authorised or accredited agencies are not allowed to request or obtain, directly or indirectly, any form of payment from workers. The reference to "fees" in the provision means any request for sums of money or any other obligation on the part of the worker (including the obligation to do or not do something). Legislative Decree 276/2003 states that whoever requests or receives payment from a worker in return for providing him with temporary employment will incur legal and financial penalties. The authorisation of the agency to carry out labour supply activities will also be revoked. This prohibition was first formulated in an ILO Convention[30] and was also included in the 2002 draft directive.[31] Italian legislation, however, contains an exception to this principle which would appear to conflict with the draft. Legislative Decree 276/2003 states that collective agreements stipulated by the most representative national or local

30 It is historically founded on the idea that the search for a job is an essential activity for the subsistence of a worker and his family and can therefore not be even indirectly exploited for profit by intermediaries.

31 Article 6, par. 3, which states that "temporary agencies shall not charge workers any fees, especially in exchange for arranging for them to be recruited by a user undertaking, or for concluding a contract of employment or an employment relationship with a user undertaking after carrying out a posting in that undertaking".

employers' and workers' associations are allowed to establish exemptions from this prohibition for specific categories of highly skilled workers or for specific services offered by authorised or accredited agencies. This facility, whereby collective agreements can identify areas in which the prohibition is not applicable, is innovative as compared with the previous Law 197/1997. It is based on Art. 7 of ILO Convention no. 181, 1997 referring to *Private Employment Agencies,* whereby states are allowed to introduce exceptions to the principle for certain categories of workers or specific services; according to this Convention these exceptions have to be sufficiently precise as regards derogation from the general prohibition against requiring payment from workers. But if and when the EU directive is approved Italy will have to adjust its legislation to bring it into line with the greater protection afforded by EU regulations, and thus eliminate the exemption from the prohibition on charging fees.

Italian legislation, like the proposed EU directive,[32] also provides regulations aiming to prevent temporary work agencies from limiting the possibility of a temporary worker being subsequently hired by a user enterprise. Any clause tending, even indirectly, to limit the possibility of a user enterprise hiring a worker on termination of a temporary assignment is considered to be null and void. It is, however, possible for collective bargaining to derogate from this provision. Legislative Decree 276/2003, in fact, establishes that the nullity sanction is not to be applied when the worker is paid adequate compensation, as laid down by the relative collective agreement.

Another respect in which agency work is subject to specific rules is safety and health regulations, where the effect of European Directive 91/383/EC is clear. The agency – that is, the formal employer – gives the worker all the necessary information about risks concerning health and safety, including specific training in the use of the equipment required for the job. But the agency and the user can state that all these duties are the responsibility of the user. In this case they have to mention it in the labour supply contract. It is, for example, the duty of the user firm if the type of work presents specific risks and requires special medical supervision. What is important to stress concerning this regulation is that the law states that the user firm has to observe all prevention rules with regard to

32 Article 6, par. 2, which states that "Member States shall take any action required to ensure that any clauses prohibiting or having the effect of preventing the conclusion of a contract of employment or an employment relationship between the user undertaking and the temporary worker after his posting are null and void or may be declared null and void. This paragraph is without prejudice to provisions under which temporary agencies receive a reasonable level of recompense for services rendered to user undertakings for posting, recruitment and training of temporary workers".

both its own employees and agency workers. This means that the user firm is responsible for infringements of safety regulations in respect of both its own employees and agency workers.

Legislative Decree 276/2003 also states that temporary workers are entitled to the same trade union rights (including right of assembly on both user firm and labour supply agency premises), laid down by Law 300, 20 May 1970 (Workers' Statute), as workers with a normal employment contract.[33] The aim of these provisions is to ensure agency workers of their entitlement to trade union rights in consideration of their risk of isolation from both workers directly employed by the user firm and other agency workers working for other user firms. Although not explicitly stated, Legislative Decree 276/2003 is also to be considered as affording temporary workers the right to strike, as enshrined in Art. 40 of the Italian Constitution. In order to allow some degree of union control over the actual modalities of recourse to temporary work, and consequently to defend the interests of the workers involved,[34] along with the collective interests of workers directly employed by the user firm, the law also obliges the user to inform the unions of the number of temporary workers used and the reasons for stipulating temporary contracts.

8. Measures to Promote Training Opportunities for Temporary Workers

The provisions on training play a significant role in the Italian temporary work regulations. As experience gained since the introduction of Law 196/1997 has shown, the success of temporary work is due to agencies' capacity to guarantee a fast, flexible supply of high quality labour. For this purpose, it is of fundamental importance for an agency to possess

33 The reference concerns both the right to trade union freedom – right of association and trade union activity, the right to non-discrimination on union grounds – and union activity rights – the right to collect union dues and carry out proselytising activities, the right of assembly, referendum, and initiatives to set up union representations in the workplace.

34 Brief mention can be made of the fact that the great spread, above all in the late 1990s, of new, more flexible forms of employment led the large union organisations to introduce specialised representation structures to protect the specific economic and normative needs of these workers (above all, the need for stabilisation of non-permanent employment relationships). Instead of including representation of these workers in conventional structures, the union confederations created ad hoc territorial structures (NIDIL, ALAI, CPO, and so on) which organised them, irrespective of the sector they belonged to, on the basis of status (which in this case was not professional status but the non-permanent nature of their position in the labour market); as far as the organisation of representation was concerned this led to the emergence of dual interests (insider/outsider) in the labour market.

competence, organisational strategies and a capacity for selection, but it is also indispensable for it to provide an adequate system of training and qualification of the workforce. Temporary workers must, that is, be suitably qualified to fit into the organisational contexts of the user enterprises and this is only possible with adequate training for the various tasks they will be required to perform.

A properly functioning system of vocational training – especially in the case of temporary work – can mean that work which to all appearances is "precarious" will, on the contrary, provide workers with significant opportunities for vocational growth and enable them to acquire labour market competitiveness. In this way temporary workers considerably increase not only their chances of longer-lasting employment but also of converting a temporary relationship with the user firm into a steady job. Training thus permits the effective insertion of a worker into the organisational context of the user enterprise and at the same time, in the case of temporary work, acts as a link in the interim between working periods, overcoming the problem of outdated skills and the consequent early loss of worker qualifications.

Considering that agency workers are mostly temporarily employed, and that their employment relationship lacks security, Italian legislation has provided them with certain forms of labour market protection since 1997. The core of this approach is the agency's contribution of 4% of agency workers' wages, paid into a special fund. This fund is used to finance vocational training for temporary agency workers, or welfare initiatives for staff leased workers in the event of dismissal, or for disadvantaged workers, or to finance measures to combat illegal work. These measures are part of a framework of policies laid down in the collective national contract for temporary work agencies, or established by means of a decree issued by the Ministry of Labour and Social Policy, after consultation with the most representative trade unions in the sector.

Bibliography

Altieri, G., and C. Oteri (2004), *Il lavoro interinale come sistema. Bilancio di un quinquennio*, Roma: Ediesse.

Bonardi, O. (2004), "La nuova disciplina della somministrazione", in *Il lavoro tra progresso e mercificazione*, Roma: Ediesse, p. 119 ff.

Chieco, P. (2004), "Somministrazione, comando, appalto. Le nuove forme di prestazione di lavoro a favore del terzo", in Curzio (ed.), *Lavoro e diritti dopo il decreto legislativo 276/2003*, Bari: Cacucci, p. 93 ff.

De Luca Tamajo, R. (2004), "Tra le righe del d.lgs. n. 276/2003 (e del decreto correttivo n. 251/2004): tendenze e ideologie", *Rivista Italiana di Diritto del Lavoro*, 4: 521ff.

Ichino, P. (2004), "Somministrazione di lavoro, appalto di servizi, distacco", in *Il nuovo mercato del lavoro,* Bologna: Zanichelli, p. 288 ff.

IRES (2005), *Dal lavoro interinale alla somministrazione di manodopera: primo monitoraggio su cosa cambia per le Agenzie per il lavoro e per le imprese utilizzatrici* (July).

Knill, C. and D. Lehmkuhl (1999), *How Europe Matters: Different Mechanisms of Europeanization,* European Integration Online Papers (EioP).

Lo Faro, A. (2002), "Fairness at work? The Italian White Paper on Italian Labour Market Reform", *Industrial Law Journal,* 2: pp. 190ff.

Lo Faro, A. (2004), "Italy: adaptable employment and private autonomy in the Italian reform of part-time work", in S. Sciarra, P. Davies and M. Freedland (eds) *Employment Policy and the Regulation of Part-time Work in the European Union,* Cambridge, 2004, pp. 156ff.

Ministero del Lavoro e delle Politiche Sociali (2005), *Lavoro interinale (o somministrato): un aggiornamento del quadro statistico* (June).

Montanino A., and P. Sestito (2003), "Le molte funzioni del lavoro temporaneo in Italia", *Rivista di Politica Economica,* 3–4: 115ff.

Nannicini, T. (2004), *The Take-Off of Temporary Employment in the Italian Labor Market,* European University Institute, ECO2004/09.

Peck, J., N. Theodore and K. Ward (2005), "Constructing markets for temporary labour: employment liberalisation and the internationalisation of the staffing industry", in *Global Networks* 5 (1), pp. 3 ff.

Speziale, V. (2004), "Art. 20. Condizioni di liceità", in E. Gragnoli and A. Perulli (eds), *La riforma del mercato del lavoro e i nuovi modelli contrattuali,* Padova: Cedam, p. 275 ff.

Tiraboschi, M. (2003), "Somministrazione, appalto di servizi, distacco", in *La riforma Biagi. Commentario allo schema di decreto attuativo della legge delega sul mercato del lavoro,* in *Guida al lavoro,* p. 69 ff.

Tiraboschi, M. (2005), "The Italian labour market after the Biagi reform", in *International Journal of Comparative Labour Law and Industrial Relations,* pp. 149ff.

Treu, T. (1993), "Italy Country Report", in R. Blanpain (ed.), *Temporary Work and Labour Law,* Kluwer Law and Taxation, pp. 201ff.

Zappalà, L. (2003), "The Temporary Worker's Directive: An Impossible Political Agreement?", *Industrial Law Journal,* pp. 310ff.

Zappalà, L. (2004), "Fixed-term contracts in Italy", in B. Caruso and M. Fuchs (eds), *Labour Law and Flexibility in Europe,* Nomos-Giuffrè, pp. 98ff.

Germany: "Premature Implementation" of the Draft Directive – In Spite of Resistance in the Council

Kerstin AHLBERG

1. Historical Background[1]

When one looks back at the history of temporary agency work in Germany and how it has developed since the end of the nineteenth century a kind of circular movement seems to present itself.

At first, the legislators made no distinction between temporary agency work and job placement, and commercial agencies could engage in both activities without many restrictions. But as unscrupulous agencies came to exploit the massive unemployment at the turn of the century, a public monopoly on job placement was developed step by step.

In 1957, a total ban on temporary agency work was introduced, as it was regarded as an infringement of the public monopoly on job placement.

Ten years later, the Federal Constitutional Court declared this absolute prohibition on commercial agency work unconstitutional and void.[2] If the worker has an employment contract with the agency, and continues to be paid for periods when he or she is not assigned to a user firm, then this is not job placement, the Court argued.

As a result, the first special legislation, the Act on Agency Work (*Arbeitnehmerüberlassungsgesetz*), was adopted in 1972. Just like the judgement from the Constitutional Court it was based on the assumption that the agencies did not – and were not allowed to – engage in job placement. Accordingly, workers must not be employed as freelancers or self-employed but as employees of the agency. Furthermore, their employment contract with the agency must be of indefinite duration and must not be restricted to the length of the assignment at a user company. This pro-

1 My account of the historical background is based on Weiss and Schmidt (1993); Weiss (1999), Schiek (2004) and Konle-Seidl and Walwei (2001).

2 BverfGE 21, No. 265, 4.4 1967.

vision, known as the ban on "synchronisation" (*Synchronisationsverbot*), also meant that they should be paid between assignments. But while the Act served the purpose of providing workers with some employment security, its aim was to keep this form of employment exceptional. Therefore, the length of assignments to a user company was restricted to three months. From the beginning, all this applied equally to all sectors of the economy. But in 1982 a total ban on temporary agency work for blue-collar workers in the building industry was introduced.

From 1985 onwards, the Act on Agency Work was changed several times in a liberalising direction, as a means of employment promotion. The maximum length of assignments was prolonged step by step. The ban on agency work in the construction industry was relaxed. In 1994 the public monopoly on job placement was repealed, partly as a consequence of the EC court's judgement in *Höfner v. Marcotron*.[3] But the main thrust of the legislation governing agency work remained the same. For example, although the theoretical justification for the ban on synchronisation – namely that private agencies must not engage in job placement – had disappeared, the ban remained.

But a comprehensive revision of the Act on Agency Work took place in the first years of the twenty first century, and with the latest amendments – which came into force on 1 January 2004 – the circle was closed. The aim of that reform is to actually encourage temporary work agencies to engage in job placement. As this development took place in parallel with and is closely linked to the efforts to create a European-level regulation of temporary agency work, I will describe it later in this chapter.

2. Economic and Social Context

In order to obtain or retain a license for hiring out labour, agencies are obliged to submit different kinds of data to the Federal Employment Office (*Bundesagentur für Arbeit, BA*) twice a year. Also, every second year since 1972 the Federal Government has to report to the *Bundestag* on the application of the Act on Agency Work. Thus, the quantity of available statistics on the nature and extent of temporary agency work in Germany is substantial.

---

3 C-41/90 [1991], ECR p. 1979, in which the Court of Justice of the European Communities ruled that the German monopoly implied an abuse of a dominant position and was contrary to EC competition rules, as it was unable to satisfy the demand in the market for services of intermediation between employers and job seekers.

2.1 The Workers

On an average day in 2004, 385,256 persons were employed in temporary agency work in Germany.[4] This means that their number had almost trebled since 1994.[5] During the same period, agency workers' share of total number of workers covered by social security contributions increased from 0.42 to 1.21%.[6] Labour turnover in the sector is extremely high, and the employment stock is statistically renewed more than twice a year.[7]

The typical agency worker in Germany is a comparatively young man working in a low skilled job in industry or manufacturing. In 2002 a little over 52% of agency workers were under 35 years old, compared to 37% of all employees in Germany.[8] The proportion of men in agency work was 72.5% compared to a little over 55% in the whole economy;[9] 46.5% were low skilled workers, compared to 17% in all occupations.[10] In 2000 the largest share, 32%, worked in the engineering and electrical industries. But this share decreased to 28% in 2004, and today "low skilled jobs [*Hilfsarbeit*] without further specification" account for the largest part, 32%. Other occupations in which temporary agency work is increasing are in the service sector, such as hotel jobs, domestic work, hairdressing, stockroom work, security and banking and insurance.[11]

2.2 The Agencies

Between 2000 and 2004, the number of natural and legal persons holding a license to hire out labour on a commercial basis increased by around 20%.[12] But the number of licence holders is not identical with the number of companies, as each branch office has to have a separate license. Also, many companies apply for a license "just-in-case", and do not in fact act as agencies. The number of companies whose exclusive or primary purpose was to provide other employers with staff for a limited

4 *Zehnter Bericht der Bundesregierung über Erfahrungen bei der Anwendung des Arbeitnehmerüberlassungsgesetzes – AÜG*, Unterrichtung durch die Bundesregierung 27.09.2005, p. 32.

5 Weinkopf (2005), p. 4

6 Kaltenborn, Knerr and Kurth-Laatsch (2004); Bellmann (2004).

7 Weinkopf (2005), p. 5.

8 *Ibid.* p. 9.

9 *Ibid.*

10 *Ibid.*

11 *Zehnter Bericht der Bundesregierung über Erfahrungen bei der Anwendung des Arbeitnehmerüberlassungsgesetzes – AÜG*, pp. 34–35.

12 *Ibid.* pp. 28–29.

period was 4,526, with 7,153 branch offices at mid-year 2004.[13] Together they employed 86% of the agency workers in Germany. Most of these agencies were small or medium-sized. Only 30% employed 50 workers or more. The figures indicate that the sector is very fragmented in comparison with the situation in other countries. The six leading companies – Randstad, Adecco, Manpower, Persona Service, DIS AG and Bindan – held only one fourth of the market in 2002.[14] But there may be signs of a structural transformation. The share of "real" agencies that employed fewer than 10 workers decreased from 25% to 16% between 1999 and 2004.[15]

Agencies established in other EU/EEA member states that want to hire out workers to employers in Germany also need a license. By the end of 2004, there were 267 foreign agencies with such a license. All but two had their offices in "old" Member States, but after EU enlargement on 1 May 2004 four Polish agencies had applied for licenses, and two of these applications had already been granted.[16]

Many of the foreign agencies post workers from Germany to other Member States, especially to Austria and the Netherlands. Since enlargement in 2004, the authorities have had an increased number of inquiries on the transnational hiring-out of workers. A trend has emerged, due to the transitory provisions restricting the free movement of workers, for workers from the new member states to be instead posted to Germany by temporary work agencies that make use of the free movement of services.[17] At the same time, posting of temporary agency workers from Spain or Portugal – previously low wage countries – was almost non-existent.[18]

13 *Zehnter Bericht der Bundesregierung über Erfahrungen bei der Anwendung des Arbeitnehmerüberlassungsgesetzes – AÜG*, table 3.

14 Weinkopf (2005), p. 6.

15 *Zehnter Bericht der Bundesregierung über Erfahrungen bei der Anwendung des Arbeitnehmerüberlassungsgesetzes – AÜG*, p. 30.

16 *Zehnter Bericht der Bundesregierung über Erfahrungen bei der Anwendung des Arbeitnehmerüberlassungsgesetzes – AÜG*, pp. 31–32.

17 One could add that Germany is one of two countries (the other is Austria) that were allowed to have transitory restrictions even on the freedom to provide services from the new Member States. These restrictions apply in three sectors: the building industry, house cleaning (*Gebäudereinigung*) and interior decoration (*Innendekoration*).

18 *Zehnter Bericht der Bundesregierung über Erfahrungen bei der Anwendung des Arbeitnehmerüberlassungsgesetzes – AÜG*, pp. 31–32.

3. Employment Conditions

3.1 Pay

In the late 1990s agency workers in Germany earned around 63% of the wages earned by comparable workers, according to the Federal Employment Service.[19] A report from 2000 speaks of wages on average 30% below the rates in comparable user firms.[20] But this refers to the situation before the radical revision of the Act on Agency Work in 2003 and 2004, which would imply an improvement of the employment conditions in temporary agency work. Later in this chapter I will describe the new collective agreements that were concluded as a result of this revision and the conditions laid down therein.

3.2 Duration of Employment with an Agency and Length of Assignments to User Enterprises

Despite the legislator's efforts to promote stable employment relationships through the ban on synchronisation and the prohibition on fixed-term contracts (which was upheld until 1997) statistics from the late 1990s show that only one third of workers had an employment relation with an agency for more than three months. Thus two thirds of contracts lasted for less than three months. Around 12% were even shorter than a week.[21] This means that agency workers had significantly shorter contracts than workers who were employed on fixed-term contracts directly by user firms.[22] In 2004, the share of agency workers whose employment contracts were of less than a week's duration had increased to 14%. On the other hand, the share that had an employment relationship of longer than three months also increased, from 37% in (2000) to 40% (2004).[23]

In light of the negotiations between EU Member States on the Directive on temporary agency work and the exemption for assignments of a certain duration that Germany called for as part of the blocking minority,[24] it would be interesting to see statistics on the duration of agency workers' assignments to user enterprises. Unfortunately, no such statistics exist. But the data on the length of their employment relations

19 Clauwaert (1998), p. 46.
20 Storrie (2002), p. 54.
21 Weiss (1999), p. 259; Clauwaert (1998), p. 50; Storrie (2002), p. 45.
22 Storrie (2002), p. 45.
23 *Zehnter Bericht der Bundesregierung über Erfahrungen bei der Anwendung des Arbeitnehmerüberlassungsgesetzes – AÜG*, pp. 33–34.
24 See Chapter 9 on the social dialogue on temporary agency work and the subsequent negotiations between the Member States.

with the agencies mentioned above give an indirect indication, as this sets an upper limit on the time workers can be assigned to work for a user company. Thus, at least 60% of the assignments must have been of less than three months duration in 2004, and 14% shorter than one week.

3.3 Other Working Conditions

As regards other employment and working conditions, such as occupational pensions, holidays, health and safety, and so on, no statistics are available. However, since 1998 the *Berufsgenossenschaft,* an insurance institution which assesses the risk of accidents at work, has applied a higher risk tariff for agency work.[25]

4. Legal Position

4.1 A New Approach

As outlined in the introduction, the traditional approach to temporary agency work in German national law was very restrictive. In order to protect regular employment, temporary agency work was to be kept to a minimum. The hiring and use of agency workers were subject to a number of restrictions that did not apply to other workers and there was a total ban on agency work in the building sector. Although the legislation was gradually liberalised, this general approach was upheld throughout the twentieth century.

But the restrictive approach had its problems. The legislation could be circumvented as in practice it was very difficult to distinguish temporary agency work from other forms of work performed by third parties, for example contract work. Also, the negative effects of the restrictions affected workers more than employers. Thus, there were several reasons why the German legislator decided to try to achieve social balance through other means than repression of agency work.[26]

At the same time as the German government was negotiating with the governments of other Member States on a EU directive on temporary agency work[27] it was preparing a revision of the German Act on Agency Work based on a completely new rationale. The revision was part of a comprehensive reform of German labour market policy, proposed on 16

25 Storrie (2002), p. 52.

26 Schiek: "Arbeitnehmerüberlassung – rechtlicher Rahmen in Deutschland und der EU", lecture October 2005.

27 See the Chapter 9 on the Social dialogue on temporary agency work and the subsequent negotiations between the Member States.

August 2002 by the Commission on Modern Services in the Labour Market, also known as the Hartz Commission.[28] As one part of the package, the public Employment Offices would set up Personnel Service Agencies (*Personal Service Agenturen*, or PSAs), independent organisational units that would engage in a form of "placement-oriented" temporary agency work, namely to hire out unemployed persons to employers with a view to this leading to a regular job. The Hartz Commission concluded that these PSAs, like the temporary work agencies, could work effectively only if the restrictions of the Act on Agency Work did not apply. Consequently, they must be repealed – on condition that collective agreements were concluded. Thus, the proposed reform would not altogether go in a liberalising direction. The lifting of the restrictions would be coupled with the introduction of a principle of equal treatment between temporary agency workers and comparable workers in the user enterprises.

On 15 November 2002 the *Bundestag* adopted the First Act on Modern Services in the Labour Market, including the amendments to the Act on Agency Work. Later, two additional Acts with the same heading were adopted (the three generally referred to as Hartz I–III). The new approach meant that temporary agency work was no longer an inferior form of employment that should be kept to a minimum, but an acceptable, even positive phenomenon that could contribute to the fight against unemployment.

4.2 "Premature Implementation" of the Draft EU Directive

The revised Act on Agency Work is more or less a blueprint of the European Commission's original proposal for a directive on temporary agency work.[29] One author calls it "a faithful implementation of the draft directive" and concludes,

> Once true to what may be referred to as a typical German tendency of overobedience … the government decided to include those provisions that it perceived as necessary to implement the draft directive on agency work. As a result, first experiences with the German legislation may be used for guidance as to which direction the renewed proposal on EU level should go.[30]

Thus, paradoxically enough, the German government seems to have used the draft Directive as an excuse for introducing measures that it consid-

28 *Moderne Dienstleistungen am Arbeitsmarkt.*

29 See the chapter on the social dialogue on temporary agency work and the subsequent negotiations between the Member States, pp. 181–252.

30 Schiek (2004).

ered necessary at national level, at the same time as it counteracted them at EU level. I shall now describe the situation as it stands at the moment.

4.2.1 License

As before, temporary work agencies must have a *license*. The article that lays down the conditions for a license (§1) defines temporary agency work as an activity where "employers" assign "employees" to third parties on a commercial basis to perform work.[31] If a worker is assigned to a third party to perform work without the agency assuming the normal obligations and risks of an employer, it is assumed that the agency is engaging in job placement, not temporary agency work. Thus, the Act rests on the presumption that the agency worker is an employee of the temporary work agency and covered by the same labour legislation as all other employees.

Employers with fewer than 50 employees may hire out workers to other employers up to twelve months without having a license, on condition that they inform the Federal Employment Service and furnish it with specified information in advance. The object of this provision is to help avoid layoffs when there is a temporary decline in demand.

Three other cases of temporary agency work are exempted from application of the greater part of the Act:

1. temporary secondment of workers between enterprises in the same sector where a collective agreement binding both enterprises allows it;
2. temporary secondment between enterprises that belong to the same group; and
3. in cases where a worker is hired out outside Germany to a transnational joint venture which is established according to international agreements and in which the agency participates.

In September 2005 there was still no such collective agreement as referred to in point 1. The exemption referred to in point 3 had no practical significance during the period 2000–2004.[32]

4.2.2 Restrictions in the Building Industry

As before, temporary agency work is as a rule not allowed in the building industry. But an exception applies if both the company hiring out the

31 If certain conditions are fulfilled, secondment between companies that are members of a consortium formed to carry out a specific work project does not fall within this definition.

32 *Zehnter Bericht der Bundesregierung über Erfahrungen bei der Anwendung des Arbeitnehmerüberlassungsgesetzes – AÜG*, pp. 26–27.

worker and the user company are building enterprises and both have verifiably been bound by the same collective agreement for at least three years. Before 1 January 2003, foreign building companies could not hire out building workers to Germany unless they too were bound by German collective agreements, which implied that they had to have an establishment there. In 2001, the European Court of Justice ruled this was contrary to EC law and that Germany had failed to fulfil its obligations under the Treaty.[33] Now building companies from other EU/EEA Member States are also allowed to hire out workers to Germany on condition that they have mainly engaged in activities that fall under the same collective agreement as the user company's activity for at least three years.

Another exception says that even other companies than building enterprises may hire out workers to the building sector, where there is a generally binding collective agreement allowing it. By the end of 2004 no such collective agreement existed.[34]

4.2.3 Restrictions in Case of Strike Action in the User Company

There is no prohibition on replacing striking workers with temporary agency workers, but the agency workers have a right to refuse to work in a user enterprise where industrial action is going on. In addition, in the case of industrial action in the user company, the agency has to inform its workers of this right. For a number of years, members of the leading organisation for temporary work agencies, the German Association of Private Employment Agencies (*Bundesverband Zeitarbeit, BZA*), have voluntarily undertaken not to assign their workers to enterprises where there is a strike.

4.2.4 No Time-based Restrictions

The most symbolic change is perhaps the fact that there are no longer any restrictions on the duration of assignments to a user company, and that the ban on synchronisation of the period of assignment and the worker's employment contract has finally been repealed. Furthermore, the rule that the agency worker must have an open-ended contract was abolished in 1997. But just like other workers, agency workers are covered by the Act on Part-time and Fixed-term Work (*Teilzeit- und Befristungsgesetz*), which contains provisions on objective grounds for and the maximum length of fixed-term contracts. One author argues that the combined effect of these provisions on temporary agency work in fact

33 C-493/99 *Commission v. Germany* (2001) ECR I-8163.

34 *Zehnter Bericht der Bundesregierung über Erfahrungen bei der Anwendung des Arbeitnehmerüberlassungsgesetzes – AÜG*, p. 18.

renders the abrogation of the ban on synchronisation "anything but convincing".[35]

German employers maintain that it is still normal practice to employ agency workers on open-ended contracts, but there are no up to date statistics on what types of contract agency workers have today.[36] On the other hand, this may not be a very accurate criterion of the quality of agency work in Germany, since, as we have already seen, agency workers have significantly shorter contracts – even if open-ended – than workers employed directly by user firms on fixed-term contracts.

4.2.5 Equal Treatment Principle

Less symbolic, but perhaps more important is the new equal treatment principle. In fact, a principle of equal treatment was introduced in the Act on Agency Work as early as 2002. It guaranteed temporary agency workers the same essential (*wesentlichen*) working conditions, including pay, as comparable workers in the user enterprise, but only after twelve months assignment in the same user enterprise.[37] But after the amendments introduced through Hartz I, the equal treatment principle applies from the first day of an assignment. This main rule, which is expressed in §§3 and 9, has two exceptions. First, if the agency employs a worker who is unemployed and has not worked for the agency before, he or she may be paid less for the first six weeks of assignment to a user company, provided that the net remuneration is at least as high as his or her unemployment benefit. Secondly, derogations are allowed through collective agreements. Where there is such a collective agreement, employers and employees not bound by it can agree to apply its provisions.

If there is reason to believe that an enterprise applying for a licence will not respect this equal treatment principle its application will not be approved. Furthermore, agreements between agencies and workers on less favourable conditions are void.

4.2.6 Promotion of Collective Bargaining

But in order to fully understand the purport of these rules one has to study the transitory provisions. The revised Act on Agency Work came into force on 1 January 2003. However, many provisions of the old act were

35 Raab (2003).

36 Arrowsmith (2005), p. 18.

37 Consequently, Germany called for a twelve-month exemption from the non-discrimination principle in the first rounds of negotiations on the Commission proposal for a Directive on temporary agency work, see Ahlberg p. 226 in this volume.

to be applied throughout 2003 on all employment relationships entered into before 1 January 2004 – unless they were within the scope of a collective agreement concluded after 15 November 2002 (the day that the Bundestag passed the parliament bill) and regulating essential working conditions within the meaning of §§3 and 9. The object of the transitory provisions was to promote collective bargaining. The new Act contained advantages for employers as well as workers, and both sides could "win" one year if they managed to conclude collective agreements on essential working conditions for agency workers.

4.2.7 From "Temp" to "Permanent"

As before, agreements that forbid workers from entering into a direct employment relationship with the user enterprise after the assignment is finished are void, as are agreements that forbid users to employ agency workers directly. Before 1 January 2004, it was debatable whether this also meant that the agency and the user enterprise could not agree that the user should pay a fee if it offered the agency worker direct employment after the assignment.[38] But this uncertainty has been cleared away with the latest amendments to the Act. Now the Act states that this does not prevent agencies and user enterprises agreeing on a reasonable (*angemessenen*) "commission fee". The German legislator explains this with the fact that it is allowed to charge a fee for job placement and that temporary agency work is often used as a means of staff recruitment. Thus, temporary agency work and job placement can be businesses that are coupled together and protected by private autonomy.[39]

4.2.8 Consultation Rights of Workers in the User Company

Before a user enterprise hires a temporary agency worker, it has to inform its works council of its plans and submit the agency's written declaration that it has the necessary license. According to §99 of the Works Constitution Act (*Betriebsverfassungsgesetz)* the works council can reject personnel measures if there are circumstantial misgivings that these measures will lead to redundancies or other disadvantages for the enterprise's own employees. Hiring of temporary agency workers is one example of situations when this codetermination right can be used. But in a given case it is very difficult for the works council to prove that this will lead to disadvantages for the permanent staff.[40]

---

38 Benkert (2004).

39 *Ibid.*

40 Raab (2003), p. 440; Weiss (2004), p. 133; Däubler, Kittner and Klebe (1996), p. 1660.

4.2.9 Sanctions

The application of the Act on Agency Work is monitored by the Federal Employment Office *(Bundesagentur für Arbeit, BA*), which is a combination of state agency and tripartite organisation.[41] The agencies are obliged to submit different kinds of statistics to the BA twice a year. Agencies or user companies that employ foreign workers without a residence permit risk terms of imprisonment; other infringements of the Act can be punished by financial penalties. There is also a sanction available for agency workers. If an agency does not have the necessary licence, the employment contracts with its workers are void, and instead they are deemed to be employees of the user companies. They also have the right to claim damages from the agency.

5. Effects of the New Legislation

5.1 Historic Collective Agreements for the Whole Sector

It is striking how the German trade unions' approach to temporary agency work changed within less than a decade. In 1995 the influential Metal Workers Union (*IG Metall)* voted for a total ban on agency work. In 1998, when the European Trade Union Confederation prepared the European-level social dialogue on temporary agency work, the German Trade Union Congress (*Deutsche Gewerkschaftsbund,* DGB) still wanted to restrict temporary agency work as far as possible.[42] In keeping with this negative attitude, German trade unions were opposed to concluding collective agreements on terms and conditions for temporary agency workers. In 1970 the white-collar union *Deutsche Angestelltengewerkschaft* concluded a collective agreement with BZA. That was the first and only sectoral agreement, and it was not renewed after 1989. The very few collective agreements concluded thereafter were only single-employer agreements. Of course, this did not encourage temporary agency workers to organise.[43]

But in parallel with the developments at EU level, the trade unions gradually started to see collective agreements as a useful tool for strengthening the position of temporary agency workers. When the Hartz commission presented its proposal, it was endorsed by the trade union movement.[44] When the new Act on Agency Work was passed, DGB

41 Clauwaert (1998), p. 45.

42 *Ibid.* p. 49.

43 Clauwaert (1998), p. 49; Weiss (2004), p. 134; Schiek (2004).

44 The trade unions had been represented in the commission, while the two most important employers' and businesses associations, Bundesvereinigung der Deutschen

President Michael Sommer welcomed it as a promising means of re-orientating temporary agency work, and demanded that employers' associations and companies start immediate negotiations with the trade unions. All trade unions affiliated to DGB had already agreed to act jointly to conclude collective agreements for the temporary agency work sector.[45]

And so it happened. On 22 July 2003, all trade unions affiliated to the DGB, for the first time in history united in a cross-sector "bargaining association", finally signed a package of three collective agreements with BZA: one general framework agreement on working conditions, one "skeleton" agreement on pay principles and pay groups, and a collective agreement on actual pay rates. A similar package was agreed with the other large association for temporary work agencies, *Interessengemeinschaft Deutscher Zeitarbeitsunternehmen* (IGZ), which represents a number of small and medium-sized enterprises.[46]

But there had been difficulties on the way.[47] A first framework agreement on standard rates of pay was reached between DGB and BZA already on 20 February. In addition it was agreed that agency workers assigned to user companies where the collectively agreed pay rate for workers on open-ended contracts was higher than the standard rate for temporary workers were to receive an extra allowance. The specific amounts of these allowances were to be negotiated separately for each sector before 31 May. But on 24 February a bargaining association of trade unions affiliated to the small Christian Federation of Trade Unions (*Christlicher Gewerkschaftsbund, CGB*) concluded a number of cross-sector collective agreements with a small regional employers' association, with pay rates considerably lower than those agreed between DGB and BZA. It also contained an "opening clause" allowing the individual agency to go under the pay rates in the sectoral agreement if it could gain the consent of the agency's works council or of 75% of the workforce. This made BZA demand that the already agreed conditions in the agreement with DGB be renegotiated. The final result differed on several points from what had been agreed in February.

Both the BZA and the IGZ agreements establish a pay scale with nine steps for work of different degrees of difficulty, from work requiring only

Arbeitgeberverbände (BDA) and Bundesverband Deutsche Industrie (BDI) had refrained from joining, see "Sweeping modernisation of labour market policy proposed", EIROnline de0209205f.html at www.eiro.eurofound.ie.

45 "New law passed on temporary agency work."

46 "Packages of collective agreements signed for temporary agency workers."

47 *Ibid.*

a short familiarisation period to work requiring a university degree and several years of work experience. Each agency worker is to be categorised in a pay group on the basis of the work predominantly performed by him or her. If a worker is temporarily assigned to perform work in a higher pay group, he or she will be paid a supplement according to the higher tariff. For 2004 the hourly rates varied between 6.85 euros to 15.50 euros in the BZA agreement and 15.43 euros in the IGZ agreement.[48] The pay levels in the first agreement were generally somewhat higher than those in the latter. In both agreements, the hourly rates for work in user companies in East Germany were 13.5% lower than for work in West Germany. As from 2006, there are no separate tariffs for East Germany.

Except for one pay group, these hourly rates are less than half of the median wage for full-time workers in Germany as a whole.[49]

After a three-month assignment at the same user enterprise, a worker is entitled to a supplement of 2% in addition to the hourly rate. This supplement is further increased after six, nine and twelve months of uninterrupted assignment to the same user enterprise. A worker who has been employed without interruption for more than one year by the agency is entitled to additional annual payments in the form of holiday and Christmas bonuses. As from 2006 this qualification period is shortened to six months.

In addition to provisions on pay, both DGB collective agreements contain, *inter alia*, provisions on average weekly working time (35 hours), the organisation of working time, on-call time, overtime, supplements for night work and work on Sundays and holidays, entering into and termination of an employment relationship, continued payment in case of illness and paid annual leave. In its final provisions the agreement between DGB and BZA states that workers shall not be assigned to companies that are directly affected by a legal strike. But in exceptional cases it is possible within the framework of an emergency service agreed upon with the user enterprise.

In this round the DGB had to give up its demands for extra allowances for agency workers assigned to user enterprises where the collectively agreed pay rate for workers on open-ended contracts was higher than the standard rate for temporary workers. Thus, if the trade union sought an agreement that guaranteed agency workers as a group an average out-

48 "Packages of collective agreements signed for temporary agency workers."

49 Weinkopf (2005), p. 14.

come close to the equal treatment principle it did not reach its goal. Also, the supplements and bonuses related to the length of assignments to the same user company or the duration of the employment relation with the agency seem to imply that agency workers have open-ended employment contracts of long duration. But this was an illusion even in the days when the legislator tried to promote such contracts by the ban on synchronisation and prohibition of fixed-term contracts. Thus, these supplements and bonuses will be of little importance if temporary agency work relationships do not change character. Nevertheless, DGB was satisfied with the outcome. Imperfect as they might be, the collective agreements with BZA and IGZ would improve working conditions in the sector compared to the situation so far. Thus it would safeguard the interests of agency workers and the industry could develop into a normal economic sector, DGB stressed.[50]

The agencies affiliated to BZA and IGZ employ a total of 42% of the agency workers in Germany.[51] But collective agreements are binding only between the employer and workers who are members of the signatory trade union, and the unionisation rate among temporary agency workers is said to be extremely low. As German employers bound by a collective agreement traditionally apply it equally to all their employees without being obliged to do so, the collective agreements for the temporary agency work sector may nevertheless be influential. The prerequisites for declaring them generally binding do not exist, however. This is possible only if the enterprises that are members of the signatory employers' associations employ at least 50% of the workers in the sector.

As already mentioned, employers and employees who are not bound by a collective agreement can agree to apply the provisions of any of these agreements and thus avoid the application of the equal treatment principle laid down in the Act on Agency Work. According to the trade unions, in the majority of cases the agreement that is least favourable for the workers is chosen.[52]

5.2 Debate on the Scope of the Exception

The possibility of concluding collective agreements that derogate from the equal treatment principle was foreseen in the European Commission's

50 "Packages of collective agreements signed for temporary agency workers."

51 Weiss (2004), p. 138.

52 Weinkopf (2005), p. 15.

53 Schüren as quoted by Schiek (2004); Raab (2003), p. 409.

54 Schiek (2004).

draft Directive on temporary agency work. In the German Act on Agency Work that "implements" the draft Directive, this provision is worded as an unconditional exception from the equal treatment principle, that is, without any reservations regarding the contents of such collective agreements. This notwithstanding, there has been a debate on whether this empowers trade unions and employers to agree on any collective agreement, or if it must guarantee workers roughly the equivalent of the wages of comparable workers in the user enterprise.[53] Schiek holds the view that the latter does not correspond either to the text of the norm or to what the legislator had in mind.[54] In addition, she argues, it is questionable if such determination of the result of collective bargaining is in line with the guarantee of trade union freedom under the German Constitution.

What the German example illustrates is how such an unconditional exemption can be (mis)used in an environment in which the rate of organisation is low and the trade union movement is fragmented. But in this concrete case it has been questioned whether the *Christlicher Gewerkschaftsbund* is in fact a trade union in the legal sense. If not, its collective agreements are void.[55]

5.3 No Infringement of Employers' Freedom of Association

But the employers have questioned whether the new Act infringes on their freedom of association as guaranteed by the German Constitution. BZA together with another, smaller employers' organisation and eight temporary work agencies lodged an appeal before the Federal Constitutional Court (*Bundesverfassungsgericht*), arguing that the provisions of the Act in practice forced them to conclude collective agreements and, in addition, put them in a weaker position than the trade union side.[56]

On 29 December 2004 the *Bundesverfassungsgericht* dismissed the case. Even if there were a restriction on the freedom of association, a question which the court left open, such a restriction would in any case be justified on constitutional grounds. The object of the legislator was to increase the acceptance and quality of temporary agency work and consequently improve agency workers' position on the labour market. The new provisions guaranteed agency workers a suitable level of protection. Especially, agency work should be used as a bridge from unemployment to employment and create new employment opportunities. The fight against mass unemployment is one of the objects of the Constitution and

55 Böhm (2003); Buchner (2004).

56 *Zehnter Bericht der Bundesregierung über Erfahrungen bei der Anwendung des Arbeitnehmerüberlassungsgesetzes – AÜG*, p. 19.

the provisions called into question are well suited to contribute to that object, as well as proportionate, the Court ruled.[57]

5.4 Will It Serve Its Purpose?

The *Bundesverfassungsgericht* quite correctly notes that the object of the "Hartz reform", with its relaxation of the restrictions on agency work, was to promote employment, and the Court itself is obviously convinced that it will serve that purpose. It is probably too early to judge the effects of the new regulation on temporary agency work. The Ministry of Economics and Labour has commissioned a number of researchers to evaluate the whole reform package.

But in its report to the Bundestag on the application of the Act on Agency Work during 2000–2004 – that is, after one year's experience of the new Act – the German Government draws a number of conclusions on the significance of temporary agency work for labour market policy.[58]

Although it has increased, the proportion of agency workers in the total workforce is still small – by the end of June 2004 it was 1.5%. One must also remember, the Government points out, that a nominal increase in the number of agency workers does not always represent new jobs. Especially in big companies there is a tendency to substitute permanent staff with agency workers. Partly, workers are fired with the purpose of hiring them back to their previous employer on inferior terms and conditions of employment through an "in-house" agency. Whole areas of production are transferred to other companies, after the employees concerned have been hired out to the new company. Consequently, this "user company" becomes a subcontractor to the workers' former employer. Also, the outsourcing of public services to newly established private companies often includes the hiring out of the staff made redundant to these new companies.

This development, that has been made possible through the abrogation of the restrictions on the length of assignments to a user company, must be closely followed, and the legislator must consider how to judge them, the Government concludes.

Nevertheless, the Government summarizes that temporary agency work offers unemployed persons in particular a better chance of re-entering the labour market. This conviction is based on the fact that by the end

---

57 1 BvR 2283/03, 1 BvR 2504/03, 1 BvR 2582/03.

58 *Zehnter Bericht der Bundesregierung über Erfahrungen bei der Anwendung des Arbeitnehmerüberlassungsgesetzes – AÜG*, p. 47.

of June 2004, 61% of the workers who were on an assignment had not been in employment immediately before they were engaged as agency workers (but had worked earlier), and that as much as 11% had been out of employment for one year or more. According to the Government, these figures show that temporary agency work offers long-term unemployed persons or persons who have taken a longer pause from working life – for example, for "family reasons" – a chance of re-entering gainful employment.[59]

Bibliography

Arrowsmith, J. (2005), *Temporary agency work in an enlarged European Union*, European Foundation for the Improvement of Living and Working Conditions.

Benkert, D. (2004), "Änderungen im Arbeitnehmerüberlassungsgesetz durch 'Hartz III'", *Betriebs-Berater* 59. jg. Heft 18 (13 May): 998–1001.

Bellmann, L. (2004), "Zur Entwicklung der Leiharbeit in Deutschland Theoretische Überlegungen und empirische Ergebnisse aus dem IAB-Betriebspanel", *Sozialer Fortschritt* 6: 135–42.

Buchner, H. (2004), "Leiharbeit: Ablösung der Verpflichtung zur Gewährung der im Entleiherbetrieb geltenden Arbeitsbedingungen (§ 10 Abs. 4 AÜG) durch Tarifregelungen – Zur Problematik der Tariffähigkeit der tarifschließenden Verbände", *Der Betrieb*, Heft 19 (7 May): 1042–44.

Böhm, W. (2003), "Billig-Tarifverträge" in der Zeitarbeit – Risiken für die Kunden", *Der Betrieb*, Heft 48 (28 November): 2598–99.

Clauwaert, S. (1998), *Survey of legislation on temporary agency work*, European Trade Union Institute.

Däubler, W., M. Kittner and T. Klebe (eds) (1996), *BetrVG Betriebsverfassungsgesetz mit Wahlordnung Kommentar für die Praxis*, 5 Auflage, Bund-Verlag.

Kaltenborn, B., P. Knerr and S. Kurth-Laatsch (2004), "Hartz-Evaluierung: Ausgangslage, Erster Zwischenbericht im Auftrag des Bundesministeriums für Wirtschaft und Arbeit", *Wirtschaftsforschung und Politikberatung* (December).

Konle-Seidl, R., and U. Walwei (2001), *Job placement regimes in Europe: trends and impacts of changes*, IAB Labour Market Research Topics No. 46, Bundesanstalt für Arbeit.

Moderne Dienstleistungen am Arbeitsmarkt (2004), Bericht der Kommission, August.

New law passed on temporary agency work, EIROnline de0212203.n.html at www.eiro.eurofound.ie

59 *Zehnter Bericht der Bundesregierung über Erfahrungen bei der Anwendung des Arbeitnehmerüberlassungsgesetzes – AÜG.*

Packages of collective agreements signed for temporary agency workers, EIROnline de0308203f.html at www.eiro.eurofound.ie

Raab, T. (2003), "Europäische und nationale Entwicklungen im Recht der Arbeitnehmerüberlassung", *Zeitschrift für Arbeitsrecht* 3: 389–446.

Schiek, D. (2004), "Agency work – from marginalisation towards acceptance? Agency work in EU Social and Employment Policy and the 'implementation' of the draft Directive on Agency Work into German law", *German Law Journal* 5 (10) (1 October).

Storrie, D. (2002), *Temporary Agency Work in the European Union*, European Foundation for the Improvement of Living and Working Conditions.

Sweeping modernisation of labour market policy proposed, EIROnline de0209205f.html at www.eiro.eurofound.ie

Weinkopf, C. (2005), The role of temporary agency work in the German employment model, paper presented to the 26th Conference of the International Working Party on Labour Market Segmentation, 8–10 September.

Weiss, M. (1999), "Germany", in R. Blanpain (ed.), *Private employment agencies. The impact of ILO Convention 181 (1997) and the judgement of the European Court of Justice of 11 December 1997*, Kluwer Law International.

Weiss, M. (2004), "Germany", in R. Blanpain and R. Graham, *Temporary agency work and the information society*, Kluwer Law International.

Weiss, M., and M. Schmidt (1993), "Germany", in R. Blanpain (ed.), *Temporary work and labour law of the European Community and Member States*, Kluwer Law and Taxation Publishers.

Zehnter Bericht der Bundesregierung über Erfahrungen bei der Anwendung des Arbeitnehmerüberlassungsgesetzes – AÜG, Unterrichtung durch die Bundesregierung (27 September).

The New Member States: Regulating a New Phenomenon

Kerstin AHLBERG

1. Introduction

After the enlargement of the European Union on 1 May 2004, an increasing number of temporary agency workers are being posted from the new member states to the "old" ones within the framework of the freedom to provide services.[1] But there was not – as some had foreseen – an abundance of agencies in Latvia, Hungary, Estonia and the other new members eagerly awaiting the starting signal. In general, temporary agency work was a new phenomenon in the acceding countries, on a small scale even within their own territories. Not surprisingly, only five of them had specific legislation on temporary agency work, and in all five this legislation had come into force quite recently.

This does not mean that temporary agency work did not exist in the new member states. But statistical data on its nature and incidence remain scarce. To the extent that statistics exist, it is not always possible to distinguish temporary agency work from other forms of temporary employment or from contract work, that is, where the "user" buys a *work result*.

Also, the fact that there is no specific legislation on temporary agency work does not mean that it is completely unregulated. For example, leg-

1 This chapter is primarily based on the results of a survey I carried out among the national correspondents of the European Industrial Relations Observatory (EIRO) in October 2004. The national correspondent for Cyprus did not answer the survey. The respondents were: Inga Blaziene, Institute of Labour and Social Research, Lithuania; Ludovit Cziria, Bratislava Center for Work and Family Studies, Slovakia; Manwel Debono, Malta Workers' Participation Development Centre, Malta; Raita Karnite, Institute of Economics, Latvian Academy of Sciences, Latvia; Lászl6 Neumann, National Employment Office, Research Unit, Hungary; Kaia Philips, Institute of Economics, University of Tartu, Estonia; Stefan Skledar, Institute of Macroeconomic Analysis and Development, Slovenia; Piotr Sula, Institute for Public Affairs, Poland; and Renáta Vaskov*á*, Research Institute for Labour and Social Affairs, the Czech Republic. Some of these results were used in a publication of the European Foundation for the Improvement of Living and Working Conditions, 'Temporary agency work in an enlarged European Union'.

islation on fixed-term work, which may restrict the grounds for recourse to temporary employment, as well as the number and/or length of fixed-term contracts, may be applicable also to temporary agency work, and agencies may also have to abide by provisions regulating the activities of private employment services.

2. The Regulation of Temporary Agency Work

Specific legislation on temporary agency work exists in the *Czech Republic*, *Hungary*, *Poland*, *Slovakia* and *Slovenia*.

In the *Czech Republic*, the new Employment Act (sb. 435/2004) that came into force on 1 October 2004, together with the amendment to the Labour Code, was a long-awaited legislative amendment concerning the regulation of temporary agency work. Until then, there had been a legislative vacuum in terms of agency work in the Czech Republic. Assigning agency workers to user enterprises did not exist legally.

In *Hungary*, temporary work agencies began to proliferate in the 1990s. However, legal regulation lagged behind company practices until 2001. Then the Act XVI of 2001 amended the Labour Code in order to implement a number of European Directives. Among other major changes it included a new chapter on temporary work agencies – translated literally "employee leasing". In 2003 minor changes were made to the regulation of temporary work agencies, as the amendment to the Act on Labour Inspection clarified that the Labour Inspectorate is entitled to investigate both agencies and user companies in order to reveal unlawful practices. In September 2005, the Government proposed that the provisions on temporary agency work be further amended in order to curb undeclared work and introduce an equal treatment principle.[2]

Collective agreements in Hungary normally have no provisions on agency work: as a rule neither the use of agencies nor the working conditions of agency workers are regulated by collective agreements (one notable exception was the IBM plant, which closed down in 2002).

In *Slovakia* the activities of temporary work agencies are regulated by Act No. 5/2004 on Employment Services and on Changes and Supplements to Some Laws, in force since 1 February 2004.

In *Slovenia* temporary agency work is regulated mainly in two laws. As early as 1998 the *Law on Employment and Unemployment Insurance* was amended so as to allow the operation of private employment agen-

2 *New Legislation proposed on temporary agency work.*

cies and temporary work agencies.The new *Law on Labour Relations*, in force since 1 January 2003, regulates temporary agency work in a special subchapter (Articles 57–62). Provisions deal with issues such as the nature of the contract (open-ended or fixed-term), details of the employment contract, rights, duties and responsibilities of the user enterprise and of the worker, and the relationship between the user enterprise and the agency.

In *Poland* the legal basis for temporary work in general is provided in the Act on the Employment of Temporary Workers, which came into force on 1 January 2004 and applies to agency workers, as well as to workers with other types of temporary employment. Temporary employment agencies operate on the basis of the Act on the Promotion of Employment and Labour Market Institutions of 20 April 2004.

In *Latvia*, there is neither special legislation nor collective agreements (sectoral or cross-sectoral) regulating temporary agency work. However, temporary workers are subject to the general regulations of the Labour Code and other legislative norms that regulate employment relations. Also, there is legislation regulating the activities of recruiting companies, that is, companies that work as intermediaries between job seekers and employers with vacancies. Such companies may also operate as temporary work agencies.

In *Lithuania* there are neither legislation nor sectoral/cross-sectoral collective agreements specifically regulating temporary agency work. However, since ratification of ILO Convention No. 181 on Private Employment Agencies, with effect from 1 March 2005, the Ministry of Social Security and Labour has been preparing for the legal regulation of temporary agency work.

The absence of specific legislation and sectoral or cross-sectoral collective agreements does not mean that the issue of agency work is completely unregulated in Lithuania. The Labour Code provides for an employee to be sent to another enterprise to work. Enterprises engaged in staff leasing have to comply with these legal norms – they take on an employee by concluding an individual (employment) contract and conclude a service provision agreement with the user enterprise. Also, a few enterprise-level collective agreements have been concluded in food industry enterprises where the term "agency work" is mentioned.[3] These

3 Here agency work is defined as work performed by employees sent by one enterprise to work or provide services for another enterprise with which it has concluded an agreement for the provision of civil services.

agreements specify that it is forbidden to use agency work to replace employees who are on strike or employees who were fired as a result of workforce reductions. They seem to be inspired by the collective agreement format developed by Lithuanian Trade Union Confederation and published by the Ministry of Social Security and Labour, which has a similar wording, namely: "it is forbidden to use agency work in order to replace employees who are on strike, when the jobs have hazardous, very hazardous or dangerous conditions, or to replace employees who have been dismissed as a result of workforce reductions unless six months have elapsed after the dismissals. Employees working under such agreements are covered by the CA".

In *Estonia*, the debate on the lawfulness of temporary agency work received an impetus in August 2005 when the company Elcoteq wanted to employ 500 new workers in its factory in Tallinn, most of them as temporary agency workers.[4] This prompted the Labour Inspectorate to declare that, in the absence of specific legislation, temporary agency work is illegal as it is used as a cover for improper employment contracts. Needless to say, this triggered a strong protest from the Estonian Employers' Confederation. However, it is said to be the common understanding that Estonia must regulate temporary agency work in the near future. The government is preparing legislation and a government bill is expected to be presented to Parliament in 2006–2007.

2.1 Conditions for Establishing and Running Temporary Work Agencies

All five countries that have specific legislation on temporary agency work have laid down some kind of licensing/authorisation or registration conditions.

All five impose conditions related to the natural or legal person wanting to establish a work agency. In addition, in *Poland* the agency has to provide security for its financial obligations to a minimum value of 50 times the average wage in the national economy for the preceding quarter. It is also obliged to provide the authorities with comprehensive information on its operations during the past year.

In *Slovakia* each license is restricted to a certain territory and certain occupations. When deciding whether to grant a license or not, the authorities take into account the number of unemployed workers in the relevant region and the number of agencies already holding a licence there.

4 *The legality of temporary agency work under discussion.*

In some countries that do not have specific legislation on temporary agency work, for example *Latvia* and *Estonia*, companies operating as agencies must still obtain a license, as this follows from the legislation on private employment services.

2.2 Restrictions on the Use of Temporary Agency Work

It seems from the questionnaires that *none* of the new member states restrict temporary agency work to *certain occupations or sectors of the economy.* In the *Czech Republic*, the Ministry of Labour and Social Affairs has a possibility to prohibit temporary agency work in certain occupations when deciding whether to authorise agencies. Until now it has not exercised this power. In *Slovakia* the individual agency can only operate within the territory and scope of occupations specified in its license.

However, *Poland* and *Slovenia* prohibit the use of agency work in three *specific situations*. Agency workers must not be assigned:

1. to replace workers on strike,
2. to replace employees of the user enterprise who have been made redundant within a given timeframe; or
3. to particularly dangerous jobs (which can include the building sector).

These are the same three prohibitions as in the collective agreement format developed by *Lithuanian* Trade Union Confederation and published by the Ministry of Social Security and Labour mentioned above.

In addition, the Law on Labour Relations in *Slovenia* stipulates that temporary agency work can be restricted in other situations through sectoral collective agreements.

In fact, the *Polish* legislation is stricter than emerges from the above, as *valid grounds* for using temporary agency work are restricted: for example, for seasonal, periodic and ad hoc work; for work that cannot be performed by the user's own employees; and to replace employees who are temporarily absent.

The use of agency workers to replace workers on strike is also prohibited in *Hungary*.

Three countries have specific conditions limiting *the extent of agency work for the same user company,* normally to twelve months.

The Labour Code of the *Czech Republic* limits the maximum total duration of assignments with the same user enterprise to twelve successive months. This limitation does not count if the assigned worker himself asks the agency to allow him to stay at the same user enterprise longer. The replacement of an employee taking parental leave is another objective reason for longer duration of assignments.

In *Poland*, the total length of assignment for the same user company must as a rule not exceed 12 months within a reference period of 36 months. But if the agency worker is a substitute in the absence of one of the user company's own employees, the maximum period is 36 months.

In *Slovenia* the condition of use is a maximum total duration of successive assignments. Article 59 of the LLR reads: "The employer may not provide workers to the user continuously or with interruptions of up to one month for more than one year if the same work is performed by the same worker all the time."

2.3 Legal Status of the Agency Worker

In *Cyprus* and *Lithuania* the legal status of agency workers is uncertain.[5] In the other countries (with the possible exception of *Latvia*) the normal state of affairs is that the agency worker is an employee and the agency his/her employer.

In *Slovenia*, this is not just normal, but obligatory, and follows from the LLR which says: "The employer who, in accordance with the regulations on employment and unemployment insurance on the basis of a concession contract can perform the activity of providing workers to another employer (hereinafter referred to as "the user") shall conclude an employment contract with such workers."

In *Hungary*, the agency signs a contract with the employee on a special sort of employment relationship (it must be indicated in the contract that its purpose is to fulfil temporary agency assignments), while it has a commercial contract with the user. During this special employment relationship, the employer's rights and duties are shared between the agency and the user company. The employer's main functions, however, are fulfilled by the agency, such as hiring, termination of the employment relationship, paying wages, and so on. The user company for its part is responsible for working time arrangements and directs and supervises the work.

In the *Czech Republic* agency workers normally have the status of employee and the agency is the employer. But it is not explicitly forbidden for agencies to play an intermediary role for self-employed persons.

In *Latvia* the agency worker may be either self-employed or an employee of the agency. For example, persons working for the largest agency in Latvia in 2004, Temporary Work Agency Ltd in Riga, were self-employed.

5 Arrowsmith (2006), p. 25.

In all five countries that have specific legislation on temporary agency work, the agency worker can have either a fixed-term or an open-ended employment contract. But fixed-term contracts seem to dominate. Only in *Hungary* do open-ended contracts seem to be common (60% in 2004).[6]

2.4 Regulation of Terms and Conditions of Employment

As regards pay and other terms and conditions of employment, four of the five countries that have specific legislation on temporary agency work favour the principle that agency workers must not be treated less favourably than workers employed directly by the user enterprise.

In *Slovenia* pay and other terms and conditions of employment of agency workers are regulated through legislation, collective agreements (indirectly) and individual contracts. In the employment contract, the employer and the worker must establish that the wage and compensation shall depend on the work actually performed at the user company, taking into account the collective agreements and "general acts"[7] that bind the individual user. Thus, even if there are no specific collective agreements covering temporary agency workers, according to the LLR, agency workers are guaranteed that their pay and compensation shall be determined by the same collective agreements and general acts as apply to comparable employees in the user enterprises. The LLR also stipulates that agency workers who have open-ended employment contracts must continue to be paid between assignments, and that this pay must not be lower than 70% of the minimum wage.

According to the Labour Code of the *Czech Republic* information on pay and other terms and conditions of employment must be included in the contract between the two enterprises, that is, the agency and the user enterprise. They have a shared responsibility for guaranteeing the agency worker the same pay and other conditions as comparable workers in the user enterprise. However, in the last instance it is the agency that has to ensure equal treatment. As Czech agencies normally employ their workers just after having been promised a concrete assignment at a user enterprise and arrange their employment contracts accordingly, agency workers usually do not continue to be paid between assignments.

In *Poland*, the execution of an employment contract between the agency and its employee must be preceded by an agreement between the agency and the user enterprise, which lays down the type of work, the qualifications required, the anticipated duration of the placement and the time and place of work. In addition, the user enterprise must inform the

6 Neumann (2005a).

7 Unilateral regulations of the employer.

agency of the remuneration for the work in question stipulated in the user's internal regulations, as well as the occupational health and safety conditions. For the duration of his/her assignment with the user enterprise, the agency worker must not receive less favourable treatment as regards employment conditions and other aspects of work than workers employed directly by the user enterprise in the same or a similar capacity. In the event of a breach of this rule, the agency worker may advance claims for damages against the agency. The user may also assume other duties pursuant to its contractual agreement with the agency. All the arrangements reached between the agency and the user must be communicated to the agency worker.

In *Slovakia*, the terms and conditions of employment of agency workers are regulated through individual "allocation employment agreements". Agency workers must not be discriminated against compared to workers employed directly by the user enterprise. However, if the assignment is shorter than six months, the law allows for some exceptions, provided that the agency worker is properly protected by the company collective agreement.

The exception, so far, is *Hungary*. The legislation on temporary agency work does not contain any provisions on non-discrimination or equal treatment. It is true that it does not suspend the general equal pay principle, which is guaranteed in the Constitution, but in practice neither the same wages nor the same conditions of employment are guaranteed as for comparable workers at the user enterprise. However, in September 2005 amendments were proposed to the Labour Code, including a principle of equal treatment between agency workers and workers directly employed by the user enterprise.

3. Nature and Extent of Temporary Agency Work

3.1 Agency Work in the National Context

So far, only four of the new member states have official statistics on temporary agency work: Hungary, Poland, Slovenia and Slovakia.

In *Poland*, which has the longest tradition of temporary agency work, there are several dozen temporary employment agencies operating at present. In 1994, the first entity of this sort is said to have assigned 21 people to temporary placements. Ten years later, agencies engaged some 167,000 workers, which corresponds to 0.4% of the economically active population in Poland.[8] However, not all of them – only 64% – were

8 Arrowsmith (2006), p. 11.

engaged on employment contracts; the remaining third had other types of contract. From 2003 to 2004 the members of the Union of Temporary Employment Agencies (ZAPT) registered a 40% increase in turnover and a 9% rise in the number of workers employed by them.

Temporary agency workers are typically engaged for periods ranging from one week to three months. The vast majority are low-skilled workers, who work in industry (nearly 80,000); the second largest group is warehouse staff (around 26,500 persons).[9]

In *Hungary* there were 282 registered agencies in 2002. In 2004 this had increased to 505, concluding contracts with 52,584 employees.[10] Although this was a 30% increase compared to the previous year, in total temporary agency workers represented only 1.35% of the employed population. Agency work is evenly distributed among men and women. Almost 90% were manual workers, and only a fifth of them were skilled.

As regards sectoral distribution, the biggest users of temporary agency work are companies in manufacturing (58% in 2004), sports and other services (14%), transport and telecommunications (8%), commerce (7%) and construction (5%).[11]

Unlike in the other countries, a majority (60%) of agency workers in Hungary had open-ended contracts, and the average length of their assignments was 108 days. The average duration for workers with fixed-term contracts was shorter, at 60 days.[12]

Although no data are available on wages for temporary agency workers in Hungary, not surprisingly case studies have found that they earn 10–20% less than permanent workers in similar jobs. The difference is even bigger in terms of the non-wage elements of compensation.

As in Poland and Hungary, a rapid growth in the demand for temporary agency work is reported from *Slovenia*, with an annual increase of 20 to 30%. Although there were as many as 145 licensed agencies in 2004, three multinational companies – Adecco, Manpower and ISS – accounted for almost all temporary agency work and employed around 90% of the 3,694 workers. Here, too, most of them work for user companies in manufacturing industry.[13] Their share of the working population in Slovenia is 0.5%.

---

9 Sula (2005).

10 Arrowsmith (2006), p. 12.

11 Arrowsmith (2006).

12 *Ibid.*

13 *Ibid.* p. 11.

Since temporary agency work was legalised in *Slovakia* only in 2004, there are still no statistics on the evolution of the sector. However, during that first year 74 agencies were licensed, of which only 31 were active; 10,828 workers were assigned, the vast majority (87%) in the Bratislava region. Altogether, temporary agency workers represented around 0.5% of all employees in the country – but approximately 1.5% of all employees in manufacturing. Nearly 80% were employed for less than six months.[14]

Statistics from the *Czech Republic* will become available in 2007: the new legislation obliges agencies to report certain data to the authorities.

The first temporary work agency in *Estonia* was established in 2002. Two years later there were over 180 companies licensed to perform employment mediation services, although only 12 of them were active as temporary work agencies.[15]

3.2 Transnational Posting of Temporary Agency Workers

All member states except Sweden, Ireland and the UK introduced transitory provisions to restrict the free movement of workers from the new member states (except Cyprus and Malta) during the first two years after enlargement. Only two member states – Germany and Austria – were allowed to apply similar restrictions to the freedom to provide services as well. Thus from the very first day, temporary work agencies could post workers to the old member states. Our survey carried out late in 2004 indicated that, with a few exceptions, they were not immediately inclined to make use of this freedom. However, in the two years that have passed since then, an ever increasing number of agency workers have been posted over the borders between new and old member states.

Among the companies that were waiting for the starting signal was the largest agency in *Latvia*, Temporary Work Agency Ltd.

Another example was the *Lithuanian* company Baltic WorkForce, with offices in Vilnius and Copenhagen. It commenced activities in 2004 and offered labour for such activities as fruit picking, horticulture, agriculture, industrial production and building. It described itself in the following manner: "Baltic WorkForce employs Lithuanian staff in many different trades. We are organised in well managed, qualified, and top motivated crews of five workers or more, who do odd jobs on contract for clients throughout the EU. The pay for a crew from Baltic WorkForce

14 Arrowsmith (2006), p. 11.

15 *Ibid.*

starts at 8 euros per hour. We take on assignments which our staff can fulfil without language skills."

However, reliable statistics on the incidence of transnational hiring out of workers are hard to find. A rare exception is *Slovakia*, where 902 workers were registered as posted to other EU countries in 2004, the vast majority of them to the Czech Republic (693) and Hungary (180) that have common borders with Slovakia.[16]

Also in 2004, 8,554 agency workers were posted from *Poland* to foreign user companies, which were not specified.[17] Some of them may have gone to Germany, which granted two Polish agencies a license in 2004 (see Chapter 5 on Germany in this volume).

Otherwise, one has to rely on estimates. For example, the Finnish Building Workers' Union and its counterpart on the employers' side estimate that around 10,000 foreign agency workers, mainly from *Estonia*, work in the Finnish construction industry during the summer season.

4. Adaptation to "EU Standards"

Given that temporary agency work is a rather new phenomenon in most of the member states that joined the EU in 2004, it may be more surprising that half of them actually have specific legislation on such work than that it is still unregulated in the other five countries. Three of them have also ratified ILO Convention No. 181 on Private Employment Agencies: the *Czech Republic* (2000), *Hungary* (2003) and *Lithuania* (2004).

When you examine this legislation you can see that to a large extent they seem to be influenced by the Commission's original proposal for a Directive on temporary agency work. The preparatory drafts in Hungary and Slovenia explicitly refer to the ILO Convention and the practice of most EU member states. That is a little surprising in respect of the Hungarian legislation, which does not contain the principle of equal treatment of agency workers. However, just like the draft Directive, legislation in the other four countries has the double function of legitimising temporary agency work as a means of promoting employment and integrating unemployed people into the labour market and of protecting the workers through an equal treatment principle.

Moreover, in September 2005 the Hungarian Government proposed a Labour Code amendment to bring it more in line with the draft Directive.[18]

16 Cziria (2005).

17 Sula (2005).

18 Neumann (2005b).

The background was that sectoral social dialogue committees in metalworking, engineering, chemicals and hotels/catering had called for action to combat undeclared labour and what they saw as the abuse of temporary agency work by companies that use agency workers permanently and set up companies specialised in providing the parent company with agency workers. Their worries were shared by a newly established trade organisation for temporary work agencies, the Hungarian Federation of Personnel Management Advisors.

According to the amendments proposed by the Hungarian Government, agencies will have to provide user companies with proof of agency workers' lawful employment. If the agency itself does not meet the legal criteria, or if the workers do not have proper employment contracts, it is presumed that they are employees of the user company. This should work as an incentive for user companies to force agencies to adhere to the law. Also, an equal treatment principle will be introduced. Agency workers are to be paid the same as comparable workers directly employed by the user company, but only if the assignment is longer than six months. An important novelty is that the amended legislation would prohibit any kind of ownership between the agency and the user enterprise. Thus companies will no longer be able to set up their own in-house agencies. Also, it will be prohibited to employ a person as an agency worker in a user company from which he or she was dismissed during the previous six months.

As already mentioned, similar to developments in Hungary, employers' wish to use temporary agency workers as more or less permanent staff has led to calls for legislation in *Estonia*.

In *Lithuania*, the Ministry of Social Security and Labour is preparing legislation to regulate temporary agency work. The Government's attitude towards agency work is generally positive. However, it means that it has to be regulated in order to prevent potential discrimination against agency workers with respect to working hours, rest time, pay and safety and health at work.

In *Latvia*, the draft Directive on working conditions for temporary agency workers has been much discussed. So far, the Government has not proposed legislation, but it has expressed an official opinion on the proposal: the Government supports the version of the Directive that provides the highest possible level of protection for workers. But since implementation of the equal treatment principle might cause additional costs for entrepreneurs, the Government supports the proposal that a period of six weeks be allowed for gradual implementation of the equal pay condition.

In sum, adoption of the draft Directive on temporary agency work may have failed so far. Nevertheless it has already had a considerable impact in the new member states. While temporary agency work is a comparably young phenomenon in these states, its use and rapid growth in the last couple of years have occasioned legislators to act.

Bibliography

Arrowsmith, J. (2006), *Temporary agency work in an enlarged European Union*, Dublin: European Foundation for the Improvement of Living and Working Conditions.

Cziria, L. (2005), "Temporary agency work – the case of Slovakia", EIROnline sk0506103t.doc at www.eiro.eurofound.eu.int

Neumann, L. (2005a), "Temporary agency work (TAW) in Hungary", EIROnline hu0506106t.doc at www.eiro.europfound.eu.int

Neumann, L. (2005b), "New legislation proposed on temporary agency work", EIROnline hu0511102f.html at www.eiro.eurofound.eu.int

"New legislation proposed on temporary agency work", EIROnline hu0511102f.html at www.eiro.eurofound.eu.int

Sula, P. (2005), "Questionnaire on the thematic features of temporary agency work in an enlarged European Union – the case of Poland", EIROnline pl0506105t.doc at www.eiro.eurofound.eu.int

"The legality of temporary agency work under discussion", EIROnline ee0509101n.html at www.eiro.eurofound.eu.int

Part II

The European Context

Legislative and Judicial Approaches to Temporary Agency Work in EU Law – An Historical Overview

Loredana ZAPPALÀ

1. Introduction

Temporary work – including temporary agency work – has increased considerably in the last ten years. But the general quality of temporary work and the prevailing working conditions are still worse than those enjoyed by workers with a standard employment contract. In light of this development, it is easy to understand why temporary work has been in the focus of Community action to harmonise the conditions for temporary workers to guarantee minimum standards.

At the same time, with the achievement of the single market, in particular as regards freedom to supply services between Member States, a new form of worker mobility has emerged, quite distinct from the mobility of migrant workers explicitly addressed in the EC Treaty and in secondary legislation concerning the free movement of workers.[1] The dynamic environment created by the single market, with its economic freedoms, is encouraging undertakings to develop their transnational activities and increasingly to provide transnational services. The situation of employees posted temporarily to another Member State to perform work under a service contract on behalf of their employer has raised all sorts of legal questions.

For these reasons, EU transnational regulation of temporary agency work was directed towards the harmonisation of different national labour standards governing temporary work in the EU Member States, to eliminate unfair competition among the employers of agency workers and to secure decent terms and conditions of employment for temporary agency workers. In this context protection of labour standards is not regarded as an obstacle to free movement of services, but as a condition of free movement itself. At the same time, EU transnational regulation of temporary

1 For more detail see the chapter by Brian Bercusson and Niklas Bruun in this book.

agency work was also directed towards establishing labour standards applicable where there is transnational movement of temporary agency workers between EU Member States.

2. The First Draft Directives in the 1980s: Apparent Interest in Promoting Steady Employment

The origins of the interest shown by European institutions in atypical jobs in general and temporary work in particular are in fact highlighted in EU documents from the late 1970s onwards. In its Resolution of 18 December 1979 on the adaptation of working time[2] the Council asked the Commission to present 'specific communications ... regarding part-time work and temporary employment' (par. 2, Final Provisions).

In this document the Council recognised that part-time and temporary jobs had spread considerably, becoming a reality in the labour markets of most Member States; it was therefore highly appropriate to take action 'to ensure that temporary work is supervised and that temporary workers receive social protection' (par. 5). There appear, however, to be few indications as to the real reasons for Community intervention.[3]

The importance of the implications, both economic and social, of regulating temporary jobs was not stated clearly until a few years later, first in the Resolution of the European Parliament of 17 September 1981 on employment and the adaptation of working time,[4] and then in the 1982 draft directive on temporary employment.[5]

The 1981 European Parliament Resolution is one of the first Community documents to address the problems of unemployment in Europe, the reorganisation of production resources and the restructuring of working hours, including measures concerning part-time and temporary employment.[6]

Given the aspirations and transversal nature of the issues addressed, the document would appear to be a precursor of recent employment policy, as it addressed the issue of employment and competitiveness in the

---

2 *OJ 1980 C 2/1.*

3 See the Resolution's aim of pursuing an 'overall strategy aimed at increasing growth potential, competitiveness and innovation, improving the employment situation'.

4 OJ 1981 C 260/54.

5 Presented to the Council by the Commission on 7 May 1982, in OJ 1982 C 128/ 2.

6 This kind of work in particular was said to be exhibiting a very worrying development: it was therefore necessary to discourage firms from using this type of work as a means to escape from contractual or legislative provisions regarding the protection of employment, as well as to prevent misuse.

production system in relation to economic, structural and social factors, as well as changes in company organisation models that had led to such high unemployment levels in Europe.

But it contained no trace of any prospects of Community action. It was merely a recognition of the problems affecting the labour market in the late 1970s. At this stage, in fact, although the commitments undertaken by the Treaty of Rome included 'guaranteeing a high level of employment', the Community did not have the tools and functional powers it needed to pursue an active employment policy, except for limited incentives provided by European Social Fund resources.

On reading these documents one can, however, perceive in connection with the issue of temporary employment the tension caused by the continuous search for balance between economic objectives and those of social policy, which was a prominent feature of Community action from the very beginning.

The tension between the 'social ambitions' of the Community and the need to ensure negative market integration emerges in particular from the *Considerations* of the first draft directive on temporary work in the early 1980s. Although point 3 of the Explanatory Memorandum recognises that temporary employment – in the dual sense of both temporary and fixed-term work – does not always clash with the interests of workers (in that it often responds to the requirements of certain categories of workers, such as the young, women, senior citizens, and so on), there was a clear awareness in the 1982 draft directive that this type of employment was being increasingly *forced* on a number of workers in search of steady employment. Temporary workers were, in fact, considered to be victims of numerous forms of discrimination, above all the precarious nature of their jobs as compared with those of permanent workers.

Based on this premise, two lines of intervention were traced in the draft directive, along with two forms of control over temporary employment.

The first was control over the use of temporary labour (with rigidly pre-established reasons for recourse to it, the limited duration of contracts, and so on) aiming to limit the application of this kind of contract and only allowing it to be used in order to meet companies' temporary requirements and consequently preserving the central role of steady employment.

The introduction to the draft directive recalled that the need for a clear definition and precise rules governing temporary work were indispensable to prevent 'misuse' and ensure the principle whereby 'steady employment is to be the rule and temporary work the exception'.[7]

7 See above all Articles 3 and 15 of the draft directive.

Although the draft directive seemed to feature provisions aiming to safeguard permanent employment against the illicit recourse to temporary work, and thus appeared to protect steady employment as a good in itself, as opposed to the inconvenience of precarious temporary employment, the techniques to be used to keep control over temporary work belied the firmly stated objectives and in fact left it up to Member States to provide effective protection of permanent employment.

It was, in fact, evident that the regulation of temporary work had another, more direct, aim: to achieve greater unity and solidarity in the labour market by extending the social protection enjoyed by permanent workers to marginalised, disadvantaged temporary workers.

As emerges from the Report accompanying the draft directive, in view of this second objective the Commission recognised that there existed two systems for controlling temporary labour in the Member States:

(i) systems which tended to protect permanent employment by limiting the cases in which recourse to temporary labour was permitted and its duration, and thus systems which did not grant temporary workers the same social rights as permanent ones (so as to make this type of employment unattractive);

(ii) systems which opted for worker protection over permanent employment, and thus allowed employers to employ temporary workers as long as they were ensured the same 'social advantages' that permanent workers were granted by labour law, collective contracts or usual company practice in industrial relations.

The draft directive therefore allowed for derogation from the more rigid forms of control aiming to guarantee permanent employment (pre-established reasons for recourse to temporary contracts, limited duration, and so on); Member States could avoid enforcing these restrictions if they were able to ensure equal treatment, as far as social advantages were concerned, between temporary and permanent workers.

The immediate social aim being pursued was preventing discrimination against temporary workers which, in the final analysis, would distort competition between countries with worker protection legislation and countries which authorised non-uniform working conditions.

Although the draft solemnly stated its aim of guaranteeing permanent employment and thus preventing the detrimental spread of temporary employment, it had no mandatory effect.

Encountering hostility from employers' associations, some sectors of the European Parliament and above all the veto of the British Government, neither the original nor the amended version of the draft led to any outcome.

3. Proposals Made in the 1990s: A Combination of Social and Economic Objectives

The European Community showed renewed interest in temporary work in the early 1990s. The drive towards a new phase of legislative initiatives was apparently due to the predictions in the 1989 Charter of Fundamental Rights for Workers, which identified the need for action to ensure an improvement in living and working conditions as regards 'forms of employment other than open-ended contracts, such as fixed-term contracts, part-time working, temporary work and seasonal work'.

In 1990 the Commission presented three new draft directives: one aiming to finalise measures to provide health and safety protection for temporary workers, the others regarding working conditions and the distortion of competition in the case of fixed-term contracts, part-time working and temporary work.[8]

What the Commission tried to accomplish was to strike a balance between the need for firms to have flexibility and the aspirations of a number of workers on the one hand, and a number of social goals on the other, such as equal treatment in some circumstances, the protection of health and safety and freedom of movement. Other goals concerned the elimination of the distortion of competition and the increase of legal certainty in the case of trans-border temporary work.

The three directives were proposed on three different legal bases: the first, concerning health and safety, was proposed on the basis of Art. 118a (now Art. 137 EC) and was the only measure successfully adopted; the second, concerning working conditions, was proposed on the basis of Art. 100 (now Art. 94 EC); the third, concerning the more ambitious aim of creating a level playing field of indirect costs for employing atypical workers, was proposed on the basis of Art. 100a (now Art. 95 EC).

In the two proposals which never were adopted, temporary work was mainly, if not exclusively, considered as a factor of production and thus as a cost for enterprises. The Commission's intention to regulate temporary jobs in such a way as to correct market failures and in particular contribute towards eliminating distortions in competitiveness and possible misuse that might occur due to the considerable differences between the various national systems clearly emerges from the Explanatory Memorandum accompanying the proposals.

The economic objective of eliminating distortions in competitiveness did not, however, make it at all necessary to guarantee a general principle of equal treatment between standard and temporary workers.

---

8 See the three proposals and the Explanatory memorandum in COM (90) 228 final, 21 August 1990, in OJ 1990 C 224/4.

From an exclusively economic viewpoint, the differences in pay between the two types of workers could be justified by their differences in productivity, which did not ultimately jeopardise 'healthy' competition between the various Member States. There were, however, certain costs – indirect salary costs linked to the duration of contracts, seniority, annual leave, redundancy payments – which had nothing to do with productivity and which could therefore lead to unacceptable distortions in the relative competitiveness of the Member States.

The proposal for a working conditions directive thus promoted a principle of equal treatment for both standard and temporary workers only in relation to services in kind or money based on a system of social assistance or a non-contributory social security system.

This perfectly reproduced the approach adopted in the Ohlin and Spaak Reports which provided the theoretical bases for the Treaty of Rome.[9] According to the 'theory of comparative advantage', in fact, *fair competition* did not require complete harmonisation of the different cost elements: it was rather on the basis of certain differences (such as productivity-linked pay) that competition was thought to be stimulated.

What was to be corrected, on the other hand, was *unfair competition,* or a comparative advantage to be gained from lower 'indirect' labour costs, not directly paid for in terms of productivity, which existed in certain Member States due to an absence of, or difference in, legal regulations.

From the proposals made in the 1990s there emerges a weak desire to limit the development of atypical employment.

The provisions reflecting this intention to limit the recourse to temporary work, or at least make it more transparent, include the requirement in the working conditions proposal that employers should indicate in temporary agency-brokered contracts the reason for recourse to these kinds of contract or the invitation to Member States – in the proposal regarding competition – to set limits on renewals of fixed-term contracts.

The regulation was, however, very low profile: not only did it set no limits on the absolute arbitrariness or discretionary powers employers were granted in employing temporary labour, but it also provided no guarantee of application of a general principle of equal treatment for standard and temporary workers.

9 The 1956 Ohlin Report for the ILO 1956 (Social Aspects of European Economic Cooperation, in *International Labour Review*, no. 99, 105 ff.) and the Spaak Report, also published in 1956 (Comité Intergouvernemental Créé par la Conférence de Messine, Rapport des Chefs de Délégation aux Ministres des Affaires Etrangères, Brussels).

4. Directive 91/383/EEC Supplementing the Measures to Encourage Improvements in the Safety and Health at Work of Temporary Workers

As mentioned above, Directive 91/393/EEC of 25 June 1991 was the only one of the proposals presented to the Commission in the early 1990s to be approved, and it is still in force.

The measures outlined in Directive 91/383 refer to both workers with fixed-term contracts and workers who have temporary employment relationships with a temporary employment business and are assigned to work for and under the control of an undertaking and/or establishment making use of its services.

As stated in the premise to the Directive, the rationale behind the regulations is that workers in temporary employment relationships are, in certain sectors, more exposed to the risk of accidents at work and occupational diseases than other workers.

These additional risks in certain sectors are in part linked to particular modes of integrating new workers into the undertaking and so can be reduced through adequate provision of information and training for temporary workers from the beginning of the employment relationship.

By applying the principle of equal treatment, the Directive requires temporary workers to be given the same level of health and safety protection as other workers in the user undertaking. It states that the existence of a temporary employment relationship cannot justify different treatment with respect to working conditions inasmuch as the protection of safety and health at work is involved, especially as regards access to personal protective equipment.

As Directive 91/383 refers exclusively to health and safety measures for temporary workers, it contains no indications as to the need for objective reasons legitimising the recourse to temporary employment; it confines itself to inviting Member States to prohibit temporary workers from being used for certain tasks which would be particularly dangerous to their safety or health, and in particular for work which requires special medical surveillance.

If Member States do not avail themselves of the option of prohibiting temporary work, the directive states that measures must be taken to ensure that these workers are under appropriate special medical surveillance both while at work and beyond the end of the employment relationship.

The directive also establishes the right to *information* and *training* for temporary workers; before starting work they are to be informed by their employer (or user undertaking) of the connected risks (above all as regards the need for special qualifications, professional skills or medical surveillance) and, if necessary, receive adequate training.

Finally, temporary employment agencies are required to inform workers of the characteristics of the work to be done and the professional qualifications required, according to indications provided by the user undertaking (Member States can require these indications to be included in the relevant contracts). The peculiarity of this type of work is stressed, specifying that while it is being carried out the user undertaking is considered responsible for health and safety conditions in the workplace.

5. The Notion of a Temporary Employment Relationship and the Responsibilities of the Temporary Employment Business and the User Concerning Health and Safety at Work

Article 1 of Directive 91/383 defines its scope stating that the Directive shall apply to temporary employment relationships between a temporary employment business, which is the employer, and the worker, where the latter is assigned to work for and under the control of an undertaking and/or establishment making use of his services.

The legal scheme contemplated by the directive thus features a triangular relationship between a temporary employment business, which merely supplies labour, a worker who actually does the work, and a user who draws benefits from his services.

A temporary worker thus comes under the external control of the user undertaking, which is formally not his employer.

The situation the Directive addresses is therefore one in which the common principle of a single employer no longer applies: there is a radical split between the legal principle of the employment relationship – that is, the employment agency – and the firm actually using and managing the worker's services (that is, the user undertaking).

Whereas the Directive states that the employment relationship is between the temporary employment business and the worker, no mention is made of the nature of the relationship between the user undertaking and the worker. However, although the user undertaking is not formally the worker's employer, it enters into a specific relationship with him and thus takes on certain significant legal obligations.

In view of the complexity of this triangular setup, EU regulations set forth a system of safety requirements which the agency and/or user have to meet. To do so they have to actively collaborate as, in the final analysis, they are jointly responsible for the conditions governing performance of the work for the duration of the assignment.

More specifically, although the Directive views the agency as the employer, the user undertaking where the work is actually done is held to be responsible for safety measures as it is more capable of managing not only the performance of the work itself but also the necessary levels of safety.

The Directive ensures temporary workers of the right to *information* and *training*: before commencing the work they are to be informed by their employer or the user of any connected risks (with reference above all to specific professional qualifications or skills, or the need for special medical surveillance) and, if necessary, receive adequate training.

In addition, before workers with a temporary employment relationship are supplied, a user undertaking is required to specify to the temporary employment business, inter alia, the occupational qualifications required and the specific features of the job to be filled; the temporary employment business will then bring all these facts to the attention of the workers concerned.

But given that the employment business may be unable to provide information about the safety measures adopted by the user, of which it may have no knowledge, and therefore the worker may be at risk of being sent to perform work without any idea of the potential risks he may encounter, the Directive states that Member States may require that the details to be given by the user undertaking to the temporary employment business appear in a contract of assignment.

Indication in the contract of assignment of risks, if any, to the health and safety of workers, as well as the precautionary measures adopted, thus assigns the user undertaking, *ab initio,* a directly active role: as it is surely better informed of the reality of working conditions in the undertaking it is required to notify any risks to worker safety.

6. Temporary Agency Work and Freedom to Provide Services

Although there are no EU regulations governing working conditions – apart from health and safety – for temporary workers, there have been cases in which the Court of Justice has had to deal with temporary work in particular or more general issues connected with the supply of labour in the context of the freedom to provide services.

The origins of the notion of temporary agency work adopted by Directive 91/383 go back some way: as early as 1970, in fact, the Court of Justice addressed the triangular relationship between an employment agency, a user undertaking and a worker, identifying the agency as the worker's employer.

In *Manpower vs Caisse Primaire d'Assurance Maladie Strasbourg,*[10] the Court was called upon to analyse a situation in which the main actor was

10 Judgment of the Court of 17 December 1970, Case 35/70.

> an undertaking having its normal activity in a member state which, according to the general conditions of its contracts, engages workers to post them to other undertakings in order to provide for temporary needs for qualified personnel. For this purpose it stipulates, with the personnel in question, a contract of employment providing reciprocal rights and obligations between it and its temporary workers for work to be done by latter in the hiring undertakings.

The Court ruled that

> although under the contract each temporary worker is required to comply with the working conditions and discipline laid down by the internal rules of the establishment to which he is sent, it appears from an examination of the file that this fact does not affect the maintenance of the worker's relationship with the undertaking which has engaged him. It is thus the latter undertaking which is at the centre of different legal relationships, because it is at the same time a party to the contract with the worker and to the contract with the hiring undertaking.

According to the Court, 'the object of the undertaking is not to do work but to engage workers to put them for a consideration at the disposal of other undertakings'. In the legal framework of the *Manpower* case,

> the undertaking which has engaged the worker remains their sole employer. The maintenance of the worker's relationship with such an employer for the entire duration of employment arises in particular from the fact that it is the employer who pays the salary and can dismiss him for any misconduct by him in the performance of his work with the hiring undertaking. Further, the hiring undertaking is indebted not to the worker but only to his employer.

In *Webb*[11] the European Court ruled that the activity of contracting out workers constitutes a provision of services within the meaning of the Treaty, but

> it must be noted in this respect that the provision of manpower is a particularly sensitive matter from the occupational and social point of view. Owing to the special nature of the employment relationships inherent in that kind of activity, pursuit of such a business directly affects both relations on the labour market and the lawful interests of the workplace concerned. That is evident, moreover, in the legislation of some of the member states in this matter, which is designed first to eliminate possible abuse and secondly to restrict the scope of such activities or even prohibit them altogether.

According to the Court, it follows that it is permissible for Member States, and amounts for them to a legitimate choice of policy pursued in the public interest, to subject the provision of manpower within their borders to a system of licensing in order to be able to refuse licences where there is reason to fear that such activities may harm good relations on the

---

11 Judgment of the Court of 17 December 1981, Case 279/80.

labour market or the interests of the workplace affected are not adequately safeguarded.

As regards posted workers within the context of the EC Treaty, the Court of Justice has been requested on several occasions to clarify their situation in the context of the freedom to supply services as referred to in Article 49 of the Treaty. In the cases decided by the ECJ, the issue was always that the country in which employees worked had created statutory rules whereby the employees posted to those countries enjoyed special social protection. The companies posting the employees in those countries invoked their fundamental freedoms and believed that they could not be subject to the standards in those countries, as their country of origin imposed its own rules for employee protection. The Court of Justice classifies the activities of a company temporarily operating in a foreign country as a service covered by the freedom to provide services pursuant to Article 49 EC, even if this is for a period of over one year. The provisions of the country which subject the foreign companies to its labour law or to the collective agreements there are regarded by the ECJ as restrictions of the freedom to provide services, regardless of whether they apply without discrimination on grounds of nationality or not. Article 49 EC covers both discriminatory and non-discriminatory forms of restriction. Thus, they can only be justified by overriding requirements relating to the public interest, insofar as the interest is not safeguarded by the rules to which the provider of the services is subject in the state where he is established. Social protection of workers is part of this 'public interest'. In a number of cases the Court of Justice has taken the opportunity to develop criteria, first and foremost to distinguish between freedom to supply services and freedom of movement of workers.

For example, mention must be made of the *Commission* v. *Italy* case,[12] concerning Italian provisions on the activities of temporary work agencies. As a precondition for their activities in Italy, they were obliged to establish their domicile or a branch office there. Referring to its consistent line of rulings in the past, the ECJ declared this form of restriction of the freedom to provide services to be inadmissible, the protection of workers intended through this requirement was said to be achievable also through a lesser degree of restriction. Furthermore, the temporary work firms were obliged to provide financial security for wage claims and social contributions. This was also considered by the ECJ to be a non-discriminatory restriction of the freedom to provide services. In the opinion of the EJC, this was not justified as it failed to take account of whether this protection was already ensured through the law of the State where the undertaking has its domicile. Furthermore, the ECJ ruled that the provi-

12 See Judgment of 7 February 2002, *Commission v. Republic of Italy*, Case C-279/00.

sions requiring security to be furnished through banks in Italy were inadmissible. The Court regarded this as a restriction on the movement of capital prohibited by Article 56(1) EC and as a restriction of the freedom to provide services according to Article 49 EC.

As regards the employment conditions applicable during the period of posting, however, the Court has recognised that Community law does not preclude Member States from extending their legislation, or collective labour agreements entered into by both sides of industry, to any person who is employed, even temporarily, within their territory, no matter in which country the employer is established, on condition that the rules of the EC Treaty, and in particular Article 49, are complied with.[13]

7. Directive 96/71/EC Concerning the Posting of Workers in the Framework of the Provision of Services

Since the middle of 1990, EU regulation of transnational posting of agency workers has existed in the form of Directive 96/71/EC on the posting of workers within the framework of the provision of services.

In order to facilitate the free movement of services it was deemed necessary and advisable to coordinate the laws of the Member States affected by this Court of Justice case law and thus lay down, at Community level, a nucleus of mandatory minimum protection rules to be observed in the host country by employers who post workers to perform temporary work in the territory of the Member State where the services are provided. Directive 96/71/EC concerning the posting of workers, which is based on Articles 47 (ex. 57), paragraph 2 and 55 (ex. 66) of the EC Treaty, establishes this Community catalogue of minimum rules deemed mandatory.

It aims to abolish the obstacles and uncertainties that impede implementation of the freedom to supply services by improving legal certainty and facilitating identification of the employment conditions that apply to workers temporarily employed in a Member State other than the Member State whose legislation governs the employment relationship. It endeavours to strike a balance between the economic freedoms bestowed by the EC Treaty and employees' rights during their period of posting.

The Directive applies to undertakings which post workers to work temporarily in a Member State other than the State whose laws govern the employment relationship. It covers three transnational posting situations, namely: posting under a contract concluded between the undertaking doing the posting and the party for whom the services are intended; posting to an establishment or an undertaking owned by the group; post-

13 See Judgment of 27 March 1990, *Rush Portuguesa*, Case C-113/89.

ing by a temporary employment undertaking to a user undertaking operating in a Member State other than that of the undertaking making the posting, with the proviso, in all three situations, that there is an employment relationship between the undertaking doing the posting and the posted worker.

Whatever the law applicable to the employment relationship, the Directive seeks to guarantee that posted workers enjoy the application of certain minimum protective provisions in force in the Member State to which they are posted. To this end, Article 3(1) of the Directive lays down the mandatory rules to be observed by employers during the period of posting in regard to the following issues: maximum work periods and minimum rest periods; minimum paid annual holidays; minimum rates of pay; the conditions of hiring-out of workers, in particular the supply of workers by temporary employment undertakings; health, safety and hygiene at work; and protective measures with regard to the terms and conditions of employment of pregnant women or women who have recently given birth, of children and of young people.

8. Attempts to Regulate Temporary Agency Work at the Beginning of the New Century

After the failure of the directives proposed at the beginning of the 1990s, in July 1994 the Commission published the White Paper on the future of European social policy, whereby the commitment to further develop European social policy, as well as the intention to bestow the highest priority on the Council's adoption of proposals concerning atypical jobs were reasserted. Once the lack of improvements by the Council was ascertained, the Commission decided to start the procedure provided for in Article 3 of the Agreement on social policy, attached to the protocol (no. 14) on social policy, enclosed in the Treaty instituting the European Community. On 27 September 1995, the Commission set up the consultation with social partners, the latter seeming to broadly agree on the fundamental principle of non-discrimination against workers employed within the framework of new work flexibility models in order to ensure them equal treatment compared with full-time and comparable permanent workers. This development leads us into the process of social dialogue which is described in detail in Chapter 9 in this book. The social dialogue was followed by an attempt to legislate, from the side of the European Commission, which is dealt with by Ahlberg in Chapter 9.

Transnational Soft Regulation of Temporary Agency Work and Adaptability Policies

A Future of Guidelines with No Rights?

Loredana ZAPPALÀ

1. What Type of Regulation for Temporary Agency Work in the European Union?

Two perspectives connected with the regulation of temporary work – increasing employment and ensuring a system of worker protection limiting the abuses connected with it – have been at the centre of the European debate in recent years.

Atypical forms of employment, along with the issue of equal opportunities, are one of the most important areas in which it is possible to find an overlapping of topics dealt with in the Treaty of Amsterdam: in Title VIII concerning employment policies and Title XII on social policies. For this reason, a single issue may at the same time be the subject of procedures of *coordination* and legislation oriented towards *harmonisation.*[1]

In this new normative framework, outlined after the Treaty of Amsterdam came into force and despite the reinforcement of the EU's decision-making power, there is no doubt that the classic method of normative harmonisation[2] did not produce any particularly meaningful outcome. This method is deemed to have failed to impose regulatory standardisation, thus consolidating national variations. According to a different interpretation, oriented towards the EU's social dimension, regulatory standardisation also threatens national social models and demo-

---

1 See Sciarra (1999). On the European Employment Strategy see "The European Employment Strategy, Multi-level Governance, and Policy Coordination: Past, Present and Future", in Zeitlin and Trubek (2003), pp. 59ff.

2 The notion of "classical Community method" recently stated in the White Paper on Governance as well (see COM (2001) - 428 def. of 5 August 2001, *La Governance europea – Un Libro Bianco,* 8ss) is investigated by Scott and Trubeck (2002), pp. 1ff.

cratic governments' capacity to preserve their own characteristics. It is commonly held that in the "new paradigm for social policy" the scope for harmonising national systems – considered crucial in the Treaty of Rome – has been reduced, if not completely removed.[3]

Thus, in the 1990s a new regulatory period was inaugurated in Europe in which the coordination of objectives, mainly utilising non-binding forms in the best Community *soft law* tradition, supplemented – and sometimes replaced – normative harmonisation. This is a phase of "regulatory minimalism" in which *hard law* is increasingly being shunted aside by *soft law*,[4] an expression of a *new governance* model that, with its flexible rules, would seem to be – at least at the moment – the only instrument capable of governing and reregulating complexity.[5]

According to the White Paper on Governance,[6]

> use of the [open method of coordination] must not upset the institutional balance nor dilute the achievement of common objectives in the Treaty or the political responsibility of the Institutions. The open method of coordination should be a complement, rather than a replacement, for Community action [...]. It should not be used when legislative action under the Community method is possible.

As already mentioned, employment flexibility has given rise to a complex of regulatory competences and techniques in accordance with Title VIII on employment policy and Title XI on social policy in the Treaty of Amsterdam. In relation to such things as flexible jobs, subject to regulation by harmonising legislation according to Art. 137 EC, directives could and should have firmly underpinned the employment objectives with firm social rights, providing rules able to enshrine the objective of quality jobs in the realm of rights.

By legislation through directives – the classic Community method – it would have been possible to set up safeguards to prevent possible debasement of guidelines, creating a transparent and effective counterbalance between soft and hard law. From this viewpoint, part of the doctrine has indeed aspired towards a closer connection between guidelines and hard law in order to strengthen objectives which are hard to implement in national action plans[7] through the open method of coordination.

3 Szyszczak (2001), pp. 1125ff.

4 Simitis (1997), pp. 609ff; Sciarra (2004), pp. 3ff.

5 Scott and Trubeck (2002), p. 6.

6 COM(2001) 428 cit., 22.

7 Cf. Scharpf (2002), pp. 662ff. The prospect of strengthening employment strategy through social law, has also been supported by Goetschy (2001), pp. 151ff; Bercusson (2001), pp. 101ff; Bruun (2001), pp. 309ff.

While on the one hand it is true that from some points of view legislation through directives helped to strengthen some objectives of employment strategy (for instance, the statement of the principle of equal treatment in Directive 99/70/EC), on the other it cannot be denied that, in keeping with the worst predictions about the future of European social legislation, the open method of coordination is spreading like a virus in the areas where the EU has legislative competence, eroding this competence in the field of social policy.[8]

In this sense the vicissitudes of temporary work agencies are emblematic, giving us an opportunity to examine whether, through the combination of these two regulatory instruments – *new governance*, in the form of the open method of coordination, and *old governance*, that is, regulation through directives – some sort of accommodation between flexibility and security can be achieved.

Temporary work has been a focus of Community action, both via the open coordination procedure, as a tool for adaptable job creation, and in order to issue a harmonisation directive that will guarantee minimum working condition standards for the workers involved.

In this sense, a reading of the proposed directive on working conditions for temporary workers presented by the European Commission on 20 March 2002 and subsequently modified in November of the same year[9] offers various points for reflection.

The proposed directive on temporary work has a dual core: on the one hand, it is inspired by social policy aims in the establishment of a network of protection and rights for temporary workers; on the other hand, it contains employment policy aims in the form of provisions expressly oriented towards improving the functioning of the labour market.

Alongside a series of protection measures, which still leave states a certain amount of discretion as to implementation, some of the points in the proposed directive – above all those inspired by employment aims – have an essentially propulsive role, actively encouraging structural reform of the labour market.

---

7 Cf. Scharpf (2002), pp. 662ff. The prospect of strengthening employment strategy through social law, has also been supported by Goetschy (2001), pp. 151ff; Bercusson (2001), pp. 101ff; Bruun (2001), pp. 309ff.

8 To learn about the debate see Trubek and Trubek (2003).

9 See European Commission, COM (2002) 149 final of 20 March 2002 and the subsequent proposal of a modified Directive, COM (2002) 701 of 28 November 2002.

2. Flexicurity and Transitional Labour Market

The aim of promoting temporary work in the proposal, however, does not appear to contradict the concept of "flexibility and security" which has inspired a number of Commission *guidelines*.

Initially the subject of theoretical debate and then encapsulated in an innovative linguistic coinage the concept of *flexicurity* represents a fascinating oxymoron which has inspired much of the European Employment Strategy (EES) since the Council of Luxembourg. The concept developed out of a series of positive experiences in labour market and employment relations reform introduced in Holland,[10] Denmark and other Scandinavian countries[11] in the late 1990s. Following a phase of deregulation, awareness gradually increased in certain European countries of the social and economic unsustainability of a process of flexibilisation that eroded workers' fundamental rights, causing social unrest. The theoretical basis was thus laid for the creation of a new political paradigm for labour policies.

Flexicurity has been defined as "a political strategy that tries, in a synchronous and *coordinated* fashion, to increase on the one hand flexibility in the labour market, the organisation of labour and employment relationships, and on the other to increase security – *employment security* and *social security* – for the weaker groups inside and outside the labour market".[12] This definition implies that flexicurity strategies cannot be achieved by labour market or work relationship intervention unless it provides for parallel development of forms of flexibility and the relevant "counterweights" in terms of security.

Flexicurity is, in fact, the result of a new model of regulation to enhance competitiveness, which tries to reconcile market values with personal ones and presupposes, according to what has been defined as the

10 The idea of combining social security issues with active labour market policies was developed in Holland from 1994 onwards under the Government led by Wim Kok. With the well-known slogan "*Jobs, jobs and jobs!*" it led to a new way of viewing flexibility in the light of social security issues. The need was felt to find a way to stem the effects of flexibility; in December 1995, the then Minister for Social Affairs and Labour, Ad Melkert, presented a *memorandum* entitled "Flexibility and Security" (*Flexibiliteit en Zekerheid*) containing a series of proposals for reconciling the two, apparently conflicting items (for example, by improving protection for temporary workers), which were later developed by subsequent legislation and a whole series of collective agreements. See Wilthagen (1998), pp. 8ff, where it is recalled that the combination of the two terms into the single concept of *flexicurity* only came about later, when the policy spread to other countries.

11 For the Danish experience, see Larsen (2004).

12 Wilthagen and Rogowski (2002), pp. 250ff.

capabilities approach, a welfare model that will guarantee workers' freedom of action and choice and thus a real capacity to take an active part in the working world and social life. In particular, this involves the synchronisation and coordination of measures aiming to introduce flexibility into the labour market and employment; but it also includes social security reform to increase security on the job market, and reasonable coordination between legislative reforms and deregulated bargaining policies based on multilevel governance, as presupposed by the *flexicurity* policy.[13] The idea of mild, sustainable flexibility, *flexisecurity* and adaptability (as flexibility is referred to in the jargon of the European Employment Strategy) refers to a widespread necessity which is being transformed – in various ways and guises, according to national context – into concrete policies and new visible, ordered ways of regulating labour. The aim of this commendable attempt is to trigger off a drive towards convergence – although in different ways – on a sort of ideal, still mobile boundary between social-oriented flexibility on the one hand, and useful flexibility in economic and organisational terms, on the other.[14]

In this perspective it is important to point out that the aim of flexicurity strategies is not that of protecting job stability or guaranteeing a career with a certain firm. They presuppose a change of perspective from "security in a job" to the "security of a job". This is the shift from *job security* to *employment security* or *social security,* described in the Supiot Report.[15]

In this theoretical approach, a notion closely connected to the concept of flexicurity is that of *transitional labour market.*[16] In a society in which having a job no longer protects workers from the risks connected with losing their job and consequently the danger of social exclusion, *transitional labour markets* represent institutionalised mechanisms that accompany and support workers during their working lives, making sure that in passing from one state of employment to another they do not fall into poverty, see their occupational capabilities diminished or set off on the path towards exclusion from active society.[17]

13 For a detailed analysis of the *flexicurity* paradigm, see Wilthagen (2003); Wilthagen and Tros (2003); Wilthagen, Tros and Van Lieshout (2003).

14 Caruso (2004).

15 Supiot (1999).

16 Schmid (2000), pp. 223ff.

17 The "transitions" taken into consideration in this theory can be of different kinds: from school to work, from one more or less skilled job to another, or to self-employment, or again to a period of training, from a period of employment to a "transitory" period of unemployment (with state support), from *full-time* employment to *part-time* and vice versa, from a period devoted to family commitments to paid employment, and so on.

As already mentioned, the concept of "flexibility and security" spread through Europe following the Council of Luxembourg on employment. Embracing the pillars of employability, adaptability[18] and entrepreneurship, the attempt was made to achieve a "soft" flexibility that guarantees workers' rights of access to education and training and at the same time paves the way towards modernising the organisation of labour, not least by defining flexible forms of contract within the framework of acceptable security standards. In this context, the EES assigns a key role to the "most adaptable" types of contract, which imply an internal differentiation in the traditional model of subordinate employment, with the dual aim of enhancing the productivity and competitiveness of enterprises and ensuring adequate levels of job security for the workers involved.

It is only in the 2000s, however, that forms of employment that combine flexibility and security have become associated with "quality work". Since the European Councils in Lisbon in March 2000 and Stockholm in March 2001, a new, ambitious strategic objective has emerged: that of modernising the European social model[19] by investing in people and building an active social state. According to the conclusions of the President of the Lisbon Council, this objective can be achieved by developing a knowledge-based economy in which the provision of employment for all does not mean concentrating exclusively on the creation of new jobs but also on better jobs, and it is in this perspective that the European Union proposes to define common approaches to maintain and improve the quality of work as one of the general aims of employment policy. As emerges from indications given by the European Commission, if it is taken to mean precariousness, uncertainty or mediocre employment with no prospects, flexibility should be considered as a "negative value" to be avoided. Although the discussion here will be confined to the implications as far as adaptability is concerned, it should be pointed out that this turning point has tightened the margins of the compromise behind the strategy adopted to weaken labour market constraints: the aim of reconciling flexibility and security has to be seen no longer, or not only, as a necessary combination of the two terms in which "security" has to be reconciled with and adapted to the superior claims of "flexibility", but – with a view to achieving the quality mentioned above – has much

---

18 Ashiagbor (2000), pp. 373ff.

19 On the evolution of the European social model from the Second World War to the present, and the distribution of competencies in Europe between the supranational community and the Member States as regards social policy, see the interesting reconstruction by Giubboni (2003). For reflections on the future development of the European social model, see Scharpf (2002), pp. 645ff; Streeck (2000), pp. 3ff; and Trubek and Mosher (2003), pp. 33ff.

stronger and more radical implications, that is, that *flexible employment of quality* is either "secure" in the sense that it guarantees adequate social protection for workers in a context of continuous change or, more simply, does not exist.

The objective of "flexibility and security", together with that of "quality employment" set forth at the Lisbon Council should thus be considered as prevailing over the objective of full employment. The concept of "full employment" by no means qualifies the "nature" of employment, it is not a synonym for *social inclusion,* and it says nothing about whether employment is precarious or insecure, thus affecting the social situation of individual workers. The concepts of *flexicurity* and *transitional labour markets*, on the contrary, have strong connections with the objectives of *social integration* and the development of opportunities for participation in society.[20]

3. Regulation's Strategies of Complexity

Those who have deeply studied the *flexicurity* strategy, as well as *transitional labour markets,* agree that the pursuit of labour policies inspired by such objectives cannot leave out of consideration forms of social regulation which are more or less structured and/or innovative. Regulation can be an instrument that – depending on the circumstances – can foster or curb the transition process, thus balancing flexibility and security. Normally such strategies are supposed to be implemented via what has been called *flexible multilevel governance*,[21] that is, management of flexibility negotiated between institutions and social partners at any level.

As regards possible legislative intervention, *flexicurity* theorists hope for the use of less substantive, less detailed, more procedural and more generally controllable regulatory forms, according to a strategy which is described as "*reflexive governance*",[22] with a view to governing complexity and diversity in an elastic and dynamic manner.

Once the intrinsic complexity of individual forms of reconciliation of flexibility and security in different welfare systems is ascertained, such a strategy evokes the notion of "reflexive law", as developed by Gunther

---

20 On the creation of new forms of employment without increasing the numbers of the "working poor" see Ferrera and Hemerijck (2003), pp. 87ff.

21 Wilthagen, Tros and Van Lieshout (2003), pp. 23ff, which underlines the need to encourage phenomena of *"positive coordination", "integrative bargaining", "positive-sum games"*, as well as practices of "*negotiated flexibility, enabling mutual gains to be achieved and better enabling achievement of the double requirement of flexibility and security. Mutual trust, based on an understanding for mutual interests, forms a crucial factor here.*"

22 Wilthagen and Tros (2003), p. 17.

Teubner in the 1980s.[23] At that time, the keen debate on deregulation did much to clarify the limits of the law's effectiveness in the management of complexity. In order to overcome the "legal crisis" as regards *welfare*, Teubner proposed adopting an "autopoietic" perspective, in which law can be understood as an instrument intended to regulate, not so much social behaviour, as organisation, procedures and distribution of competences within society, dealing with social conflicts, thus ensuring "discursive consensus". In this light, law does not appear to be a system of obligations, but an ensemble of opportunities which become available under determinate conditions. These conditions can vary, but not so much that they can eliminate the benefits that, from time to time, can be achieved.[24]

But as Teubner himself underlines, the "proceduralisation" of the law should not be misunderstood to mean that, in the perspective of so-called "reflexive law",[25] the legislator should renounce juridical rules and rely totally on procedural law. On the contrary, the "proceduralisation" formula should be understood as an attempt to bring substantive juridical rules, which cannot be renounced, together with mechanisms of procedural cross-referencing and autoregulation by various other possible actors which would be able to adapt substantive rules to the functional differentiation of complex societies.

On this approach, *flexicurity* strategies, through the "*reflexive governance*" model, can be the object of both "reflexive re-regulation" and "reflexive deregulation" processes.[26]

Through the first process, *flexicurity*-inspired regulation tries to provide inputs to transform and re-regulate normative systems in the light of new and innovative forms of reconciliation of economic and social targets, introducing boundaries and limits in the action of private citizens, but at the same time providing them with new opportunities and action models which make it possible to balance flexibility and security. By means of "reflexive deregulation" – not to be confused with neo-liberal deregulation *tout court*[27] – it is possible to reduce the excessive complex-

23 Teubner (1987), pp. 3ff.

24 On the notion of "reflexive law" as applied to labour law see Rogowski and Wilthagen (2004), pp. 305ff.

25 Teubner (1987), pp. 3ff.

26 Wilthagen and Rogowski (2002), pp. 233ff.

27 On the importance of not running the risk of putting "reflexive law" on the same level as neo-liberal notions and deregulation strategies, see Teubner (1996), pp. 99ff, who states that "autopoiesis cannot mean letting things simply take their course. Autopoietic control rather signifies establishing the structure and interaction of systems to be controlled and developed, so that they can auto-regulate and control one another".

ity that sometimes characterises normative systems. According to this perspective, in certain cases, only by reducing complexity by means of a limited and indeed reflexive deregulation, it will be possible to create and/or foster trans-national labour markets, where *flexicurity* strategies can be realised.[28]

4. "Reflexive Deregulation" or Merely Liberalisation?

In terms of flexicurity and transitional labour markets what emerges from the Commission's proposal on temporary work of 2002 is the enhancement of the role played by temporary work agencies, in the sense that they are implicitly considered to be tools that will contribute towards creating work opportunities for workers outside the labour market who have a "real" preference for temporary work. There are, however, signs of an awareness that temporary work – as stated on p. 5 of the *Explanatory Memorandum* – will not be able to act as a driving force for job creation unless it provides sufficient guarantees for workers and the unemployed, that is, unless it offers quality employment that will compensate for its temporary nature.

Although quality work and flexicurity are key objectives, the proposal does not dictate prescriptive models whereby these objectives can be achieved, but confines itself to providing minimum indications on some aspects of quality of work (relating to non-discrimination, training, and so on). So although the *social policy* aims pursued are evident, the lack of clear indications as to the elements that will ensure security for workers gives rise to a whole series of doubts as to how to interpret it and the scope of the directive's *employment policy*-inspired measures.

One of the most problematic areas in this respect is Article 4, which is entirely inspired by *employment policy* objectives. The Article states that

> Prohibitions or restrictions on the use of temporary work are justified only on grounds of general interest relating in particular to the protection of temporary workers, the requirements of health and safety at work and the need to ensure that the labour market functions properly and abuses are prevented. The Member States, after consulting the social partners (...), shall review any restrictions or prohibitions mentioned above in order to verify whether they are justified on the grounds given in paragraph 1. If not, the Member States shall discontinue them. The Member States shall inform the Commission of the results of that review. (cc. 1 and 2)

It seems undeniable that this provision is an expression of the desire to remove – in Member States where such legislation is in force – constraints which limit the spread of temporary work. Its aim is not to estab-

28 Wilthagen and Rogowski (2002), p. 239.

lish minimum *standards* of protection for the workers involved, but – through a *soft* formulation of the indications given to Member States, imitating the contents of the *guidelines* – to provide *input* for more efficient regulation of the temporary labour market in accordance with the objectives of the European Employment Strategy.

But in the Commission *guidelines* relating to adaptability, the tool used to guarantee an efficient labour market is not deregulation but re-regulation, which takes specific circumstances into account and, if necessary, provides protection against labour market malfunctioning in Member States.

With Article 4 the Commission is trying to clarify the degree of acceptance of greater flexibility among the Member States. It clearly has no intention of attempting to harmonise national legislation: in the re-regulation process the Member States do not have to remove all constraints and restrictions on temporary work *tout court*, but to evaluate – in collaboration with the social partners – "in order to verify whether they are justified". Each system, according to the "reflexive de-regulation" model previously mentioned, will therefore have to ascertain whether it possesses the necessary "antibodies" that will make greater flexibility tolerable and coherent with the aim of ensuring quality employment.

In this sense, Article 4, cc. 1 and 2, states that restrictions and prohibitions are only justifiable "on grounds of general interest relating in particular to the protection of temporary workers, the requirements of health and safety at work and the need to ensure that the labour market functions properly and abuses are prevented".

Nothing is laid down concerning the parameters on the basis of which Member States are to assess the permanence of legislative restrictions on temporary work. This apparent gap can be bridged by a teleological-systematic hermeneutic operation which leads to an interpretation of EU law in accordance with the aim of the provision and coherently with the principles and objectives of the Treaty and the European Employment Strategy, the effectiveness of which – as we have seen – the proposed Directive aspires to strengthen.

On this basis, the problem of interpretation is easily solved: there can be no deregulation without a blend of flexibility and security, flexibility and certainty of employment. To be coherent with the objectives of the directive and the employment strategy, liberalisation is possible *on condition that* Member States not only introduce certain minimum worker protection standards (for example, the principle of equal treatment), but also find a fair balance ensuring quality of temporary work.

The grounds of general interest – mainly worker protection, health and safety requirements and/or the proper functioning of the labour market – which will not allow Member States to remove all restrictions on temporary work, should thus be identified as a sort of mechanism for guaranteeing security in the labour market and/or in employment relationships.

As regards the evaluation of these grounds, Member States are left free to choose the most suitable solution for the specific features of their markets and welfare systems.

However, although no uniformity is imposed or even sought, thus giving Member States great discretionary power, it is also true that certain combinations of flexibility/security do emerge from a systematic interpretation of the Commission guidelines within the framework of the EES and the binding provisions contained in the proposal.

For example, in ascertaining the existence of "reasons of general interest" which would require them to maintain restrictions on the use of temporary jobs, Member States will have to assess the "sustainability" of the spread of this kind of employment given their national social protection system. For this reason, as emphasised by the proposed Directive with a view to ensuring not only an increase in employment levels but also work of quality, *only* states that can guarantee active support (via training and/or re-qualification mechanisms, systems to bridge information gaps, and so on) and/or passive support (the provision of unemployment benefits for workers who have been employed for short periods of time, thus favouring their reinsertion in the labour market) will be able to contemplate eliminating the constraints and restrictions on temporary work.

4. A Future of Guidelines with No Rights?

The amended proposal presented by the Commission in November 2002 was submitted for discussion by the Council on three different occasions (2–3 December 2002, 6 March 2003 and 2–3 June 2003). Although initially it seemed that approval would not take long, during the work on social issues carried out by delegations from the various countries it proved all too difficult to reach an agreement on certain crucial points.

Some delegations, in fact, did not agree with the "appropriacy" of introducing the provision whereby states were obliged to re-examine restrictions and prohibitions; others wished for further clarification concerning the "reasons of general interest" the Commission would accept for maintaining such restrictions; others again asked for them to be totally removed. The Commission declared its willingness to "reformulate" Art. 4 of the proposal if agreement was reached on the other points. Consensus was not reached on one of the most debated points of the pro-

[29] Cf. the work of the *Social Questions Working Party,* 8 January 2003 (5332/03 SOC 14 CODEC 36), 4 February 2003 (5772/03 SOC 33 CODEC 91), and 21 February 2003 (6526/03 SOC 71 CODEC 178).

posal, however: the principle of non-discrimination and the relevant exceptions. It was the provision contained in clause 4 of Art. 5 examined above – regarding the possibility of legitimising exceptions to the principle of equal treatment for work lasting less than 6 weeks – that led the delegations to become aware of the impossibility of reaching an agreement.[30]

As a result, the Council meeting of 2 June 2003 brought the proposal for a directive on temporary work to a temporary halt.[31]

If this was yet another failed attempt to *harmonise* temporary work regulations, the same cannot be said about the *coordination* of Member States' activities relating to the European Employment Strategy.

Five years after the introduction of the Lisbon strategy, and despite the sophisticated "conceptualisation" of the notion of *flexicurity* the Commission has recently achieved, it does not appear that the objective of reconciling flexibility and security has had particularly significant results.[32] On the contrary, as stated by the EU institutions themselves:

> *Working life is becoming more complex* as working patterns become more irregular. A number of *transitions now* need to be accounted for, including the transition between school and working life, between jobs, between different working statuses, between working life and retirement and between work and training, career breaks and care periods (…). The *balance between flexibility and security* is becoming a tangible concern for an increasing share of the labour force.[33]

It is finally being admitted that the "security component is difficult to measure".[34] Up to now, as we have frequently mentioned, *employment security* has been taken in a dynamic perspective to mean an individual's capacity to remain and progress in the labour market. This involves a decent salary, access to training opportunities, good working conditions,

---

30 See the COREPER to the Council on 27 November 2003 (9739/03 SOC 220 CODEC 714), from which it emerges that, with a view to achieving a compromise, most delegations declared a willingness to accept a derogation from the principle of equal treatment for work lasting less than 6 weeks, for a transitory period of 5 years. Denmark, Germany, Ireland and the UK, on the other hand, opposed any compromise relating to the transitory nature of the exception, stating that it should be permanent.

31 See the *Dossier sulle proposte in codecisione sotto la Presidenza irlandese,* 18 December 2003, which "annotates" the directive proposal of November 2002 as a "dossier without evolution".

32 The first results of the EES were evaluated on the basis of "indicators" outlined at the Council of Laeken in December 2001.

33 COM(2003) 6 final of 14 January 2003, 6 ff.

34 Cf. COM(2003) 728 final of 26 November 2003, 14 ff.

support in the event of job loss, the right to transfer acquired social rights in the event of switching jobs, and so on. Although it is recognised that fixed-term jobs may help certain categories of workers to enter the labour market, it is admitted that reality draws a much darker picture of the results achieved by *flexicurity* policies: "the evidence so far is that employees under these forms of contracts risk discrimination in pay and pensions and have fewer opportunities to participate in continuous training and to improve their career prospects".[35]

In *Impact Evaluation 2002*, in which the Commission analysed the effects and results achieved in the first five years of the Employment Strategy, it recognises the partial failure of adaptability-inspired policies to modernise the organisation of labour via a combination of flexibility and security. As emerges from recent statistics taken into consideration in *Impact Evaluation 2002*, data referring to fixed-term employment would appear to support a rather pessimistic view of the situation. Only a third of fixed-term workers accepted this kind of contract *voluntarily*; despite the principle of equal treatment laid down by Directive 99/70/EC, fixed-term workers receive lower salaries than workers on permanent contracts; 58% of fixed-term workers declared themselves willing to forego an "interesting job" if they had the opportunity to sign a permanent contract.[36]

It has also been pointed out that there remains a close connection between temporary employment, poor job quality, social exclusion and poverty. This is due to the serious effects of a worker's previous employment status (especially unemployment) and the characteristics of the work done. Although in some cases – above all in the most vulnerable groups – temporary jobs represent an opportunity to get back into the labour market, working on a temporary contract (as opposed to a full-time permanent contract) substantially reduces a person's probability of later finding full-time employment. "In the presence of unfavourable transitions out of flexible working arrangements, it increases the probability of, often permanent, unemployment and labour market exclusion".[37]

In this complex context, the European Council meeting held in Brussels in March 2003 called on the Commission to set up a *European*

---

35 COM(2003) 728 final of 26 November 2003, 16 ff.

36 Cf. *Impact Evaluation 2002*, where it is stated on p. 246 that "[i]t is evident that, for many employees, flexible forms of employment are often associated with reduced quality of work and with reduced security, despite the fact that the different types of employment are treated almost equally in legal terms".

37 V. COM(2003) 728 final of 29 November 2003, 7.

Taskforce on Employment under the presidency of former Dutch Prime Minister Wim Kok, whose remit was to report to the Commission about possible practical reforms that would have a more direct and immediate impact on implementation of the Employment Strategy. In November 2003 the Taskforce presented a detailed report on the possible paths to be taken in the sphere of employment.[38] As emerges from the report, the employment taskforce focused on the need to intensify both employment and productivity growth, and identified four "keys to success": (i) enhancing the adaptability of workers and enterprises; (ii) attracting a larger number of people to the labour market; (iii) investing more – and more wisely – in human resources; and (iv) assuring effective implementation of reforms by means of better *governance.* The Taskforce then identified action priorities of general relevance to the Member States for each of these points and outlined specific messages regarding the reforms needed in each of the fifteen current Members and the ten new ones.

In the report the Taskforce also dealt with temporary agency-brokered work. It pointed out that temporary work can be seen as a stepping stone for new entries to the labour market, thanks to the intermediary role played by agencies.[39] Despite this positive assessment, however, the Taskforce pointed out the numerous obstacles and legislative restrictions that prevent Member States from encouraging the spread of this type of contract. Given the "evident" advantages of temporary work in terms of *job opportunities* and *job matching*, the Kok report indicated as one of the primary objectives to be pursued in the Employment Strategy the removal of "obstacles to the setting up and development of temporary work agencies as effective and attractive intermediaries in the labour market, offering improved job opportunities and high employment standards".[40]

At the same time, this process of removing obstacles should – according to the report – be accompanied by a guarantee of "minimum levels of

38 Kok (2003).

39 See Kok (2003), p. 29, "Temporary agency work can be an effective stepping stone for new entrants into the labour market and hence contribute to increased job creation, for example by facilitating recruitment instead of overtime. Acting as human capital managers – rather than mere manpower suppliers – these agencies can also play the role of new intermediaries in the recruitment and management of both qualified and unqualified staff, offering employers an attractive alternative to traditional recruitment channels. Temporary work agencies should have their place in a modern labour market as new intermediaries that can support flexibility and mobility of firms and of workers, while offering security for workers in the form of improved job opportunities and high employment standards, including in terms of pay, working time and training opportunities."

40 Kok (2003), pp. 9, 27.

protection and access to training for temporary workers would be required to ensure equal treatment of all workers and to raise the attractiveness of agency work".[41]

The Council of Europe meeting in Brussels in December 2003 then called on the Commission and Council to take the *Taskforce* report into account in preparing the common report on employment, and so both the Joint Employment Report 2003/2004[42] and the new Commission *guidelines* on employment were born and expressly declare themselves to have been inspired by the proposals made in the Kok report.[43] It is immediately clear that the pages quoted from the Kok report recall the debated Art. 4 of the proposal examined above and in general can be considered as a sort of "surrogate" of the Directive.

It could be seen, in fact, that the report – retracing parts of the draft Directive – recommends that EU institutions insert into the *guidelines* the objective of "removing restrictions on temporary work" and at the same time of guaranteeing "minimum levels of protection" and "training opportunities" for workers hired with this type of contract.

This evolution is a puzzling one, however. The failure of the Directive and the "transfer" of some of its provisions to the open method of coordination would appear to confirm the worries expressed regarding the future regulation of temporary work in Europe. Given the evident difficulty of *hard* regulation, the open method of coordination seems to act as a *virus,* capable of both attacking the form and contents of legislation aiming at harmonisation, and eroding, if not quite expropriating, the legislative competencies of the Union.

On an issue like this – the living and working conditions of workers employed by agencies – the Union in fact renounces, at least temporarily, the possibility of setting any kind of *labour standard,* any kind of more or less *hard* protection, and entrusts the "promotion" of principles like equal treatment or the right to training to *guidelines* that are not bind-

41 Kok (2003), p. 28.

42 COM(2004) 24 final of 21 January 2004, *Draft Joint Employment Report,* 4 ff., in which it is stated that "the Taskforce identified priorities for action of general relevance for Member States under each of these headings and specific messages on the reforms needed for each of the fifteen current and the ten new Member States. The Employment Taskforce's assessment and policy messages are shared by the Commission and the Council and, since they are fully consistent with the European Employment Strategy Guidelines, have been closely integrated into this Joint Employment Report".

43 COM(2004) 239 final of 7 April 2004, *Strengthening the implementation of the European Employment Strategy,* containing the proposal from the Commission to the Council regarding *"guidelines for the employment policies of the Member States".*

ing for Member States. The call to remove obstacles to temporary work is made without seeking any kind of "real", effective trade-off between flexibility and security, without any warning to Member States to maintain restrictions justified by reasons of general interest, such as the need to protect workers, health and safety, and the prevention of misuse in general. In all likelihood the model of "reflective deregulation" that appeared to have inspired Art. 4 of the proposal will also disappear. It is no coincidence that the Commission's proposal for the new *guidelines* refers to the need to promote temporary work *tout court* in some countries.[44]

What would happen if a state were to pursue adaptability too enthusiastically, deregulating *tout court* the conditions applying to recourse to temporary work? What guarantee would the EU have of a real blend of flexibility and security and the spread of quality employment? What rights would workers enjoy as regards the principle of equal treatment and the right to training? What weapons could be used against employers who misuse this kind of contract? These questions obviously take us back to the current debate – which cannot be dealt with thoroughly here – regarding the nature and effectiveness of the open method of coordination, the possibility of anchoring it to the fundamental rights enshrined in the Charter, the theoretical difficulties of "justiciable" enforcement of *soft law* in the light of the "horizontal provisions" of the Charter, and so on.

For the time being it is only possible to point out that the possibility of an immediate future made up only of *guidelines*, in a sphere in which the EU has the competence to legislate, establish standards and guarantee legal rights, cannot but call into question the path taken in the last few years by EU integration. If, from one point of view, the report has the general merit of encouraging certain forms of work, such as temporary work, and discouraging others, such as short-term work, the tacit resignation of EU institutions to abandoning with such ease the language of rights is alarming. Nor, in the case of temporary work, can the abandonment of the "classical" technique of harmonisation in favour of coordination be seen as an obligatory step for the Commission. On the contrary, its acceptance of the shifting of the most contested provisions of the Directive (revision of restrictions and the principle of equal treatment) to the open method of coordination may well have the effect of strengthen-

44 See COM(2004) 239 final of 7 April 2004, cit. and the recommendations to Greece (p. 14) and Spain (p. 16) in which the country is called on to "revise the regulatory framework to make permanent contracts more attractive for employers and to discourage the use of fixed-term contracts so as to counter the segmentation of the labour market; remove obstacles to part-time work and make temporary agency work more attractive for companies and workers".

ing and further legitimising the attitude of states which are reluctant to accept harmonisation on social issues, aware that it is sufficient to "resist" any attempt at harmonisation for the Commission to fall back on more innocuous coordination, not only as regards employment policy but also in other areas in which the EU has striven to introduce the possibility of decision-making by a qualified majority, as established by Art. 137 EC.

In the case of temporary work the evident difficulties connected with the deregulatory prescriptions contained in the draft Directive are destined – as we have seen – to change into real pessimism towards the "shifting" of some of the contents of the draft to the open method of coordination.

Given this "ambiguous" attitude on the part of EU institutions, hedged in between evident regulatory difficulties and perhaps too weak an abandonment of any attempt at harmonisation, one should not be surprised at the risk of "opportunistic" behaviour by Member States applying arbitrary scraps of legislation and *soft law* that may go against the overall *ratio* of the "flexibility and security" model as weakly pursued by EU institutions.[45]

Bibliography

Ashiagbor, D. (2000), "'Flexibility' and 'adaptability' in the EU Employment Strategy", in H. Collins, P. Davies and R. Rideout (eds), *Legal regulation of employment relations*, Kluwer Law International.

Ashiagbor, D. (2004), "Soft harmonization: the 'open method of coordination' in the European Employment Strategy", *European Public Law*, 2.

Bercusson, B. (2001), "Institutional reform and social and labour policy", in U. Mückenberger (ed.), *Manifesto social Europe*, ETUI.

Bruun, N. (2001), "The European Employment Strategy and the 'acquis communautaire' of labour law", *The International Journal of Comparative Labour Law and Industrial Relations*, 3.

45 On the Italian situation see Caruso (2004: 11ff) who notes that the "never-ending demand for a further wave of flexibility in the system (without security) from certain sectors of entrepreneurs has been taken up by the centre-right government which came to power at the beginning of this century. On coming to power, the government published a White Paper proposing reforms based on a type of flexibility which was said to comply with the indications given by EU institutions. The proposals were then transformed into a Parliamentary text (Delegatory Act n. 30/03), which came into effect on 24 October 2003 (Legislative Decree 276/2003) directly drawn up by the Government. In this transition from a statement of policy to concrete legislative implementation, all homgin remains merely formal".

Caruso, B. (2004), "Flexibility and labour law reforms in Italy", in B. Caruso and M. Fuchs (eds), *Flexibility in employment and labour market legislation in Europe: comparing Italy and Germany*, Milan: Nomos-Giuffrè.

Ferrera, M., and A. Hemerijck (2003), "Recalibrating Europe's welfare regimes", in J. Zeitlin and D. Trubek (eds), *Governing work and welfare in a new economy*, Oxford University Press.

Giubboni, S. (2003), *Diritti sociali e mercato*, Bologna: Il Mulino.

Goetschy, J. (2001), "The future of the European Employment Strategy", in U. Mückenberger (ed.), *Manifesto social Europe*, ETUI.

Kok, W. (2003), *Jobs, jobs, jobs. Creating more employment in Europe*, Report of the Employment Taskforce chaired by Wim Kok (November).

Larsen, F. (2004), "The importance of institutional regimes for active labour market policies – the case of Denmark", Paper presented at TLM workshop work package 5: "Active labour market policies and escape routes from unemployment", Rotterdam (26–27 April).

Rogowski, R., and T. Wilthagen (2004), *Reflexive labour law*, Deventer: Kluwer.

Scharpf, F. (2002), "The European Social Model: coping with the challenges of diversity", *Jour. of Comm. Mark. St.*, 4.

Schmid, G. (2000), "Transitional labour markets. A new European Employment Strategy", in B. Marin, D. Meulders and D. Snower (eds), *Innovative employment initiatives*, Aldershot: Ashgate.

Sciarra, S. (1999), "The Employment Title in the Amsterdam Treaty. A Multi-language Legal Discourse", in D. O'Keeffe and P. Twomey (eds), *Legal Issues of the Amsterdam Treaty*, Hart Publishing, pp. 157 ff.

Sciarra, S. (2004), "New discourse in labour law. Part-time work and the paradigm of flexibility", in S. Sciarra, P. Davies and M. Freedland (eds), *Employment policy and the regulation of part-time work in the European Union*, Cambridge.

Scott, J., and D. Trubek (2002), "Mind the gap: law and new approaches to governance in the European Union", *European Law Journal*, 1.

Simitis, S. (1997), "Il diritto del lavoro ha ancora un futuro?", *Diritto del Lavoro e delle Relazioni Industriali.*

Streeck, W. (2000), "Il modello sociale europeo: dalla redistribuzione alla solidarietà competitiva", *Stato e Mercato*, 58, Bologna: Il Mulino.

Supiot, A. (1999), *Au-delà de l'emploi*, Paris: Flammarion.

Szyszczak, E. (2001), "The new paradigm for social policy: a virtuous circle?", *Common Market Law Review.*

Teubner, G. (1987), "Juridification – concepts, aspects, limits, solutions", in G. Teubner (ed.), *Juridification of social spheres*, Berlin: Walter de Gruyter.

Teubner, G. (1996), *Il diritto come sistema autopoietico*, Milan: Giuffrè.

Trubek, D., and J.S. Mosher (2003), "New governance, employment policy and the European Social Model", in J. Zeitlin and D. Trubek (eds), *Governing work and welfare in a new economy*, Oxford University Press.

Trubek, D., and L. Trubek (2003), "Hard and soft law in the construction of Social Europe", Paper presented at the workshop on 'Opening the Open Method of Coordination', Florence (July).

Wilthagen, T. (1998), "A new paradigm for labour market policy reform?", Flexicurity Research Programme FXPaper No. 1, OSA/Institute for Labour Studies, Tilburg University,

Wilthagen, T. (2003), "The flexibility–security nexus: new approaches to regulating employment and labour markets", Flexicurity Research Paper FXP 2003 – 2, OSA/Institute for Labour Studies, Tilburg University.

Wilthagen, T., and R. Rogowski (2002), "Legal regulation of transitional labour markets", in G. Schmid and B. Gazier (eds), *The dynamics of full employment: social integration through transitional labour markets*, Cheltenham: Edward Elgar.

Wilthagen, T., and F. Tros (2003), "The concept of 'flexicurity': a new approach to regulating employment and labour markets", Flexicurity Research Paper FXP 2003 – 3, OSA/Institute for Labour Studies, Tilburg University.

Wilthagen, T., F. Tros and H. Van Lieshout (2003), "Towards 'flexicurity'?: balancing flexibility and security in EU member states", Flexicurity Research Paper FXP 2003 – 3, OSA/Institute for Labour Studies, Tilburg University.

Zeitlin, J., and D. Trubek (eds) (2003), *Governing work and welfare in a new economy*, Oxford University Press.

Part III

Failure or Success? EU Regulation of Temporary Agency Work and the Transnational Provision of Services

A Story of a Failure – But Also of Success

The Social Dialogue on Temporary Agency Work and the Subsequent Negotiations between the Member States on the Draft Directive

Kerstin AHLBERG

1. Prologue

The story that you are about to read is the story of a failure. At the same time, it is a story of success – success for those actors who do not want EU legislation on temporary agency work.

Some might say that it is also a narrative about how the European Trade Union Confederation (ETUC) missed a historic chance to improve conditions for temporary agency workers by rejecting what would have been good in its pursuit of the very best. Others might call it an account of how the same organisation was stabbed in the back by European Commission officials with their own political agenda.

In any case, this story is an illustration of the difficulties involved in creating a transnational regulation that not only fits in with (at that time 15, now 27) very different industrial relations systems, but also is able to win the approval of as many governments of differing political colours. And some readers may be surprised to learn how Members States' governments, Commission officials, trade unionists and employers act behind closed doors when EU legislation is being negotiated.

Because these processes are to a large extent excluded from public control. Normally, records of proceedings and draft texts are not at all, or only partially, accessible to the public, and information that has decisive significance for the understanding of the process is classified. By securing access to as many of these documents as possible from different sources and through interviews with persons directly engaged in the social dialogue on temporary agency work and the subsequent negotiations between the Member States, I hope to have made up some small part of this deficiency.

Now, let the play begin.

2. From 1982 to 1999 – Changing Circumstances

Like many other legislative initiatives in the history of the European Union, the efforts to regulate temporary agency work have been long drawn out. In 1982 the EEC Commission presented the first draft directive "concerning temporary work".[1] The Commission justified its initiative with the fact that the legislation on agency work varied considerably between the Member States, which leads to unfair competition within the single market. The purpose of the Directive would be to prevent abuse of temporary employment in the form of agency work (and fixed-term work) and to "protect workers with open-ended contracts from excessive use of agency work". Furthermore, temporary work agencies must be prevented from using the free movement of services and the free movement of workers to avoid the application of more stringent provisions in other Member States. Consequently, the draft directive contained a catalogue of conditions for the operation of temporary work agencies, inspired by the legislation in those Member States that had the most elaborate provisions. In order to operate, work agencies must have a license from the authorities; they must be subject to public control; agency work must only be used in certain situations; missions must not last longer than three months; missions must only be renewed once; the user company must not successively employ more agency workers for the same job, and so on.

However, as unanimity was required in the Council, it was practically impossible to adopt legislation in these years, and the Commission had to withdraw its proposal.

The setting had changed considerably when, almost two decades later, the process that is the subject of this study started. Not only could the Council adopt labour law directives by qualified majority vote, but with the Amsterdam Treaty a completely new procedure for regulation in the social policy field had been inscribed in Articles 138 and 139 of the EC Treaty. It meant that, besides the European Commission, which has exclusive competence to propose legislation, and the Council, which adopts it, trade unions and employers' organisations can in practice decide the material contents of European legislation.

Thus, every time the European Commission considers submitting a proposal in the social policy field it must first consult "management and labour" – that is, trade unions and employers' organisations at European

1 COM(82) 155 final, OJ No. C 128, 19.5.1982, p. 2. The title was later amended to Council Directive concerning the supply of workers by temporary employment businesses and fixed-duration contracts of employment (COM(84) 159 final, OJ No C 133, 21 May 1984, p. 1.

level – "on the possible direction" of Community action. If, after that, the Commission considers Community action advisable, it must consult the social partners once more, this time on the content of the envisaged proposal. When they respond to this second stage of consultation, they can inform the Commission that they will try to negotiate an agreement on the subject in question. If so, the Commission will temporarily interrupt the legislative process and give them nine months to reach an agreement. If both parties feel that some additional time could be useful, the Commission can extend the nine-month period.

What happens after that depends on the outcome of the negotiations. If the parties succeed in reaching an agreement, they can jointly ask the Commission to propose a Directive that would make the agreement binding for the Member States.

Until 1999, this procedure led to the conclusion of three interprofessional agreements between ETUC and its counterparts on the employers' side, the Union of Industrial and Employers' Confederations of Europe (UNICE) and the European Centre of Enterprises with Public Participation and of Enterprises of General Economic Interest (CEEP), and there was little reason to believe that they would not succeed a fourth time – with the negotiations on temporary agency work.

In addition to the revision of the legislative procedure, there had been other changes. Since the first draft Directive, the Community legislator had managed to regulate some aspects of agency work. In 1991 a directive was adopted that was designed to guarantee agency workers the same conditions of health and safety as the workers of the user company.[2] And according to the "posting" directive adopted in 1996, agency workers posted from one Member State to another shall enjoy the basic working and employment conditions in force in the country where they perform the work.[3] Thus, part of the needs that the Commission foresaw in the draft directive of 1982 had already been taken care of.

However, obviously more important for how the negotiations would end was another development: since 1982 temporary work agencies had been gaining more and more acceptance. In the middle of the 1990s, the International Labour Organisation had started to formulate a new standard that would replace the C 96 Fee-charging Employment Agencies Convention of 1949 (and 1933). The background was that more and more

2 Directive 91/383/EEC of 25 June 1991 supplementing the measures to encourage improvements in the safety and health at work of workers with a fixed-duration employment relationship or a temporary employment relationship.

3 Directive 96/71/EC of the European Parliament and the Council of 16 December 1996 concerning the posting of workers in the framework of the provision of services.

countries were dissatisfied with the public employment services' monopoly on job placement, and that private employment services were prepared to offer services that the public institutions could not provide.[4] Thus, in 1997 the ILO adopted a Convention (C181) and a Recommendation (R188) on Private Employment Agencies, which implied a total shift in attitude in relation to temporary agency work. It was based on a compromise, which would satisfy governments' wish to use agency work as a tool for employment promotion, meet with the agencies' want for recognition and guarantee agency workers' better protection. Thus, while the object of the old Convention was the abolition of fee-charging employment agencies, the new Convention referred to "the importance of flexibility in the functioning of labour markets" and recognised "the role which private employment agencies may play in a well functioning labour market". Consequently, it recognised and legalised private employment services as providers, *inter alia*, of services consisting of employing workers with a view to making them available to a third party, referred to as a user enterprise, which assigns their tasks and supervises the execution of these tasks. The Recommendation complementing the Convention encourages cooperation between public employment services and private employment agencies. At the same time the Convention underlined the need to protect workers against abuses. It would still be possible under certain circumstances to prohibit private employment agencies from operating in respect of certain categories of workers or branches of economic activity. Also, the greater part of the Convention and of the Recommendation consists of provisions aimed at protecting agency workers' individual and collective rights.

In parallel with this evolution within the ILO, several EU Member States had liberalised their legislation, some of them radically. But as we will see, some governments had adopted the idea that agency work is a useful tool for employment promotion more than others had done.

3. Social Dialogue 2000–2001

3.1 A Tardy Start[5]

I said that there was little reason to believe that ETUC, UNICE and CEEP would not succeed in reaching an agreement for the fourth time.

4 For a detailed account of the background to the abolition of the old Convention and the adoption of Convention No. 181 and the Recommendation No. 188, see Phan (1999) and Nakayama and Samodorov (2004).

5 My record of the negotiations on temporary agency work, including its preludes and reverberations, is based on internal documents of the participating organisations and on interviews with persons with direct insight into the negotiations, the names of whom

Well, that may not be entirely true after all. There were signs that might have indicated that these negotiations would be more difficult than the earlier rounds.

First of all, one should remember that in its response to the Commission's 1995 consultation on "Flexibility in working time and security for workers", UNICE had declared that there was no need for European regulation on either of the three forms of "atypical" work – part-time, fixed time and temporary agency work – that the consultation dealt with.[6] Not surprisingly, the ETUC was of the opposite opinion. However, in its consultation, the Commission had already made clear that it thought European level action necessary. Thus, for both sides, the decision whether to enter into negotiations or not was dependent on whether that was likely to lead to a more satisfactory outcome than if the Commission drafted a Directive.[7]

Secondly, during the negotiations on fixed-term work several of the trade union delegates advocated that temporary agency work should be covered by the same agreement.[8] However, in the agreement on fixed-term work concluded by ETUC, UNICE and CEEP on 18 March 1999 temporary agency workers were explicitly excluded from its scope of application. From the trade union point of view, the reason was simply practical: it would be too complicated to regulate them both at the same time as the "triangular" character of temporary agency work requires different legislative solutions than those governing bilateral contracts. For the employers, however, the exclusion of temporary agency work from the scope of the fixed-term work agreement may have had a wider purpose. In the preamble of the agreement the parties declared that they would "consider the need for a similar agreement relating to temporary agency work". In other words, what they committed themselves to do was to "consider" the issue – it was not given that they would actually decide to enter into negotiations.

---

will not be given. Where I refer to something as an established fact it is confirmed by two or more sources independently of each other, and not contradicted by others. Unfortunately, the employers' side has not been as communicative as the trade union side. In other words, I have more sources from the latter.

6 Flexibility in working time and security for workers UNICE response to first-stage consultation with the social partners, 15 December 1995.

7 In the light of what happened after the negotiations broke down, it is obvious that they should also have considered the possibility that, irrespective of what the Commission might propose, it would not gather a sufficient majority in the Council. The question is to what extent they took that possibility into account.

8 Ahlberg (1999), p. 25.

Opinions differed, not only on the employers' side but also among the trade unions. The ETUC secretariat had its position clear: it wanted to enter into new negotiations, and intended that it must be done without any waste of time. However, there were affiliates which were not very satisfied with the agreement on fixed-term work, and which wanted to wait until the agreement on fixed-term work had been implemented before deciding whether or not to negotiate on agency work. The secretariat insisted. It was unlikely that the Commission would rush to step in, should the "social partners" decide not to negotiate, and any prolonged gap in regulating temporary agency work would stimulate this form of employment in countries where it was not regulated, the secretariat argued. In addition, any legislative proposal from the Commission would probably not differ very much from the agreement on fixed-term work. The ETUC Executive Committee was convinced, and on 2 December 1999 it unanimously decided in favour of negotiations.

The employers apparently had greater difficulties in deciding. On the very same day as the ETUC Executive Committee met, UNICE's Council of Presidents had a meeting in Helsinki, where it was expected it would decide whether or not to enter into negotiations on temporary agency work. However, it took another four months, until 3 May 2000, before UNICE decided to give a positive answer to ETUC's call for negotiations.

CEEP had already declared that it was in favour of a European agreement in its response to the Commission's consultation.[9]

A factor that most likely influenced both sides to decide in favour of negotiations after all was the appearance of a new actor on the industrial relations scene: the International Confederation of Temporary Work Businesses (CIETT). In recent decades, CIETT has lobbied successfully for deregulation and liberalisation of temporary agency work by working hard to improve the image of the sector. In its annual report for 1998 CIETT consequently declared that it "would be happy to discuss EU legislation on Temporary Work provided that such legislation would have as its main objectives the liberalisation of TWB, as well as the protection of workers".

Also, in 1999 CIETT had established a sectoral social dialogue committee with one of ETUC's industry federations, Euro-fiet (as from 1 January 2000 UNI-Europa), which represents temporary agency workers in the service sector. Now, a perfectly conceivable scenario was that CIETT and Euro-fiet/UNI-Europa would start to negotiate a sectoral

9 Flexibility in working time and security for employees (other than full-time open ended working patterns). Second stage consultation with the social partners pursuant to Article 3(3) of the Agreement on Social Policy.

agreement, had UNICE/CEEP and ETUC decided not to negotiate with each other. In ETUC's view this would be unacceptable, as Eurofiet/UNI-Europa could not speak for temporary agency workers in all sectors. From the employers' point of view, CIETT could not represent the interests of the user companies, which were likely to be indirectly affected by a sectoral agreement.

3.2 Diverging Agendas

After the ETUC Executive Committee had decided in favour of starting negotiations, the national confederations and industry federations had three months for consultations on the mandate among their members. On 13–14 January 2000 ETUC arranged a "technical seminar" for all the affiliates concerned to discuss the secretariat's draft mandate. Among other things, the seminar stressed the importance of marginalising temporary agency work. It emphasised that any agreement must not impose liberalisation in the Member States, and underlined that it must include a non-regression clause that would prevent Member States from calling existing restrictive regulations into question. Another conclusion was that both collective agreements and legislation are important for regulation of temporary agency work.

However, it seems that it was more difficult to agree on the mandate on temporary agency work than it had been to settle the mandates before the previous negotiations. The character of temporary agency work varies much more from Member State to Member State than the character of fixed-term or part-time work, and so do the trade unions' strategies for safeguarding agency workers' interests. While some trade unions intended that the minimum European standard should be that every agency worker would have the right to an open-ended contract with the agency, unions from other countries would under no circumstances accept that, since open-ended contracts would mean the normalisation of agency work. Another point of dispute was whether or not agency workers should have the right to collective representation in the user enterprise, as well as in the agency. The mandate finally – and unanimously – adopted on 22 March 2000 was a rather detailed wish list covering two pages.

On the employers' side, the agencies' confederation CIETT made its own wish list in the form of a complete draft directive, negotiated article by article among the organisation's national affiliates. CIETT would be represented in the negotiations on the employers' delegation and the text was "used by UNICE as source of inspiration", but formally the employers' organisations acted under one joint UNICE mandate when they met the ETUC at the negotiating table. As we shall see, the trade union delegation nevertheless got the impression that there were two separate agendas on the employers' side.

3.3 The Organisation of the Negotiations

The ETUC elected a negotiating team of 31 persons in all: one representative per Member State/EEA state, eight persons representing the industry federations, one from the women's committee, one from Eurocadres and two from the secretariat. Among them, a drafting committee of eight persons was designated: Dave Feickert (TUC, United Kingdom), Miguel Gonzalez (CCOO, Spain), Catelene Passchier, (FNV, the Netherlands), Jorma Rusanen (SAK, Finland), Bart Samyn (European Metalworkers' Federation), Bernadette Tesch-Ségol (UNI-Europa), and from the secretariat Deputy Secretary General Jean Lapeyre and his assistant Penny Clarke. As he had done in all three European level negotiations so far, Jean Lapeyre would again act as spokesperson for the trade union side.

On the employers' side the organisation for private employers, UNICE, and that for public employers, CEEP, had a joint negotiating team, with one representative per EU/EEA state for UNICE and nine for CEEP. However, the employers' delegation also included five representatives for the agencies' confederation CIETT, and, for the first time, two observers representing the European organisation for small and medium-size companies, UEAPME. The employers' drafting committee consisted of Susan Anderson (CBI, United Kingdom), Wilfred Beirnaert (chairman of UNICE's social affairs committee) Jytte Fredensborg (CEEP), Fred van Haasteren (CIETT), Renate Hornung-Draus (BDA, Germany) Thérèse de Liedekerke, (UNICE secretariat), Jørgen Rønnest (DA, Denmark) and Liliane Volozinskis (UEAPME). Wilfred Beirnaert was the employers' spokesperson and was new in this role in European-level negotiations.

The negotiations would be organised as in earlier negotiating rounds.[10] The delegations would meet in plenary about once a month. This meant that there would be over 60 persons in the room, all of whom could ask permission to speak and express his or her opinion. However, mostly the two spokespersons would do the speaking. The task of the drafting groups, which could meet whenever it was deemed useful, would be to draft texts on issues that had been agreed in plenary, to explore possible compromises and to clarify issues that had to be clarified.

A characteristic of European-level negotiations is that the Commission supports them with all kinds of practical arrangements. It pays for the interpreters, it organises meeting rooms, and so on. Another characteristic is that the negotiations are chaired by an outsider – an impartial chair. Impartial chair during the negotiations on temporary agency work was

10 See Ahlberg (1999), p. 16ff.

Mr Jean Degimbe, who had also chaired the negotiations on fixed-term work. Mr Degimbe had an assistant, Mr Diego Mellado, an official at the Commission's Directorate General for Employment and Social Policy. The role of the impartial chair and his/her assistant is to give the negotiating parties any kind of assistance that they ask for, but nothing apart from that. For example, it is a rule that the parties ask for opinions from the Commission's Legal Service on the interpretation of Community law, since they must act within the scope of the Treaty if they want to have their agreements made binding for the Member States through a decision by the Council. Such requests for legal advice are normally conveyed by the chairperson and his or her assistant. Both the Commission and the impartial chair have to perform a delicate balancing act between assisting and interfering in the negotiations.

A third characteristic is that the parties only have a limited time in which they can negotiate this type of agreement. After they have decided to enter into negotiations, the Commission suspends the normal legislative process for nine months. If they have not reached an agreement by then but feel that it may be within their grasp, they may apply for some additional time.

3.4 The First Round: Presentation of the Mandates

The first bargaining round took place only on 23 June 2000. In plenary, the two spokespersons presented their mandates. Both spokespersons referred to the European employment strategy and the objective of full employment. Apart from that, they had little in common.

ETUC Deputy Secretary General Jean Lapeyre stressed that recognising the existence of temporary agency work and its place in the operation of the labour market did not necessarily constitute acceptance of the conditions under which it was developing. Thus, the trade unions' main starting point was that the quality of temporary work must be improved on the basis of two principles, first, establishing the conditions under which temporary agency work can be used, and second, ensuring equal treatment for the workers concerned. The conditions of use should firmly establish temporary agency work as marginal to the operation of the labour market. Therefore, any agreement should reiterate the statement from the fixed-term work agreement that open-ended contracts are and will remain the general form of employment. Generally, a European Union regulation on temporary agency work should go further than the ILO Convention 181 on private employment agencies.

Mr Lapeyre finished by pointing to three considerations that, from the trade unions' point of view, were important for a satisfactory European agreement:

1. it should stimulate structured negotiations of collective agreements in the sector;
2. it should "tie in" with the posting directive;
3. the principle of subsidiarity should be applied in a manner that ensures that national social partners are genuinely in a position to transpose the agreement via national collective agreements.

In response, the employers' spokesperson, Wilfred Beirnaert, stressed that an agreement must achieve an equitable balance between flexibility and security for workers. Therefore it must recognise the positive contribution of temporary agency work to employment and remove existing obstacles to agency work. Beirnaert presented statistics to support his statement: one third of agency workers get full-time jobs later on; more than half of them were unemployed before they were employed by an agency; and 64% of agency workers are first-time job seekers. The principle of subsidiarity would play an important role, including in determining who are comparable workers for the purposes of equal treatment.

On the face of it, the situation was very similar to the situation at the opening plenary of the negotiations on fixed-term work two years earlier: the employers were prepared to discuss a non-discrimination/equal treatment clause. Given the fact that non-discrimination would be guaranteed, there would be no need for conditioning the use of agency work, the employers argued. For the trade union side, both elements were equally important.

3.5 The UNI-Europa/CIETT Joint Declaration

After the first meeting the negotiators went on their summer holidays, and there was a long pause till the next bargaining round.

But in the meantime the agencies' confederation CIETT and its counterpart in the sectoral social dialogue, UNI-Europa, took a joint initiative that caused a stir on the trade union side.

As already mentioned, about a year earlier CIETT and UNI-Europa had established a sectoral social dialogue committee where they had met once or twice and started a discussion on training of agency workers. When it was confirmed that UNICE and ETUC would start cross-sectoral negotiations on temporary agency work, CIETT and UNI-Europa decided to stop meeting at sectoral level until the negotiations were finished. However, on 3 July 2000 the two organisations made a joint declaration "on the Sectoral Social Dialogue on Agency Work". First, they stated that they recognised each other as representative organisations in the sector. They continued:

> Both organisations are hopeful and confident that the sectoral Social Dialogue will have positive effects on this important industry which will benefit all parties involved in Europe – employees, agencies and user enterprises … On the

basis that agency work may play a positive role in the labour market, the sectoral social dialogue should work towards improving the quality and the operation of the European labour market, the employment and working conditions of agency-supplied workers, as well as the further professionalisation of the sector.

They finished by declaring that they supported ongoing negotiations between UNICE/CEEP and ETUC and would seek to play an active role in their progression.

When the ETUC delegation met immediately before the second plenary with the employers, this declaration was subject to an animated debate. UNI-Europa was convinced that the declaration would have a positive impact on the negotiations, but several other members of the ETUC delegation doubted that. They were especially critical of the fact that the declaration acknowledged that temporary agency work could constitute a positive contribution to the labour market.

3.6 Second Round: A Restart

The second plenary did not take place until 11–12 September. It consisted mainly of deepened presentations of the mandates. Because of the long break, it was almost a restart of the process.

ETUC's spokesperson Jean Lapeyre described what the trade union side saw as similarities between temporary agency work and other forms of "atypical" work and in what respects temporary agency work requires specific solutions.

The employers' spokesperson Wilfred Beirnaert once again stressed the twofold objectives of the employers – to promote employment and ensure a balance between flexibility and security. Notably, the employers would under no circumstances accept an agreement speaking about "prevention of abuse" as in the fixed-term work agreement, as this would imply that the use of temporary agency work is synonymous with "abuse".

3.7 The First Drafts on Non-discrimination

The third bargaining round took place on 11–12 October. This time, each side presented a list of points to be included in the negotiations.

The ETUC list went into two pages, enumerating among other things twelve points under the heading "Conditions of use for temporary agency work". The employers' list was half as long. Under the heading "Enhancing job opportunities" it stated that the agreement should contain a clause inviting Member States and/or social partners to review and eliminate restrictive conditions of use which limit job opportunities.

The lists also displayed another conflict of interests that would prove to be decisive at a later stage: the trade union side wanted an agreement that covered agency workers with open-ended contracts with the agencies as well as those with fixed-term contracts. According to the employers, only temporary employment relationships should be covered.

Both also presented their first drafts for a clause on non-discrimination.

The ETUC draft read as follows:

Principle of non-discrimination

1. Temporary agency workers shall not be treated in a less favourable manner than comparable workers, unless different treatment is justified on objective grounds

2. With regard to the following employment conditions the comparable worker is considered to be the worker in the user-enterprise unless explicitly regulated otherwise by collective agreement at the national or sectoral level:

- remuneration;
- working conditions, including working time and rest periods;
- health and safety, taking into account the Directive 91/383 EEC.

3. In regard to other employment conditions Member States, after consultation with the social partners and/or the social partners at national or sectoral level, shall define in which cases the comparable worker is that of the user enterprise and in which cases that of the temporary work agency.

4. The arrangements for the application of this clause shall be defined by the Member States after consultation with the social partners and/or the social partners having regard to Community law, national law, collective agreements and practice.

The employers answered with the following draft:

Employers proposals on non-discrimination

1. In respect of employment conditions, temporary agency workers assigned to work for and under the control of an undertaking or establishment shall not be treated in a less favourable manner than a comparable worker, defined in accordance with point 4, unless different treatment is justified on objective grounds, and without prejudice to length of service or seniority criteria relating to particular benefits.

2. Where appropriate, the principle pro rata temporis shall apply.

3. The modalities of application of this clause shall be defined by the MS and/or SP having regard to national law, collective agreements or practice.

4. The responsibility to define the term comparable worker is incumbent upon MS and/or SP.

5. Temporary employment agencies established in one MS assigning a worker to work for and under the control of an undertaking/establishment established in another MS shall respect the provisions of Directive 96/71.

The texts reflected a fundamental disagreement that the parties never really managed to overcome until it was too late.

For the trade unions, the only conceivable standpoint was that, as regards certain employment conditions, agency workers must be guaranteed equal treatment with the workers in the *user* company, unless they are otherwise guaranteed decent employment conditions – for example, through a collective agreement for the sector. And in fact, this principle was already applied in many of the Member States. However, the employers would not make it binding on all Member States. Instead, they wanted to leave the definition of who is a comparable worker to the Member States or the national social partners, including at company level.

The employers were also opposed to specifying different employment conditions in the agreement. More specifically, they did not want any explicit reference to the issue of pay.

To understand the implications of this standpoint one has to go back to the agreement and Directive on fixed-term work. During the negotiations on fixed-term work there was a common understanding between employers and trade unions that the concept "employment conditions" includes pay. For example, this was the reason why the British employers, the CBI, fought hard to have pensions explicitly excepted from the non-discrimination principle in that agreement. The CBI did not get their way, but when the Council eventually adopted the Directive that implemented the agreement, the UK Government made a declaration to the minutes. It said "This Directive can implement the framework agreement only on matters other than pay, the right to strike and the right to impose lock-outs, which (as this Directive is proposed under Article 139(2)) are excluded under Article 137(6)[11] of the Treaty".

Thus, by not specifying to which employment conditions the non-discrimination principle in an agreement on temporary agency work would be applicable, the British employers could hope that their Government (and any other party concerned) would once again rule out pay from the application of a Directive implementing the agreement.

The employers' attitude made the ETUC question whether they were at all prepared to stick to what was already agreed in the previous agreement. It stressed that if no agreement could be reached on equal treatment, an overall agreement would not be possible. The employers agreed to that, but argued that the ETUC drafts were not flexible enough. The ETUC answered that the employment strategy calls not only for more, but also for better jobs, which was why the trade union side could not accept anything that would promote temporary agency work.

---

11 Article 137(5) after the coming into force of the Nice Treaty.

3.8 First Meeting of the Drafting Groups

The fourth negotiating round took place in November without any progress. In December, almost six months after the first round, the parties had still not started real negotiations and their drafting groups had not had a single joint meeting. This was in sharp contrast to how the negotiations on fixed-term work had developed, where the drafting groups started to draft texts together almost immediately, even if the parties were very far from reaching agreement on any point.

Already at an early stage, the ETUC delegates had decided that, even if the conditions of use of temporary agency work were important, the non-discrimination clause was of primary importance, and gradually they realised that it would be useful to discuss both issues in context. Therefore, when the parties met for the fifth time on 11–12 December 2000, ETUC presented a comprehensive text, almost a complete draft agreement, to the employers.

The employers answered with a compromise proposal for a non-discrimination clause. Now they accepted that workers in the user company should be the comparators with regard to certain working conditions, namely maximum working time, minimum resting periods and health and safety protection. However, with regard to other employment conditions (for example – although not explicitly mentioned – pay), they would still entrust the Member States and/or the social partners with defining the comparable worker.

By presenting a full text, the ETUC delegation had hoped that it could persuade the employers to do likewise, but the employers tabled no drafts apart from that on non-discrimination. However, it was agreed that the drafting teams of both sides would at last have their first meeting.

The drafting groups met on 18 December. The ETUC presented a reviewed version of its draft agreement. Apart from clauses on Purpose, Scope, Definitions and Principle of non-discrimination (which was unchanged) it contained clauses on Measures to promote quality "TEB work",[12] Information and employment opportunities, Conditions of use, Information and consultation and Provisions on implementation.

As one of the *measures to improve the quality of agency work*, Member States were to clarify the legal status of agency workers and the applicability of labour legislation to them with a view to ensuring their labour protection. The motive for this provision was the fact that in Ireland and the UK many agency workers are regarded as self-employed

12 Here the notion 'temporary agency' was replaced by 'Temporary Employment Business', 'TEB'.

or as having a contract *sui generis* and not as employees of either the agency or of the user company.

According to the second paragraph under the same heading, the social partners at the appropriate levels were to promote collective agreements to cover agency workers as a means of improving their situation. Such collective agreements should in particular improve access to training opportunities both in the temporary employment businesses and in the user companies.

The clause on *information on employment opportunities* was copied from the fixed-term work agreement.

The *conditions-of-use* clause (one and a half pages) began with a paragraph that built on the same formula as the clause on measures to prevent abuse in the fixed-term work agreement, that is, a choice between objective reasons for renewal, a maximum total duration or a maximum number of renewals of missions. In addition, Member States were to:

- ensure that these conditions are not circumvented by an agency and a user enterprise alternately employing a worker to do the same job in the user enterprise, or by one or more agencies posting one or more agency workers alternately to the same job in the user enterprise;
- take adequate measures to control and supervise temporary employment businesses, for example through authorisation or licensing or certification;
- ensure the employment protection of migrant workers, for example by preventing fraudulent practices in their recruitment, placement and employment;
- prohibit the posting of agency workers to a user enterprise in which there is a strike;
- prohibit agencies from asking a fee, directly or indirectly, from agency workers;
- prohibit agencies from hindering agency workers entering into a direct labour contract with the user enterprise or another enterprise.
- In addition, the agreement should explicitly allow Member States to restrict or prohibit the use of agency work in particular sectors of the economy or for particular categories of workers, as foreseen in ILO Convention No. 181.

As regards *information and consultation*, Member States were to promote the exercise of individual and collective rights of agency workers, including trade union rights, both in the user company and in the temporary employment business. Similarly, agency workers must be taken into consideration in calculating thresholds above which workers' representative bodies are provided for, both in the user undertaking and in the temporary employment business. Also, user enterprises should provide appropriate information to workers' representative bodies about temporary agency work in the undertaking.

The employers were not able to respond, but announced that they would present a compromise proposal to the next plenary.

3.9 A Possible Opening?

The sixth bargaining round took place on 11–12 January 2001. In their compromise proposal the employers had taken up some of the ideas put forward by the ETUC, although in most cases worded in a way that limited their scope.

In the preamble they recognised, as in the fixed-term work agreement, that employment contracts of an indefinite duration are, and will continue to be, the general form of employment relationship.

They would include a clause saying that agency workers shall have access to information about vacancies in the user undertaking to the same extent as the undertaking's own employees.

They also agreed that agencies must not charge workers any fees for assignments.

Neither would the agencies be allowed to introduce clauses in employment contracts that forbid agency workers to enter into a direct employment relationship with the user undertaking.

As regards information and consultation, the employers agreed that agency workers must be taken into consideration in calculating thresholds above which workers' representative bodies are provided for in the agency.

Also, the user undertaking should include appropriate information about temporary work in the undertaking when providing information on the employment situation to existing workers' representative bodies.

However, on the central issues there was no change. The material contents of the non-discrimination clause were the same as in earlier drafts from the employers' side, and there was not a word on conditions of use. Instead, the employers repeated that Member States and social partners respectively "should identify and review obstacles of a legal or administrative nature which may limit the opportunities for temporary agency work and, where appropriate, eliminate them".

Other important differences between the ETUC draft and the employers' proposal were:

Scope: the employers insisted that an agreement should apply only to workers with *temporary* employment contracts with the agency.

The role of collective bargaining: ETUC's idea that collective bargaining and collective agreements would play an important role in improving the quality of agency work – especially to improve access to training opportunities – met no reaction from the employers.

Trade union rights: the paragraphs in the ETUC proposal saying that Member States should promote the exercise of individual and collective rights of agency workers, including trade union rights, had no counterpart in the employers' draft. Neither had the provision that would prohibit the posting of agency workers to a user enterprise in which there is a strike.

Nevertheless, the ETUC spokesman initiated a discussion on conditions of use. The ETUC wanted to make clear that it was prepared to be more flexible on the issue of conditions of use, if only the employers would accept a non-discrimination clause that met the requirements of the trade union side, and the spokesperson Jean Lapeyre mentioned two points that were especially important to them:

1. The possibility to restrict or prohibit agency work in certain sectors or for certain categories of workers.
2. Agency workers must not be used to replace workers on strike.

The employers were prepared to discuss the last issue. However, they questioned whether it would be consistent with Article 137.6 of the Treaty[13] to say something about strikes in the agreement. Both sides agreed to postpone the proceedings and ask the Commission's Legal Service for advice. At the same time, they would take the opportunity to ask whether or not, in the Legal Service's view, the concept "employment conditions" includes pay. The inquiry would be conducted by the impartial chair Jean Degimbe.

3.10 "Real Negotiations Start Now"

On 9 February 2001 the agencies' confederation CIETT's European Committee arranged a meeting for its members to discuss how the negotiators should proceed. Representatives of the national confederations were informed that the parties had had six plenary sessions and one drafting committee meeting – "but real negotiations start now". According to the CIETT negotiators, the following meeting would be crucial to see whether the gap between the two sides could be bridged.

The CIETT representatives stated that no agreement could be reached within the current mandates. There were four "make-or-break" points:

1. the scope of the agreement;
2. the non-discrimination clause;
3. the conditions of use;
4. the issue of strike breaking.

13 Article 137(5) after the coming into force of the Nice Treaty.

On the first point, CIETT's position was the same as that of the trade union side, namely that the agreement should cover workers with open-ended contracts as well as those with temporary contracts, while UNICE wanted to restrict the scope to workers with temporary contracts only.

On the second point too, CIETT took a slightly different position from UNICE. CIETT had no problems with mentioning pay in an agreement, but like UNICE it meant that, as a rule, the comparator should be a worker with the same or similar job in the agency. But it should be possible to apply the principle of comparison with the user company's workers after a certain period of qualification, defined by the Member States.

The third point was the only where CIETT and UNICE shared exactly the same view.

Finally, the employers were divided on the issue of strike breaking as well. UNICE was against any reference to strike breaking in an agreement, while CIETT was ready to accept it.

The rapporteur concluded that even CIETT's position on pay might be unacceptable to ETUC. On the other hand, there was clearly room for negotiations on the conditions of use. And if the issue of strike breaking turned out to be the breaking point it would not be CIETT's fault.

Now the CIETT affiliates were confronted with three options:

The first was to go for an agreement "at any price", which was synonymous with accepting that agency workers should have the same pay as comparable workers in the user companies. This would have as positive effects to bring credibility for the sector, and probably also allow for more flexible conditions of use. Negative effects would be that wage costs would increase in a number of countries, and that the agencies would not be fully recognised as normal employers.

The second option was to try to reach an agreement, but not at any price. This could, for example, mean an agreement which guaranteed agency workers the *minimum* pay applicable in the user company, or some other compromise. It would be cheaper than the first option, but would probably limit the room for compromise with the ETUC on conditions of use for temporary agency work.

The third option was to give up the idea of a European agreement. This alternative would involve several risks, and the positive effects would be rather uncertain.

CIETT's negotiators obviously took the view that a European agreement on agency work would be of great value.

3.11 Unwanted Advice

On 13 February the impartial chair Jean Degimbe brought back a message from the Commission's Legal Service. It was an oral message – the Legal Service did not want to give a written opinion.

On the first question, it advised the parties not to refer to strikes in the binding clauses of an agreement, although, eventually, they might be mentioned in the preamble.

As regards "employment conditions", the Legal Service did indeed interpret the concept as including pay. Nevertheless, in the absence of case law from the EC Court on the scope of Article 137.6 of the EC Treaty,[14] it was not advisable to mention the word "pay" (or remuneration) in the body of the text.

However, the Legal Service did not confine itself to responding to the two questions that it had been asked to answer. It also took a stand on the requirement that agency workers should be paid as comparable workers in the user company. Since it was an oral opinion, there are different versions of the exact wording, but the message delivered by Jean Degimbe was clear: to state that the comparison should be made with the user company would mean that the agreement regulated the wage level for the sector, which would clearly be contrary to Article 137.6.

This was a severe setback to the ETUC delegates. In their opinion, the Legal Service had not only "advised" the parties on an issue that it had not been asked to comment on, but they even doubted that this interpretation was correct.

However, as it seemed, the employers could now count on having it their way on this important issue, should the negotiations fail and the initiative go back to the Commission. The ETUC delegation noted a hardening position on the employers' side, and again it felt that they were even prepared to back out of what had been agreed in the fixed-term agreement regarding the concept "employment conditions". But it also saw signs of division between user enterprises and agencies in the employers' group.

Jean Degimbe closed the plenary with a summary of the tasks ahead of the negotiators, and finished by suggesting that the parties would restrict themselves to include in the agreement an obligation for the Member States to "do something" about equal treatment with regard to either the user or the agency.

The following day the trade union delegates met with the ETUC Steering Committee to discuss how to proceed. They proposed that

---

14 Article 137(5) after the coming into force of the Nice Treaty.

ETUC should make a last attempt to take the negotiations out of the impasse. This attempt would be based on proposals which maintained the two main elements equal treatment and conditions of use, but at the same time allowed for rebalancing these elements in giving priority to the quality of the non-discrimination clause and simplifying the conditions of use. The Steering Committee thought that it was worth a try.

Now the members of the ETUC drafting team started to work on drafts based on differentiation between "basic" employment conditions, for which the comparable worker would be a worker in the user undertaking (unless adequate protection was guaranteed otherwise by collective agreements) and "other" employment and working conditions. The idea was that the word "pay" or "remuneration" should not be mentioned in the core agreement, while remuneration/basic wages would be explicitly referred to in the preamble, as part of the term "basic" or elementary employment conditions.

The employers too had consultations within the UNICE social affairs committee that met on 20 February, together with the delegates from CIETT and the observers from UEAPME.

3.12 Final Breakdown?

The eighth negotiating round took place on 26–28 February 2001, and was the last within the nine-month period.

First the drafting groups met.

The employers' consultations had not changed their position on comparability or other key points, such as scope, interpretation of the notion "employment conditions" and conditions of use. But they were more positive on the issue of training, and they were still prepared to discuss the use of agency work in strike situations.

ETUC reported on the discussion in its Steering Committee and insisted on two main points: (i) reference to the user company for basic employment conditions and (ii) the need for a clear indication from the employers that pay is included in that concept.

Finally, the employers' spokesperson Wilfried Beirnaert declared that he, as spokesperson, had been fully aware that the concept covered remuneration and that the interpretation of the previous agreements was not called into question. As it appears from the wording, the trade union side could not be sure that he expressed the view of the whole employers' delegation. In any case, the ETUC delegation asked Mr Beirnaert to repeat his statement in a plenary with the full delegations, which he did.

After this small step forward, ETUC tabled a new draft on non-discrimination at 8.30 p.m. on 27 February: For "basic employment conditions", the comparable worker would be a worker in the user company, "unless explicitly regulated otherwise by a collective agreement concluded by the social partners at the national or sectoral level assuring the principle of non-discrimination". A second paragraph was specifically designed to match the wishes of the British employers. It said:

> In Member States where there is no system ensuring the conclusion of collective agreements between the social partners at national or sectoral level, Member States *together* (italics added) with the national social partners and/or the social partners at national level, may decide if and under which conditions other tripartite arrangements or collective agreements concluded by the social partners at levels other than specified in [the above] clause … may be considered as providing for equivalent protection.

While the employers were considering this proposal, the ETUC delegation worked on a text on conditions of use that would be more acceptable to the employers. First, it would recognise the role that the agencies could play in a well functioning labour market. Instead of "conditions of use" it would talk about "Measures to improve the quality" of agency work, and the conditions actually mentioned would on the whole be copied from ILO Convention 181 of 1997 on private employment agencies. Finally, the Member States might review prohibitions and restrictions on agency work periodically to ensure that they remain justified.

However, this text was never given to the employers. When the employers refused to make any concessions on non-discrimination before they had received a global text from ETUC, the trade union side's patience was exhausted. Throughout the negotiations the ETUC delegation had felt that the trade union side had tabled nearly all the compromise texts, without the employers giving anything in return.

As the nine-month period had come to an end, the employers nevertheless suggested that the parties ask the Commission for three additional months to try to reach an agreement. The ETUC negotiators refused, but agreed to ask for one month's extension, to have time to consult its Executive Committee.

In the meantime, impartial chair Jean Degimbe would talk to both sides to see whether there was still a chance of bridging the gap between the parties, or whether the negotiations had definitely broke down.

3.13 The Last Stumbling Block: Scope

On 14 March 2001 Jean Degimbe reported back to the two delegations. His conclusion was that there was no room for further compromises, and that an agreement on temporary agency work was beyond reach.

Within a few days ETUC addressed two questions to UNICE's Council of Presidents in order to verify whether Mr Degimbe's conclusion was correct:

- Could the employers accept the user enterprise as the first reference for the non-discrimination principle?
- Were they ready to discuss a clause on prevention of abuse of temporary agency work based on the same logic – as opposed to the same wording – as in the agreement on fixed-term work?

UNICE's Council of Presidents responded on 21 March.

- On the first question, it repeated that it accepted that the comparison should be made with the user company for health and safety conditions and maximum working time and minimum rest periods. But it still thought that ETUC's insistence that a worker in the user company should be the first reference for other employment conditions was unjustified.
- On the second question it declared that, in a spirit of compromise, UNICE was prepared to include a clause whereby Member States could ban or limit temporary agency work in specific sectors or activities for specific reasons, provided that such limitations were regularly reviewed to check if they are still justified.

On the basis of this answer, UNICE's Council of Presidents called on the trade union side to continue negotiations. But on the same day the ETUC Executive Committee confirmed that the negotiations had been terminated and that the initiative was again in the hands of the Commission.

On the same occasion both organisations met in Stockholm at a "Social Dialogue mini Summit". During a pause President Romano Prodi asked the Commissioner Anna Diamantopoulou to arrange a meeting with the social partners in order to verify whether in fact all possibilities for reaching an agreement were exhausted, before the Commission launched its legislative initiative.

On 6 April UNICE President George Jacobs, spokesperson Wilfried Beirnaert, UNICE Director of Social Affairs Thérèse de Liedekerke, ETUC President Emilio Gabaglio, spokesperson Jean Lapeyre and his assistant Penny Clarke met at the Commissioner's office. She asked them to try one last time to try to find a compromise. She pointed out that if the traditional legislative procedure were followed they would have no guarantee of achieving their objectives.

On two occasions after that, the ETUC secretariat had informal discussions with Wilfried Beirnaert, without consulting the rest of the ETUC delegation or even its drafting group. And they actually made some progress. Now Beirnaert indicated that the employers would accept the principle that the agency worker's basic employment conditions, including pay, should be the same as in the user company – provided that this principle apply only to workers with fixed-term employment contracts with the agency, but not to workers with open-ended contracts.

Although the employers moved a step closer to the trade union position, ETUC could not accept that workers with open-ended contracts be excluded.

On 10 May, the parties met with the Commissioner again to report back on their deliberations. In a last attempt, the Commissioner herself suggested a compromise: Would it be possible to allow exceptions to the principle of equal treatment in basic employment conditions with comparable workers in the user enterprise, where this was justified by objective reasons, such as an adequate level of protection by other means?

ETUC were not enthusiastic about the proposal, but the matter was never brought to a head. The employers rejected it completely, since it would still mean that agency workers with open-ended contracts were covered by the non-discrimination principle.

Consequently, the Commissioner announced that she would launch a legislative initiative very soon. That would prove to be more difficult than she anticipated.

3.14 Why Did the Negotiations Fail?

Many were taken by surprise when the agreement on fixed-term work was concluded early in 1999. How could ETUC accept an agreement that seemed so weak and far from the original mandate? And how could the employers' delegation accept clauses on measures to prevent abuse which they under no circumstances were supposed to do? The answer given to me by most of the people I interviewed then was: They reached an agreement because, for several reasons, both sides had a very strong wish to do so.[15]

One might easily believe that the same was true for the negotiations on temporary agency work. It was clear from the outset that the Commission would draft a directive of its own if the negotiations failed, and none of the parties could know beforehand what this directive would be like. In addition, one of the actors on the employers' side, CIETT, was very anxious to gain recognition as "normal" employers that can offer good employment, and saw a European agreement on agency work as a means of achieving such recognition.

So, in what respects were the negotiations on temporary agency work different from those on fixed-term work? Why could the two sides not overcome their disagreement on the principle of non-discrimination and conditions of use for temporary agency work, when they managed to do so in relation to fixed-term work?

15 Ahlberg (1999), p. 30ff.

There are a number of factors that characterise and complicate European-level negotiations in general. In the case of temporary agency work, there were some specific circumstances which made the general complicating factors have a more decisive impact to the negative.

On the other hand, in European-level negotiations there are a number of general factors that have the function of encouraging the parties to attempt to reach an agreement. However, in the case of temporary agency work, there were specific circumstances that weakened those driving forces.

A general difficulty in negotiations at European level is to find a solution that fits in with the (at that time) 15 national legal and industrial relations systems. This is the more difficult, the greater the differences are at national level. A specific circumstance in this case was (and is) that the character and the regulation of temporary agency work differed much more between the Member States than the character and regulation of fixed-term work and part-time work. Most continental countries have extensive and detailed regulation of both agencies (they must have a license, they are subject to public control, and so on) and agency work (agency work is permitted only where there are objective reasons, restrictions regarding the length of assignments, and so on). The Scandinavian countries, on the other hand, have practically no specific legislation of either agencies or agency work. Instead, agency workers are protected by general labour law and by collective agreements. Now, one might expect that the rate of agency work as a percentage of total employment would be lower in countries with extensive statutory regulation, but that is not always the case: for example, Belgium, France and Luxembourg have relatively high rates of agency work, while they are low in the Scandinavian countries.[16] Nor is there a simple correlation between extensive statutory regulation and a high standard of employment and working conditions for agency workers. Thus, it would have necessitated an extremely flexible solution at EU level in order to safeguard decent working conditions for agency workers in need of more protection, without disturbing national systems that function relatively well.

Part of the problem is that, in all European-level negotiations so far, both sides have had to spend a disproportionate amount of energy on the demands of two countries, the UK and Ireland. On the UNICE side, especially the British but also the Irish employers have tended to have specific requirements that become stumbling blocks in the negotiations, probably because they are the two countries where any European labour leg-

16 Storrie (2002), p. 27ff.

islation will have the greatest impact. The standard UNICE solution is to propose to the trade unions that these issues be resolved by the Member States after consultation with the social partners or by the social partners themselves. In some cases, this could be a perfectly acceptable solution to the majority of ETUC's national confederations, at least as a means of allowing for exceptions from a basic rule in the agreement. However, it seldom works for the British trade unions. First, from the trade unions' point of view the British Government is too inclined to listen to the employers when it consults the social partners. Secondly, in the British context, referring issues to the social partners means referring them to company level. There simply does not exist a structure for bargaining at national or sectoral level. And to entrust the definitions of concepts in European legislation to individual employers and company trade union branches, or to authorise deviations from the European norm through such agreements would mean a total loss of control.

Another complicating factor was that the national trade unions' attitudes to temporary agency work varied a lot more than their attitudes to fixed-term work or part-time work. While the French Force Ouvrière "is and will always be against the use of temporary work, since it is merely an instrument of flexibility",[17] and the German IG Metall voted for a total ban on temporary agency work as recently as 1995,[18] trade unions in the UK and Sweden have a more permissive approach and concentrate their efforts on improving employment and working conditions for agency workers. As one of the members of the ETUC negotiating team says: "These negotiations really demonstrated how difficult it still is for trade unions from different countries to understand each other – to understand the culture and the development concerning agency work in various countries, to understand what is at stake at European level." Another ETUC delegate says:

> Fixed-term work and part-time work are rather considered a part of normal working relations in most countries – even though not all trade unions may say so openly – but the legal and public acceptance of temporary agency work varies much more. It was much more difficult to reach a common mandate, and as a consequence, the mandate was much more fixed and less flexible once we had reached it.

And that, of course, makes negotiations more difficult.

Yet another circumstance that distinguished these negotiations from those on fixed-term work was that there were twice as many organisations on the employers' side this time – apart from UNICE and CEEP

17 Clauwaert (1998), p. 42.

18 *Ibid.* p. 49.

also CIETT and UEAPME – and that they had partly conflicting interests. The ETUC delegations saw clear indications that the agencies' organisation CIETT, with its wish to enhance the image of the industry, was more inclined to compromise on issues that would improve the situation of agency workers.[19] But each one of these improvements would make agency work more expensive for the user companies represented by UNICE/UEAPME, which consequently was less willing to compromise.

Actually, a similar divide, although informal, is said to have existed on the trade union side, where some delegates seem to have focused primarily on protecting permanent employment in the user companies, while others concentrated on what would be in the interest of the agency workers. To give an example: with the first focus, assignments should be as short as possible in order not to repress permanent employment, while, if you focus on the situation of the agency worker, longer assignments are preferable as this gives the worker a more secure income. "It is a real challenge for trade unions to make sure that they are capable of simultaneously representing workers with 'normal' contracts and workers who are employed through agencies", says one of the ETUC delegates.

A specific circumstance in these negotiations was that the employers had a new spokesperson. Also, to the trade union side it was striking that the employers acted very differently and "illogically" in relation to the negotiations on fixed-term work. Very few draft texts were exchanged between the parties. The majority of the texts were drafted by the ETUC group and it was only shortly before the nine-month period came to an end that the drafting groups of the two sides met. How should one interpret this changeover? Was it a deliberate change of strategy on the employers' side? And to what extent, if any, did these practical differences contribute to the failure?

In my view, they were probably mere symptoms of other problems, and as such not the immediate reason why the negotiations failed. First, one reason why the employers did not table many texts may have been, as shown earlier, that they could not agree among themselves. Secondly, my interviews have given me the impression that the trade union side may have overlooked – or underestimated the importance of – another essential difference between these negotiations and those on fixed-term work (or part-time work). While the latter merely concerned certain types of employment contracts, the negotiations on temporary agency work

19 This impression is confirmed by the report given by CIETT's own representative at the meeting on 9 February 2001 referred to above.

concerned the market access and consequently the future of a whole industry, namely the temporary employment business sector. In other words, there were bigger interests at stake this time. This must have made it more important for the employers' side to win the battle on conditions of use. In turn, this may explain why they were not ready to compromise very much on the non-discrimination principle until they had seen what they could get on conditions of use. Or as two members of the employers' delegation expressed it, "When you negotiate with people who want to eradicate the whole sector it is not a question of drafting".

On the other hand, the employers may have underestimated how important the principle of comparison with pay levels in the user company was for ETUC. From a trade union point of view an agreement that guaranteed agency workers equal pay with other workers in the same agency would be completely without meaning. It would be a bit like saying that equal treatment for women means that women should be paid equally to other women.

The primary factor that normally stimulates the will to negotiate at European level and efforts to reach agreement is that neither party knows if things will go its way, should the negotiations fail and the Commission resume the initiative. All they know is that the Commission will propose legislation. In that perspective, and provided that the proposed legislation is likely to gain the majority needed in the Council, an agreement the contents of which you control is preferable. However, in addition to the fact that the employers seemed to have difficulties deciding in favour of even starting negotiations on temporary agency work, a remarkable incident happened that must have encouraged the employers' resistance to compromise during the negotiations. The Commission's Legal Service – without being asked – interfered with advice that meant that the parties simply could not agree on a non-discrimination principle of the type that ETUC was calling for since that would be contrary to Article 137.6 of the EC Treaty. This may have had a decisive influence on the outcome of the negotiations!

This was all the more remarkable, as the Legal Service would take another position when – a couple of months later – the Commission worked out its proposal for a Directive on temporary agency work.

Finally, many have witnessed that an important incentive for the parties to reach agreement in the preceding negotiating rounds was their wish to demonstrate their capability as actors in the social dialogue. However, since they had now concluded three such agreements (on parental leave, part-time work and fixed-term work), this driving force was not as strong in the negotiations on temporary agency work as before. Instead, the pressure had increased, especially on ETUC, to prove that it would not accept an agreement at any price. As already mentioned,[20] some of ETUC's affiliates, among them the European Metal Workers' Federation, were reluctant even to start negotiations until the Directive concerning the agreement on fixed-term work – which they deemed unsatisfactory – had been implemented. The fixed-term work agreement had also been subject to scathing criticism by members of the European Parliament. In her draft report for the Parliament's Committee on Employment and Social Affairs, rapporteur Karin Jöns condemned its material content in its entirety.[21] Even though the resolution finally adopted by the Parliament expresses its dissatisfaction more in terms of regret than of criticism,[22] ETUC was deeply shaken by this reaction.

4. The Legislative Phase

4.1 Start of the Legislative Phase

After the negotiations had broken down, the next concern of all parties was to influence the coming legislation as much as possible by lobbying national governments and EU institutions.

Both sides handed over all their draft texts to the Commission – including those that ETUC had never given to the employers – and now ETUC saw it as constituting something of an advantage that the trade union side had worked on many more texts than the employers.

In addition, the Commission had a good insight into the arguments of both sides through its official Diego Mellado, who had served as a secretary to the impartial chair Jean Degimbe during the negotiations. However, as a matter of principle, the Commission official responsible for the subsequent work with the draft Directive is never the same person who has been a secretary during the negotiations. Thus, after Diego Mellado had informed his colleagues, another official took over the responsibility.

4.2 Another UNI-Europa/CIETT Joint Declaration

During the negotiations there had been two organisations – CIETT on the employers' side and UNI-Europa on the trade union side – that had had a special urge to reach an agreement. After the negotiations had broken down, they resumed their work in the sectoral social dialogue committee, and their first project was to see if they could make a joint declaration on

20 See p. 196.

21 Draft report on the framework agreement on fixed-term work concluded by UNICE, CEEP and ETUC, 12 March 1999, PE 230.208.

22 Resolution on the Commission proposal for a Council Directive concerning the framework agreement on fixed-term work concluded by UNICE, CEEP and ETUC (COM(99)0203 C4- 0220/99) A4-0261/99.

what the objectives of a future directive should be. Considering the criticism that their joint declaration of 3 July 2000 had provoked within ETUC, UNI-Europa was very anxious to involve ETUC in their plans. UNI-Europa's representative informed the ETUC Executive Committee and Steering Committee, and Penny Clarke of the ETUC secretariat participated in all the meetings of the sectoral social dialogue committee. By the end of September, when the parties had managed to draw up a draft, UNI-Europa's Regional Secretary Bernadette Tesch-Ségol had a separate meeting with ETUC's Deputy Secretary General Jean Lapeyre, after which the text was further amended.

On 8 October 2001, CIETT and UNI-Europa published their second joint declaration. The moment was chosen with care – a couple of days later the Commission would have a meeting with national governments' experts, at which they would discuss the possible direction of a European directive on agency work.

The basis of the joint declaration was that both organisations were in favour of European legislation. However, it was not worded as a directly applicable agreement, its purpose was to communicate to the EU institutions CIETT's and UNI-Europa's common views on the *objectives* to be pursued by the Directive.

Among other things the joint declaration stated that the objectives should be:

- To reiterate that non-agency employment and contracts of indefinite duration remain the most common forms of employment, while at the same time the directive should recognise that agency work can contribute to the European Union's employment and economic objectives.
- To recognise that agency employment can be a means of enhancing job opportunities and integration in the labour market for special and/or disadvantaged groups, for instance through training and development opportunities.
- A principle of equal treatment should be established at two levels: the equal treatment obligations which arise from the employment relationship between the agency, being the employer, and the agency worker, being the employee, and the equal treatment obligations which arise from the fact that agency workers are assigned to work for and under the control of a user enterprise.
- As regards conditions of use for agency work, the directive should, on the one hand, ask Member States to identify and, where appropriate, eliminate obstacles of a legal or administrative nature which might limit the opportunities for agency work to play a positive role on the labour market; while on the other hand, it should also recognise that certain prohibitions, restrictions and/or regulations might be necessary in order to prevent potential abuses, "such as the

potential undermining of employment conditions of workers in the user enterprise and/or any other worker in non-agency employment".

- In addition, it should ensure that employment agencies do not make workers available to replace workers who are on strike.
- Contrary to the attitude of the employers' side during the negotiations, CIETT had also accepted that the directive should encourage the social partners to negotiate implementation of the principles included in the directive.

Accordingly, the declaration said nothing about which company – agency or user company – would be the appropriate comparator for which employment conditions. On the other hand, the fact that "the potential undermining of employment conditions of workers in the user enterprise and/or any other worker in non-agency employment" was mentioned as an example of abuse of agency work obviously constituted an argument for comparing the central employment conditions (including pay) with those applied in the user company, with the object of preventing a further undermining of these employment conditions.

4.3 The Commission's Draft Directive

It would take more than five additional months for the Commission to work out a proposal for a Directive. The issues that had been controversial in the social dialogue were controversial also within the Commission. For example, according to an information sheet[23] distributed to Member State governments before the meeting with the national experts on 15 October 2001, the Directorate General for Employment and Social Policy intended to propose a directive that would allow the Member States and the social partners to restrict or prohibit the use of temporary agency work in certain occupational categories or certain areas of economic activity (as foreseen in ILO Convention 181 on Private Employment Agencies), restrictions that, however, should be reviewed periodically to ascertain whether they continue to be justified. When the Commission's final proposal for a Directive[24] was presented on 20 March 2002, only the part that would oblige the Member States to review and discontinue existing restrictions remained. On the other hand, the draft Directive also met the demands of the trade union side on vital points.

23 Information sheet for persons attending the meeting organised by Employment DG for the presentation of a preliminary draft Directive on temporary agency work.

24 Commission proposal for a Directive of the European Parliament and the Council on working conditions for temporary workers, COM(2002) 149 final, OJ No. C 203 E, 27 August 2002, p. 1.

The *aim* of the Directive, as expressed in Article 2, was

a) to improve the quality of temporary work by ensuring that the principle of non-discrimination is applied to temporary workers;

b) to establish a suitable framework for the use of temporary work to contribute to the smooth functioning of the labour and employment market.[25]

As regards the issues that had been stumbling blocks during the negotiations between the social partners the proposal involved the following:

Scope (Article 1): The directive would apply to temporary workers with open-ended contracts, as well as to those with fixed-term contracts with the agency, and to both private and public undertakings engaged in economic activities, irrespective of whether they operate for gain. However, Member States would have the possibility not to apply its provisions to workers participating in public or publicly supported training, integration or vocational training programmes.

Restrictions on the use of agency work (Article 4): Under the heading "Review of restrictions or prohibitions" Member States would be instructed to periodically review any restrictions or prohibitions on temporary agency work for certain groups of workers or sectors of economic activity, in order to verify whether the underlying conditions are still in being. If they are not, they must be discontinued.[26] If restrictions or prohibitions are maintained, the Member States must inform the Commission why they consider that they are still necessary and justified. In order to be maintained they must be justified on grounds of general interest regarding, in particular, the protection of workers. Thus, it is true that in principle the Directive would allow Member States to restrict or prohibit agency work, but the basic assumption expressed by this provision is that such restrictions are a bad thing.

The non-discrimination principle (Article 5): Here, the Commission's Legal Service had obviously changed its mind since its informal advice to the social partners. In Article 5(1) the draft Directive stated that temporary agency workers should receive at least as favourable basic working and employment conditions as a comparable worker in the user enterprise, unless different treatment is justified by objective reasons. And what is more, in Article 3, the concept "basic working and employment conditions" was explicitly defined as including pay!

However, Member States could allow exemptions from this principle in three situations:

---

25 In its first draft the Commission used the expressions 'temporary work' and 'temporary worker'.

26 The English and Portuguese versions were not consistent with the other language versions, and the word 'periodically' was later corrected to 'at least every 5 years'.

1. when agency workers with permanent contracts with the agency continue to be paid between postings (Article 5(2));
2. when agency workers are covered by collective agreements that provide for "an adequate level of protection" (Article 5(3));
3. for assignments on jobs that can be accomplished within six weeks (Article 5(4)).

In its explanatory memorandum, the Commission claimed that the proposal was "largely" based on points on which UNICE/UEAPME/CEEP and ETUC had been able to reach consensus. This statement appears somewhat divorced from reality. As is clear from the above, it is doubtful whether one could say that UNICE/UEAPME/CEEP and ETUC had actually reached consensus on any matter of importance, and not surprisingly, with one exception, the stumbling blocks from the negotiations would continue to cause trouble in the Council.

4.4 First Deliberations in the Council Working Party: "General Reservations"

On 11 June 2002 the Council's Social Questions Working Party met to hear the Commission's presentation of the proposal and to give the Member States' first reactions.[27]

The Council's working parties consist of diplomatic officials and experts from the Member States' governments, and their task is to prepare

[27] The outcome of the proceedings in the working party is recorded in documents in which the positions of different Member States on the details of a proposal are given. My record of the negotiations in the Council is based on these and other official documents from the EU institutions. These sources are problematic in two respects:

First, since the EU institutions still regard the dossier on temporary agency work as an open dossier, they will only give the public access to the documents after having deleted all references to the names of individual Member States. Thus, from these documents it is possible to acquaint oneself with the arguments and standpoints expressed during the negotiations, but not to which Member State a certain opinion is to be attributed. However, I have had access to some early documents in which the names of individual Member States are not deleted. Thanks to the principle of public access to official records enshrined in the Swedish Constitution I have also gained access to the standpoints of the Swedish Government. Thus, to some extent, I have been able to identify the positions of individual Member States after all.

The second problem is that the contents of the Member States' comments and positions are reproduced in concise – and not always very accurate – terms. For example, it may well be that two Member States which seem to share the same view have quite diverging opinions. Therefore, I have refrained from reproducing standpoints that seem odd or inexplicable, and have tried to understand the position of individual Member States as it appears from consecutive documents. The reader may notice that I have elaborated more on the standpoints of the Swedish delegation. The simple explanation is that I have a better knowledge of these.

items that will later appear on the agenda of the Coreper (which consists of the Member States' Permanent Representatives/Ambassadors) and the Council. The meetings are chaired by officials from the Presidency's Permanent Representation. A number of Commission officials also participate in each meeting.

As the chair or a Commission representative presents the proposal paragraph by paragraph, or as new proposals are put on the table, the officials and experts from the Member States make comments and enter reservations on all points that they are not (yet) prepared to accept.

There are various types of reservations, the most fundamental one being the "general" reservation. When a delegation enters a general reservation, it means that the Member State calls the proposal in its entirety into question, for example because of lack of legal basis. Nevertheless, it is customary that it continues to take part in the negotiations on the individual provisions. An illustrative example was when the UK managed to force through a number of exemptions in the Working Time Directive (93/104/EC), whereupon it brought an action against the Council and called for the annulment of the Directive.

While general reservations are not very frequent, Member States regularly enter "scrutiny" reservations on different elements of the proposal. This indicates that the Member State in question cannot yet take a position on a particular point. It may even be an issue on which it has to consult its national parliament, in which case it enters a "parliamentary scrutiny" reservation.

As the negotiations proceed, the Member States successively withdraw their reservations one by one. However, since it is a negotiation, a Member State often formally maintains its reservations on certain points even after they have been solved in a way acceptable, in principle, to that Member State, withdrawing them only after the Member States have reached a compromise on other important outstanding issues. Thus, if the Member States manage to overcome a major stumbling block, the scenario can change very quickly and a large number of reservations be lifted at a time.

Already at the first meeting of the Social Questions Working Party on temporary agency work, three delegations (the UK, Ireland and Germany or Denmark) entered general reservations on the main thrust of the proposal and doubts on whether there was any need at all for Community

---

It goes without saying that in order to get a complete picture of the negotiations between the Member States one must also take into account the many bilateral contacts taken by them or by the Commission between the meetings of the Council working party or the Council itself. I have not been able to cover these contacts in this study.

legislation in this area.[28] They considered that the proposal lacked balance and proportionality, as it did not sufficiently take account of the different legislative situations in the various Member States. The UK added that the initiative could be at odds with the Lisbon Strategy as it could increase the administrative burdens and costs for both agencies and user enterprises, in particular the small and medium-sized ones. A fourth delegation (Germany or Denmark) also doubted that regulation was needed, but indicated that it would contribute constructively to the debate.

Also, it was clear from this first meeting what would be the main issues of concern in the negotiations to come.

To begin with, there was a debate on *the legal basis* of the proposal. One delegation (the UK?) doubted that the directive could be based on Article 137 of the Treaty as it would explicitly cover pay, which is excluded from EC competence under Article 137(6).[29]

A number of delegations were worried about the implications and scope of Article 4 on *review of restrictions and prohibitions* on agency work. In particular, one delegation took the view that there was an imbalance between this Article and Article 5 on the non-discrimination principle, as some Member States would have to take radical steps to comply with Article 5, while other Member States might not be required to take any positive steps according to Article 4. Another delegation felt that unless a deadline was set for reviewing restrictions this Article would amount to mere window-dressing. The complaint about *unfairness* between the Member States would continue to echo through the course of negotiations until they finally broke down a year later.

As in the social dialogue the year before, there was disagreement over who would be *the comparable worker* for the purpose of the non-discrimination principle. Several delegations indicated that they would have difficulties with using a permanent worker in the user undertaking as comparator. In Germany, for example, this principle was applied only if the agency worker had an assignment for more than 12 months with the user enterprise. Another delegation suggested that agency workers should be compared with permanent workers in the same sector, but were contradicted by delegations from Member States where sectoral collective bargaining is an unfamiliar phenomenon. Sweden was not against the principle of the comparator being a worker in the user company, but it foresaw practical problems with implementing such a provision. Although over 90% of Swedish workers are covered by sectoral collec-

28 Outcome of proceedings of the Social Questions Working Party, 10131/1/02 REV1, SOC 321 CODEC 789, 2 July 2002.

29 Article 137(5) after the coming into force of the Nice Treaty.

tive agreements, fixed pay scales or standard rates are getting more and more unusual. As from the late 1990s, the individual worker's wage is normally negotiated at workplace level according to principles laid down in the sectoral agreement, and it consists of a number of components, some of which are related to individual factors, such as the worker's performance, responsibility, and so on. This makes it difficult to identify which workers are comparable.[30]

A large number of delegations had problems in one way or another with the proposed *exemptions from the non-discrimination principle*. Some questioned the possibility of making exemptions by means of collective agreements, while others argued that the possibility of exempting agency workers carrying out assignments not exceeding six weeks could open the door to misuse. One delegation also questioned the economic justification for this exemption. Others, on the other hand, called for the exemption to cover a significantly longer period.

In addition, two delegations – the UK and Sweden – for very different reasons questioned whether it was at all appropriate to use the concept of non-discrimination in this context. The UK argued that the Directive was an instrument of labour market policy, and as such not analogous with protection against discrimination under Article 13 of the Treaty. Sweden's doubts were of a theoretic-systematic nature: it questioned whether it is correct to say that an employer discriminates against an employee in relation to another employee whose conditions the employer cannot control as he is not the employer of the latter employee. If the concept of discrimination were applied to such situations, it would be watered down, Sweden feared. Different Member States' differing interpretations of the concept of discrimination continued to cause misunderstandings throughout the process in the Council.

As a conclusion, the Presidency felt called upon to point out that the Directive was aimed at regulating the future labour market in the EU, and that therefore it should not just reflect the current situation in the Member States.

On 25 June and 16 July the working party met again and started to discuss the individual provisions of the draft Directive.[31]

---

30 For an account for the individualisation of wage formation in Sweden since the 1990s see Ahlberg and Bruun (2005).

31 Outcome of proceedings of the Social Questions Working Party; 10425/02 SOC 335 CODEC 825, 11 July 2002, Outcome of proceedings of the Social Questions Working Party, 10586/02 SOC 339 CODEC 857, 24 July 2002, Corrigendum to Outcome of the proceedings of the Social Questions Working Party, 10586/02 COR 1 SOC 339, 25 July 2002.

On *scope* (Article 1) Ireland asked for a clarification of the implications of the phrase "a temporary agency, which is the employer". It seemed to confirm that there is an employment relationship between the agency and the worker, which is not always the case in Ireland. The Commission responded that if the agency were not the employer, the Directive would not apply at all. Germany insisted that non-profit making companies – for example, hospitals – should be excluded, as German legislation did not cover such companies. The Commission, for its part, found it difficult to understand why hospitals should have to comply with the working time directive, but not with this one.

There was an animated debate on the very *aim* of the Directive (Article 2). Again, the non-discrimination principle as such was questioned. Ireland declared that even if it did not disagree with the aims, it was concerned about how these aims were developed in Articles 3 and 4 and about the practical difficulties of implementing the principle of non-discrimination. The UK reiterated its view that non-discrimination was not the only way to regulate the labour market. It stressed that its greatest cause for concern was that the agency worker would be compared with an employee in the user undertaking from the first day. This was unreasonable, as one could not compare a person who had been out of a job for a long time with a permanent worker.

Sweden, in consequence of its perception of the concept of discrimination, preferred to identify the primary aim of the Directive as "improving the basic working and employment conditions" of agency workers.

Germany did not question the principle of non-discrimination as such, but supported the general approach of the UK that people should be given a chance to get a foothold in the labour market, which would only be likely if they could be paid less than a permanent worker in the user undertaking. Thus, in its view, the conditions of the user enterprise should not be applicable until after an assignment of at least 12 months.

France, Greece and Luxemburg agreed with the aims and pointed out that the inclusion of workers in the labour market should go hand-in-hand with maintaining the quality of working conditions. Luxemburg added that the primary role of work agencies was not to reinsert workers into the labour market, but to provide other companies with workers.

The Commission upheld its view that the non-discrimination principle must be included. But it pointed out that the proposal only provided for a limited application of this principle. Due to the possible exemptions, up to 60% of agency workers would not be covered.

As regards the last paragraph in Article 2, which stated that the purpose of the Directive was to contribute to the smooth functioning of the labour and employment market, Germany, Ireland, Italy, France, Greece and Sweden stressed that the aim of increasing *levels* of employment must also be highlighted. France and Greece added that both quality working conditions and improving the employment situation were part of the Lisbon goals and not in contradiction with each other.

In Article 3 on *Definitions*, there were two issues in particular that caused debate. On the definition of "*comparable worker*" France, Spain and Sweden expressed support for the Commission's proposal, even though Sweden had some doubts about the practical application in its national context. However, the UK pointed out that it would raise substantial difficulties in the UK and affect it disproportionately, as it had no tradition of collective agreements and a comparator in the user company would have to be found for each specific worker. Therefore, it suggested an approach based on minimum standards. Ireland agreed with the UK on many points, but would prefer an approach that allowed Member States to choose between the different comparators.

There was also a debate on which factors that should be taken into account when deciding whom the comparable worker is. Spain, Sweden, Belgium and Portugal questioned the need to take account of "seniority, qualifications and skills" as mentioned in the draft and also saw difficulties of applying this in practice. The UK, Ireland and Austria all favoured the reference to "seniority", although they admitted that it might induce practical problems. Austria suggested that experience should also be taken into account. Here, the Commission was willing to clarify the draft or to refer to "experience" rather than "seniority".

The second point of conflict in Article 3 concerned the definition of the concept "*basic working and employment conditions*". The UK and Ireland could not accept that the non-discrimination principle would cover pay, as pay is excluded from EC competence under Article 137(6) of the Treaty.[32] The working party agreed that this issue would be discussed at a later occasion in the presence of the Council's Legal Service. Apart from that, Denmark, Finland, Germany, Ireland and Sweden asked the Commission to clarify what was included in the concept of pay, for example in relation to Community legislation on equal pay. Notably, Sweden felt that certain elements, such as pension entitlements, should not be covered. France did not want the scope and content to be clarified further and wanted to stick to national legislation in this area. The Commission agreed, and answered that the definition of the concept of pay itself would be left to the Member States. It also stated that it had not intended to cover additional social security benefits.

The debate on *the restrictions on the use of agency work* (Article 4) hovered between the opinion that there was an imbalance, in terms of binding requirements, between this Article and the Article on non-dis-

32 Article 137(5) after the coming into force of the Nice Treaty.

crimination (Ireland), and the view that the provision was not justified at all in this Directive and should be deleted or referred to a recital only (France, Italy and Luxembourg). As temporary agency work was subject to some restrictions in legislation or collective agreements in most Member States, several delegations asked for clarification on what reasons the Commission would accept for maintaining such restrictions and prohibitions. Austria and Sweden were of the view that agency workers should not be used to replace workers on strike or where there have been lay-offs. The Commission responded that Article 4 was based on the agreement reached between the social partners, the ILO Convention 181 on Private Employment Agencies and case law from the European Court of Justice. It pointed out that even though it did not consider every restriction, such as that in the construction sector in Germany, to be wrong it felt that they should nevertheless be reviewed.

When the details of the *principle of non-discrimination* (Article 5) were debated, Ireland, Portugal and the UK once again questioned whether the objective of protecting agency workers would be best served by application of a fundamental principle of non-discrimination, while at the same time a wide range of exemptions were allowed. On the contrary Belgium, France, Spain and Greece expressed their general support for this principle. The Commission pointed out that the exemptions provided for in Article 5 were not exemptions from the fundamental non-discrimination principle. Ireland, Italy and the UK also wanted the Commission to clarify what were the "objective reasons" that would justify differences in treatment. However, the Commission did not want to draw up a list of reasons and had deliberately left this term vague to allow Member States more leeway.

When it came to *the first exemption* (Article 5(2)) from the main rule, Sweden and Greece voiced concern that if agency workers with "permanent" contracts who continue to be paid between postings were exempted, they could end up having worse conditions than those with fixed-term contracts. Germany, which was the primary addressee of this provision, rather wanted to delete the word "permanent" and have the possibility of applying the exemption to workers with fixed-term contracts as well, since both categories receive continuous pay between assignments in Germany.

The second exemption (Article 5(3)), which allowed derogations where agency workers are covered by collective agreements that ensure adequate protection, was generally supported by Denmark, France and Sweden. However, France, Belgium and Luxembourg asked the Commission to confirm that the exemptions in paragraphs 2 and 3 were exemptions from the principle of comparability with the user enterprise rather than exemptions from the general principle of non-discrimination. The Commission confirmed that this was the case. Ireland, Portugal and the UK were also concerned about the nature of this provision and asked for clarification about the extent of the freedom given to the social partners. The UK pointed out that the overall formulation appeared to interfere with the autonomy of the social partners. Luxemburg expressed concern whether this provision meant that the social partners in the user enterprise could define a regime for the agency workers. Austria suggested that the word "adequate" should be replaced by "comparable". The Netherlands asked who would be responsible for checking whether a collective agreement provided sufficient protection. The Commission pointed out that this provision was similar to provisions in the working time Directive and that derogations were acceptable if they were agreed under collective bargaining.

As many as eight delegations (Austria, Belgium, Spain, France, Greece, Luxembourg, the Netherlands and Sweden) were against the possibility of *exempting assignments of up to six weeks* (5(4)) from application of the non-discrimination principle, both because they foresaw difficulties when implementing and a risk of abuse of such an exemption period. In contrast, Germany, Ireland and the UK welcomed such a provision, even if they would prefer an even longer qualifying period. Italy indicated that it had no problems with this optional provision.

Among the final provisions, Article 9 stated that the Directive would not prejudice Member States' right to apply or introduce *provisions which are more favourable to workers*. Neither would it constitute sufficient grounds for justifying a *reduction in the general level of protection of workers*. France and Portugal questioned whether this Article was coherent with Article 4, which prescribed that restrictions and prohibitions on temporary agency work must be reviewed and discontinued. The Commission made it clear that Member States could change its existing legislation provided that the minimum requirements were applied.

Several of the other provisions of the Directive were debated as well, such as Article 6(2), according to which Member States must ensure that clauses hindering agency workers from taking up employment direct with the user enterprise may be declared null and void; Article 6(5), which would oblige Member States to take measures in order to improve agency workers' access to training; and Article 7 on collective representation of agency workers. But the disagreement on these issues seems to have been manageable. In order to make my account of the negotiations in the Council more readable, I will omit the debate on these issues and concentrate on the stumbling blocks.

4.5 Interaction with the Parliament

In parallel with the work in the Council Working Party, the European Parliament's Committee for Employment and Social Affairs was preparing its report for the Parliament's first reading. Often, the debate in the

Council pays little attention to the proposals discussed in the Parliament until matters are brought to a head, ultimately referred to conciliation between the Council and the Parliament. However, this time it was different. As will be seen from the minutes of the meeting of the Social Questions Working Party on 16 September 2002, the Commission in particular put forward several ideas inspired by the EP rapporteur.[33]

It was understood that all delegations maintained their general, scrutiny and parliamentary reservations from the very first meeting, and the Presidency asked them not to repeat their positions on the key issues unless they had modified them. This meeting was devoted to examining the details of the proposal, and the Working Party would try to advance on the formulation of individual provisions and the structure of the Directive, irrespective of the disagreement on the points of principle.

On one point, there was immediate agreement: all further debate on Article 2 on the *aim* of the Directive would be left until the discussions of the contents of the proposal were completed.

When it came to the definition of "*comparable worker*" it was as difficult to reach agreement on the details as on the basic principles. For the first time, the idea of a hypothetical comparison was raised, and awakened the interest of several delegations.

Also, as some delegations had questioned whether it was possible to cover *pay* in a Directive based on Article 137 EC, a representative of the Council Legal Service attended the meeting and gave an oral opinion on this matter. The official record of this meeting does not reveal what he or she said. However, the Legal Service was asked to resume and develop its interpretation in a written opinion to a later meeting.

On 8 October 2002 the proposal for a Directive on temporary agency work was on the Council's (Employment, Social Policy, Health and Consumer Affairs) agenda for the first time.[34] At this stage, the actual negotiations were still handled by the Social Questions Working Party and had not yet been lifted to the political level. The Danish Presidency simply reported on the progress achieved so far and mentioned which issues had to be solved in the months ahead, such as the principle of non-discrimination and the concept of "comparable worker". The Presidency concluded by informing the ministers that it intended to return to the issue at the Council meeting at the beginning of December.

33 Outcome of proceedings of the Social Questions Working Party, 1222/02 SOC 395, CODEC 1132, 25 September 2002.

34 12746/02 (Presse 306), 2454th Council Meeting, Employment, Social Policy, Health and Consumer Affairs.

On 15 October 2002 the Social Questions Working Party made progress on a number of issues, all but one of minor importance.[35]

First, it was agreed that the term "temporary worker", which until then had been used throughout the draft, should be replaced by "*temporary agency worker*".

Three new *definitions* were inserted in Article 3. Another amendment in the same Article made clear that the definition of the concepts of "*worker*" and "*pay*" was to be left to the Member States, even though Ireland and the UK still insisted on excluding pay from the scope of the Directive.

Hoping to get round the difficulties with regard to the *non-discrimination principle*, the Commission suggested that the Working Party should follow the line under consideration by the Parliament's rapporteurs. Their idea was to concentrate not on who is the comparable worker, but on ensuring that the treatment of temporary workers is at least equivalent to the treatment given to a worker directly employed for the same duration by the user enterprise. Such a text in Article 5 would also make the definition of "*comparable worker*" in Article 3 superfluous. The majority of the delegations were generally open to considering this approach and the Commission would work on a simplified version till the next meeting.

However, none of the general, scrutiny or parliamentary reservations from the very first meeting was lifted.

On 23 October 2002 the European Parliament's Committee for Employment and Social Affairs tabled its report for the Parliament's first reading. The report included 54 amendments to the Commission's proposal.[36] A general remark made by the rapporteur Ieke van den Burg was that the Commission should have built more on existing regulatory texts. For example, it had not referred to either the ILO Convention (C181) and Recommendation (R188) on Private Employment Agencies or to the joint declaration of UNI-Europa and CIETT. Also, it had used expressions and terms that were close to provisions in, for example, the Fixed-term Work Directive, the Directive on Posting of Workers and the ILO Convention, but still slightly different from these. This might cause interpretative problems and barriers in implementation, application and jurisdiction. Therefore, many of the amendments were intended to bring definitions and obligations more into line.

---

35 Outcome of proceedings of the Social Questions Working Party, 13291/02 SOC 453 CODEC 1294, 18 October 2002, Note to Social Questions Working Party, 12898/02 SOC 423 CODEC 1228, 10 October 2002, Note to Social Questions Working Party, 12899/02 SOC 424 CODEC 1229, 10 October 2002.

36 A5-0356/2002.

Other amendments were intended to formulate the aims and objectives of the Directive more clearly, and to ensure that agency workers – apart from the protection provided for by the non-discrimination clause – are guaranteed basic protection by labour law and social security, which cannot under any circumstances be exempted or derogated from.

On 4 November the Council's Social Questions Working Party met again.[37] By now, the Working Party had also received the written opinion from the Council's Legal Service on the purport of Article 137(6),[38] which says that the provisions of Article 137 shall not apply to pay.[39] The Legal Service states that the purpose of this provision is to exclude the adoption of uniform provisions for the Member States where such provisions consist primarily of setting the level and method for calculating pay, for example, setting a minimum guaranteed wage. However, it does not rule out the possibility of adopting measures intended to improve the working environment, measures on working conditions, on information and consultation or on integrating people excluded from the labour market, even if these measures have an impact on pay. The purpose of the proposed Directive was to introduce non-discriminatory treatment of temporary workers, but it was not intended to regulate the level or method of setting workers' wages. Thus, these issues would continue to be governed by national law and collective agreements. With regard to the UK's concerns about the autonomy of the social partners the Legal Service concludes that although they are in principle free to negotiate and conclude agreements, they must observe the limits set by national and Community laws just like any other economic operator. In this case, they would be authorised to conclude agreements which derogate from the principle of equal treatment set out in the Directive as long as an adequate level of protection is provided. With regard to wage negotiations for individuals, the Legal Service found that it was flexible enough as it would enable employers to treat agency workers differently from comparable workers in the user enterprise where there is objective justification for such treatment. The Legal Service concluded that it would not be incompatible with Article 137(6) of the EC Treaty to refer to pay in the Directive.

37 Outcome of proceedings of the Social Questions Working Party, 13975/02 SOC 496 CODEC 1394, 12 November 2002, Corrigendum to Outcome of proceedings of the Social Questions Working Party, 13975/02COR 1, SOC 496 CODEC 1394, 20 November 2002.

38 Article 137(5) after the coming into force of the Nice Treaty.

39 Legal Service contribution to the proceedings of the Working Party on Social Questions on 14 October 2002, 13756/02 JUR 433 SOC 482 CODEC 1366, 4 November 2002.

Nevertheless, Ireland and the UK informed the Working Party that they maintained their substantive reservations on the inclusion of pay until they had had the opportunity to examine the Legal Service's opinion more closely. However, without prejudice to their reservation on pay, Ireland and the UK stressed that *if* pay was included, the text should make clear that occupational pensions were excluded. This opinion was supported by Denmark and the Netherlands.

At the same meeting, the Commission presented an amended version of the Parliamentary Committee's draft on *the non-discrimination principle*. It read: "The basic working and employment conditions applicable to a temporary agency worker shall be at least those which would apply to such a worker if he/she were employed by the user undertaking to occupy the same post." The majority of the delegations were generally open to considering this approach, even though Germany, Ireland, the UK and Sweden had reservations. Sweden noted that the concept of a hypothetical comparable worker would be difficult to apply in the Swedish context. The UK pointed out that its position with regard to this paragraph was directly linked to the outcome of discussions on the definition of "*basic working and employment conditions*", that is, that pay should be excluded.

In many respects, the debate was a repetition of what had been said at previous meetings. As regards the possibility to make *derogations by way of collective agreements* "as long as an adequate level of protection is provided", there was a division between those delegations which seemed to fear that there would be too much room for the social partners' own discretion, and those – like Finland and the UK – that expressed concern about the implications of this provision for collective autonomy. Ireland noted that this exemption would be likely to work to the advantage of only some countries.

4.6 The Parliament's First Reading

On 21 November the European Parliament debated the report of the Committee for Employment and Social Affairs in plenary, and adopted 61 amendments to the Commission's proposal for a Directive.[40]

In Article 1 on *scope*, the Parliament wanted to introduce a new paragraph, obviously intended to satisfy Germany's interests. It would allow Member States – where it is customary in national law and practice – not to apply the non-discrimination principle on specific public and private undertakings engaged in non-profit-making activities.

40 PED T5-0562/2002, Working conditions for temporary workers.

Another amendment had the purpose of making clear that trainees in general – for example, persons who participate in programmes geared to integrating problem groups into the labour market – should not fall within the scope of the Directive.

Several amendments were made to Article 4 on *restrictions on the use of agency work.* The first paragraph was reworded, so that it would explicitly allow Member States to maintain and introduce restrictions in line with the ILO Convention.

Secondly, the grounds that could justify the maintaining of restrictions and prohibitions were further specified to include the protection of temporary agency workers, the health and safety and other risks posed to certain groups of workers or sectors of economic activity, the proper functioning of the labour market and the need to prevent potential abuses. Here, reference was made to the joint CIETT–UNI-Europa declaration.

Thirdly, a new paragraph stated that the provisions on review and discontinuation of restrictions and prohibitions would be without prejudice to reasonable arrangements for registration, licensing, certification, guaranteeing or monitoring of agency work.

Fourthly, in line with ILO Convention 181 on Private Employment Agencies, restrictions and prohibitions should be maintained or introduced to prevent agency workers from being used to replace workers engaged in collective action.

The most vigorous debate centred on *the non-discrimination principle* and the possible exemptions from that principle.

The basic principle in Article 5(1) was reworded in line with the proposal from the Committee for Employment and Social Affairs (see above).

"*The German exemption*" in Article 5(2) was partly narrowed, partly extended. On the one hand, the exemption for workers with permanent contracts could be used only for "pay and specific pay elements", not for other basic working and employment conditions. On the other hand, it would be applicable both to agency workers with permanent contracts and to those with "other" contracts, however, on condition not only that they are guaranteed continuous payment between assignments, but also that the pay is "adequate".

On the initiative of one of the Danish Members of Parliament Article 5(3), which would allow for *exemptions by way of collective agreements* as long as they ensure adequate protection, was amended with reference to legal certainty and to the autonomy of the social partners. Interference with existing collective agreements must be avoided, and neither party should be able to create uncertainty by appealing to the Court of Justice to set aside the agreement on grounds of inadequate protection, she argued. As a consequence the reservation "as long as an adequate level of protection is provided" was deleted.

The last exemption, the *six-week qualification period* in Article 5(4), was as controversial in the Parliament as in the Council's working party. In opposition to those Members of the Parliament who argued that six weeks was far too short, the majority took the view that the qualification period was in conflict with the very nature of agency work, which by definition can be for a very short period, and that the qualification period would, in fact, completely exclude the majority of agency workers from equal treatment. Thus, this paragraph was deleted.

Notwithstanding the fact that the Parliament rejected the six-week qualification period, it drafted a transitional provision to be added to Article 11 on implementation of the Directive. It implied that in Member States (in fact Ireland and the UK) where the principle of non-discrimination is not laid down when the Directive enters into force and where the exemptions provided for in 5(2) and 5(3) are not normal practice, the state may – for a transitional period up to the planned evaluation of the Directive – decide not to apply this principle with respect to pay for assignments up to six weeks, as long as an "adequate" level of pay is provided from day one.

4.7 The Presidency's Four Questions

On 26 November the Danish Presidency sent a note to the Council (Employment, Social Policy, Health and Consumer Affairs) that would meet a week later.[41]

According to the note the dossier on temporary agency work had been a priority for the Danish Presidency and there had been a lot of progress on the issue in a very short time. At the same time, the Presidency had noted a number of outstanding issues. They were:

- *Review of restrictions and prohibitions* in Article 4: a number of Member States had questioned whether this Article was appropriate in this Directive. The Presidency saw two alternatives to accommodate those countries: either the Article should be deleted, or it should be confined to an obligation to register such restrictions and prohibitions at intervals. Another possibility was to explore the approach of the European Parliament, which provided for an explicit permission for Member States to introduce or maintain restrictions and prohibitions.
- *Duration of the so-called exemption or "grace-period"* in Article 5(4): a large group of Member States either wanted to maintain the

41 Note from the Presidency to Council (Employment, Social Policy, Health and Consumer Affairs), 14681/02 SOC 557 CODEC 1521, 26 November 2002.

six-week period as a maximum or rejected it completely, while others called for a considerably longer period. Here, the Council could examine the possibility of allowing an exemption from the pay obligation or an extension of the "grace period", either for all countries or for those countries where the present proposal would be especially burdensome in terms of changes to the national system. Another possibility could be to introduce an approach based on minimum protection for a certain period. The Presidency also drew attention to the Parliament's amendments which replaced the general exemption in Article 5(4) with a transitional provision for the period up to the evaluation of the Directive.

- *Temporary agency work as a labour market instrument:* some Member States questioned whether the *scope* of the Directive, as expressed in Article 1(3), would allow Member States to use temporary agency work in a sufficiently flexible manner as an instrument of their national labour market policies. Therefore, the wording of the Article remained to be examined in detail.
- *Principle of non-discrimination and the concept of comparable worker* in Article 5(1) and Article 3(1)(b): here the Presidency noted that the Social Questions Working Party had made progress on a possible solution that would build on the concept of a hypothetical worker in the user enterprise, and added that the Parliament had proposed a similar solution which would obviate the need for a definition of "comparable worker". However, the definite drafting of this provision was still to be agreed.
- *The role of the social partners*: several delegations had expressed concern about the implications of the provision in Article 5(3) (exemptions from the basic rule on non-discrimination by way of collective agreements) with regard to the autonomy of the social partners. The Presidency concluded that the details of this provision would be discussed further in light of these concerns and the amendment that the Parliament had made to Article 5(3).

Against this background, there were four questions that the Presidency wanted to discuss:

- Did Member States agree that Article 4 on restrictions and prohibitions should not imply an actual duty on Member States to change national legislation or collective agreements in this field?
- Were there any ways of reaching a compromise solution on the exemption period in Article 5(4)?
- How should the Directive take account of temporary agency work used as an instrument of national labour market policy?
- And finally, did the Member States agree that all five outstanding issues mentioned above should be part of an overall compromise solution, with Article 4 and 5(4) being the key elements?

4.8 The Commission's Amended Proposal

Two days later, on 28 November, the Commission presented its amended proposal for a directive.[42]

Out of 58 amendments adopted by the Parliament, the Commission had accepted 31, some of them in full and others "in principle" – the latter meaning that it agreed with the tenor but would modify the formulation.

A new recital was included which said that the provisions on restrictions or prohibitions on agency work would be without prejudice to national legislation or practices prohibiting agency workers being used to *replace workers on strike*. However, there was no corresponding provision in the Directive itself.

Unlike the Parliament, the Commission had not met the wish of Germany to exclude non-profit-making undertakings from *the scope* of the Directive (Article 1).

However, three new elements were added to Article 2 on the *aim* of the Directive: to ensure the protection of agency workers, to recognise temporary agencies as employers and to contribute to job creation.

An amendment to Article 3 meant that the *definition of the concept "pay"* would be left to the Member States.

Article 4 on *restrictions and prohibitions* had been thoroughly rewritten in line with the amendments adopted by the European Parliament. Now it began with a paragraph that specified on what grounds restrictions or prohibitions would be justified, namely "on grounds of general interest relating in particular to the protection of temporary workers, the requirements of health and safety at work and the need to ensure that the labour market functions properly and abuses are prevented".

The provisions on the review of such restrictions and prohibitions had been made less stringent and placed in a second paragraph. The requirement that the review should be made "regularly" or "within five years" was deleted.

Finally, a third paragraph made clear that the paragraphs mentioned above were without prejudice to national requirements with regard to registration, licensing, certification, financial guarantees or monitoring of temporary agencies.

The *principle of non-discrimination* (Article 5(1)) built on the draft that the Commission had presented to the Council's Working Party on 4 November and read: "The basic working and employment conditions of

42 Amended proposal for a Dir lective of the European Parliament and the Council on working conditions for temporary workers, COM(2002) 701 final.

temporary workers shall be, for the duration of their posting at a user undertaking, at least those that would apply if they had been recruited directly by that enterprise to occupy the same job."

The exemptions from the principle in Article 5(1) had on the whole been made more stringent, compared to the Commission's original proposal.

Now, the *"German" exemption* in Article 5(2) would only be applicable to pay, not to other working and employment conditions. The other amendments made to this paragraph by the Parliament were rejected by the Commission.

Nor did it accept the deletion of the last sentence of Article 5(3), which specified that *exemptions by way of collective agreements* could be made on condition that "an adequate level of protection is provided".

The option for Member States to allow *exemptions for assignments up to six weeks* was still there, although according to the amended proposal it would only apply with regard to pay, not to other basic working and employment conditions.

4.9 Further Deliberations in the Council's Working Party

When the Council met on 2–3 December, the Ministers had an in-depth debate on the issues raised by the Presidency.[43] The Presidency concluded that all five issues should form part of an overall compromise package, the two overriding issues to be taken into account in order to achieve a political agreement under the Greek presidency being the prohibitions and restrictions on the use of temporary agency work and the possible period of exemption from the principle of non-discrimination. What does not emerge from the minutes is that the Swedish minister had declared that Sweden was prepared to block the whole Directive unless the autonomy of the social partners to conclude collective agreements as they see it was guaranteed.

This was the last Council meeting under the Danish Presidency. After the turn of the year, Greece took over.

In January 2003 the Social Questions Working Party met twice to examine the Commission's amended proposal for a Directive.[44]

---

43 Draft Minutes 2470th meeting of the Council of the European Union (EMPLOYMENT, SOCIAL POLICY, HEALTH AND CONSUMER AFFAIRS), 15071/02.

44 Outcome of proceedings of the Social Questions Working Party, 5332/03 SOC 14 CODEC 36, 16 January 2003, Outcome of proceedings of the Social Questions Working Party, 5772/03 SOC 33 CODEC 91, 4 February 2003, Corrigendum to Outcome of proceedings of the Social Questions Working Party, 5772/03 COR 1 SOC 33 CODEC 91, 7 February 2003.

At least two delegations still maintained their general reservations on the text, while a large number maintained scrutiny reservations on specific provisions.

Nevertheless, the delegations had made enough progress to be able to resume the debate on the *aim* of the Directive (Article 2), which they had not discussed since September 2002. Again, the debate reflected a fundamental disagreement on what was to be achieved. Some delegations, including the Swedish, objected to the putting of job creation and the functioning of the labour market, as mentioned in the second paragraph, on an equal footing with the protection of agency workers. To these delegations, the protection of workers was the main aim of the Directive. One delegation commented that job creation should be a consequence of this, rather than an aim in itself. On the contrary, other delegations regarded agency work primarily as a labour market measure and argued that the correct legal basis for the Directive would be Article 126 EC on the Member States' employment policy rather than Article 137 that authorises the EC to adopt Directives on social policy.[45]

The debate on the substantive provisions confirmed that they were still far from coming to an agreement.

Irrespective of the opinion of the Council's Legal Service, Ireland and the UK insisted that the definition of *basic working and employment conditions* in Article 3 should not include "*pay*".

A large number of delegations welcomed the Commission's new approach, inspired by the European Parliament, to Article 4 on *review of restrictions and prohibitions*. However, many of them still thought that the Article should be made less obliging, if not deleted. The motivations varied from a total rejection of the mandatory review and the obligation to discontinue restrictions, to concerns about the right of social partners to conclude collective agreements. Some delegations were concerned that the term "on the grounds of general interest" as justification for restrictions was too vague and difficult to apply. Somebody raised the idea of asking the Council's Legal Service to give its opinion on how to interpret the new wording.

As the direct comparison with a worker in the user enterprise had been sorted out with the new wording of Article 5, there was broad support for changing its heading from "*The principle of non-discrimination*" to "*The principle of equal treatment*". However, when it came to the exemptions from the main rule, disagreement persisted. The Swedish delegation sharpened its tone in accordance with the Swedish minister's declaration

---

45 In fact, neither Article 126 nor any of the other Articles in the 'Employment chapter' (Title VIII) authorises the EU to adopt d*irectives* on employment policy.

in the Council of 2–3 December. Till then, little attention had been paid to Sweden's concerns for *the autonomy of the social partners,* but now it indicated that its overall position on the Directive would depend on a satisfactory solution in this respect. Supported by Denmark and Finland, it called for a deletion of the phrase "as long as an adequate level of protection is provided" in Article 5(3) and suggested a new wording of the exemption, intended to safeguard the right to conclude collective agreements and to prevent such agreements from being subject to judicial examination by the European Court of Justice. The Commission for its part was prepared to accept it if there was general consensus on the text and if it allowed Sweden to lift some of its other reservations. Still, one delegation (Luxemburg) felt that there was a need to add some kind of safeguard clause (for example "sous réserve de garantir l'effet utile de cette directive"). And Ireland and the UK maintained their reservations on this paragraph because of their general concern about the imbalance in the proposal in respect of derogations which would be to the advantage of some Member States but not to others.

Germany stated that, in its view, Article 5(4), allowing *exemptions for assignments not exceeding six weeks*, was the most important provision, as it would provide the necessary flexibility to integrate people into the labour force. Therefore the transitional provisions proposed by the European Parliament were not acceptable. In a spirit of compromise, Germany would accept a shorter period than the twelve months that it had originally advocated, but it must be significantly longer than six weeks. Also, it should apply to all working conditions and not only to pay. In order to prevent abuse, the "grace" period should be in the form of a qualifying period, as it would remove the possibility of a post being reclassified. It proposed a text according to which Member States would be allowed not to apply Article 5(1) "until a temporary worker has worked on an assignment or series of assignments with the same user enterprise for a continuous period of (x) months". A couple of delegations supported the demand for a longer period and this draft text. Another group of delegations could accept some form of compromise, such as the transitional arrangements proposed by the Parliament. However, five delegations were opposed to any derogation even if it was limited to pay, and called for the deletion of paragraph 4. The Commission for its part stated that it could not accept more than six weeks in Article 5(4). No progress was made.

On one point, though, the delegations could more or less agree. A new final paragraph should be added to Article 5 in order to clarify that the principle of equal treatment would not apply to occupational social security schemes, including occupational pensions and sick pay, or to financial participation schemes.

The following meeting of the Working Party took place on 11 February 2003.[46] The delegations took a rest from the debate *on review of restrictions or prohibitions* and *the principle of equal treatment*, and tried to make progress on, *inter alia*, Article 1 (Scope) and Article 2 (Aim).

One of the delegations that took a special interest in the function of agency work as a labour market measure wanted to narrow *the scope* of the Directive, and drafted an amendment to Article 1(3) which would give Member States the option to exclude not only "public or publicly supported" training and integration programmes from its application, as proposed by the Commission, but also other measures specifically aiming at integrating unemployed workers. A couple of delegations were open to exploring possible compromises in this direction.

A new draft on Article 2 was tabled. According to this draft, *the aim* of the Directive would be to ensure the protection of temporary agency workers "*while taking into account*[47] the need for establishing a suitable framework for the use of temporary agency work with a view to contributing effectively to the creation of jobs and to the development of flexible forms of working". Thus, job creation would not be an aim in itself, but an interest that had to be taken into account.

4.10 Progress on Two Points

On 21 February the Social Questions Working Party reported to the Permanent Representatives Committee (Coreper) on the outcome of proceedings so far.[48]

It concluded that, in spite of much progress having been achieved by the Working Party, there were two issues of principle relating to Articles 4 and 5(4) that could only be resolved at the political level. Moreover, further progress on a number of other outstanding issues was likely to be difficult until a satisfactory solution had been found on these key issues. The key issues were the review of restrictions and prohibitions and the duration of the exemption from the principle of equal treatment. The positions were as follows:

As regards Article 4 on *restrictions and prohibitions*, a large number of delegations still had difficulties, as they did not consider it appropriate to change their national legislation or collective agreements on restrictions on the use of agency work. Three of them called for the deletion of the whole Article, while another (Sweden) maintained scrutiny reserva-

46 Outcome of proceedings of the Social Questions Working Party, 6316/03 SOC 65 CODEC 152, 14 February 2003.

47 My italics.

48 Report from the Social Questions Working Party to the Permanent Representatives Committee (Part 1), 6526/03 SOC 71 CODEC 178, 21 February 2003.

tions in this respect. Certain other delegations had expressed difficulties with the second paragraph of the Article on mandatory *review and discontinuation* of restrictions and prohibitions. One of them would prefer to delete the whole paragraph, while two other delegations were in favour of deleting the last two sentences of that paragraph, with the effect that there would be no obligation to *discontinue* restrictions or prohibitions, only to *review* them. On the other hand, four delegations could only consider deletion of the requirement that the Member States inform the Commission of the results of the review. The Commission, for its part, had indicated that it was willing to be flexible in order to find a solution that all delegations could accept.

The positions of the delegations on *the six-week exemption period* in Article 5(4) remained diametrically opposed. As many as eleven delegations took the view that the equal treatment principle should apply to pay from day one. Of these, four had indicated that by way of compromise they would consider some form of transitional arrangement in line with the Parliament's proposal. On the other hand, Denmark, Germany, Ireland and the UK wanted a significantly longer exemption period. Two of them called for a period of around twelve months in the form of a qualifying period. A third delegation had indicated that it wanted an exemption period of at least six months, while the fourth had mentioned the possibility of other compromise solutions, such as a "phasing-in" approach.

In addition, the Working Party mentioned two other outstanding questions: *temporary agency work as a labour market instrument,* and *the autonomy of the social partners.* The first referred to the wish of some delegations to be able to exclude various types of measures aimed at integrating unemployed workers from the scope of the Directive. The second alluded to the matter of principle of the Nordic countries that collective agreements according to Article 5(3) should not be subject to judicial examination by the European Court of Justice.

Besides these key, or outstanding, issues, different delegations still had reservations on almost every Article. However, many of them were linked to their opinions on the main outstanding issues and were likely to be lifted if satisfactory solutions could be found for them. For example, it seems that no severe objections remained to Article 5(1) that laid down the equal treatment principle (earlier the principle of non-discrimination), even though there were still some "technical" problems with how to define what "basic working and employment conditions" were in situations where no collective agreements or general provisions exist.

Coreper met on 27 February 2003. The Council's Legal Service was invited to this meeting to give its opinion on how to interpret the new wording of Article 4. More specifically it was asked to comment on the Presidency's suggestion to delete the last two sentences of the second paragraph, which obliged Member States to discontinue *restrictions and prohibitions on the use of agency work*, and to inform the Commission of the results of their reviews.[49]

The representative of the Legal Service concluded that the deletion of the two sentences would have no influence on the legal obligations of Member States. Since the first paragraph of Article 4 provided that prohibitions and restrictions were justified only on grounds of general interest, it was implied that Member States must discontinue them if the reasons for their justification disappear. Consequently, the second paragraph only made explicit this obligation. If it was deleted, Member States would still have to discontinue prohibitions and restrictions not justified on the grounds mentioned in the first paragraph.

As a result of the statement by the Legal Service representative the debate on Article 4 flagged. As regards the exemption period in Article 5(4), the positions remained the same as before.

However, some progress was made at the Coreper meeting, particularly on one point.[50] The delegations accepted Sweden's position on Article 5(3), meaning that the social partners would be free to conclude collective agreements establishing other arrangements concerning basic working and employment conditions than those referred to in the first paragraph of Article 5, without these agreements being subject to judicial review. Only Ireland and the UK made their approval conditional. They would not lift their reservations unless the "imbalance" in respect of derogations working to the advantage of some Member States and not others was compensated.

Also, the new wording drafted on 11 February of Article 2 on *the aim* of the Directive was approved in principle.

4.11 Three Issues Still Unresolved

On 6 March the Council (Employment, Social Policy, Health and Consumer Affairs) was expected to hold a debate on the proposal for a Directive. After the informal exchange of views by the Ministers over lunch, the Greek Presidency announced that even though there was general recognition of the importance of the issue and broad agreement on the need for a Directive, further work was required before it would be

---

49 Contribution of the Legal Service to the proceedings of the Committee of Permanent Representatives (First part), 6920/03 JUR 105 SOC 101 CODEC 231, 28 February 2003.

50 Report from Permanent Representatives Committee (Part I) to Council (Employment, Social Policy, Health and Consumer Affairs), 6892/03 SOC 99 CODEC 222, 28 February 2003.

possible to reach a political compromise.[51] The views on the degree of regulation and the role of the social partners, as well as the relative importance and characteristics of temporary agency work in the Member States, were too divergent. However, the Presidency announced its ambition to work for a political agreement in public deliberation at the next Council meeting. It was agreed that a compromise had to be worked out on the following three Articles:

- Article 1(3) on *scope*, about how to address the wish of some Member States for a specific derogation with a view to promoting the integration of unemployed persons into the labour market;
- Article 4 about reviewing and possibly removing *restrictions and prohibitions* to temporary agency work;
- Article 5(4) about *the nature and the length of the qualifying period* for implementing the principle of equal treatment.[52]

The Greek Presidency accordingly prepared a draft "compromise package". It contained the following elements:

- A minor amendment was made to Article 1(3) on scope.
- The last two sentences of the second paragraph of Article 4 – that the Legal Service had deemed superfluous – were deleted.
- Article 5(4) that provided for a permanent exemption for assignments not longer than six weeks was deleted. Instead, the Presidency proposed that a new paragraph be added to Article 11 on implementation of the Directive, which contained a transitional arrangement in line with the European Parliament's proposal. It meant that for five years following the implementation of the Directive, Member States could refrain from applying the equal treatment principle for assignments up to [an unspecified number of] months. Before the expiry of the transitional period, the Commission should submit a report on the effects of the exemption. On the basis of this report, the Parliament and the Council could decide to extend the transitional period.[53]

The Presidency's proposal was examined by the Social Questions Working Party and Coreper on a number of occasions in April and May.

---

51 2492nd Council meeting – Employment, Social Policy, Health and Consumer Affairs, 6678/03 (Presse 55).

52 Report from the Presidency to Permanent Representatives Committee (Part I), 8812/03 SOC 175 CODEC 551, 2 May 2003.

53 Report from the Presidency to Permanent Representatives Committee (Part I) 8812/03 SOC 175 CODEC 551, 2 May 2003, Corrigendum to Report from the Presidency to Permanent Representatives Committee (Part I) 8812/03 COR 1 SOC 175 CODEC 551, 5 May 2003, Report from the Presidency to the Social Questions Working Party, 9140/03 SOC 188 CODEC 617, 12 May 2003.

In contrast to the polite tone that prevails in the earlier documents, the reports and minutes from these meetings reflect an increasing irritation and sarcastic arguments.

Eleven delegations could accept the main thrust of the compromise package, subject to some adjustments to the drafting of Article 4 on review of restrictions and prohibitions on agency work. However, Denmark, Germany, Ireland and the UK considered that their main concerns about the effect of the Directive on their labour markets had not yet been adequately addressed.[54] A number of delegations, among them Sweden, had serious doubts about the utility of the Directive if it were to be further watered down by any more concessions regarding the principle of equal treatment. The Commission also shared the concern about the need to ensure that the Directive had a useful effect. Another delegation pointed out that a number of important concessions had already been made to take into account the different situations in the various Member States. In particular, the principle of equal treatment was now much more flexible than in the original Commission proposal as it did not require the user undertaking to find a comparable worker. Several delegations also queried why "certain" Member States continued to have difficulties with this provision and wanted to know the real extent of the problem.

At the Coreper meeting on 19 and 21 May 2003 new texts on the transitional provisions, as well as on Article 4, were tabled.[55]

After the Council's Legal Service had stated that, according to the first paragraph of Article 4, Member States would be obliged to discontinue *restrictions and prohibitions* on agency work which are not justified on grounds of general interest, irrespective of whether this was said explicitly in the second paragraph or not, the arguments concerning Article 4 focused on the need to ensure the autonomy of the social partners. Thus, one delegation proposed a text that would oblige Member States to review existing restrictions or prohibitions on agency work *once and for all* by the time the Directive had to be implemented in their national law. The second paragraph read: "If such restrictions or prohibitions are laid down by collective agreements, Member States should encourage the social partners to review them in order to verify whether they are justified". Another delegation, supported by Sweden, suggested that the whole of Article 4 should be replaced by the following: "Member States … should identify and review obstacles of a legal or administrative nature which may limit the opportunities for temporary agency work and,

54 Report from the Social Questions Working Party to Permanent Representatives Committee (Part I) 9355/03 SOC 196 CODEC 649, 16 May 2003.

55 Extract from Summary Record, 9636/03 EXT 2 CRS/CRP 23 SOC 217 CODEC 700, 22 May 2003.

where appropriate, eliminate them", thus avoiding having to specify the grounds on which such obstacles would be justified.

The Presidency presented a compromise text for a revised transitional provision, hoping to be able to bridge the gap between, on the one side, Denmark, Germany, Ireland and the UK, that still were seeking a permanent derogation in Article 5(4), and on the other, those that could accept a transitional period. It added a new paragraph to the Article on transitional provisions which meant that, as long as the Parliament and the Council did not take a decision on what to do on the basis of the Commission's evaluation of the effects of the qualification period, Member States would have the opportunity not to apply the equal treatment principle for assignments up to (an unspecified number of) weeks, for three additional years after the expiry of the transitional period.

Denmark, Germany, Ireland and the UK on their part presented a joint position paper where they stated that:

- They were not interested in a mere transitional arrangement. The qualifying period (not simply a derogation) for equal treatment should be permanent. They could accept six months, but it should apply to all working conditions, not just pay.
- The qualifying period would remain at six months unless and until the Council and Parliament agree otherwise on the basis of a proposal by the Commission.
- However, "in the spirit of compromise" they could accept that the Directive made provision for the Commission to review and report on the workings of the qualifying period, once the Directive has been implemented and after "a reasonable number of years' experience (5–10 years)" of how it has worked. The Directive could also make provision for the Commission to present its report to the Council and, if necessary, bring forward proposals.
- They added that "to assist" other Member States they would suggest that the Article state explicitly that Member States do not *have to* apply the qualifying period.

4.12 Two Outstanding Issues Remain

On 27 May 2003 Coreper submitted a report on the state of play of the key outstanding issues plus the text of the draft Directive as it stood, in preparation for the Council meeting a week later.[56]

[56] Report from the Permanent Representatives Committee to the Council (Employment, Social Policy, Health and Consumer Affairs), 9739/03 SOC 220 CODEC 714, 27 May 2003, Addendum to report from the Permanent Representatives Committee to the Council (Employment, Social Policy, Health and Consumer Affairs), 9739/03 ADD 1 SOC 220 CODEC 714, 27 May 2003.

It concluded that, as the delegations had in principle accepted the Presidency's compromise proposal on Article 1(3) on *the scope* of the Directive, only two key issues of principle remained.

As regards the *review of restrictions and prohibitions*, neither the Presidency's proposal nor the texts proposed by delegations gained general support. As regards the *exemption from the principle of equal treatment*, eleven delegations – that is, all but the blocking minority – had indicated that they could accept a transitional period of five years, even though seven of them had difficulties of varying degrees with the review mechanism. On the other hand, Denmark, Germany, Ireland and the UK could not accept the Presidency compromise, as it would allow the exemption to elapse unless the European Parliament and Council had decided otherwise. The Commission had declared that it was open to examine the Presidency compromise and the amendments suggested by the four delegations, provided that the qualifying periods were short enough to ensure that the Directive still had a useful effect.

4.13 The Final Breakdown

The ambition of the Presidency was to reach a political agreement on a common position in public deliberation at the Council meeting on 2–3 June. The debate focused entirely on the nature and duration of the exemption from the principle of equal treatment.[57] A clear majority of the delegations were willing to accept a transitional period of five years during which Member States would be allowed an exemption from the principle of equal treatment for assignments up to six weeks, in view of the specific conditions characterising their labour markets. However, the Presidency went another step in the direction of the minority and suggested that the exemption might be continued pending a future decision of the Council and the Parliament. This alternative was unacceptable to the majority, as it would make the "transitional" period permanent if the Parliament and the Council could not reach an agreement. Also, it was acceptable to the minority only if the qualifying period was at least six months, not six weeks.

As a last, desperate try after the public session, the Presidency arranged a restricted session at which only the Minister and the highest-ranking diplomat from each Member State were allowed to participate. Here the debate could be more explicit and less diplomatic, and a lot of proposals were put forward. However, the restricted session merely confirmed the deadlock. The Presidency had to recognise that fundamental differences remained and that the Council was unable to reach a political agreement.

57 2512th Council meeting (Employment, Social Policy, Health and Consumer Affairs), 9688/1/03 REV 1 (Presse 152).

4.14 An Open Dossier

Greece had been extremely anxious to close the dossier on temporary agency work, but now its Presidency was coming to an end. The Italian and the Irish Presidencies that followed made no attempt to advance the issue. On 1 May 2004 ten new Member States joined the European Union, a fact that was not likely to facilitate efforts to regulate temporary agency work at European level.

Nevertheless, the Commission and the Council still regard this as an open dossier. At the beginning of 2004 the rumour was that the Commission was looking for a trade off between the working time Directive that is subject to revision and the Directive on temporary agency work. More specifically, the Commission would be prepared to support the UK's wish to maintain the "individual opt-out" on the working time Directive if it accepted the Commission's amended proposal for a directive on temporary agency work. A look at the register of Council documents seems to confirm this rumour. From the register you can see that the file on the Directive on temporary agency work (2002/0072(COD)) includes documents concerning the proposal for a Directive amending the working time Directive as well.

The Dutch Presidency tried to breathe fresh life into the process. On 1 September 2004, the Social Questions Working Party re-opened the examination of the proposal in order to see whether the situation had changed after the accession of the new Member States.[58] The Presidency asked delegations to indicate their view on four points:

- Should the "transitional" period be a fixed period in two stages (five years plus an additional three years maximum) or an open-ended period in two stages (five years plus a further period until a decision is taken by the Parliament and the Council)? Here 18 delegations were opposed to an open-ended period but could accept a fixed transitional period, even though several thought that eight years was too long. In contrast, Denmark, Germany, Ireland and the UK plus two of the new Member States were seeking a permanent exemption or an open-ended transitional period "with a view to providing a sufficient level of flexibility in the labour market so as to encourage job creation and address unemployment". One of these delegations added that it was currently reviewing its national

58 Outcome of proceedings of the Social Questions Working Party, *(cont. on next page)* *(cont. from previous page)* 11950/04 SOC 377 CODEC 959, 9 September 2004, Corrigendum to Outcome of proceedings of the Social Questions Working Party, 11950/04 COR 1 SOC 377 CODEC 959, 10 September 2004, Corrigendum to Outcome of proceedings of the Social Questions Working Party, 11950/04 COR 2 SOC 377 CODEC 959, 14 September 2004.

legislation which had been based on the Commission's original proposal, as it had not been successful in addressing these aims.[59] Finally, one delegation could not give a firm position pending the outcome of a case related to temporary workers currently before its Constitutional Court.[60]

- How long should the qualifying periods laid down in the transitional provision be? The six seeking a permanent exemption called for at least six months, one of them recalling that this was already a substantial concession on its part. Seven delegations were open to a "reasonable" period (three–four months). However, eight other delegations could only accept a short period, while some could not give a firm view at this stage. Sweden indicated that its position would depend on the various components in the compromise solution.
- Should the exemption apply only to pay, or should it be extended to other essential working conditions? Eleven delegations were in favour of the first alternative, while seven wanted the exemption to be widened to include some other working conditions. Six other delegations, among them the Swedish, indicated a certain level of flexibility in the context of a compromise solution.
- Which of the texts concerning the review of restrictions and prohibitions on agency work did the delegations prefer, the compromise text put forward by the Greek Presidency (deletion of the last two sentences of Article 4) or that proposed by one delegation which would oblige Member States to review existing restrictions or prohibitions on agency work *once and for all* by the time the Directive had to be implemented in their national law? This issue had not been exhaustively discussed in the final Council meeting during the Greek Presidency, but it was still an outstanding issue and had to be part of an overall compromise. Here, eight delegations opted for the last mentioned proposal, which best protected the rights of the social partners, while just as many could not accept it and preferred the text of the original Commission proposal of March 2002. One delegation still insisted that the whole Article should be deleted. The rest were more undecided. In this context, a number of delegations also raised the issue of the link between this Directive and the

59 Five of these countries have legislation that is very similar to the Commission's original proposal: Germany, Poland, Slovakia, Slovenia and the Czech Republic (see the chapters on Germany and on the new Member States). None have reviewed their legislation since then.

60 In Germany, organisations representing temporary work agencies had filed a complaint to the Constitutional Court, arguing that the new German legislation infringed their freedom of association (see the chapter on Germany).

Directive on Services in the Internal Market that had been proposed by the Commission in January 2004. In response, the Commission representative pointed out that the two questions were separate, as Article 4(3) of the draft Directive on temporary agency work made clear that this Directive would not affect questions of registration, licensing, certification, and so on. One delegation in particular maintained reservations in this respect.

The Dutch Presidency put the issue on the agenda of the Council of 4 October 2004 in order to determine whether the conditions for a compromise solution and a possible political agreement at the December Council existed.[61] The Presidency recalled that the report of the Employment Taskforce had underlined that equal treatment of temporary agency workers contributes to the development of the sector and in this way also to flexibility in the labour market (job opportunities and job matching).[62] It put forward the following issues for discussion:

- Should the Council focus on the elements that were now on the table, that is, the length and nature of the transitional period itself and the qualifying periods?
- Or should it alternatively/additionally also take into account the distinctive characteristics of the industrial relations systems in a number of Member States in view of the limited use they can make of the exemption through collective agreements. If so, under what conditions could this be achieved?
- If the number of possibilities for exemptions was extended, would a special provision be justified to prevent Member States from making use of all the exemptions at the same time?

The debate revealed that further efforts would be needed to enable the Council to reach a compromise that was acceptable for all delegations.[63]

The subsequent meeting of the Social Questions Working Party on 10 November dealt exclusively with Article 4 on the review of restrictions and prohibitions.[64] However, the discussion confirmed that the positions were as locked as ever.

---

61 Note from the Presidency to the Council (EPSCO), 12449/04 REV 1 SOC 402 Codec 1008, 22 September 2004.

62 'Jobs, jobs, jobs. Creating more Employment in Europe', report of the Employment Taskforce chaired by Wim Kok, November 2003.

63 Press release 2606th Council Meeting Employment, Social Policy, Health and Consumer Affairs, 12400/04 (Presse 264).

64 Outcome of proceedings of the Social Questions Working Party, 15011/04 SOC 553 CODEC 1269, 22 November 2004.

In the operational programme of the Council for 2005 the incoming Presidencies Luxemburg and the United Kingdom declared that they would "use their best endeavours to reach a settlement on the Temporary Agency Work Directive".[65] However, Luxemburg had to strike the item off the agenda of the Council meeting on 3 March 2005, and so far (as I write in December 2006) nether the Social Questions Working Party nor Coreper has discussed temporary agency work since November 2004. The incoming German Presidency has indicated that it will put the issue of temporary agency work on the agenda during the first half of 2007, but much creativity is required if it is to succeed.

4.15 Why Did the Efforts Fail?

There are many possible theories concerning why the Member States failed to reach an agreement on a Directive on temporary agency work. Considering the far-reaching exemptions called for by Denmark, Germany, Ireland and the UK, one might suspect that at least a couple of them never had the political will to regulate temporary agency work at European level. A directive that permanently allowed Member States to provide for a six-month (or even longer) qualifying period would have given protection to a very small proportion of Europe's agency workers – and exclude those who typically would have the greatest need for protection. Could they actually believe that the majority would swallow the bait? Also, remember that at the very first meeting of the Social Questions Working Party in June 2002 these four delegations questioned whether there was a need for Community legislation in this area. However, as we cannot look into other souls and minds, I will base my analysis on the arguments given by the delegations as if they expressed their real motives, and try to enter into the position of each Member State when I seek to understand why the negotiations failed.

The main problem, as described by Coreper, was to find

- the right balance between protecting temporary agency workers and providing sufficient flexibility in the labour market,
- while at the same time respecting the different practices and traditions at national level.[66]

The last point is a major issue every time the EU legislates in the social field. When you scrutinise the arguments put forward in the negotiations

[65] Note from the Luxembourg and United Kingdom Delegations to Delegations, 116299/04 POLGEN 57, 22 December 2004.

[66] Report from Permanent Representatives Committee (Part I) to Council (Employment, Social Policy, Health and Consumer Affairs), 6892/03 SOC 99 CODEC 222, 28 February 2003.

on temporary agency work, you can easily get the feeling that *every* Member State wanted a directive that had as little impact on its own regulation as possible. For example:

- most of the Member States where agency work is restricted fiercely opposed any obligation to review and, possibly, discontinue the restrictions;
- Germany called for exemptions from the equal treatment principle for all situations that were exempted under German law;
- Sweden, where terms and conditions of temporary agency workers are regulated by collective agreements, was prepared to block the directive unless it guaranteed the social partners' right to conclude collective agreements without interference by the state or the European Court of Justice;
- and the UK and Ireland, that had almost no regulation on agency work, either by legislation or collective agreements, called for a qualifying period that would have enabled them to exempt most of their agency workers from application of the Directive.[67]

These were all political arguments. But there were also arguments of a more practical nature. It is obvious that it is more difficult to apply a principle of non-discrimination/equal treatment where wages are individually set than where sectoral collective agreements lay down fixed pay scales. Not only the UK foresaw practical problems in this respect. Sweden too indicated that it would have practical problems with identifying who the comparable worker would be according to the original non-discrimination principle, as today the individual worker's wage is normally negotiated at the workplace according to principles laid down in the sectoral agreements and it consists of a number of components, some of which are related to individual factors such as the worker's performance, responsibility, and so on. However, for Sweden's part the problem would be minimised with the possibility of deviating from the main rule by means of collective agreements. This possibility seemed unjust to Ireland and the UK since, as they reiterated, it would work "to the advantage of some Member States but not others". In other words, they felt that they would be treated unfairly if they did not get "their own" exemption.

67 According to Arrowsmith (2006) p. 7, 57% of the temporary work assignments in the UK were shorter than six months and 81% of the assignments in Ireland were shorter than five months in 2004. One could add that, as pointed out both by the Irish government (see p. 226) and the European Parliament, many agency workers in Ireland and the UK are regarded as self-employed or as having a contract *sui generis* and not as employees of either the agency or of the user company, which means that they would be excluded from the scope of the Directive for that reason alone.

However, derogation by means of collective agreements is *another method of regulating* terms and conditions – a method that can be very effective if the trade unions are strong and collective bargaining has high coverage. In Sweden, for example, collective agreements are covering an increasing share of the agency work sector, and a Directive would probably serve as an incentive for even more agencies to join the employers' association. On the contrary, a permanent exemption or qualification period as advocated by the minority would have left the conditions of a large proportion of agency workers in countries with liberal legislation and no collective agreements *unregulated.*

True, most social policy directives that aim at regulating (as opposed to deregulating) are likely to affect Ireland and the UK more than other Member States, simply because they have more liberal legislation and no tradition of sectoral collective agreements. With this in mind it is understandable that these two countries often resist, both in the social dialogue and in the negotiations in the Council.[68] But it would be of little use to adopt a comprehensive European regulation that has so many exemptions that it is deprived of most – if not all – of its effect. That explains why the majority, supported by the Commission, would not comply with the minority's calls for a long and permanent qualification period.

The motives for Denmark's and Germany's resistance to the Directive are less evident.

As a country in which temporary agency work is regulated almost exclusively through collective agreements, Denmark could have made use of the same exemption as Sweden. Thus, it would only have to adopt supplementary legislation to guarantee the effect of the Directive for the relatively small share of the labour market that is not covered by collective agreements (as would Sweden). However, today it is no secret that the Danish government was very much against the idea of European legislation on temporary agency work from the beginning, as this would go against the "Danish flexibility" that the liberal/conservative government values so highly. As a government official puts it: "Why do the French always have to impose their model on us, which does not work even in their own country?" However, because Denmark held the Presidency when the Member States began to examine the provisions of the draft directive in the second half of 2002, it could not act openly against it until later. In fact, not even the Danish trade unions were enthusiastic over the proposed Directive. At least some of them feared that it would undermine their collective agreements.

68 A trade union representative whom I interviewed for a project on the social dialogue on fixed-term work aired her dissatisfaction with 'always having to bargain for two countries alone'.

The German Government is said to have shared the Danish Government's feeling that the Franco-Roman model would be imposed on it. Nevertheless, the position that it took in the Council is downright astonishing. In parallel with the social dialogue and, later, the negotiations in the Council, Germany reformed its legislation on agency work. The general thrust of the reform was liberalising, but, as one author writes,

> Once true to what may be referred to as a typical German tendency of over-obedience … the government decided to include those provisions that it perceived as necessary to implement the draft directive on agency work. As a result, first experiences with the German legislation may be used for guidance as to which direction the renewed proposal at EU level should go.[69]

Thus, as from 1 January 2004 under the new German legislation a temporary agency worker is entitled to the same essential working conditions, including remuneration, as comparable employees in the user enterprise. However, this does not apply for the first six weeks if the worker was previously unemployed and is paid net remuneration that is at least the amount he or she had received as unemployment benefit.[70] In the Council, Germany had originally advocated a qualifying period of twelve months, and it refused to compromise on less than six months!

There was one thing that Germany, Ireland and the UK had in common from the very beginning and which was reflected in the discussion on the scope and aim of the directive, as well as on the equal treatment principle. They all saw temporary agency work very much as an instrument for creating jobs and integrating unemployed people into the labour market. This made them stress the flexibility issue. One might say that they had moved further in the direction of the new ILO Convention on private employment services than many of the other delegations.[71]

Thus, judging from the arguments put forward by the Member States' governments, the fundamental reason for the failure to reach an agreement on temporary agency work was this disagreement over what political aim the Directive would fulfil and where, consequently, the emphasis should be – flexibility or security? And it is from this perspective that even the German government's inconsequent behaviour makes sense.

69 Schiek (2004).

70 See Ahlberg, p. 128 in this volume.

71 However, unlike several countries in the majority, none of the countries in the blocking minority had ratified Convention No. 181. At the time of the negotiations, five of the 'old' Member States had ratified it, namely Finland (1999), Italy (2000), the Netherlands (1999), Portugal (2002) and Spain (1999). Among the new Member States, it has been ratified by Czech Republic (2000), Hungary (2003) and Lithuania (2004).

According to a person who participated in the work of the Social Questions Working Party, the German unemployment problem was so huge that the Government did not dare to bind itself to the contents of the Directive until it had been able to evaluate whether the "premature implementation" of it had had the intended effects on employment.

According to rumour, the German position may have an additional explanation. Supposedly, the German Government made a "dirty deal" with the UK and agreed to support the British Government in its resistance to the directive on temporary agency work in exchange for British support on the issue of workers' participation in the Directive on takeover bids. This type of barter exists, but for obvious reasons it is never visible in the documents. Thus, I have not been able to verify if the rumour is true or not.

5. Conclusions

My record of the social dialogue on temporary agency work and the subsequent negotiations between the Member States has demonstrated the many difficulties encountered by efforts to create transnational labour regulations. What conclusions can be drawn from a comparison of the two processes?

5.1 The Commission Influences Both Processes

It is self-evident that the Commission, which has the exclusive right according to the Treaty to initiate legislation, participates actively when new legislation is negotiated in the Council's working parties. However, the only role conferred by the Treaty on the Commission in relation to the social dialogue is that of facilitator. Also, in the Commission's oratory much reverence is paid to the autonomy of the social partners. At the very least, the negotiations on temporary agency work have nevertheless confirmed that the Commission has an influence not only on the legislative process but also in the social dialogue. First, the Commission's Legal Service "advised" the parties on an issue that it had not been asked to comment on, which strengthened the employers and may have had a decisive influence on the outcome of the negotiations. Second, after the formal breakdown of the negotiations, the Commission intervened again as Commissioner Diamantopoulous urged the parties to try to find a compromise and underlined her appeal with a "threat": they would have no guarantee of achieving their objectives if the traditional legislative procedure was followed. Her intervention in fact led to renewed discussions between the two spokespersons, and they also made some further progress before they finally concluded that the negotiations had broken down.

5.2 The Ultimate Stumbling Blocks Can Differ

As regards the contents of both processes, the most obvious similarity is that the question of the comparator for the purpose of the non-discrimination/equal treatment principle and the issue of restrictions and prohibitions on the use of temporary agency work were the most controversial. Another common feature was that a disproportionate amount of time and energy during both processes was spent on discussing the special demands of the UK and Ireland and their insistence on "pay" being exempted from the scope of the agreement/directive.[72] And yet it was not these issues that finally determined the failure of the social dialogue or the negotiations in the Council.

After Anna Diamantopoulous' intervention in the social dialogue in May 2001, it seemed as if the only matter of principle on which there was still unbridgeable disagreement between the two sides was the scope of the agreement: the employers insisted that workers with open-ended contracts should be excluded from the scope, which the trade union side would not accept in any circumstances.

Why was this issue decisive in the social dialogue? In most countries agency workers are normally employed on fixed-term contracts, with Sweden and Germany as the most prominent exceptions (at least when the social dialogue on temporary agency work took place). Thus, an agreement which excluded workers with open-ended contracts would still cover the majority of temporary agency workers. From the employers' perspective it could be argued that workers with open-ended employment contracts who continue to be paid between assignments are in exactly the same position and covered by the same labour legislation as any other employee, which means that they do not need any specific protection simply because they are employed by a temporary work agency. From the trade unions' point of view that may be true if the open-ended contract provides the worker with more stable employment than a fixed-term contract according to national law. However, this is not always the case. For example, even though temporary work agencies in Germany were obliged to employ their workers on open-ended contracts, these workers had significantly shorter employment contracts than workers who were employed on fixed-term contracts directly by user firms. Also, their wages were on average 30% below the rates in comparable user firms.[73] Consequently, an agreement that deprived German agency workers of protection was unacceptable for the trade union side, and especial-

---

72 The same thing happened in the negotiations on fixed-term work, see Ahlberg (1999), p. 13ff.

73 See Ahlberg, p. 123 in this volume.

ly for the German trade unions, which (at least when the social dialogue started) were among the most hostile to temporary agency work as such.

In the negotiations between the Member States that followed the breakdown of the social dialogue this was no big issue. The Commission's draft directive allowed Member States to make exemptions from the principle of non-discrimination for workers with open-ended contracts who continue to be paid between assignments. A couple of delegations voiced concern over this exception early in the process, but it was never the object of any major conflicts. It is true that this exemption did not go as far as excluding workers with open-ended contracts from the Directive in its entirety (which would have been the effect if the employers had had their way in the social dialogue), but it did mean that they could not invoke the most central Article from a worker's perspective. The Commission, which had drafted the Directive, knew very well how controversial this was between the social partners. To what extent the Member States' governments were aware of this is more uncertain – they never even mentioned the social dialogue during the negotiations in the Working Party or in the Council. However, if they knew, this was obviously a price they were ready to pay in order to facilitate adoption of the Directive.

Instead, the ultimate stumbling block in the negotiations in the Council was the minority's calls for a permanent exemption meaning that the principle of equal treatment would be applicable only after a worker had been assigned for six months in the same user enterprise. During the social dialogue no such provision was even discussed. You could say that this is not surprising as the social partners never reached agreement on the non-discrimination principle as such, and that, consequently, there was no reason to start discussing exemptions. On the other hand, the employers tabled a couple of drafts on the non-discrimination principle, none of which included any exemptions.

The idea that assignments of a certain length could be exempted was introduced by the Commission, perhaps as a "compensation" for the fact that it had sided with ETUC's view that the point of reference for the non-discrimination principle should be a worker in the user enterprise. But instead of pleasing those governments that had the biggest problems with this non-discrimination principle, it turned out to be the straw that broke the camel's back. Why was precisely this provision decisive in the Council? Again, remember that on the very first meeting of the Social Questions Working Party in June 2002 the UK, Ireland, Germany and Denmark questioned whether there was at all a need for Community legislation in this area. Perhaps they just needed a pretext for blocking the whole directive, and this was the point at which they could find one another?

Having said that I must add that, naturally, the debate in the Council can take another direction than the social dialogue, simply because governments have to safeguard the interests of society as a whole. These are not always and in every respect identical with the interests that the social partners are primarily concerned with.

5.3 Technical Debate in the Council, Principal Debate in the Social Dialogue

A striking difference was that the debate in the Council's Working Party was much more technical than the deliberations during the social dialogue. Partly this is a consequence of the fact that the Council's Working Party negotiated over a complete draft directive, while ETUC, UNICE/UEAPME and CEEP hardly reached the stage where they started to draft texts. However, an example illustrates that this is only part of the explanation: During the negotiations between the Member States the Swedish delegation repeatedly pointed out that, although it supported the non-discrimination principle as proposed by the Commission, it foresaw practical problems with applying it in the Swedish context. However, the Swedish trade unions, who would be the first to know these practical problems, obviously supported the same non-discrimination principle in the social dialogue without reservations. Even though more states (including EEA members) are represented in the social dialogue than in the Council, each side has to speak with one voice, which probably leads to concentration on the principal issues. This in turn is likely to help the parties to agree on the texts once they have reached agreement on matters of principle. For example, the agreement on fixed-term work was finalised in four days after the two spokespersons had met and reached a compromise on two major issues.[74] In contrast, in the Council's Working Party each Member State is supposed to take a stand on each provision. Thus the character of the debate is influenced by the way the negotiations are conducted.

5.4 A Memento for the European Parliament

The fact that neither of the two processes resulted in an agreement occasions another reflection.

As already mentioned, members of the European Parliament levelled severe criticism against the fixed-term work agreement concluded between UNICE, CEEP and ETUC in 1999. In its resolution, the Parliament also criticised the procedure under Articles 138 and 139 of the Treaty, namely the social dialogue. Although it may be useful in some cases – especially to overcome an impasse in the Council – it must not in

74 Ahlberg (1999).

any circumstances be allowed to be a systematic replacement for the normal legislative process, the resolution stated.[75] The Parliament considered that the procedure was too time-consuming and extremely cumbersome, and that its own rights had been restricted by how the procedure had been applied by the social partners. In addition, it hinted that the traditional legislative procedure would have led to a more satisfying result, as the Parliament and the Council can decide by a qualified majority, while the social dialogue is likely to result in an agreement only on a consensus basis.

My study of the social dialogue on temporary agency work and the subsequent negotiations in the Council does not support the conclusion that the procedure under Articles 138 and 139 is more time-consuming than the traditional legislative process – rather the contrary. UNICE, CEEP and ETUC started their dialogue with a blank paper and negotiated for a little more than ten months until they gave up. After that, the Commission needed ten months to produce a draft Directive. Thus, the Member States' governments could start with a complete draft text. After one year of negotiations, they were as close to (or rather as far from) reaching an agreement as the social partners had been.

Also, it is evident that it can be just as difficult to reach the necessary majority in the Council as to reach consensus in the social dialogue. In both processes the outcome is dependent on political realities rather than formalities.

5.5 Different Risks

But would ETUC, UNICE/UEAPME and CEEP have succeeded in reaching an agreement on temporary agency work if only the trade union side had agreed to exclude agency workers with open-ended contracts from the scope? We will never know the answer. The employers' might have introduced new elements in the negotiations that the trade union side could not accept. What we do know, however, is that ETUC took a double risk when it decided to leave the negotiating table. Not only did it risk that the Council would adopt a directive that was even less satisfactory than an agreement would have been, but also that there would be no European legislation on temporary agency work at all. In contrast, a Member State that stubbornly blocks the adoption of a directive in the Council takes no risk at all.

Another question is whether the trade unions considered the risk that the failure of the social dialogue would be followed by another failure in the Council? Had they actually decided whether a situation with no European legislation on temporary agency work at all was preferable to

75 See p. 218.

a Directive implementing an agreement which covered the majority of Europe's agency workers but excluded a minority from its scope? I have not found a definite answer. What they had decided, though, was that they would not conclude an agreement at any price. They must obtain something of what was in their mandate. If the alternative was a "bad" directive drafted by the Commission or no legislation at all, it would not be the responsibility of the ETUC.

6. Epilogue

You have just read the story of how several hundred persons have been engaged for years in the efforts to create European legislation on temporary agency work. As their efforts have been fruitless, it must be called a failure. But has it been a complete failure? Bear in mind that, in parallel with the negotiations in the Council, Germany "implemented" the Commission's original proposal for a Directive.[76] Furthermore, a number of the new Member States have adopted legislation apparently inspired by the same draft.[77] Bear in mind also that, in Sweden, important steps were taken in order to integrate temporary agency workers in the collective bargaining system – would all that have happened independently of what took place around the negotiating tables in Brussels?[78]

To me it appears as if all these developments are manifestations of an informal, voluntary harmonisation process triggered by the debate at EU level. And it may still be going on.

Bibliography

Ahlberg, K. (1999), "The negotiations on fixed-term work", in C. Vigneau, K. Ahlberg, B. Bercusson and N. Bruun, *Fixed-term work in the EU. A European agreement against discrimination and abuse*. SALTSA, Stockholm: National Institute for Working Life.

Ahlberg, K., and N. Bruun (2005), "Sweden: Transition through collective bargaining", in R. Blanpain, T. Blanke and E. Rose (eds), *Collective bargaining and wages in comparative perspective*, Bulletin of Comparative Labour Relations 56, Kluwer Law International.

Arrowsmith, J. (2006), *Temporary agency work in an enlarged European Union.* Dublin: European Foundation for the Improvement of Living and Working Conditions.

Clauwaert, S. (1998), *Survey of legislation on temporary agency work*, Brussels: European Trade Union Institute.

76 See Ahlberg, p. 119 in this volume.

77 See Ahlberg, p. 139 in this volume.

78 See Ahlberg and Bruun, p. 37 in this volume.

Nakayama, J., and A Samodorov (2004), "Public and private employment services: from co-existence to cooperation", in R. Blanpain, and R. Graham (eds.), *Temporary agency work in the information society*, Bulletin of Comparative Labour Relations 50, Kluwer Law International.

Phan, T (1999), "ILO convention on private employment agencies (No. 181)", in R. Blanpain (ed.), *Private employment agencies*, Bulletin of Comparative Labour Relations 36, Kluwer Law International.

Schiek, D. (2004), "Agency work – from marginalisation towards acceptance? Agency work in EU social and employment policy and the 'implementation' of the draft Directive on agency work into German law", *German Law Journal*, vol. 5, no. 10 (October).

Storrie, D. (2002), *Temporary agency work in the European Union*, European Foundation for the Improvement of Living and Working Conditions.

Free Movement of Services, Transnational Temporary Agency Work and the *Acquis Communautaire*

Brian BERCUSSON and Niklas BRUUN

1. Introduction: Transnational Regulation of Temporary Agency Work and the Free Movement of Services in the European Union

Temporary agency work links the performance of work within the framework of an employment contract between employer and employee with the provision of services within the framework of a commercial contract.[1] This form of service provision by employed workers has specific features which have led to special regulation by labour laws in Europe.

The national reports in this book show that the dominant pattern in the evolution of *national* labour regulation, supported by *international* regulation in the form of ILO Convention 181, is to protect labour standards while accepting the use of labour in the specific form of provision of services, a framework seeking to combine flexibility and security.

Free movement of services across national borders is one of the four freedoms of the internal market protected by the law of the European Union (EU). Transnational temporary agency work is an important component of the free movement of services in the EU. *Transnational* labour regulation in the EU already governs certain aspects of transnational temporary agency work: health and safety[2] and the posting of workers.[3] But the fierce debate over the Commission's proposal to liberalise the transnational market in services,[4] which led eventually to the exclusion

1 Between a temporary agency business and the user enterprise (business-to-business (b2b)).

2 Council Directive 91/383 of 25 June 1991 supplementing the measures to encourage improvements in the safety and health of workers with a fixed-duration employment relationship or a temporary employment relationship, OJ 1991 L206/19.

3 Directive 96/71/EC concerning the posting of workers in the framework of the provision of services. OJ 1996, L18/1.

4 Proposal for a Directive on Services in the Internal Market, COM (2004) 2 final/3, adopted 13 January 2004. Now Directive 2006/123/EC of the European Parliament

of provision of services by temporary work agencies from the scope of the directive,[5] arguably exposed the need for specific transnational regulation of temporary agency work in the EU.

As with regulation of temporary agency work in general, the debate over the proposed Services Directive focused on the crucial issue of how to balance the economic dimension of the internal market (freedom to provide services) with the social dimension (protection of employees, but also of national industrial relations models). The Commission was revealed as having failed to address the complex task of balancing the economic and social dimensions of the EU.

After this introduction (Section I), this chapter begins by contrasting different perspectives (economic market-oriented v. social policy-oriented) on the relationship between freedom to provide services and protection of labour standards, including those applied to temporary agency workers. The contrast serves to highlight the Commission's exclusively market-oriented perspective, evident in the "country of origin" principle in the proposed Services Directive (Section II).

The proposed Services Directive, through its "country of origin principle", came into conflict with the *acquis communautaire* of EU labour law. It also aroused great concern through its potential impact on the labour laws of the host Member States where transnational workers were to be employed, by excluding to a large extent labour standards established in the national labour law of the host Member State.[6]

---

and of the Council of 12 December 2006 on services in the internal market, OJ L376/26 of 27 December 2006.

5 Directive 2006/123/EC, Article 2(2): "This Directive shall not apply to the following activities: (c) services of temporary work agencies". The proposed Directive had provided in Article 2 – Scope: "This Directive shall apply to services supplied by providers established in a Member State." Article 4 – Definitions, provided "'service' means any selfemployed economic activity, as referred to in Article 50 of the Treaty, consisting in the provision of a service for consideration". The proposed Directive did not cover temporary employment agencies as such, but labour market services were not excluded from its scope, and in its considerations (no. 14), the Commission expressly referred to "recruitment agencies, including employment agencies". Given the broad definition of services, the proposed Directive had covered temporary employment services. However, the European Parliament's amendments, voted on during the first reading of the Directive on 16 February 2006, excluded temporary work agencies. Although initially the Commission declared (on 2 March 2006 in a high level Council Working Group) that it would not accept the removal of temporary work agencies, it acceded to the Parliament's position in its revised proposal of 4 April 2006. See the account of this ongoing struggle in Kowalsky (2006), pp. 240, 243.

6 Article 16(1) of the proposed Directive, headed "Country of origin principle", read: 'Member States shall ensure that providers are subject only to the national provisions

The proposed Services Directive purported not to "aim to address issues of labour law as such". It asserted that it was only "abolishing certain disproportionate administrative procedures, while also improving the monitoring of compliance with employment and working conditions in accordance with Directive 96/71/EC".[7] However, the very next Recital of the Preamble to the proposed Directive stated:[8]

> *as regards employment and working conditions* other than those laid down in Directive 96/71/EC, *it should not be possible for the Member State of posting to take restrictive measures against a provider established in another Member State.*[9]

This was a radical change to transnational labour regulation in the EU. It was based on the fundamental misapprehension that the "country of origin" principle was consistent with existing EU labour law, and that it was sufficient if some limited derogation could be made to this principle to accommodate Directive 96/71/EC. On the contrary, a major change in policy was being proposed.

---

of their Member State of origin which fall within the coordinated field. Paragraph 1 shall cover national provisions relating to access to and the exercise of a service activity, in particular those requirements governing the behaviour of the provider, the quality or content of the service, advertising, contracts and the provider's liability'. Article 16(2): 'The Member State of origin shall be responsible for supervising the provider and the services provided by him, including where services are provided in another Member State'. As explained in Recital 37: 'In order to secure effective implementation of the free movement of services [...] it is necessary to establish the principle that a provider may be subject only to the law of the country in which he is established. That principle is essential in order to enable providers, especially SMEs, to avail themselves with full legal certainty of the opportunities offered by the internal market'. Recital 38: 'It is also necessary to ensure that supervision of services activities is carried out at source, that is to say, by the competent authorities of the Member State in which the provider is established'. COM(2004) 2 final/3, 2004/0001(COD), Brussels, 5 March 2004, Corrigendum.

7 Preamble, Recital 58.

8 Italics added. Preamble, Recital 59, which began: 'In order to avoid discriminatory or disproportionate administrative formalities, which would be a disincentive to SMEs in particular, it is necessary to preclude the Member State of posting from making postings subject to compliance with requirements such as an obligation to request authorisation from the authorities. The obligation to make a declaration to the authorities of the Member State of posting should also be prohibited. However, it should be possible to maintain such an obligation until 31 December 2008 in the field of building work in accordance with the Annex to Directive 96/71/EC. In that connection, a group of Member State experts on the application of that Directive are studying ways to improve administrative cooperation between Member States in order to facilitate supervision. Furthermore [...]'.

9 The intention stated in this Preamble text is implemented by Article 17 (General derogations from the country of origin principle) which states that Article 16 (the 'country of origin' principle) shall not apply to 'matters covered by Directive 96/71/EC'.

The chapter contrasts the one-sided approach of the "country of origin" principle with established principles of the *acquis communautaire social* as revealed in EU legislation and the case law of the European Court of Justice (ECJ). By seeking to apply the "country of origin" principle to labour law[10] the proposed Services Directive called into question fundamental principles of the *acquis communautaire social*.

Not surprisingly, in light of its pursuit of liberalisation of the internal market in services while disregarding the social policy implications and, in particular, ignoring the *acquis communautaire social*, the proposed Directive encountered a barrage of criticism and hostility. The chapter continues with a short account of the legislative struggle which led to the deletion of the "country of origin" principle. Article 16 of the proposed Directive, formerly entitled "Country of origin principle", is now headed "Freedom to provide services". Despite the proposed Directive's initial assurance that it did not "aim to address issues of labour law as such", amendments were inserted in the final text of the Directive aiming to restrict the scope of application of the Directive from the field of labour law (Section 3).[11]

Following this, each of these elements of the *acquis communautaire social* will be examined. In each case, we shall describe how the amendments to the proposed Directive, now in the final text adopted by the Council on 12 December 2006, re-established the principles of the *acquis communautaire social*. The underlying principle upheld was the reaffirmation of the equal treatment of workers by providing that the subject

10 In contrast, it was recently rejected by the Council as regards consumer protection in relation to the adoption of a common position on the proposal for a Directive concerning unfair business-to-consumer commercial practices in the Internal Market, amending earlier Directives; COM (2003) 356 final.

11 Recital 14: "This Directive does not affect terms and conditions of employment, including maximum work periods and minimum rest periods, minimum paid annual holidays, minimum rates of pay as well as health, safety and hygiene at work, which Member States apply in compliance with Community law, nor does it affect relations between social partners, including the right to negotiate and conclude collective agreements, the right to strike and to take industrial action in accordance with national law and practices which respect Community law, nor does it apply to services provided by temporary work agencies. This directive does not affect Member States' social security legislation". Recital 15: "This Directive respects the exercise of fundamental rights applicable in the Member States and as recognised in the Charter of Fundamental Rights of the European Union and the accompanying explanations, reconciling them with the fundamental freedoms laid down in Articles 43 and 49 of the Treaty. Those fundamental rights include the right to take industrial action in accordance with national law and practices which respect Community law". Article 1, "Subject matter", provides in Article 1(6): "This Directive does not affect labour law, that is any legal or contractual provision concerning employment conditions, working conditions,

matter of the Directive on free movement of services does not affect labour law, including employment and working conditions and the relationship between employers and workers which Member States apply in accordance with national law (Section 4). This was expressly confirmed by a number of provisions, mostly in the form of amendments introduced by the European Parliament, which aimed to prevent "social dumping" (Section 5). These included (a) the explicit protection of collective agreements, (b) the acknowledgment of protection of workers as an overriding reason relating to the public interest, and (c) the re-affirmation of fundamental labour rights.

Finally, despite its apparent support for the Posting of Workers Directive, the proposed Directive rather sought to circumscribe its effects by reducing it to a minimum set of labour standards (Section 6). In doing so, while ignoring the implications of the Rome Convention on the law applicable to contractual obligations (Rome I), it made the determination of the labour standards applicable to transnational temporary workers impossibly complex and difficult (Section 7). The approach adopted in the proposed Services Directive was at odds with that of the European Court of Justice towards the application of national labour standards to workers temporarily employed in a Member State (Section 8). Finally, the proposed Services Directive threatened to undermine the ability of

---

including health and safety at work and the relationship between employers and workers, which Member States apply in accordance with national law which respects Community law. Equally, this Directive does not affect the social security legislation of the Member States". Article 1(7): "This Directive does not affect the exercise of fundamental rights as recognised in the Member States and by Community law. Nor does it affect the right to negotiate, conclude and enforce collective agreements and to take industrial action in accordance with national law and practices which respect Community law". Finally, Article 16, 'Freedom to provide services', provides in Article 16(3): 'The Member State to which the provider moves shall not be prevented from imposing requirements with regard to the provision of a service activity, where they are justified for reasons of public policy, public security, public health or the protection of the environment and in accordance with paragraph 1. Nor shall that Member State be prevented from applying, in accordance with Community law, its rules on employment conditions, including those laid down in collective agreements'. Cf. the definitions in Article 4(7): '"requirement" means any obligation, prohibition, condition or limit provided for in the laws, regulations or administrative provisions of the Member States or in consequence of case-law, administrative practice, the rules of professional bodies, or the collective rules of professional associations or other professional organisations, adopted in the exercise of their legal autonomy. Rules laid down in collective agreements negotiated by the social partners shall not as such be seen as requirements within the meaning of this Directive.' Article 4(8): '"overriding reasons relating to the public interest" means reasons recognised as such in the case law of the Court of Justice, including the following grounds: [...] the protection of [...] workers; [...] social policy objectives [...]'.

Member States to effectively enforce, through surveillance and control, the labour standards applicable to temporary workers (Section 9).

In conclusion, the chapter argues that the Directive is likely to produce difficulties on a scale which will require further legislation dealing specifically with the labour law applicable to transnational provision of services, including temporary agency work. We elaborate a number of principles of EU labour law which should be taken into account when such legislation is proposed (Section 10).

The substantial revision, in particular by the European Parliament, of the Commission's initial draft of the proposed Services Directive demonstrates that a legitimate and successful development of the internal market is conditional on taking into consideration the social consequences and implications of proposals. Nor is it satisfactory to leave this task exclusively to legal developments in the European Court of Justice. Yet the current position under the Services Directive produces uncertainty about the labour standards applicable to transnational provision of services and, in particular, those applicable to temporary agency workers. Inevitably, litigation will follow.[12]

The European Parliament's insistence on the explicit exclusion of temporary agency work from the scope of the proposed Directive, against the opposition of the Commission, which initially proposed and persisted in seeking to include such workers within the ambit of the Directive, is significant. Its implications are twofold. First, the affirmation in the Services Directive of the *acquis communautaire social* reinforces the case for ensuring that its protection extends also to temporary agency work. Secondly, the recognition that temporary agency work is a special case, not to be governed by the rules applicable generally to free movement of services, makes it clear that transnational temporary agency work, and by implication temporary agency work in general, requires specific regulation. This simply confirms the recognition evident already in the 1991 Directive on health and safety of temporary agency workers, the decision of the social partners in 1999 to attempt to negotiate an agreement on temporary agency work through the social dialogue, and the Commission's proposal in 2002 of a directive on temporary agency work.

12 Doubts remain as to the protection of labour standards by the *acquis communautaire social* due to continuing attempts through litigation to use the free movement provisions of the Treaty to achieve the same objective sought by the "country of origin" principle. Case C-438/05, *Viking Line Abp OU Viking Line Eesti v The International Transport Workers' Federation, The Finnish Seamen's Union;* Case C-341/05, *Laval un Partneri Ltd v Svenska Byggnadsarbetareförbundet, Svenska Byggnadsarbetareförbundet, Avdelning 1, Svenska Elektrikerförbundet.* See Ahlberg, Bruun and Malmberg (2006), Blanke (2006) and Bercusson (2007).

There can be little excuse now for failure by the EU institutions and the Member States to adopt the necessary regulation of temporary agency work, respecting the principles of the *acquis communautaire social*.

Consequently, the Commission and the Member States urgently need to consider comprehensive regulation of transnational temporary agency work. This chapter's analysis of, on the one hand, the debates on the conflicting principles of the *acquis communautaire social*, and on the other hand, on the proposed draft and finally adopted text of the Services Directive regulating the transnational movement of workers providing services, aims to provide valuable lessons for the future transnational labour regulation of temporary agency work. Therefore we also have chosen to deal in detail with some aspects of the draft proposal for the Services Directive in spite of the fact that they were explicitly rejected in the legislative process.

2. The Services Directive: Different Perspectives

On 13 January 2004, the Commission published a proposal for a draft directive liberalising the market in services.[13] The proposed Directive aimed to enhance and guarantee the freedom to provide services in the internal market in accordance with the EC Treaty.[14] Its underlying assumption was that barriers at the national level cannot be removed solely by relying on the direct application of Articles 43 and 49 of the Treaty. Comprehensive secondary legislation was needed.

At the heart of the proposed Services Directive was the so-called "country of origin" principle.[15] This principle has wider implications, but became the subject of fierce debate as to its merits in principle and its proposed application in practice, specifically regarding the labour standards of workers engaged in transnational provision of services.[16]

13 Proposal for a Directive on Services in the Internal Market, COM (2004) 2 final/3, adopted 13 January 2004.

14 Services account for over two-thirds of employment in the EU. Explanatory Memorandum to the proposed Services Directive, Section 1: "Necessity and objective", *ibid.*, p. 5: "Services are omnipresent in today's economy, generating almost 70% of GNP and jobs [...]".

15 *Ibid.*, Article 16.

16 For details of the controversy, and its wider institutional legislative implications, see Kowalsky (2006), pp. 212–13. "For the first time ever the ETUC has succeeded in ensuring that a draft Directive has been brought to the attention of the European public and the media prior to being finally approved", and "The question of services goes beyond the significance of the issue itself and is of considerable importance for the general position of the European Parliament within the institutional triangle [...] the European institutional system has become more democratic".

This section analyses the differences between a market-oriented and a socially oriented perspective, taking into account what might have been the potential implications of the proposed Directive for the labour standards of temporary agency workers. The market-oriented argument is marked with an *M*, the social policy-oriented one with an *S*.

Free Movement of Goods vs Services

M: The European common market aims to achieve free movement of goods, services, capital and labour with no discrimination on grounds of nationality. The draft Services Directive aimed to remove obstacles to free movement of services between Member States by applying the same principles used to remove obstacles to free movement of goods.

S: Services are not the same as goods. Services involve persons; in particular, the workers who provide the services. Different principles should apply. "Labour is not a commodity".[17]

"Mutual Recognition" Principle vs "Country of Origin" Principle

M: The principle governing free movement of goods is the "mutual recognition" principle. Goods produced lawfully in one EU Member State (the "country of origin") must be allowed to circulate freely in the common market. Each EU Member State must extend mutual recognition to the rules of other Member States. Similarly, free movement of services should not be obstructed because another Member State has different rules from those of the country of origin. The same principle should be applied to services and, therefore, to the workers providing them.

S: The "mutual recognition" principle in EU law on free movement of goods is balanced by the "rule of reason": Member States may justify restrictions on free movement of goods where these are based on an open-ended category of "mandatory requirements of public policy".[18] In contrast, the "country of origin" principle (Article 16 of the draft

17 International labour law has its most important source in the norms promulgated by the International Labour Organisation (ILO), established in 1919, which declared as one of its principles that "labour should not be regarded merely as a commodity or article of commerce". Article 427 of the Treaty of Versailles, 1919, which contained the first ILO Constitution. The Constitution was revised in 1944, and Article 1 declared its aims and purposes to be those of the Declaration annexed to the Constitution, which "reaffirms the fundamental principles on which the Organisation is based and, in particular, that – (a) labour is not a commodity". O'Higgins (1997), p. 225.

18 The *Cassis* "rule of reason" justifications: *Rewe-Zentral AG v. Bundesmonopolverwaltung für Branntwein, ("Cassis de Dijon")* [1979] ECR 649. "Although in the area of goods, these open-ended exceptions have generally been referred to as 'mandatory requirements', we see that in the field of services the term 'imperative requirements' or the generic term 'objective justifications' is more often used. The origins of

Directive) did not allow Member States to justify restrictions on free movement on policy grounds. Instead, there was a closed list of "derogations" (such as the Posting of Workers Directive[19]) allowed from the principle (Article 17).

EU Centralisation vs Subsidiarity

M: In the absence of harmonised rules laying down minimum standards for the provision of services in the internal market, the country of origin principle provided a single and simple rule for regulation of the internal market in services.

S: The country of origin principle displaced national standards on the provision of services. Unlike the mutual recognition principle, national courts could not use mandatory requirements of public policy to justify restrictions on free movement of services. Member States could not apply their national rules to regulate service providers from other Member States operating on their territory.

Discrimination between Service Providers vs Discrimination between Workers

M: Requiring service providers to comply both with their own national rules and with those of other Member States where they provide services imposes a double burden of compliance compared to service providers based only in one Member State. It discriminates against them on grounds of their nationality. Requiring compliance only with the rules of their country of origin removed this discrimination.

S: Requiring providers of services in another Member State to comply only with the labour law of their country of origin means the workers providing the services are treated differently from other workers in the Member State where the services are provided. Preventing discrimination against service providers on grounds of nationality does not justify discrimination against workers on grounds of nationality.

Minimum vs Maximum Protection of Labour Standards

M: The Posted Workers Directive 96/71/EC was and is one of the derogations allowed by Article 17 of the draft Directive. Directive 96/71/EC provides that national legislation and (only in the construction sector) generally applicable and binding collective agreements protect workers

---

this approach in the services context can be found in the case of *Van Binsbergen* [Case 33/74, *Van Binsbergen v. Bestuur van de Bedrijfsvereniging voor de Mataalsnijverheid* [1974] ECR 1299]". Craig and de Búrca (2003), p. 767.

19 Directive 96/71/EC concerning the posting of workers in the framework of the provision of services. OJ 1996, L18/1.

posted to a host country by a service provider based in the country of origin.

S: The Posted Workers Directive aims to provide minimum protection. The draft Services Directive transformed this into maximum protection. There was to be no protection against lower labour standards outside the minimum standards required by the Posted Workers Directive.

Advantages for Consumers vs Disadvantages for Workers

M: Removing barriers to free movement of services would benefit consumers by allowing competition between service providers in different Member States, thereby increasing choice and lowering prices.

S: The draft Services Directive, by allowing competition between service providers in different countries over wages and working conditions, would have meant that workers would suffer as labour standards were driven down without any protection by EU minimum standards.

Quality of Services vs Quality of Labour

M: The draft directive on Services and other EU law (for example, mutual recognition of qualifications), recognised that minimum standards are required for the provision of services by certain professions (doctors, lawyers, architects…). It thus allowed Member States to lay down requirements, including collective rules set by regulated professional bodies, prescribing standards for professional workers providing services.

S: No such protection was envisaged by the draft Services Directive in the case of services provided by workers. There was no recognition of standards, including those in collective agreements, prescribed for workers providing services. In the absence of such EU standards, price competition would drive both service standards and labour standards down to the lowest level.

Administrative Simplicity vs Effective Protection

M: The exclusive application of the standards of the country of origin eliminated the need to compare standards of different Member States to see if they are compatible. The responsibility of the country of origin to supervise compliance with its own standards meant efficient administration of standards through a one-stop shop.

S: The supervision of home country labour standards in the host country where services are provided could not be effectively performed by authorities in the country of origin. Enforcing labour law is difficult enough in relation to workers who are nationals of the host Member State; it is more difficult to ensure that national labour law protects workers who are not nationals; it would be even more difficult to ensure that "country of origin" labour law protects workers outside the country of origin, especially where enforcement is not by the authorities in the Member State where they are working, but by the authorities in their country of origin.

Simplicity vs Complexity of Identifying Relevant Regulations

M: The country of origin principle allowed for the simple and easy identification of the relevant rules applicable to service providers. Once the Member State of the service provider is established, the relevant rules, including the rules of labour law applicable to the workers providing services, could be applied.

S: The problem of identifying where a service provider is really established was underestimated. The derogations to the country of origin principle (including Rome I on choice of law rules and the Posted Workers Directive) leave much scope for dispute as to whether the rules of the home country (of origin) apply to the workers providing services. There would be many disputes over whether the rules of the country of origin apply or those under the permitted derogations.

Summing Up

The point of this introductory illustration of different perspectives on liberalisation of services in the EU is not to argue that one is wrong and the other right. Rather, all arguments presented above are relevant within the context of existing EC law. A comprehensive legal approach needs to balance the market and social policy aspects with each other in order to achieve consistency with the law of the common market and the *acquis communautaire social*. Much of the debate aroused by the proposed Services Directive was due to the fact that the Commission gave primacy to the market-oriented aspects and neglected the social policy dimension. It took a prolonged struggle by the European Parliament and many others, not least the European Trade Union Confederation, to achieve a semblance of balance.

3. The Legislative Progression of the Services Directive

Following the Commission's proposal of the Services Directive in January 2004, in January 2005 a preliminary report on the proposed Directive was issued by the rapporteur of the European Parliament's Internal Market Committee, Evelyne Gebhardt. This proposed replacing the "country of origin" principle with that of "mutual recognition".[20] In mid-May 2005, the European Parliament's Employment and Social Affairs Committee presented its report. The rapporteur, Anne Van

20 *European Industrial Relations Review*, No. 378 (July 2005), p. 20.

Lancker, specifically concerned with the "country of origin" principle, stated that national legislation in the area of labour law and social protection should be respected: "I have written clearly and explicitly that social legislation, labour law rules and collective agreements are a priority in all Member States". Accordingly, she too proposed replacing the "country of origin" principle with that of "mutual recognition". This specified that where there is no minimum level or European harmonisation or minimum rules in force in each Member State, the host Member State should determine the relevant conditions of access and exercise of services.[21]

It transpired, however, that the position in the Parliament's Internal Market Committee was subject to contention. On 4 October 2005 the Committee announced that it had postponed a vote on the draft report due to internal conflicts between left-wing and right-wing MEP groups which had produced different proposals. In contrast to the proposal in Gebhardt's draft report to replace the "country of origin" principle, the other proposal wished to retain the principle.[22] When the vote was eventually held in the Internal Market Committee on 22 November 2005, a compromise prevailed. The Committee supported a provision that the service provider should be subject only to home country regulations: the "country of origin" principle. However, "labour law" was to be excluded from the scope of the proposed Directive.[23]

This exclusion of labour law, despite the apparent reaffirmation of the "country of origin" principle, highlighted the specific and exceptional sensitivity of its application to labour standards. This was confirmed when the vote on the first reading of the proposed Services Directive took place in the plenary of the Parliament on 16 February 2006. The Parliament voted to remove the "country of origin" principle and replaced it with a provision entitled "freedom to provide services". Neither the country of origin nor the host country was specifically mentioned. Rather, Member States were enjoined to respect the right of the service provider to supply services and to guarantee to the provider "free access to and free exercise of a service activity within its territory". One commentator stated: "Crucially, from an employment policy perspective, the EP"s text does not include labour law: Member States will continue to apply their own rules on conditions of employment, including those laid down through collective bargaining agreements".[24] Not least, the text also excluded "sensitive sectors" such as temporary work agencies.

21 *European Industrial Relations Review*, No. 377 (June 2005), p. 2.

22 *European Industrial Relations Review*, No. 382 (November 2005), p. 2.

23 *European Industrial Relations Review*, No. 383 (December 2005), p. 2.

24 *European Industrial Relations Review*, No. 386 (March 2006), p. 2.

On 4 April 2006 the Commission presented a revised proposal for a Services Directive. In its most significant concession, the Commission removed the "country of origin" principle. On the other hand, the text did not require a cross-border service provider to comply with the rules of the host country. The text excluded temporary agency work.[25] But there was considerable and continuing debate over the precise wording and scope of the exclusion of labour law.[26] The legislative process eventually forced the Commission and the Council to engage with the social policy dimension. Through the amendments by the European Parliament, the final Directive reflects a balance of the freedom of service providers in the internal market with the *acquis communautaire social* protecting workers. The proposed Services Directive had aimed to eliminate restrictions on the provision of services by postulating the "country of origin" principle, preventing Member States applying their national rules to service providers from outside. The "country of origin" principle clashed with the *acquis communautaire social.* Instead, the final Directive incorporates central elements of this *acquis.*

It reflects the underlying principle of the equal treatment of workers by specifically authorising the host Member State to apply its rules on employment conditions and collective agreements, not those of the country of origin (Article 16(3)). It provides that the subject matter covered by the Directive does not affect labour law, employment conditions, collective agreements or industrial action (Article 1(6) and 1(7)). It aims to prevent "social dumping" by providing explicit protection for collective agreements, acknowledging protection of workers as an overriding reason relating to the public interest and re-affirms fundamental rights of labour. Finally, it respects the EU law prescribing minimum labour standards, as in the Posting Directive. Each of these elements of the *acquis communautaire social* will now be examined as they appear in the final text of the Services Directive.

---

25 Amended Proposal for a Directive of the European Parliament and of the Council on Services in the Internal Market, COM (2006) 160 final.

26 For example, a draft from the General Secretariat of the Council proposes an amendment to Article 1(6) as follows (amendment in italics): "This Directive does not affect labour law, that is any legal or contractual provision concerning employment conditions, working conditions, including health and safety at work and the relationship between employers and workers, which Member States apply *in accordance with national law* in compliance with Community law [...]". Council of the European Union, Interinstitutional File: 2004/0001 (COD), Doc. 9612/06, Brussels, 22 May 2006. For details of the legislative process up to this point, see Kowalsky (2006).

4. Transnational Employment, Services and the *Acquis Communautaire Social*: The "Country of Origin" Principle vs the Equal Treatment Principle

A central feature of the freedom to provide services in the internal market is that the provision of services, in contrast to free movement of goods, usually involves *employees* of the service provider crossing borders to perform the services. So *in practice* the free movement of *services* shares many characteristics with the free movement of *workers*.[27]

Labour is not a commodity. The proposed Services Directive used a legal technique to reverse this fundamental social value: it classified the proposed directive as free movement of services, not workers. Yet services are provided by workers.[28] Workers *moving from* one Member State to another encounter different working conditions, laid down in legislation, collective agreements and other legal sources. The fundamental principle of equal treatment regardless of nationality means that workers are entitled to the same terms and conditions regardless of nationality. Workers are entitled to equal treatment under the laws of the host Member State.[29]

Instead, the proposed Services Directive asserted the "country of origin principle" in Article 16(1) (italics added):

> Member States shall ensure that providers are subject *only to the national provisions of their Member State of origin* which fall within the co-ordinated field.

---

27 Whatever the parallels in practice, from the *formal legal* viewpoint, as confirmed by the European Court of Justice (ECJ), the freedoms affecting services and workers are analytically quite distinct: "The Court has held that workers employed by a business established in one Member State who are temporarily sent to another Member State to provide services do not, in any way, seek access to the labour market in that second state, if they return to their country of origin or residence after completion of their work". *Finalarte Sociedade de Construção Civil Lda and Others v. Urlaubs- und Lohnausgleichskasse der Bauwirtschaft*, Cases C-49-50/98, C-52/98, C-54/98, C-68/98 and C-71/98, [2001] ECR I-7831, p. 22. It is essential, however, whatever the *formal legal* analytical distinction, to take into account the fact that, *in practice*, movement of *workers* is a, if not the central feature of cross-border *service* provision in the internal market. A starting point of principle in this respect is Article 50 of the EC Treaty (italics added): "the person providing a service may, in order to do so, temporarily pursue his activity in the State where the service is provided, *under the same conditions as are imposed by that State on its own nationals*."

28 Workers working *in* one Member State are not affected by free movement. Their terms of employment are governed by the law of the Member State in which they work. Similarly, service providers operating exclusively in one Member State, and their employees, are not affected.

29 A primary principle governing free movement of workers is equal treatment and non-discrimination on grounds of nationality. Article 39 EC: "1. Freedom of movement for

> Paragraph 1 should cover national provisions relating to access to and the exercise of a service activity, in particular those requirements governing the behaviour of the provider […] contracts and the provider's liability.[30]

The proposed Services Directive prescribed that the *behaviour* of service providers as regards their employees, their *contracts* with their employees and their *liabilities* towards their employees will all be governed by the law of the Member State of origin. Behaviour, contracts and liability (that is, terms and conditions of employment of the employees of service providers) are determined by the nationality of the service provider. Employees of service providers are denied equal treatment with employees in the Member State to which they move because of the nationality of their employer. In practice, this will frequently result in discrimination, direct and indirect, based on the nationality of the employees (as when the service provider imports employees from the country of origin).[31] The

---

workers shall be secured within the Community. 2. Such freedom of movement shall entail the abolition of any discrimination based on nationality between workers of the Member States as regards employment, remuneration and other conditions of work and employment. 3. It shall entail the right, subject to limitations justified on grounds of public policy, public security or public health: […] (c) to stay in a Member State for the purpose of employment in accordance with the provisions governing the employment of nationals of that State laid down by law, regulation or administrative action […]". This is elaborated in Regulation 1612/68, Title II, "Employment and Equality of Treatment", Article 7: "A worker who is a national of a Member State may not, in the territory of another Member State, be treated differently from national workers by reason of his nationality in respect of any conditions of employment and work, in particular as regards remuneration, dismissal, and should he become unemployed, reinstatement or reemployment". Regulation (EEC) No. 1612/68 of the Council of 15 October 1968 on freedom of movement for workers within the Community OJ Sp. Ed. 1968, No. L257/2, p. 475, as amended. The principle of equal treatment is extended to nationals of third countries by the EU Charter of Fundamental Rights 2000, Article 15(3): "Nationals of third countries who are authorised to work in the territories of the Member States are entitled to working conditions equivalent to those of citizens of the Union". Re-numbered in the proposed Constitutional Treaty as Article II-75(3). See the detailed commentary on Article 15(3) by Christophe Vigneau in Bercusson (2006), pp. 189–92.

30 The principles of the proposed directive on free movement of services conflicted with the principles governing free movement of workers. Arguably, the principle of free movement itself is subverted by the "country of origin" principle. The country of origin principle may promote free movement of service providers from countries with low labour standards wishing to exploit their labour cost advantage, but equally it is an obstacle to free movement of service providers, and their employees, from countries with high labour standards, disadvantaged by the higher labour standards of their country of origin (in both cases subject to the possible derogation of Article 17(20): "the freedom of parties to choose the law applicable to their contract").

31 Subject to the derogation in Article 17(5) of "matters covered by Directive 96/71/EC", the Posting of Workers Directive.

country of origin principle is premised on unequal treatment of workers on grounds of nationality and thereby conflicts with Articles 39(2) and 39(3)(c) EC and violates Article 7 of Regulation 1612/68.[32]

The proposed Services Directive was concerned with service providers, and their employees, operating in more than one Member State. The draft Directive prescribed the reverse of equal treatment: employees of service providers moving to another Member State were *not* entitled to equal treatment, but were with some exceptions subject to the principle that they are governed by the rules of their country of origin. The purpose of the draft Services Directive was to ensure that different rules applying in different Member States do not obstruct the free movement of service providers. Equal treatment of workers was to be sacrificed on the altar of free movement of service providers. Under the guise of application of the rules of the service provider's country of origin, the contracts of workers with service providers in the host Member State were to be governed by the law of the country of origin. Employees of service providers were to be denied equal treatment with workers of the host country.

It was not surprising that the application of the "country of origin" principle to employment conditions should have aroused the opposition of those concerned to protect the principle of equal treatment of workers. The outcome was an amendment of the European Parliament which deleted the "country of origin" principle from Article 16 of the proposed Directive and substituted the following provision (Article 16(3), italics added):[33]

---

32 That the "country of origin" principle also conflicts with the EU Charter Article 15(3) (now Article II-75(3) of the proposed Constitution) has, ironically, the result that better protection is extended to migrant workers who are third country nationals than to migrant workers from other Member States.

33 As finally adopted, the Services Directive sets out rules on freedom of establishment and free movement of services. Article 1 ("Subject matter"), provides in paragraph 1: (italics added) "This Directive establishes general provisions facilitating the exercise of the *freedom of establishment* for service providers and the *free movement of services*, while maintaining a high quality of services". The "general provisions" facilitating these freedoms are spelled out in Articles 14, 15 and 16. The Directive does this by prescribing that free movement is not to be subject to *requirements*, (Article 14 ("Prohibited *requirements*") provides in paragraph 1: "Member States shall not make access to, or the exercise of, a service activity in their territory subject to compliance with any of the following: 1) discriminatory *requirements* based directly or indirectly on nationality [...]"), existing *requirements* are to be evaluated, (Article 15 ("*Requirements* to be evaluated") provides in paragraph 1: "Member States shall examine whether, under their legal system, any of the *requirements* listed in paragraph 2 are imposed and shall ensure that any such *requirements* are compatible with the conditions laid down in

> The Member State to which the provider moves shall not be prevented from imposing requirements with regard to the provision of a service activity, where they are justified for reasons of public policy, public security, public health or the protection of the environment and in accordance with paragraph 1. *Nor shall that Member State be prevented from applying, in accordance with Community law, its rules on employment conditions, including those laid down in collective agreements.*[34]

As amended, the Services Directive therefore provides that the rules on free movement of services are not to affect the national labour law and employment conditions of the host Member State. This is spelled out in Article 1 ("Subject matter"), paragraph 6:[35]

---

paragraph 3 [non-discrimination, necessity and proportionality]. Member States shall adapt their laws, regulations or administrative provisions so as to make them compatible with those conditions"); and freedom to provide services is not to be subject to *requirements* as to access or exercise unless these respect certain principles (Article 16 ("Freedom to provide services") provides in paragraph 1: "Member States shall respect the right of providers to provide services in a Member State other than that in which they are established. The Member State in which the service is provided shall ensure free access to and free exercise of a service activity within its territory. Member States shall not make access to or exercise of a service activity in their territory subject to compliance with any *requirements* which do not respect the following principles: (a) non-discrimination: the *requirement* may be neither directly nor indirectly discriminatory with regard to nationality or, in the case of legal persons, with regard to the Member State in which they are established; (b) necessity: the *requirement* must be justified for reasons of public policy, public security, public health or the protection of the environment; (c) proportionality: the *requirement* must be suitable for attaining the objective pursued, and must not go beyond what is necessary to attain that objective").

34 Thereby reiterating the principle laid down by the ECJ in Case C-113/89, *Rush Portuguesa* [1990] ECR 1417, and going beyond the limitations of the Posting Directive 96/71/EC, OJ 1996 L18/1, which otherwise prevails over the Services Directive (Article 3(1)(a)) or is otherwise merely a derogation from the freedom to provide services (Article 17(2)). See also Recital 86: "This Directive should not affect terms and conditions of employment which, pursuant to Directive 96/71/EC [...] apply to workers posted to provide a service in the territory of another Member State". Recital 86 includes the following penultimate sentence regarding Directive 96/71/EC (italics added): "This not only concerns terms and conditions of employment which are laid down by law but also those laid down in collective agreements or arbitration awards that are officially declared or *de facto universally applicable* within the meaning of Directive 96/71/EC". See also Hellsten (2006).

35 See also Recital 14: "This Directive does not affect terms and conditions of employment, including maximum work periods and minimum rest periods, minimum paid annual holidays, minimum rates of pay as well as health, safety and hygiene at work, which Member States apply in compliance with Community law, nor does it affect relations between social partners, including the right to negotiate and conclude collective agreements, the right to strike and to take industrial action in accordance with

> This Directive does not affect labour law, that is any legal or contractual provision concerning employment conditions, working conditions, including health and safety at work and the relationship between employers and workers, which Member States apply in accordance with national law which respects Community law. Equally, this Directive does not affect the social security legislation of the Member States.

The proposed Services Directive should have respected the *acquis communautaire social*. The proposed Directive conflicted with the *acquis* in the social sphere; in particular, it was a violent break with the fundamental principle of equal treatment embodied in many aspects of the *acquis*. The policy and principle of equal treatment guaranteed to workers exercising freedom of movement to work in other Member States, challenged by the proposed Directive, was re-affirmed in the amended text of the Directive finally adopted. This aspect also provides a good base for any future design of a specific legal instrument harmonising the transnational regulation of temporary agency work in the EU.

5. Transnational Temporary Employment and Social Dumping

The principle of equal treatment, non-discrimination, is rooted in the *acquis* of EU labour law.[36] The proposed Services Directive proposed to break with this established *acquis* by explicitly allowing different conditions to apply to workers doing the same work – on the grounds that they are employed by service providers subject to the law of their country of origin. This contradicted not only the equal treatment principle of the *acquis communautaire*, but threatened to undermine terms and conditions of employment, including collective agreements and fundamental labour rights established as public policy in the labour laws of many Member States: in other words, it promoted "social dumping".

This can be seen as a straight conflict of interests. On the one hand, service providers wish to exploit the comparative advantage of lower labour costs in their country of origin. On the other hand, their employees seek equal treatment with workers in the host country. This encapsulates a conflict between two principles underlying the EU: free move-

national law and practices which respect Community law, nor does it apply to services provided by temporary work agencies. This Directive does not affect Member States' social security legislation".

36 It is manifest in numerous directives on sex discrimination, on discrimination on other grounds, and in the case of different categories of workers (part-time workers, fixed-term workers, teleworkers).

ment of services and equal treatment of workers. It is the clash between economic and social visions of the EU. Either "labour is a commodity", and competition over terms and conditions of employment, including those of migrant workers, is an inherent element of the common market. Or "labour is not a commodity", and the common market's rules on competition do not apply to workers involved in free movement of services.

The principles of equal treatment, the public interest in protection of workers and fundamental rights were acknowledged as applicable to transnational employment in the most important EU legislation concerning movement of workers in the context of provision of services: the Posting of Workers Directive.[37]

On 1 August 1991, the Commission published a Proposal for a Council Directive concerning the posting of workers in the framework of the provision of services.[38] This was concerned to implement the commitment in the Commission's Action Programme relating to the Community Charter of the Fundamental Social Rights of Workers, as regards the "working conditions applicable to workers from another State performing work in the host country in the framework of the freedom to provide services, especially on behalf of a subcontracting undertaking".[39]

The Commission posed the question "as to which national labour legislation should be applied to undertakings which post a worker to carry out temporary work in a Member State".[40] Formally, the solution depends on conflict of law rules, but given that these vary among Member States, the outcome may give rise to distortions of competition between national and foreign undertakings. The Commission therefore proposed to coordinate the laws of the Member States "to eradicate practices which may be both detrimental to fair competition between undertakings and prejudicial to the interests of the workers concerned".[41] The element of competition between firms as regards labour conditions was described as follows:[42]

> A particular problem arises, however, where a Member State places obligations, notably with regard to pay, on firms based in and working on its territory, and these firms are faced with competition – for a specific task carried

37 Directive 96/71/EC concerning the posting of workers in the framework of the provision of services. OJ 1996, L18/1.

38 COM(91) 230 final, SYN 346, Brussels, 1 August 1991.

39 Action Programme, COM(89) 568 final, Brussels, 19 November 1989, Part II, Section 4B.

40 Explanatory Memorandum, paragraph 2.

41 *Ibid.*, paragraph 3.

42 *Ibid.*, paragraph 9 bis.

> would certainly affect fair competition between undertakings and equality of treatment between foreign and national undertakings; it would from the social point of view be completely unacceptable.

"Social dumping", which was "from the social point of view [...] completely unacceptable" to the Commission in 1991, had become socially acceptable to the Commission in 2004 when it proposed the Services Directive.

Fortunately the European Parliament did not share the view of 2004. Not only did the Parliament retain the *acquis communautaire social* in the Posting Directive, but it reiterated the position that "social dumping" was unacceptable by providing that the rules in the Services Directive on free movement of services in general were not to affect the national labour law and employment conditions of the host Member State.

Further amendments to the proposed Directive expanded this social vision by (i) the explicit protection of collective agreements, (ii) the acknowledgment of protection of workers as an overriding reason relating to the public interest, and (iii) the reaffirmation of fundamental rights of labour.

5.1 Protection of Collective Agreements

The Services Directive sets out rules on freedom of establishment and free movement of services. The Directive does this by prescribing that free movement is not to be subject to *requirements*, existing *requirements* are to be evaluated, and freedom to provide services is not to be subject to *requirements* as to access or exercise unless these respect certain principles.[47]

The target of the Services Directive is those *requirements* which are deemed to violate the rules on free movement. Article 4 ("Definitions") in Article 4(7) stipulates that collective agreements are *not* such requirements: (italics added)

> "*requirement*" means any obligation, prohibition, condition or limit provided for in the laws, regulations or administrative provisions of the Member States or in consequence of case-law, administrative practice, the rules of professional bodies, or the collective rules of professional associations or other professional organisations, adopted in the exercise of their legal autonomy. *Rules laid down in collective agreements negotiated by the social partners shall not as such be seen as requirements within the meaning of this Directive.*[48]

---

47 See the text of these provisions in Articles 1 and 14–16 in footnote 33 above.

48 A question is raised by the provision in Article 16(3): "Nor shall that Member State be prevented from applying, in accordance with Community law, its rules on employment conditions, including those laid down in collective agreements". While this further supports the non-restrictive nature of collective agreements as far as free movement

The Directive's rules on free movement do not apply to collective agreements.[49]

There is no specific provision in the Services Directive declaring collective agreements to be non-discriminatory *per se*. But it follows from the wholesale exclusion from the subject matter of this Directive on free movement of services of "rules laid down in collective agreements negotiated by the social partners"[50] that an interpretation of the provisions of the Directive as a whole which is both effective and consistent is that agreements concluded in the context of collective negotiations between management and labour must be regarded as falling outside the scope of the Directive.[51] This can only be interpreted to mean that collective agreements are not discriminatory *as far as rules on free movement are concerned*.[52]

The European Parliament's view clearly differed from the position taken by the Commission. The same hostile approach of the Commission to the application of collective agreements is highlighted by contrast with

---

is concerned, if "rules laid down in collective agreements" are not "requirements", why is the reference to collective agreements in Article 16(3) necessary?

49 Collective agreements are distinguished not only from State measures, but also from those of professional bodies or associations. As they lack the regulatory effect to be deemed *requirements* subject to the Services Directive's rules on free movement of services, the same argument should apply to Articles 43 and 49 EC. The link is made through the legal basis of the Services Directive: "Having regard to the Treaty establishing the European Community, and in particular the first and third sentence of Article 47(2) and Article 55 thereof". Further, Recital 5: "It is therefore necessary to remove barriers to the freedom of establishment for providers in Member States and barriers to the free movement of services as between Member States [...]"; Recital 6: "Those barriers cannot be removed solely by relying on direct application of Articles 43 and 49 of the Treaty [...]".

50 These not being deemed "requirements" (Article 4(7)).

51 As put by the European Court of Justice in *Albany International BV v. Stichting Bedrijfspensioenfonds Textielindustrie*, Case C-67/96; with Joined cases C-115/97, C-116/97 and C-117/97; [1999] ECR I-5751, paras. 59–60: " [...]the social policy objectives pursued by such agreements would be seriously undermined if management and labour were subject to Article 85(1) [Articles 43/49] of the Treaty when seeking jointly to adopt measures to improve conditions of work and employment. It therefore follows from an interpretation of the provisions of the Treaty as a whole which is both effective and consistent that agreements concluded in the context of collective negotiations between management and labour in pursuit of such objectives must, by virtue of their nature and purpose, be regarded as falling outside the scope of Article 85(1) [Articles 43/49] of the Treaty".

52 Not being "requirements", rules laid down in collective agreements are not prohibited as "discriminatory requirements" (Article 14(1)), they need not satisfy the principle of non-discrimination (Article 16(1)(a)), and they are justifiable under the provision in Article 16(3). The same principle applies to Articles 43 and 49 EC.

the approach of the European Court of Justice in *Commission vs Germany*, where the Court accepted in principle restrictions on the hiring-out of manpower in the construction industry in Germany.[53] As such, the case throws light on the current Commission's perspective on regulation of labour standards in transnational employment.

A Commission Communication of 2001 stated that the European Court has accepted that worker protection justifies derogation from the freedom to provide services, though "purely administrative considerations would not justify such a derogation". However:[54]

> Exclusion from participation in a public procurement contract of an undertaking established in another Member State because it was not affiliated to a national collective agreement in force in the relevant sector in the country of the contracting authority would thus not only be contrary to the public procurement directives, but might also be an infringement of the freedom to provide services and, in certain cases, of the right of establishment. [Footnote 86 states: "See in, this context, the conclusions of the Advocate-General in Case C-493/99, *Commission v. Germany*, of 5.4.2001"].

The Communication does not state that the mandatory application of labour standards, because they are embodied in a collective agreement, violates EC law. EC law poses no obstacle to collective agreements embodying labour standards being made mandatory on all employers and workers in a Member State. This was the undisputed conclusion of the European Court in *Rush Portuguesa*.[55]

The problems arise where the undertaking is excluded from affiliation to the collective agreement, or affiliation is made more difficult for undertakings established in another Member State, and this precludes participation in the public procurement process. This was the position in the case cited as authority in the Communication: Case C-493/99, *Commission v. Germany*.[56] German law prevented hiring out of employees among construction undertakings unless they were party to collective agreements for the industry, and undertakings could be party to the col-

53 Case C-493/99, [2001] ECR I-8163.

54 Interpretative Communication of the Commission on the Community law applicable to public procurement and the possibilities for integrating social considerations into public procurement, COM(2001) 566 final, Brussels, 15 October 2001, p. 21.

55 "[…] Community law does not preclude Member States from extending their legislation, or collective agreements entered into by both sides of industry, to any person who is employed, even temporarily, within their territory, no matter in which country the employer is established; nor does Community law prohibit Member States from enforcing those rules by appropriate means". *Rush Portuguesa Lda v. Office Nacional d'Immigration,* Case C-113/89, [1990] ECR I-1417, paragraph 18.

56 [2001] ECR I-8163.

lective agreements only if they had a subsidiary in Germany employing construction workers.

In an Opinion of 5 April 2001, Advocate-General Ruiz-Jarabo Colomer agreed with the Commission that the German legislation entailed covert discrimination on grounds of nationality (paragraph 14) since German undertakings "need only subscribe to the agreement [...] whereas undertakings from other Member States have to establish a permanent subsidiary" (paragraph 16).

The German government sought to justify the requirement on the basis that the restriction was minimal, the objective of protection of workers from abuses required adherence to collective agreements, and the requirement was proportionate, necessary and appropriate. Nonetheless, the Advocate-General concluded (paragraph 26):

> I would not deny that I sympathise with the reasoning deployed by the German government [...] I would disagree with it, however, insofar as it considers that the threat to workers' rights in the hiring out of employees, which is particularly acute in the construction industry, is sufficient to justify covert discrimination.

Unfortunately, the Advocate-General's conclusion as to the violation of EC law took the following form (paragraph 35):

> by requiring that, in order to hire out employees, all undertakings of a consortium set up in order to carry out construction work should be party to all the national collective agreements for the construction sector [...]

This appears to have been duly reflected in the Commission's Communication of 15 October 2001. Ten days later, however, the European Court, in deciding the case on 25 October 2001, formulated its condemnation of the German legislation more carefully (paragraph 22):

> it must be concluded that the requirement to have an establishment in the Member State in which the services are to be provided, such as that under the legislation in question, goes beyond what is necessary to attain the objective of providing social protection for workers in the building industry.

In other words, the Court targeted *not* the collective agreement setting the labour standard, but the requirement to have an establishment, which is a condition of affiliation to the collective agreement, and thereby constitutes an infringement of the freedom to provide services. Hence, if the German law had allowed for affiliation to the collective agreement *without the requirement of establishment,* it would not have violated EC law on the freedom to provide services. Labour standards can condition the transnational provision of services.

The provisions of Directive 96/71/EC (the Posting Directive) reinforce the important principle established by *Rush Portuguesa.* The Commission's Communication of 2003 on the implementation of the Posting Directive acknowledges the significance of collective agreements in the context of transnational provision of services by posted workers:[57]

> The question of the applicability of collective agreements is particularly important, since wages are chiefly determined by collective bargaining. Most Member States' legislations provide for the application or extension of universally applicable collective agreements to posted workers. Some Member States do not have universally applicable collective agreements. Consequently, the only rules that these States apply to posted workers are those contained in the law or in other legislative texts.

It would appear that it is vital, therefore, to reinforce national collective bargaining systems. The provisions of the Posting Directive were not entirely satisfactory in this respect. Article 3(1) of the Directive provides:

> Member States shall ensure that, whatever the law applicable to the employment relationship, the undertakings referred to in Article 1(1) guarantee workers posted to their territory the terms and conditions of employment covering the following matters which, in the Member States where the work is carried out, are laid down:
>
> – by law, regulation or administrative provision, and/or
> – by collective agreements or arbitration awards which have been declared universally applicable within the meaning of paragraph 8, insofar as they concern the activities referred to in the Annex [...].[58]

Article 3(8) provides:

> "Collective agreements or arbitration awards which have been declared universally applicable" means collective agreements or arbitration awards which must be observed by all undertakings in the geographical area and in the profession or industry concerned.
>
> In the absence of a system for declaring collective agreements or arbitration awards to be of universal application within the meaning of the first subparagraph, Member States may, if they so decide, base themselves on:
>
> – collective agreements or arbitration awards which are generally applicable to all similar undertakings in the geographical area and in the profession or industry concerned, and/or

---

57 Commission of the EC, Communication from the Commission, *The implementation of Directive 96/71/EC in the Member States*, COM(2003) 458 final, Brussels, 15 July 2003, p. 9, Section 3.1.

58 Article 3(10), 2nd indent allows Member States the option to extend such collective agreements to apply to "activities other than those referred to in the Annex". A Communication from the Commission on Guidance on the Posting of Workers in the framework of the provision of services (MEMO/06/151 of 4 April 2006) states: "Terms and conditions in collective agreements that are generally applicable must be applied to posted workers in the construction sector. However, Member States may choose to apply these collective agreements to posted workers in other sectors. In fact, most Member States have chosen to do so in all sectors".

- collective agreements which have been concluded by the most representative employers' and labour organizations at national level and which are applied throughout the national territory.[59]

But the present Commission goes in quite the other direction. Far from encouraging extension of workers' protection by collective agreements, the Communication goes out of its way to undermine them:[60]

> Insofar as the absence of identification of "mandatory rules" is to be interpreted as meaning that the totality of the legislation in the field of labour law applies to posting situations, it should be pointed out that the Directive in no way permits Member States to extend all their legislative provisions and/or collective agreements governing terms and conditions of employment to workers posted on their territory, and that the application of such rules must be in compliance with the EC Treaty, in particular Article 49.

Specifically as regards collective agreements:

> Not all the transposing legislation has addressed the question of determining the collective agreements applicable to posting situations. The Commission intends to look more closely and examine the criteria used for determining the collective agreements applicable to national undertakings on the one hand and undertakings from other countries on the other. (p. 12)[61]

It continues by addressing the case of there being no collective agreements of universal application:

> The group of experts [...] was of the opinion that if Member States, in the absence of a system for declaring collective agreements or arbitration awards to be of universal application, decide to base themselves on the two other categories of collective agreements referred to in Article 3(8), i.e. generally applicable collective agreements or collective agreements concluded by the most representative employers' and labour organisations, they must make explicit mention thereof in their legislation implementing the posted workers Directive. If their implementing legislation makes no reference to this effect,

---

59 One question was whether Member States are *obliged* to include these latter agreements among the standards imposed on undertakings employing posted workers. Or merely, as put by the Explanatory Memorandum to the original proposal, "to *allow* Member States, in the absence of the abovementioned collective agreements (or awards), to include those which are complied with [...]". Although the word "*may*" would seem to preclude an obligation to observe generally applicable collective agreements, there are arguments that the Member States are so obliged. See Bercusson (1996), chapter 27, "Free Movement and Social Dumping", pp. 397–412, at pp. 404–7.

60 COM(2003) 458 final, p. 11, Section 4.1.1.

61 The Commission continues: "As the Court of Justice emphasised in the joined Cases C-49/98, C-40/98, C-52/98 to C-54/98 and C-68/98 to C-71/98 [Judgment of 25 October 2001, '*Finalarte*', points 76-83, ECR 2001, p. I-7831] these criteria may have different practical consequences in the case of 'mixed businesses', i.e. businesses which carry out activities in a variety of sectors".

> Member States may not oblige undertakings established in another Member State which post workers to their territory to observe the collective agreements referred to in the second subparagraph of Article 3(8).[62]
>
> Since no Member State's transposing legislation makes any mention of the options offered by the second subparagraph of Article 3(8), the Commission concludes that those Member States which do not have collective agreements declared to be universally applicable within the meaning of the first subparagraph of Article 3(8) of the Directive do not apply the terms and conditions of employment laid down in collective agreements to workers posted on their territory. In those countries, therefore, only the terms and conditions of employment laid down in legislative provisions apply to workers posted on their territory. (p. 12)

Instead of supporting the fundamental rights that were established in the EU Charter of December 2000 – to fair and just working conditions (Article 31) and to "negotiate and conclude collective agreements at the appropriate levels" (Article 28) – the Commission appears to demand that Member States justify the social protection of workers by collective agreements.[63]

In the draft Services Directive, under gestation at the same time as the Commission's review of the Posting Directive, the ideological shift became fully apparent. This vision, however, was not shared by the European Parliament. The amendments led to the final text of the Directive protecting collective agreements from being undermined by free movement of services.

---

62 This view of the Commission's group of experts has been challenged by the Commissoin's Legal Service in its submission to the pending Case C-341/05, *Laval un Partneri Ltd v. Svenska Byggnadsarbetareförbundet, Svenska Byggnadsarbetareförbundet, Avdelning 1, Svenska Elektrikerförbundet*, referred to the ECJ by the Swedish Labour Court, JURM(06)2007 31 January 2006. See also Ahlberg, Bruun and Malmberg (2006); also Eklund (2006).

63 For another example, see the joint letter from the leaders of the social partners in Sweden (Urban Bäckstrom and Erland Olauson) and the Netherlands (N.J. van Kesteren and P. Gortzak) in the *Financial Times* of 19 July 2006, p. 18: "The European Commission has proposed a directive that aims to improve labour mobility by creating more convergence in supplementary pensions schemes […] In our view, the Commission's reasoning is severely flawed in a number of aspects. In our countries, [these] issues […] are primarily regulated through voluntary collective agreements between the social partners. These systems have developed over time and reflect all the relevant aspects of our labour market […] by intervening in an area which in our countries is the primary responsibility of social partners, the proposal seriously undermines the liberty and incentives for social partners to continue to agree on supplementary pensions".

5.2 Protection of Workers as an Overriding Reason Relating to the Public Interest

Member States *are* permitted to restrict cross-border provision of services:[64]

> [The freedom to provide services] as one of the fundamental principles of the Treaty, may be restricted only by rules justified by *overriding requirements related to the public interest* and applicable to all persons and undertakings operating in the territory of the state where the service is provided, in so far as that interest is not safeguarded by the rules to which the provider of such a service is subject in the Member State where he is established. (italics added)

Protection of workers is accepted by the European Court as an overriding public interest.[65] Hence, the protection of posted workers, including those despatched by a foreign temporary employment agency, would be allowed to justify restricting the cross-border provision of services.[66]

The final text of the Services Directive contains various provisions concerning public interest justifications for restricting free movement.[67] Article 4(8) provides one definition:

> "overriding reasons relating to the public interest" means reasons recognised as such in the case law of the Court of Justice, including the following

64 *Arblade v. Leloup and Sofrage SARL*, Cases C-369/96 and C-276/96, [1999] ECR I-8453, para. 34,

65 Night work in bakeries: *Oebel*, Case 155/80, [1981] ECR 1993; Sunday working: *Conforama*, Case 312/89, [1990] ECR 997; working hours, health and safety not subject to economic considerations: *Sindicato de Médicos de Asistencia Pública (Simap) v. Conselleria de Sanidad y Consumo de la Generalidad Valenciana*, Case C-303/98, [2000] ECR I-7963.

66 Paul Davies (2002: 302) notes that "Most Member States, when enacting or strengthening their domestic laws, would probably have said, if asked, that they were doing so to protect their domestic businesses and the employees of those businesses from being undermined by competition from foreign enterprises relying on cheap posted workers. Indeed, the German legislator, with its customary commitment to honesty and transparency, said so in its explanatory memorandum to the relevant law. The difficulty here is that, as formulated, this is an economic aim and, as such, does not fall within the scope of an overriding public interest. In short, the justification for domestic legislation has to be found, rather bizarrely, by assessing whether it protects *the posted workers* (*Finalarte*, paras. 38–41)".

67 Some of these are implicit in the many exclusions from the subject matter of the Directive in Article 1 and from the scope of the Directive in Article 2. The general exclusion of "labour law" from the subject matter of the Directive in Article 1(6) is arguably an indication that there is a public interest justification for the non-application of the rules on free movement of services to the sphere of employment and industrial relations. The general exclusion of the "services of temporary work agencies" from the scope of the Directive in Article 2(2)(e) is another such indication.

> grounds: […] the protection of […] workers; […] [and] social policy objectives […][68]

The concept of "overriding reason relating to the public interest" appears in a number of contexts.[69] Most important, in Article 15(3)(b), requirements restricting free movement must be evaluated in light of the criterion of "necessity", which is defined in terms of "an overriding reason relating to the public interest".[70]

Despite the exclusion by Article 4(7) of "rules laid down in collective agreements" from the definition of "requirements", the Directive in the second sentence of Article 16(3) provides what seems an unnecessary permission:

---

68 Recital 40 expands this: "The concept of 'overriding reasons relating to the public interest' […] has been developed by the Court of Justice in its case law in relation to Articles 43 and 49 of the Treaty and may continue to evolve. The notion as recognised in the case law of the Court of Justice covers at least the following grounds: […] the protection of workers, including the social protection of workers […]". Recital 66 refers to the concept in terms including "social policy".

69 See Article 10(2)(b): a condition for the Member States making access to a service activity subject to granting of authorisation; Article 11(1)(c): a condition for unlimited duration of authorisations granted.

70 So "protection of workers" and "social" policy objectives are grounds for evaluating restrictive requirements as "necessary" and would be available to justify requirements, including labour law and collective agreements protecting workers (were these deemed to be "requirements", but they are not so deemed under Article 4(7) of the Directive). The concept of "necessity" is defined differently, however, in Article 16(1)(b): Member States must respect the principle of "necessity" if they wish to impose restrictions on the provision of services. "Necessity" is not defined in terms of "overriding reasons relating to the public interest". Rather: "the requirement must be justified for reasons of public policy, public security, public health or the protection of the environment". Social policy objectives and protection of workers are not specified. Article 16(3) spells out identical grounds on which a Member State may justify the imposition of requirements ("[w]here they are justified for reasons of public policy, public security, publichealth or the protection of the environment". Similarly, in Recital 78. Again, social policy objectives and protection of workers are not specified.) But Article 16(3) adds: "Nor shall that Member State be prevented from applying, in accordance with Community law, its rules on employment conditions, including those laid down in collective agreements". At best, there is an overlap here with the concept of "overriding reasons relating to the public interest", which includes social policy objectives and protection of workers. Contrast the scope of justifications available under Article 12(3), concerning Member States' selection from among several candidates requiring authorisation to provide services. Member States "may take into account, in establishing the rules for the selection procedure […] social policy objectives, the health and safety of employees or self-employed persons". Social policy objectives remain, but the protection of workers is limited to health and safety; there is no reference to rules on employment conditions.

> The Member State to which the provider moves shall not be prevented from imposing requirements with regard to the provision of a service activity, where they are justified for reasons of public policy, public security, public health or the protection of the environment and in accordance with paragraph 1.[71] Nor shall that Member State be prevented from applying, in accordance with Community law, its rules on employment conditions, including those laid down in collective agreements.

The matter may be clarified by Recital 82:

> The provisions of this Directive shall not preclude the application by a Member State of rules on employment conditions. Rules laid down by *law, regulation or administrative provisions* should, in accordance with the Treaty, be justified for reasons relating to the protection of workers and be non-discriminatory, necessary and proportionate, as interpreted by the Court of Justice, and comply with other relevant Community law.. (italics added)

Notably, there is no explicit reference to rules laid down "in collective agreements". It seems, therefore, that rules laid down in collective agreements (as *per se* not discriminatory "requirements" as far as free movement is concerned) need not be justified. [72]

---

71 Paragraph 1 of Article 16 (formerly including the now deleted "country of origin" principle) reads: "Member States shall respect the right of providers to provide services in a Member State other than that in which they are established.

The Member State in which the service is provided shall ensure free access to and free exercise of a service activity within its territory.

Member States shall not make access to or exercise of a service activity in their territory subject to compliance with any requirements which do not respect the following principles:

(a) non-discrimination: the requirement may be neither directly nor indirectly discriminatory with regard to nationality or, in the case of legal persons, with regard to the Member State in which they are established;

(b) necessity: the requirement must be justified for reasons of public policy, public security, public health or the protection of the environment;

(c) proportionality: the requirement must be suitable for attaining the objective pursued, and must not go beyond what is necessary to attain that objective."

72 Employment conditions laid down by law, regulation or administrative provisions, however, are "requirements" and must be justified as, *inter alia*, "necessary", presumably as the latter concept is defined in Articles 16(1)(b) and 16(3). Viz. "the requirement must be justified for reasons of public policy, public security, public health or the protection of the environment". The definition of "public policy" might offer a prospect for protection of workers if it is interpreted consistently with the definition in Article 4(8) of : "overriding reasons relating to the public interest" as "including the following grounds: [...] the protection of [...] workers; ... [and] social policy objectives". On the other hand, Recital 41 provides: "The concept of 'public policy', asinterpreted by the Court of Justice, covers the protection against a genuine and sufficiently serious threat affecting one of the fundamental interests of society and may

5.3 Affirmation of the Fundamental Rights of Labour

Justifications for restrictions on the freedom to provide services might include consideration of fundamental rights, in this case, those of labour.[73] The Commission's position was expressed in the Preamble to the proposed Services Directive:[74]

> In addition, any restriction of the freedom to provide services should be permitted, by way of exception, only if it is consistent with fundamental rights which, as the Court of Justice has consistently held, form an integral part of the general principles of law enshrined in the Community legal order.[75]

The contrast is clear with the text of Article 1(7) of the final Services Directive (italics added):

> This Directive does not affect the exercise of fundamental rights as recognised in the Member States *and by Community law*.[76] Nor does it affect the right to negotiate, conclude and enforce collective agreements and to take industrial action in accordance with national law and practices which respect Community law.

There is clear acknowledgment in the first sentence that "fundamental rights [...] [are] recognised [...] *by Community law*".[77] The other rights referred to are arguably these specified in the second sentence (*eiusdem generis*): Community law protects "the right to negotiate, conclude and enforce collective agreements and to take industrial action in

---

include, in particular, issues relating to human dignity, the protection of minors and vulnerable adults and animal welfare. Similarly, the concept of public security includes issues of public safety". Protection of workers is not explicitly mentioned.

73 *Omega Spielhallen- und Automatenaufstellungs-GmbH v. Oberbürgermeisterin der Bundesstadt Bonn*, Case C-36/02, decided 14 October 2004.

74 Recital 40.

75 In this connection notice should be taken of Article 31 of the EU Charter of Fundamental Rights, "Fair and just working conditions", the first paragraph of which states: "Every worker has the right to working conditions which respect his or her health, safety and dignity". See the detailed commentary on Article 31 by Thomas Blanke in Bercusson (2006), pp. 357–77.

76 The rights concerned are not the economic freedoms in Articles 43 and 49, since these are the legal basis of the Directive, which aims to supplement their inadequacies. See footnote 49 above.

77 Compare Council Regulation (EC) No. 2679/98 of 7 December 1998 on the functioning of the internal market in relation to the free movement of goods among the Member States. OJ L337/8 of 12.12.98; Article 2, which does not refer to fundamental rights recognised by Community law: "This Regulation may not be interpreted as affecting in any way the exercise of fundamental rights as recognised in Member States, including the right or freedom to strike. These rights may also include the right or freedom to take other actions covered by the specific industrial relations systems in Member States".

accordance with *national* law and practices which respect Community law".[78]

This is an interpretation consistent with Recital 15:

> This Directive respects the exercise of fundamental rights applicable in the Member States and as recognised in the Charter of Fundamental Rights of the European Union and the accompanying explanations, reconciling them with the fundamental freedoms laid down in Articles 43 and 49 of the Treaty. Those fundamental rights include the right to take industrial action in accordance with national law and practices which respect Community law.

Recital 15's explicit reference to the EU Charter is significant. The reference to reconciliation with fundamental freedoms in Articles 43 and 49 may be read as confirming that, in particular, the right to take industrial action *can be reconciled* with Articles 43 and 49 on freedom of establishment and free movement of services.[79]

6. Transnational Temporary Agency Work, Services and the Posting of Workers Directive

Directive 96/71/EC applies a specific social policy to workers posted within the framework of free movement of services.[80] Directive 96/71/EC specifies minimum terms and conditions of employment which must apply to workers posted to the host country. Furthermore, the employer is obliged in general to observe those of the host country's labour law provisions which have a public policy character[81] and that Member State's public law regulations.[82]

---

78 The second sentence (and, in particular, its last phrase: "which respect Community law") may be interpreted as meaning that insofar as *national* law and practices do *not* respect fundamental rights recognised by *Community* law they *are* affected by the Directive. The provisions of the Directive which will affect national law and practices on collective bargaining and action are the Directive's provisions which stipulate that rules laid down by collective agreements do *not* violate free movement provisions. I.e. if *national* rules were to stipulate that collective agreements or collective action *contravene* free movement rules, this *would* violate Community law's protection of these fundamental rights.

79 The position is further elaborated, if not clarified, by Recital 83, concerning derogations from the freedom to provide services and exceptional measures against a given provider: "In addition, any restriction of the free movement of services should be permitted, by way of exception, only if it is consistent with fundamental rights which form an integral part of the general principles of law enshrined in the Community legal order".

80 Directive 96/71/EC concerning the posting of workers in the framework of the provision of services. OJ 1996, L18/1.

81 Article 3(10).

82 The limitation to application of the labour law of the host Member State is that it cannot require service providers to pay "double": "National rules which require a

What the draft Services directive called a "general derogation" (Article 17(5)) was rather a recognition that the principles it initially proposed conflicted with the Posting of Workers Directive 96/71/EC. Directive 96/71/EC is not an exception to be allowed for by derogation. It arose from precisely the same context of debates regarding working conditions of the employees of service providers. The decision of policy and principle was clear: the employees of enterprises, including service providers, are not to be subject to the law of the country of origin. Instead, they are entitled to equal protection of the mandatory rules of the host Member State, including collective agreements. Working conditions are to be taken out of competition, whatever the consequences for free movement.

The derogation for posted workers means the country of origin principle does not apply to *temporary* service providers. If the workers are *permanently* posted, they may be regarded as effectively migrant workers entitled to equal treatment under the labour law provisions of the host state, even though their employer is based outside the host state. The Services Directive as initially proposed was an unsatisfactory half-way house. If employees of service providers are posted workers, they are covered by the Posting Directive. If these workers are permanently posted and treated as migrant workers, they are entitled to equal treatment under host country rules. But in between, as employees of service providers, the "country of origin" principle denied them the protection of host country standards (subject to derogations).

The proposed Services Directive thus created a separate category of employees of service providers subject to special rules. The new legal classification of employees of service providers had the serious consequence of denying to such workers the principle of equal treatment guaranteed by the *acquis communautaire* on free movement of workers. Furthermore, it created great uncertainty. Posted workers were covered, but only as far as the protection extended by Directive 96/71/EC: certain terms and conditions of employment and certain types of collective agreement. As regards other terms and conditions of employment, they must look to the country of origin. This was an impossibly complex analysis in practice.[83]

---

service provider [...] to pay employers" contributions to the host Member State's fund, in addition to those he has already paid to the fund of the Member State where he is established, constitute a restriction on freedom to provide services". *Arblade v. Leloup and Sofrage SARL*, Cases C-369/96 and C-276/96, [1999] ECR I-8453.

83 As remarked concerning a similar exercise whereby the ECJ in *Mazzoleni*, Case C-165/98, [2001] ECR I-2189, insisted that national authorities "determine whether

The clash between the policy underlying the Posting Directive and that of the country of origin principle lies in the changing political ideology and values of the Commission. This was clear in the Commission's 2003 review of the Posting Directive's implementation.[84] The policy shift can be illustrated by the Commission's position on what constitutes mandatory labour law standards required by national public policy to apply to posted workers. The Communication was concerned with the potential extension by Member States of protective labour standards to other conditions of work beyond those in Article 3(1)(a)–(g) of the Posting Directive.[85] Article 3(10) of the Directive allows for this by providing:

> This Directive shall not preclude the application by Member States, in compliance with the Treaty, to national undertakings and to the undertakings of other States, on a basis of equality of treatment, of:
>
> – terms and conditions of employment on matters other than those referred to in the first subparagraph of paragraph 1, in the case of public policy provisions,

The question arises of what falls within the scope of "public policy provisions" (*ordre public*) within the meaning of the Directive. The Commission's Communication of 2003 begins with an invitation to a strict reading of this provision:

> The Commission considers that the first indent of Article 3(10) has to be interpreted bearing in mind the objective of facilitating the free movement of services within the Community [...] Member States are not free to impose all their mandatory labour law provisions on service providers establishing in another Member State. They must comply with the rules of the EC Treaty, and in particular Article 49, as interpreted by the Court of Justice (cf. the *Portugaia Construcoes* [Judgment of 24 January 2002, Case 164/99] and *Mazzoleni* [Judgment of 15 March 2001, Case 165/98, ECR p. I-2189] judgments [...]). (p. 13)

French and Belgian workers "enjoy an equivalent position overall in relation to remuneration, taxation and social security contributions" (para. 35). One can imagine the reaction of the Belgian court receiving this judgment". Davies (2002), p. 304.

84 Commission of the EC, Communication from the Commission, *The implementation of Directive 96/71/EC in the Member States*, COM(2003) 458 final, Brussels, 15 July 2003.

85 Maximum work periods and minimum rest periods, minimum paid holidays, minimum rates of pay, as defined by the host State's law and/or practice, including overtime (not including supplementary occupational retirement pension schemes), conditions of hiring out of workers, in particular the supply of workers by temporary work agencies, health, safety and hygiene at work, protective measures with regard to the terms and conditions of employment of pregnant women or women who have recently given birth, of children and young people, and equality of treatment between men and women and other provisions on non-discrimination.

The Communication goes on to discuss interpretation of "public policy provisions":

> the concept of public policy within the meaning of Directive 96/71/EC must be interpreted in the light of the case law of the court [...]. may vary from one country to another and from one period to another [...] must be interpreted strictly and should not be determined unilaterally by each Member State [...] recourse [...] must be justified on overriding general interest grounds, must presuppose the existence of a genuine and sufficiently serious threat affecting one of the fundamental interests of society and must be in conformity with the general principles of law, in particular fundamental rights and the general principle of freedom of expression.[86]

The Commission regards the concept of public policy in the context of workers as if it were the same as in the context of goods, services and capital. Yet there are many illustrations of the European Court taking quite a different approach to public policy when it comes to protection of workers.[87] Workers are not a commodity. Public policy has much wider implications in the context of protection of labour producers – workers – than in the context of protectionism for commodity producers of goods and services. The Commission appears to be blind to this:

> To illustrate the difference between domestic public policy provisions on the one hand and public policy provisions and mandatory provisions ["*lois de police*"] in the international context on the other, we can cite the example of the rules governing dismissal, which in some countries are domestic public order provisions. These are national mandatory rules from which the parties may not derogate by contract, and which are intended to protect a "weak" party (the worker) [...] However, these same rules are not considered to be international public policy provisions or mandatory rules within the meaning of Article 7 of the Rome Convention [Rome I], which would apply *whatever the law applicable to the contract*. Accordingly, when the employment contract is validly subject to a foreign law, the domestic public policy provisions regarding dismissal do not apply automatically. (pp. 13–14)

The example provided is ironic. Even the Commission acknowledges that fundamental rights fall within the scope of public policy provisions.[88]

---

86 The Commission does not refer, as regards changes "from one period to another" in the concept of public policy, to the Charter of Fundamental Rights of the European Union, proclaimed at the meeting of the European Council held in Nice, 7–9 December 2000, and adopted by the Commission, the Council and the Member States, OJ C 364/01 of 18 December 2000.

87 See footnote 65 above.

88 There may be a general role for the EU Charter of Fundamental Rights. Article 31 of the Charter is entitled "Fair and just working conditions", and provides: "1. Every worker has the right to working conditions which respect his or her health, safety and dignity. 2. Every worker has the right to limitation of maximum working hours, to daily and weekly rest periods and to an annual period of paid leave".

The Commission cites the example of dismissal protection as not covered as a mandatory rule under Rome I. Yet the EU Charter, Article 30, proclaims as a fundamental right "Protection in the event of unjustified dismissal".[89] The Commission appears to have neglected its own commitment to respect the Charter.[90]

An explanatory document from the Council highlighted the problems created by the application of the "country of origin" principle to labour law in the proposed Services Directive. The Council Document concerned the relationship between the proposed Directive and the rules on posting of workers.[91]

6.1 *Transforming Directive 96/71/EC from a Minimum to a Maximum Standard*

The proposed Directive totally altered the underlying assumption of Directive 96/71/EC. It transformed it, in principle, from a Directive providing a *minimum* of employment protection in the host Member State[92]

89 "Every worker has the right to protection against unjustified dismissal, in accordance with Community law and national laws and practices". See the detailed commentary on Article 30 by Bruun in Bercusson (2006).

90 The Commission's position is also at odds with recent doctrinal developments in the case law of the European Court regarding precisely "mandatory rules from which the parties may not derogate by contract". In *Pfeiffer*, the Advocate-General presented his first Opinion on 6 May 2003. In an unusual move, the Court issued an Order on 13 January 2004 re-opening the procedure, transferring the case from the sixth Chamber to the Court and ordering an oral hearing for arguments on 9 March 2004. The ECJ's Order of 13 January 2003 provides some indications of why this unusual procedural step was taken. It reveals a stance at odds with that of the Commission in its Communication of 2003 on the Posting Directive. In particular, in paragraph 9 of its Order of 13 January 2003 the ECJ emphasises the purpose of Directive 93/104: to protect workers as the weaker party to the employment contract, and adds that effective protection (*effet utile*) must be assured by both EU and national courts. In paragraph 10, the ECJ emphasises that the complaints based on Directive 93/104 are concerned with limiting daily working hours, not monetary compensation, making it difficult to launch a claim against the Member State for the harm caused by the violation of EC law (a *Francovich* claim, *Francovich and Bonfaci v. Italy*, Cases C-6/90 and C-9/90, [1991] ECR I-5357). The Commission's Communication emphasises its policy to restrict as far as possible the scope for mandatory rules of public policy protecting workers to override individual contracts of employment. In contrast, the European Court acknowledges explicitly the inequality of bargaining power inherent in the contract of employment and requires national and EU courts to look to EU labour law standards – in *Pfeiffer* concerned with working time – to protect the weaker party. See *Bernhard Pfeiffer et al. c. Deutsches Rotes Kreuz Kreisverband Waldshut eV,* Joined Cases C-397/01 to C-403/01. Opinion of Advocate-General M.D. Ruiz-Jarabo Colomer, 6 May 2003; Second Opinion, 27 April 2004, ECJ decision, 5 October 2004.

91 Council Document 2004/0001 COD, 5 July 2004.

92 The view that Directive 96/71/EC is a minimum Directive is also stated in the Preamble to Directive 2004/18/EC (public procurement). See Bercusson and Bruun (2005).

to one specifying the *maximum* protection available to employees. This was clearly stated in Recital 59 of the proposed Services Directive:

> as regards employment and working conditions other than those laid down in Directive 96/71/EC, it should not be possible for the Member State of posting to take restrictive measures against a provider established in another Member State.

On the contrary, the final text of the Directive now explicitly stipulates in Article 16(3): "Nor shall that Member State be prevented from applying, in accordance with Community law, its rules on employment conditions, including those laid down in collective agreements".[93]

6.2 Safeguarding Only Some Terms of Employment of Posted Workers

The Council document stressed that the proposed Services Directive exempted all matters covered by Directive 96/71/EC from the "country of origin" principle. In particular, the "country of origin" principle was not to affect the application of terms and conditions of employment in matters covered by Directive 96/71/EC and the application of "universally applicable" collective agreements in these areas. The host Member State was to continue to be responsible for the necessary controls on all these matters. Specifically, the document claimed that terms and conditions applicable to temporary workers were covered by Directive 96/71/EC and thus exempt from the application of the "country of origin" principle. As Recital 59 of the proposed Directive showed, however, this was at least misleading, if not wrong concerning the totality of employment and working conditions.[94]

6.3 The Problem of Self-employed Posted Workers

Similarly, the "country of origin" principle was not to affect the definition of who is a "worker". Self-employment, therefore, appeared to be a matter covered indirectly by the Posting of Workers Directive, Article 2(2) of which confirms that the law of the host country defines the notion

---

93 Recital 86: "This not only concerns terms and conditions of employment which are laid down by law but also those laid down in collective agreements or arbitration awards that are officially declared or de facto universally applicable within the meaning of Directive 96/71/EC. Moreover, this Directive should not prevent Member States from applying terms and conditions of employment on matters other than those listed in Article 3(1) of Directive 96/71/EC on the grounds of public policy".

94 Again, Recital 59: "as regards employment and working conditions *other than those laid down in Directive 96/71/EC*, it should not be possible for the Member State of posting to take restrictive measures against a provider established in another Member State."

of "worker".[95] The intention appeared to be to combat the posting of "bogus" self-employed workers. But there was a problem in that, by definition, if in host-country terms there was *no* natural or legal person in the country of origin posting the (bogus) *self*-employed person to work in the host country, such a self-employed person was not covered by the Posting Directive.[96]

7. Transnational Employment Contracts and the Rome Convention

Another explanatory document from the Council highlighted further problems created by the "country of origin" principle in the proposed Services Directive. This Document concerned the relationship between the proposal and the Rome I and draft Rome II Conventions.[97]

The Rome Convention on the law applicable to contractual obligations (Rome I) provides that the contract of employment is governed:[98]

> (a) by the law of the country in which the employee habitually carries out his work in performance of the contract, even if he is temporarily employed in another country; or
>
> (b) if the employee does not habitually carry out his work in any one country, by the law of the country in which the place of business through which he was engaged is situated;
>
> unless it appears from the circumstances as a whole that the contract is more closely connected with another country in which case the contract shall be governed by the law of that country.

Accordingly, if the posted worker is temporarily working in the host country but habitually carries out work in that Member State, the rules of that host State apply to regulate the individual employment relationship. Again, if the employee does *not* have any country where he habitually

95 It would be useful to consider whether the context of transnational employment justifies the adoption of an EU definition of "employment". Cf. the ECJ's insistence on a Community definition of worker for the purpose of the Community principle of equal pay between men and women in *Allonby v. Accrington & Rosendale College*, Case C-256/01, [2004] IRLR 224.

96 See Article 16(2)(d) of the final Directive: "Member States may not restrict the freedom to provide services in the case of a provider established in another Member State by imposing any of the following requirements: [...] (d) the application of specific contractual arrangements between the provider and the recipient which prevent or restrict service provision by the self-employed". See also Recital 87.

97 Council Document 2004/0001 COD, 25 June 2004.

98 Article 6(2).

works, the rules of the host country may apply if he is still more closely connected with that country.

But in some cases, the applicable law may instead be that of the country where the place of business of the employer is situated. The "country of origin" principle proposed in the draft Services Directive created an exponential increase in problems by prescribing (i) some home country conditions for workers employed in the host country by service providers in the home country; (ii) other host country conditions due to derogation for posted workers. The problem was determining which labour standards apply.[99] How did Rome I affect this situation?

The Council's explanatory document was explicitly said to be limited to private law issues.[100] It stated that the "country of origin" principle appears to create a choice of law rule, and that this has implications for the existing Rome I and the solutions envisaged by Rome II.[101] It was argued that, in principle, employment relationships are excluded from the scope of the proposed Directive.[102] But no real analysis was provided of the relationship between the labour law aspects of Rome I and II and the "country of origin" principle. Yet there appeared to be a clear conflict between them in situations in which the employee does not habitually work in his country of origin: Rome I allows for host country labour law to apply; the "country of origin" principle dictated the opposite conclusion. The final Directive provides in Article 3(2):[103]

> This Directive does not concern rules of private international law, in particular rules governing the law applicable to contractual and non-contractual obligations.

8. National Labour Law Conditions for the Hiring-out of Temporary Workers

The Council Document took the view that the proposed Services Directive covered "the conditions of hiring-out of workers including the

99 The equal treatment (non-discrimination) principle of the *acquis* seems blessedly simple by comparison. It operates to secure equal treatment between the employees of service providers and workers in the host Member State. The proposed Services Directive aims to halt equal treatment in its tracks. Outside prescribed boundaries of equal treatment, inequality is to be permitted insofar as the country of origin rules are different from those of the host state.

100 Council Document 2004/0001 COD, 25 June 2004, page 6.

101 *Ibid.*, page 13.

102 *Ibid.*, page 29.

103 See also Recital 90 and Article 17(15).

conditions regarding supply of workers by temporary employment agencies".[104] Again, the case law of the European Court of Justice, which has handed down a number of important decisions on cross-border temporary work, is relevant.

Thus, in *Webb* the Court acknowledged the social sensitivity of the issue of temporary agency businesses. It recognised the right of Member States to restrict temporary agency work or even to ban it. But it was necessary to take account of the evidence and guarantees already provided by the business in the Member State of its establishment.[105] In *Commission v. Italy*, the Court did not outlaw in principle a requirement to establish a financial guarantee in temporary work; but it outlawed a national scheme that did not take into account the guarantee established in another Member State.[106] In 1999, the judgment in *Webb* shaped the substantive content of a unanimous Council Resolution on the transnational hiring-out of workers.[107] Licensing was accepted and it included also a Code of Conduct for administrative cooperation.

Of particular interest is a decision of the European Court interpreting the Posting Directive 96/71/EC in *Finalarte*.[108] The case concerned challenges by employers from Member States other than Germany who posted workers to Germany. These employers had received demands to pay contributions to a paid leave fund for construction workers, and to provide information for the calculation of these contributions. The German legislation allowed for payment of the holiday entitlement directly to the workers employed by firms established outside Germany, as required by a German collective agreement.

The Court appears to have taken a more appreciative approach to the protective function of labour standards. As regards the holiday payments, the Court held that (point 50):

---

104 Council Document 2004/0001 COD, 5 July 2004, page 5. A careful reading of this explanatory document of 5 July 2004 indicates that the aim is not to apply the "country of origin" principle to conditions of hiring-out of workers. It states that this could be explained in a recital. But the conclusions of the explanatory document, where a draft text for new recitals is presented, do not cover this point. Minimum clarity of this crucial issue requires an unambiguous text, at least in a recital. Later revisions to the draft Services Directive proposed to exclude temporary agency workers.

105 *Webb*, Case 279/80, [1981] ECR 195, paragraphs 17–20.

106 Case C- 279/00, judgment of 3 February 2002. Italy at that time required a minimum share capital of ITL 1 billion for running a temporary work agency.

107 Officially headed: Fight against Social Security Fraud and Undeclared Work. See the Resolution of the Social Council of 9 March 1999.

108 *Finalarte Sociedad de Construcao Civil Lda and others v. Urlaubs- und Lohnausgleichskasse der Bauwirtschaft,*, Cases C-49-50/98, C-52/98, C-54/98, C-68/98 and C-71/98, [2001] ECR I-7831.

> the national court should balance the administrative and economic burdens that the rules impose on providers of services against the increased social protection that they confer on workers compared with that guaranteed by the law of the Member State where their employer is established.

As regards direct payment to workers:

> there are, clearly, objective differences between businesses established in the Federal Republic of Germany and those established in other Member States as regards the effective implementation of the obligation to give holiday pay. Accordingly, where a business established outside Germany ceases to provide services there, the German authorities are no longer able to ensure that it has, in fact, given holiday pay to the posted workers. It follows that it is more efficient if the fund gives holiday pay directly to the posted workers. The discrimination in treatment may be explained by those objective differences, and does not therefore constitute discrimination. (points 63–64)

Again, as regards the demand for information:

> the national court should consider whether the objective differences between the position of businesses established in Germany and that of businesses established outside Germany objectively require the additional information required of the latter. (point 75)

Together, these cases evince a positive approach by the European Court to national labour standards applicable by the host state to transnational employees. In sum, the conclusion to be drawn from the case law is that the conditions for hiring-out of manpower should not fall under the "country of origin" principle. To that extent, the proposed Services Directive seemed to be based on an inadequate perception of EC law.

9. Problems of Monitoring and Control of Labour Standards

The thinking behind the proposed Services Directive assumed that implementation and enforcement of the law could be completely separated from its material content. The Commission's position was that it did not intend to change "labour law as such", only some enforcement mechanisms. But although the Commission claimed that its intention was to improve administrative cooperation in order to facilitate enforcement, there were serious grounds for doubting that this would be the effect of the proposed changes.

The European Parliament shared these doubts, by explicitly providing that the rules in the Services Directive on free movement of services were not to affect the national labour law and employment conditions of the host Member State, and further amending the proposed Directive to provide protection of collective agreements, acknowledge protection of workers as an overriding reason relating to the public interest, and reaffirm fundamental rights of labour. This removed some of the anxieties about enforcement of national labour law on service providers from other

Member States. Nonetheless, in reflecting on transnational regulation of temporary agency work, it is worthwhile referring to three kinds of labour and social law rules which should be distinguished in the context of a discussion of enforcement mechanisms:

i. substantive labour law rules and employment standards;
ii. rules aiming to guarantee the effective implementation and enforcement of these rules (inspections, obligation to provide information and documentation, prior declarations of compliance, sanctions, and so on);
iii. rules creating administrative mechanisms to control sensitive activities in the employment field (authorisation of temporary employment agencies, and so on).

The rules in category (i) were central to the debate over the proposed Services Directive because of the introduction of the "country of origin" principle. They were of crucial importance because *national* machinery of enforcement was being required to control the application to employees on its territory of *non-national* ("country of origin") labour law standards governing employment. The problems inherent in this proposal (increased complexity, reduced transparency, confused application of EU labour law, contradiction with the *acquis communautaire*) were elaborated above.

Understandably, in the context of free movement of services, there was also a debate on control mechanisms related to category (iii).[109] In light of the exclusion of temporary agency work from the scope of the final Services Directive,[110] the issues raised by category (iii) should be dealt with in a balanced way through separate and specific harmonisation measures, such as the proposal for a Directive on working conditions for temporary workers.[111]

But the rules in category (ii) are vital to respect the principle of effectiveness of EU law and to satisfy the need for its effective enforcement. There is a very strong argument for close scrutiny of any proposals to deprive Member States of the necessary tools of implementation and enforcement provided by rules in category (ii). The following sections concentrate on issues which were raised by the proposed Services Directive in relation to rules in category (ii).

---

109 See the final Directive, Recitals 105–115 and Articles 28–34.

110 Article 2(2)(e).

111 Commission of the European Communities, *Proposal for a Directive of the European Parliament and the Council on working conditions for temporary workers*, COM(2002) 149 final, Brussels, 20 March 2002; *Amended Proposal*, COM(2002) 701 final, Brussels, 28 November 2002.

9.1 Prior Declarations

Prior declarations by service providers are simply a basic mechanism for any effective control of employment standards. National law imposes a requirement of prior declarations on service providers posting workers in Member States such as Germany, Austria, Belgium and France. As will be shown below, there are good reasons for this. Such controls are not a problem for well-organised enterprises which comply with labour standards. Abolishing prior declarations only serves those seeking to avoid any controls.

It is of course possible to review details of national systems of prior declaration; for example, those requiring a separate declaration for each site and worker, or imposing a new declaration when the worker changes site temporarily. But such fine-tuning is completely different from a proposal to ban any and all prior declarations. Contrary to the proposal in the draft Services Directive, an obligation to make prior declarations should be imposed particularly on sensitive sectors, such as construction, the cleaning industry and transport.[112] In the event, the final text of the Directive provides:[113]

> Where Member States require a provider or recipient to supply a certificate, attestation or any other document proving that a requirement has been satisfied, they shall accept any document from another Member State which serves an equivalent purpose or from which it is clear that the requirement in question has been satisfied. They may not require a document from another Member State to be produced in its original form, or as a certified copy or as a certified translation, save in the cases provided for in other Community instruments or where such a requirement is justified by an overriding reason relating to the public interest, including public order and security.

9.2 Employment Documents

The Commission proposed in the draft Directive to restrict control mechanisms by providing that Member States were no longer entitled to

112 Final Directive, Article 2(2)(d): "This Directive shall not apply to the following activities: [...] (d) services in the field of transport, including port services, falling within the scope of Title V of the Treaty". Recital 21: "Transport services, including urban transport, taxis and ambulances as well as port services, should be excluded from the scope of this Directive".

113 Article 5(3). See Recital 47: "With the aim of administrative simplification, general formal requirements, such as presentation of original documents, certified copies or a certified translation, should not be imposed, except where objectively justified by an overriding reason relating to the public interest, such as the protection of workers, public health, the protection of the environment or the protection of consumers". Further on the "public interest", see Recitals 56 and 66. On prohibition of discriminatory requirements to supply original documents, see Recital 94.

require employment documentation to be held in their territory and retained in accordance with the conditions applicable there.[114] Article 24(2) was meant to compensate for this by imposing on the country of origin the obligation to guarantee the provision of documents. Yet Article 24(1) imposed on the host Member State the duty to carry out checks, inspections and investigations, and also to take measures in respect of a service provider.

In its explanatory note of 5 July 2004[115] the Commission provided further guidance. It quoted paragraphs 61 and 62 of the European Court's judgment in *Arblade*,[116] and maintained that the proposed Services Directive "is perfectly in line with the rationale expressed in that judgment in that it reinforces that co-operation."[117] This reliance of the Commission on the judgment in *Arblade* deserved closer scrutiny.

It is of course true that the reasoning of the Court in *Arblade* reflects the provisions on cooperation between Member States required by Article 4 of the Posting of Workers Directive. But a first elementary comment is that the Court did not completely rule out the right to require documents on-site, despite the cooperation anticipated under Article 4. On the contrary, in paragraph 61 the Court was cautious about abolishing such a requirement. It used the word "particularly" to insist on the precondition of an "organised system of co-operation" *before* abandoning the requirement "that certain documents are kept on site, or at least in an accessible and clearly identified place in the territory of the host Member

114 Article 24(1)(d) of the proposed Services Directive.

115 Council Document 2004/0001 COD, 5 July 2004.

116 *Arblade v. Leloup and Sofrage SARL*, Cases C-369/96 and C-276/96, [1999] ECR I-8453. Paragraphs 61 and 62 of *Arblade* read as follows:

"61. The effective protection of workers in the construction industry, particularly as regards health and safety matters and working hours, may require that certain documents are kept on site, or at least in an accessible and clearly identified place in the territory of the host Member State, so that they are available to the authorities of that State responsible for carrying out checks, particularly where there exists no organised system for cooperation or exchanges of information between Member States as provided for in Article 4 of Directive 96/71.

62. Furthermore, in the absence of an organised system for cooperation or exchanges of information of the kind referred to in the preceding paragraph, the obligation to draw up and keep on site, or at least in an accessible and clearly identified place in the territory of the host Member State, certain of the documents required by the rules of that State may constitute the only appropriate means of control, having regard to the objective pursued by those rules".

117 Page 12 of the explanatory note. However, the Commission also makes the concession that, by virtue of a recital in the Preamble to the proposed Directive, the Member States could require the presence of "documents which in the normal course of work are established and kept at the work place such as time-sheets, etc." *Ibid.*, page 14.

State, so that they are available to the authorities of that State responsible for carrying out checks […]".

Moreover, by limiting the quotation only to paragraphs 61 and 62 of *Arblade*, the Commission created a misleading overall impression of the "rationale" of that judgment. In paragraph 63, the Court continues to elaborate this rationale:

> 63. The items of information respectively required by the rules of the Member State of establishment and by those of the host Member State concerning, in particular, the employer, the worker, working conditions and remuneration may differ to such an extent that *the monitoring required under the rules of the host Member State cannot be carried out on the basis of documents kept in accordance with the rules of the Member State of establishment.* (italics added)

Hence, requiring documents to be kept in accordance with the rules in the host Member State was not outlawed. The Court went on to state:

> 74. For the reasons set out in paragraphs 61 to 63 of this judgment, the need for *effective control* by the authorities of the host Member State *may justify* the imposition on an employer established in another Member State who provides services in the host Member State of the obligation to *keep certain documents available for inspection by the national authorities on site or, at least, in an accessible and clearly identified place in the territory of the host Member State.* (italics added)
>
> 75. It is for the national court to establish, having regard to the principle of proportionality, which documents are covered by such an obligation.

The rationale is summarised in the fourth paragraph of Court's ruling:

> 4. Articles 59 and 60 of the Treaty do not preclude the imposition by a Member State on an undertaking established in another Member State, and temporarily carrying out work in the first State, of an obligation to keep social and labour documents available, throughout the period of activity within the territory of the first Member State, on site or in an accessible and clearly identified place within the territory of that State, where such a measure is necessary in order to enable it effectively to monitor compliance with legislation of that State which is justified by the need to safeguard the social protection of workers.

It is important to point out that the reasoning and conclusion quoted from the *Arblade* case are given by the Court applying the EC Treaty. The Treaty remains unchanged and the Posting of Workers Directive is to continue to be applied in light of Article 49 [ex 59] EC.

This is demonstrated by the judgment of the Court in *Wolff & Müller v. Pereira*.[118] The case concerned the German system in which the prin-

118 Case C-60/03, judgment of 12 October 2004.

cipal contractor is the guarantor of the minimum wage. Its aim is to guarantee the remuneration owed according to the rules (laws and collective agreements) in force in the host country. In line with the statements of the Court in *Arblade*, the German system, as with any real system of control in any Member State, requires the immediate production of documents showing the amount of wages paid or due. Of course, this cannot guarantee that the worker will receive full remuneration. But it is a reasonable attempt to safeguard the worker's essential interest in receiving in any case a minimum wage.

Any other interpretation of the duty of Member States under Article 5 of the Posting of Workers Directive[119] – for example, by limiting the obligation to retaining only time sheets on-site, or in the territory of the home Member State – seriously endangers effective enforcement of the rights and duties set out in the Directive. An example would be a company from Member State A, with employees from Member State B, signing contracts in Member State C and posting workers to Member State D. Wages may be paid in different Member States, and the relevant bookkeeping operations may be undertaken in a Member State other than that of origin. In this case, the Member State of origin cannot be expected to guarantee production of documents from other countries.

Reliable and effective control of labour standards requires that documents showing at least the working conditions applicable, hours worked and wages paid are immediately, without the need for requests via authorities in the country of origin, available on the spot. A vital added advantage is that the workers at the site are in principle able to participate in the exercise of this control.[120]

A further aspect supporting the requirement that all documents relevant to pay be available without any prior request via the authorities of the country of origin is in Declaration No. 7 attached to the Council Minutes when the Posting of Workers Directive was adopted.[121] It confirms that foreign companies are *a priori* required to pay, for example, holiday pay via a social fund in the host country. This obligation is, of course, not applicable if there is an equivalent fund scheme operating in the country of origin.

---

119 Article 5, paragraph 1: "Member states shall take appropriate measures in the event of failure to comply with this Directive".

120 This approach is also in line with the rationale of Council Directive 91/533/EEC on an employer's obligation to inform employees of the conditions applicable to the contract or employment relationship. As its Article 7 shows, it is a minimum directive that does not preclude stricter national rules. Council Directive 91/533/EEC of 14 October 1991; OJ L288/32 of 18 October 1991.

121 See European Union Council 20 September 1996, File No 00/0346 SYN, ADD 1.

A requirement that Member States must obtain documents from the authorities of the country of origin simply weakens controls. Imposing obligations on the country of origin as was proposed in Article 24(2) of the draft Services Directive would be perfectly appropriate if they were complementary to the rights and obligations of the host Member State to exercise effective control. Such obligations may well be deduced from the requirements of the Posting of Workers Directive; in terms of legal technique, their correct place would be there.

In sum, the correct starting point for assessing the rights and duties of the host Member State as regards controlling entitlements to pay is Article 5 in the Posting of Workers Directive:

> Member States shall take appropriate measures in the event of failure to comply with this Directive.
>
> They shall in particular ensure that adequate procedures are available to workers and/or their representatives for the enforcement of obligations under the Directive.

This does not require the service provider to ship all employment documents to the host country. However, a minimum effective control requires that at least work contracts and documents showing, for instance, the hours worked and wages paid (per hour) are directly available in the host Member State.

In the event, as indicated in the preceding section, the final text of the Directive requires a Member State requesting documents to accept any equivalent document from another Member State, and not an original document, save where this is justified by an overriding reason relating to the public interest.[122] Only the exclusion of labour law and employment conditions from the rules on free movement of services preserves this enforcement safeguard where provided for by national law.

The general approach adopted by the final Directive to spheres outside labour standards is indicated by its provisions on the supervision of service providers by the Member State of their establishment:[123]

> the Member State of establishment shall ensure that compliance with its requirements supervised in conformity with the powers of supervision provided for in its national law, in particular through supervisory measures at the place of establishment of the provider.

However, that obligation:[124]

---

122 Article 5(3). See Recitals 47, 56, 66 and 94.

123 Article 30(1).

124 Article 30(3).

> does not entail a duty on the part of the Member State of establishment to carry out factual checks and controls in the territory of the Member State where the service is provided. Such checks and controls shall be carried out by the authorities of the Member State where the provider is temporarily operating at the request of the authorities of the Member State of establishment, in accordance with Article 31.

However, in the interest of limiting national restrictions on the transnational provision of services, Article 31 lays down strict limits on the power of Member States where the service is provided to carry out supervision activity.

9.3 Representatives

In the *Arblade* case[125] the European Court of Justice did not outlaw the obligation to appoint a representative. The Court outlawed the specific provision of Belgian law requiring a representative domiciled in Belgium, and the keeping of employment documents for five years after the work in Belgium had been carried out.[126]

Any conclusions to be drawn from the ruling in *Arblade* should be limited to the specific findings of the case. Thus, in *Arblade* the Court stated that Directive 96/71/EC would render superfluous the requirement of keeping documents in the host country *after* completion of the work.[127] The Court equally accepted the possibility that the authorities of the host Member States may show a sufficient interest in requiring the appointment of a representative.[128] Hence, in principle, requiring a representative is possible even in those legal systems (Belgium) where the implementation and execution of the Posting Directive is based upon collective agreements declared *erga omnes*.

The obligation to appoint a representative is of crucial importance in the Swedish-Danish system of regulating the labour market. Take the example of a company from Member State A, with workers from Member State B, signing contracts in Member State C and posting workers to Sweden. According to the Commission's explanatory memorandum of 5 July 2004,[129] the proposed Services Directive would not prevent Member States from requiring the employer, for the duration of the work, to appoint one of the workers to represent him and "to whom requests for

---

125 *Arblade v. Leloup and Sofrage SARL*, Cases C-369/96 and C-276/96, [1999] ECR I-8453; judgment of 23 November 1999.

126 See the fifth ruling in the case.

127 Paragraph 79.

128 Paragraph 76.

129 Council Document 2004/0001 COD, 5 July 2004, page 10.

information, demands and correspondence can be addressed". What is more, the Commission admits: "[t]his could be *clarified* in a recital".[130] The Commission does not appear to fully understand the multitude of functions such a representative might have to perform. The Swedish-Danish system illustrates the problem.

The Posting of Workers Directive recognises[131] the Swedish-Danish model of using collective agreements to regulate the labour market and protect the rights of workers under the Directive. It is also without prejudice to the law of the Member States concerning collective action to defend the interests of trades and professions.[132] The right to conduct business *without* a competent representative seriously undermines this Nordic Model. The representative of the employer is the person with whom the trade unions in Sweden and Denmark wish to (and who is the only one entitled to) conclude a binding collective agreement. It is not only for "information, demands and correspondence".

It is equally clear that the trade unions in these countries would wish to avoid any unnecessary industrial action to guarantee the application of the rules in the Posting of Workers Directive. A foreign worker, probably unfamiliar with the Swedish or Danish law and collective bargaining systems, often not proficient in English, perhaps not knowing workmates from several different countries, would be in the impossible situation of having to negotiate and conclude an agreement with the unions. Yet it is entirely possible that the employer would order him/her to sign such an agreement, and only later consider whether to regard it as valid or not. Such a system would simply serve to multiply malpractice and give rise to serious conflicts.

This is not a purely theoretical scenario. The Commission's explanatory memorandum states that Nordic countries may apply collective agreements to workers posted in their territories as long as they are *de facto* of universal application. The problem, especially in Denmark and Sweden, is that there are no mechanisms by which the State controls the application of these agreements. The social partners do it themselves. This means there must be someone for the employees and unions to negotiate with, and there must be some means for surveillance of the agreement. A prohibition of the requirement to have a representative present in the Member State might raise questions as to the lawfulness of industrial action demanding negotiations with service providers.[133]

---

130 Italics added.

131 In Article 3(8).

132 Recital 22.

133 It should be noted that this is enshrined in the European Union Charter of Fundamental Rights, Article 28 on the "Right of collective bargaining and action":

The Swedish-Danish model, in particular, requires the practical possibility of a real representative. Such an obligation is, moreover, perfectly natural in other Member States as well. It does not require a full-time person on the spot, only that there is a responsible person appointed to undertake the responsibilities of the service provider as the employer.

In conclusion: Article 24 of the proposed Services Directive ("specific provisions on the posting of workers") would have reduced the effectiveness of essential mechanisms needed to secure the implementation and enforcement of obligations relating to employment and working conditions.[134] The final Directive retains strict limitations on the host Member State's requiring service providers to be resident (Article 14(1)(b)) or to have an establishment on their territory (Article 16(2)(a)).[135]

10. Conclusions: Principles of Transnational Regulation of Temporary Agency Work

The impact of the Services Directive should be assessed against the background of greater diversity in wage levels and income within a European Union comprising 27 Member States. Free movement of services offers great opportunities, but also creates the risk of abuses and exploitation of

"Workers and employers, or their respective organisations, have in accordance with Union law and national laws and practices, the right to negotiate and conclude collective agreements at the appropriate levels and, in cases of conflicts of interest, to take collective action to defend their interests, including strike action." The Services Directive includes an explicit provision (Article 1(7)) stating: "This Directive does not affect the exercise of fundamental rights as recognised in the Member States and by Community law. Nor does it affect the right to negotiate, conclude and enforce collective agreements and to take industrial action in accordance with national law and practices which respect Community law". See the detailed commentary on Article 28 by Veneziani in Bercusson (2006), pp. 291–336.

134 To the extent that greater specification of the obligations of the country of origin of the service provider is needed in the context of posting, this can be achieved by introducing any such specifications into the Posting of Workers Directive 96/71/EC.

135 The latter, however, may be mitigated by the provision in Article 16(3): "The Member State to which the provider moves shall not be prevented from imposing requirements with regard to the provision of a service activity where they are justified for reasons of public policy, public security, public health or the protection of the environment and in accordance with paragraph 1. Nor shall that Member State be prevented from applying, in accordance with Community law, its rules on employment conditions, including those laid down in collective agreements". Recital 65: Service providers are not to be subject to requirements as to establishment, residence, domicile, etc.: "However, these criteria should not include requirements according to which a provider or one of his employees or a representative must be present during the exercise of the activity when this is justified by an overriding reason relating to the public interest".

unemployment and poverty. In its most extreme form, this can appear as trafficking, child labour, and so on.

These factors strongly support a cautious approach to restricting the operation of labour law regimes in cross-border situations. The European internal market, for good reasons, adopts a liberal approach to the creation of new company forms, such as the European company (SE) and the guaranteed freedom of establishment. The near future will also see proposals making it easier to change the registered seat of companies in Europe.

But in order to sustain a Social Europe, it is essential that social and labour law aspects are taken into account in a realistic way when introducing a regulation that has an indirect but strong impact on employees. The proposal for a Services Directive in January 2004 lacked such a realistic approach and it must be seen as an attempt to set aside already existing fundamental principles of EC labour law as well as ECJ case law.

Although the proposed Directive was significantly improved during the legislative process, the final Directive leaves many issues open concerning how to balance the economic and social dimensions of EU law. Not least, the exclusion of temporary agency work from the scope of application of the Directive signals that the Directive does not pretend to provide the answers to the problem of balancing economic and social aspects in transnational regulation of temporary agency work. Establishing a balance remains necessary when transnational temporary agency work is performed. Some guidance is needed.

This guidance should draw on the principles of the *acquis communautaire social*. Starting points for such principles are the following, some of which were acknowledged in the final text of the Services Directive.

The first principle is to insist that the social protection of workers is not to be subordinated to free movement of services and the interests of service providers, including temporary work agencies and their user-employer clients. Labour is not a commodity. Conditions of work are not to be determined by the rules applied to free movement of services. The Services Directive recognised this by providing that "This Directive does not affect labour law".[136] EU law should look to the substance: that services, the business of temporary work agencies, are provided by workers, and provide protection.

Secondly, recent decisions of the European Court expose the need for specific legal protection of workers with the status of temporary agency workers. In *Allonby v. Accrington & Rosendale College*, teaching staff employed by a college were dismissed by their employer and hired back

136 Article 1(6).

through an agency as self-employed persons.[137] Though in industrial relations practice, the case was not wholly unsuccessful,[138] the now self-employed staff were held unable to compare their terms and conditions of employment with those of employees of the college where they had been employed.[139] It was commented about *Allonby*: "Both the Commission and the Advocate General took the view that any protection to be offered agency workers should come through the legislative process and could not be developed judicially. Although they acknowledged the seriousness of the potential abuse when an employer reconfigured its operations to evade equal pay laws (para. 43), both were clearly reluctant to pre-empt the stalled directive on agency workers".[140]

Third, a central principle of the *acquis communautaire social* as regards conditions of work is equal treatment.[141] The question is how this principle should be applied in the case of transnational provision of services. One function of collective agreements is precisely to avoid the damaging effects of competition among individual workers in the labour market producing unequal treatment. Through collective organisation and action, individual workers are able to compensate for their weaker bargaining position with employers and negotiate collective agreements to ensure equality of treatment among the collectivity of workers.

---

137 Case C-256/01, [2004] *Industrial Relations Law Reports* 224.

138 The trade union promoting the case, the National Association of Teachers in Further and Higher Education (NATFHE) stated "the intention to provide a line in the sand over the extension of casualisation was largely achieved: 'we saw the end many years ago of wholesale sackings and re-employment. People like Allonby now really only provide short-term cover'". Colling (2006), p. 151.

139 Indeed, the "country of origin" principle in the proposed Services Directive only highlighted the anomaly. If the female worker hired from a temporary work agency based in the home state was imported from the home state to work alongside a male worker employed in the user enterprise in the host state, the proposed Services Directive would have denied equal pay as her rate of pay was that of her country of origin.

140 Fredman (2004), p. 283. See also *Lawrence v. Regent Office Care Ltd, Commercial Catering Group and Mitie Secure Services Ltd.*, Case C-320/00, [2002] ECR I-7325, where the Advocate General similarly looked to the adoption of the proposed agency workers directive rather than reliance on Article 141 EC. See Barrett (2006), pp. 100–1, who concludes: "A better approach is that suggested by Advocate General Geelhoed – the use of Community secondary legislation in order to provide specific remedies, e.g. against the use of agencies to avoid employment rights generally. This is an approach which – happily in the light of the rulings in *Lawrence* and *Allonby* – the Community legislature has attempted to engage in, even if agreement between the Member States on how best to provide for the rights of temporary workers has to date remained worryingly elusive".

141 See above, Section IV: "Transnational employment, services and the *acquis communautaire social*: The 'country of origin' principle v. the equal treatment principle".

This was the path first recognised by the European Court[142] and later indicated by the Posting of Workers Directive. Building on this would entail a more expansive definition of applicable collective agreements to determine working conditions for the providers of services, including temporary work agencies and their user-employer clients. As stated in the Services Directive: Member States are not to be prevented from applying rules on employment conditions "including those laid down in collective agreements".[143] Protection is to be secured by *national* collective agreements.[144]

Transnational collective agreements could achieve the same protection specifically as regards the transnational provision of services by temporary work agencies. The sectoral social dialogue is a potential forum for the negotiation of labour standards. In the context of temporary agency

140 Fredman (2004), p. 283. See also *Lawrence v. Regent Office Care Ltd, Commercial Catering Group and Mitie Secure Services Ltd.*, Case C-320/00, [2002] ECR I-7325, where the Advocate General similarly looked to the adoption of the proposed agency workers directive rather than reliance on Article 141 EC. See Barrett (2006), pp. 100–1, who concludes: "A better approach is that suggested by Advocate General Geelhoed – the use of Community secondary legislation in order to provide specific remedies, e.g. against the use of agencies to avoid employment rights generally. This is an approach which – happily in the light of the rulings in *Lawrence* and *Allonby* – the Community legislature has attempted to engage in, even if agreement between the Member States on how best to provide for the rights of temporary workers has to date remained worryingly elusive".

141 See above, Section IV: "Transnational employment, services and the *acquis communautaire social*: The 'country of origin' principle v. the equal treatment principle".

142 *Rush Portuguesa Lda v. Office national d'immigration,* Case 113/89, [1990] ECR 1417 at p. 1445.

143 Article 16(3). Article 4(7): "rules laid down in collective agreements negotiated by the social partners shall not as such be seen as requirements [subject to] within the meaning of this Directive".

144 For example, in the temporary work sector, in Germany, on 20 February 2003 a frame work agreement was reached between trade unions grouped together by the central German trade union confederation, DGB, in a bargaining cartel and the employer's organisation in the temporary work sector, BZA (Bundesverband Zeitarbeit Personal-Dienstleistungen). BZA, the largest employers' organisation in the temporary work sector, with some 1.600 members. In 2002, an estimated 4,000 private sector temporary employment agencies were operating in Germany employing some 273,000 temporary workers. "Collective agreements in place in temporary work sector", *European Industrial Relations Review* No. 354, July 2003, at pp. 22–24. See the national report by Kerstin Ahlberg in this book (Chapter 5). In Spain a national agreement was concluded in March 2005 for the telemarketing sector employing some 40,000 workers of whom some 90% are temporary. "National accord provides security for telemarketing workers', *European Industrial Relations Review* No. 378, July 2005, at pp. 27–29. For further examples of collective agreements, see the national report on the Nordic countries in this book by Kerstin Ahlberg and Niklas Bruun (Chapter 1).

work, a joint declaration of 3 July 2001 by the sectoral social partners[145] confirmed mutual recognition to each other as representative organisations, and on 8 October 2001 they announced jointly agreed objectives for draft European legislation, including recommendations for non-discrimination and potentially equal treatment between agency workers and permanent staff at user companies and trade union rights.[146]

Finally, the relevant standards should draw on the EU Charter of Fundamental Rights. The Services Directive states: "This directive does not affect the exercise of fundamental rights as recognised in the Member States and by Community Law".[147] The proposed EU Constitutional Treaty incorporates the EU Charter in Part II. It thereby promotes both relevant standards and the mechanism for achieving them: recognition of the social partners and the social dialogue at transnational European level.[148] Regulation of temporary agency work similarly should respect these fundamental rights.

These starting points, which of course have to be implemented so as to take into account the relevant internal market provisions, provide a solid base for a specific legal instrument harmonising the transnational regulation of temporary agency work in the EU. The lesson learned by the fierce debate on the draft Services Directive is that it is very difficult to achieve a balance between economic and social aspects concerning temporary agency work without specific secondary EC regulation. It is definitely time to put the adoption of a Directive on temporary agency work back on the agenda. It is urgently needed and should build upon the existing *acquis communautaire social.*

---

145 CIETT (the European Committee of the International Confederation of Temporary Work Businesses) and UNI-Europa (the European regional organisation of Union Network International).

146 See for details the account by Kerstin Ahlberg of the social dialogue on agency work in this book (Chapter 9).

147 Article 1(7). That the rights in question are fundamental labour rights is evident in the following text: "Nor does it affect the right to negotiate, conclude and enforce collective agreements and to take industrial action in accordance with national law and practices which respect Community law". Recital 15 includes specific reference to the EU Charter.

148 Article I-48: "The Union recognises and promotes the role of the social partners at its level, taking into account the diversity of national systems. It shall facilitate dialogue between the social partners, respecting their autonomy". Treaty establishing a Constitution for Europe adopted by the Member States in the Intergovernmental Conference meeting in Brussels, 17–18 June 2004, OJ C 310/1 of 16 December 2004.

Bibliography

Ahlberg, K., N. Bruun and J. Malmberg (2006), "The *Vaxholm* case from a Swedish and European perspective", *Transfer: European Review of Labour and Research* 12, (2) (summer): 155–66.

Barrett, G. (2006), "'Shall I Compare Thee to…?' On Article 141 EC and Lawrence", *Industrial Law Journal* 35 (93): 100–101.

Bercusson, B. (1996), *European Labour Law*, London: Butterworths.

Bercusson, B. (ed.) (2006), *European Labour Law and the EU Charter of Fundamental Rights*, Baden-Baden: Nomos.

Bercusson, B. (2007), "The Trade Union Movement and the European Union: Judgment Day", *European Law Journal* 13 (3): 279–308.

Bercusson, B., and N. Bruun (2005), "Labour Law Aspects of Public Procurement in the EU", in R. Nielsen and S. Treumer (eds), *The New Public Procurement Directives*, Copenhagen: Djøf, pp. 97–116.

Blanke, T. (2006), "The *Viking* case", *Transfer: European Review of Labour and Research* 12 (2) (summer): 251–66.

Colling, T. (2006), "What Space for Unions on the Floor of Rights? Trade Unions and the Enforcement of Statutory Individual Employment Rights", *Industrial Law Journal* 35: 140–51.

Craig, P., and G. de Búrca (2003), *EU Law: Text, Cases and Materials*, 3rd ed., Oxford: Oxford University Press.

Davies, P. (2002), "The Posted Workers Directive and the EC Treaty", *Industrial Law Journal* 31: 298–302.

Eklund, R. (2006), "The Laval Case. Swedish Labour Court Decision 2005 No. 49", in *Industrial Law Journal* 35: 202–208.

Eurostat (1992), "Labour costs: updating 1989–90", Luxembourg.

Fredman, S. (2004), "Marginalising Equal Pay Laws", *Industrial Law Journal* 33: 281–83.

Hellsten, J. (2006), *On the Social Dimension in Posting of Workers*, Ministry of Labour, Helsinki, Finland.

Kowalsky, W. "The Services Directive: the legislative process clears the first hurdle", *Transfer: European Review of Labour and Research,* 12 (2) (Summer 2006): 231–49.

O'Higgins, P. (1997), "'Labour Is Not a Commodity' – An Irish Contribution to International Labour Law", *Industrial Law Journal,* 26: 225.

Streeck, W. (1990), "La dimensione sociale del mercato unico europeo: verso un'economia non regolato?", *Stato e Mercato* 28 (29): 48.

Part IV

The EU and Transnational Labour Regulation

Lessons for Transnational Labour Regulation from a Case Study of Temporary Agency Work

Brian BERCUSSON[1]

Introduction

This concluding chapter summarises lessons to be drawn from this case study of the regulation of temporary agency work at national and transnational levels. While the book focuses on temporary agency work, the larger purpose of our research has been to throw light on a number of different issues which arise when efforts are made to regulate transnationally in general, and in the EU in particular.

The "lessons" are organised under six headings, focusing in turn on how transnational labour regulation may be affected by the *substance* of national regulation of labour (section 1) and the transformation of labour markets in an evolving transnational economy (section 2); then on *processes* of transnational labour regulation through transnational social dialogue and legislative procedures (sections 3 and 4). Both substance and process issues are evident in the lessons to be learned from the EU's recent adoption of a Directive aiming at regulation of the transnational market in *services* (section 5).[2] Finally, there are *lessons for the future* of transnational labour regulation envisaged by the divergent perspectives in the proposed Constitutional Treaty, incorporating the EU Charter of Fundamental Rights,[3] and the contrasting vision of the present European

1 This chapter is based on common considerations and discussions throughout the lifetime of the project and all co-authors of the book actively participated in it.

2 Directive 2006/123/EC of the European Parliament and of the Council of 12 December 2006 on services in the internal market, OJ L376/26 of 27 December 2006.

3 The EU Charter of Fundamental Rights was adopted at Nice on 7 December 2000 and published as a "solemn proclamation" of the European Parliament, the Council and the Commission in the Official Journal of 18 December 2000, OJ C 364/1. The Charter is incorporated, with amendments, in the Treaty establishing a Constitution for Europe adopted by the Member States in the Intergovernmental Conference meeting in Brussels, 17–18 June 2004, OJ C 310/1 of 16 December 2004. See Bercusson (2006).

Commission in its recent Green Paper (section 6).[4] In more detail the lessons are grouped under the following headings.

1. What have we learned about the development of the regulation of temporary agency work at *national* level in the EU Member States which helps us to address issues of transnational labour regulation in general in the EU?
2. What are the lessons of the emergence of *cross-border temporary agency work* in the EU for the regulation of labour in a transnational economy in general?
3. What does the experience of the *combined* attempts at transnational labour regulation of temporary agency work at EU level through *both the European social dialogue and the EU legislative process* teach us?
4. What does the process of European social dialogue on temporary agency work reveal about the efficacy and democratic legitimacy of social dialogue as a mechanism of transnational labour regulation?
5. What does the EU's adoption of the *Services Directive* in December 2006 teach us about the balance between market forces and the protection of labour in transnational labour regulation?
6. Finally, we offer some conclusions drawn from this research on transnational labour regulation for the *future of European labour law*, including reflections on the implications of the proposed Constitutional Treaty and the Commission's Green Paper of 22 November 2006: "Modernising Labour Law to Meet the Challenges of the 21st Century".

1. What Are the Lessons of Regulation of Temporary Agency Work at National Level for Issues of Transnational Labour Regulation in the EU?

1.1 National Diversity: An Obstacle to Transnational Labour Regulation

Diversity among the labour laws of Member States is hardly surprising. But the case study of regulation of temporary agency work at national level reveals the extent to which such diversity poses difficulties for transnational labour regulation.

4 Commission Green Paper "Modernising Labour Law to Meet the Challenges of the 21st Century", COM(2006) 798 final, Brussels, 22 November 2006.

Member state regulation of temporary agency work reveals radically different ideological perceptions of temporary agency work, ranging from the view that temporary work agencies are legitimate and, indeed, fulfil a valuable service to the labour market, to the view that the activities of such agencies are a form of illegitimate exploitation of workers and intervene to commercialise the employment relationship between worker and employer. The resulting diversity takes the form of a variety of rules which were explored in detail in earlier chapters of this book; for example, integrating temporary agency work into the general system of regulation by the social partners, including special collective agreements (Denmark), combined with a very liberal regime allowing for the operation of temporary agency work (Sweden), severe restrictions and even prohibitions (for example, in the building sector) giving way to gradual liberalisation subject to regulation (Germany), treating temporary agency workers as a normal segment of the workforce, but regulating the operations of temporary agency businesses (UK), or establishing an equilibrium involving restricted use of agency work, more security of employment contracts and a specific legal status for temporary agency workers (France).

Divergent views may be expected as regards the perspectives of the social partners, employers' organisations and trade unions, in a given Member State, but compromises may nonetheless be achieved and concretised in national legislation. It becomes very difficult to unravel hard-won national compromises in some Member States where the principles underlying them are at variance with those in other Member States.

The difficulties may be reduced or augmented depending on the practical, ideological and legal importance of the issues at stake: practical in the sense that a greater or lesser proportion of the workforce, or numbers of temporary work agencies may be engaged in the temporary agency work market and are likely to be affected by transnational regulation; ideological in the sense that the national legislation may be considered to reflect fundamental principles (temporary agency work as an "abuse" of the normal functioning of the labour market vs temporary agency work as essential to "labour market flexibility"); legal in the sense that there may be pre-existing norms established at different levels in national legal orders (constitutions, legislation, regulations, collective agreements, judicial decisions) which may have to be accommodated or else block progress. In general, where the practical consequences are great, ideological principles are considered to be at stake, and there are substantial legal obstacles to be overcome, there is less potential for transnational labour regulation.

1.2 Convergence Trends Contribute to Transnational Labour Regulation

That is not to say that compromise and convergence are not possible and trends in that direction can improve the prospects of transnational labour regulation. In the case of temporary agency work, a general trend can be perceived towards acceptance of temporary agency work as one particular flexible mode of hiring labour, but a mode that must be regulated to avoid abuses and dilution of labour conditions for weaker groups.

The trend towards convergence has been driven by the general increase in the use of temporary agency work in the Member States as problems of application of standard employment law to this growing proportion of the workforce lead to pressures for regulation. The impact of the accession of new Member States in May 2004, when provision of temporary agency workers through service providers usually avoided the restrictions imposed by the accession treaties on free movement of workers to the old Member States, stimulated a common trend towards reform of the regulation of temporary agency work.

Furthermore, the prospect of transnational labour regulation may itself be a factor promoting compromise and consensus. ILO Convention 181 on Private Employment Agencies, adopted in 1997, provided a benchmark for convergence. Pressures from the EU for harmonisation of standards and practices in the internal market, or the emergence of specific EU labour market policies, for example, encouraging certain forms of "atypical" employment across the EU, may overcome the obstacles posed by national diversity.

In the case of temporary agency work, national developments over the period highlighted in our research reveal that new Member States in particular – but also others, such as Germany[5] – were strongly influenced by the Commission's proposals on temporary agency work.

1.3 Sectoral Specificity Can Work Both for and against Transnational Labour Regulation

The extent to which a labour issue is sector-specific may affect the prospects for transnational labour regulation. In the case of temporary agency work, the particular form of labour and temporary work agencies as employers may be said to comprise a specific sector. Interests common to the sectoral actors across different Member States may improve the prospects for transnational labour regulation.

5 As pointed out by Kerstin Ahlberg, Germany wanted to try out the temporary agency work reforms at domestic level before binding themselves at EU level.

But the case for general labour regulation may be weakened where the proposals address only one sector and sectoral specificity reveals conflicts. The interests of others, whether permanent workers or user employers, may be in conflict with the temporary agency work sector and a powerful force obstructing transnational regulation. This was evident in the European social dialogue on temporary agency work where tensions emerged on the employer side between UNICE, representing user employers, and CIETT, representing temporary agency employers, and, on the workers' side, between the ETUC and UNI-Europa.

Among employers, there were probably also divisions between large multinational enterprises in the temporary agency work sector, prominent in some Member States, and seeking legitimation through harmonised transnational rules and a highly fragmented sector comprising small temporary work agencies in other Member States, concerned with the potential additional costs of transnational regulation.

1.4 Legal Concepts and Regulatory Traditions Can Pose Problems

There are difficulties for transnational labour regulation when there are important differences in legal concepts commonly used in Member States. The particularly complex triangular relationship characterising temporary agency work was highlighted in our research. The concept of whether an agency worker is a "worker" or "employee" differs among Member States, and in some, such as the UK, there is considerable dispute as to the identity of the employer: the agency or the user of the agency worker. Transnational labour regulation can contribute to a solution of these issues by providing a definition binding all Member States.[6]

But major problems can arise if it is left to the Member States to define the concept of the employment relationship delimiting the scope of application of the Directive.[7] Major discrepancies appear in the application of transnational labour regulation in Member States. Furthermore, opportunities are available for Member States to avoid it through manipulative

---

6 Either through legislation, as in Council Directive 91/383 of 25 June 1991 supplementing the measures to encourage improvements in the safety and health of workers with a fixed-duration employment relationship or a temporary employment relationship, OJ 1991 L206/19, or by judicial decision, as in Case C-256/01, *Allonby v. Accrington & Rosendale College*, [2004] IRLR 224.

7 As proposed in the draft temporary agency work Directive. Commission of the European Communities, *Proposal for a Directive of the European Parliament and the Council on working conditions for temporary workers*, COM(2002) 149 final, Brussels, 20 March 2002; *Amended Proposal*, COM(2002) 701 final, Brussels, 28 November 2002.

definitions of their domestic legal concepts, deferred to by the transnational regulation.[8]

Different regulatory traditions in Member States also have to be accommodated, in particular the different roles played in regulating the labour market by the social partners and legislative and administrative action by the state and the courts. On the one hand, transnational labour regulation in the EU has addressed these concerns by allowing for transposition of directives through collective agreements, thereby respecting the traditions established in the Nordic states.[9] Directives, including the proposed directive on temporary agency work, increasingly make reference to agreements between the social partners as a flexible means of implementing the transnational labour standards prescribed.

On the other hand, the decline or even absence of substantial collective bargaining activity in the Member States can undermine attempts to achieve flexibility by means of channelling implementation through collective bargaining. Resistance to regulation may emerge if collective bargaining becomes the sole channel available for achieving flexibility, to the detriment of those Member States without recourse to this mechanism.

1.5 Spillover Effects of Transnational Labour Regulation of One Issue to National Regulation of Other Issues

Selective transnational regulation of one issue affecting labour can spill over to affect other issues, a risk that poses potential difficulties. An example was the warning that excluding temporary agency work from the scope of the Fixed-Term Work Directive could lead to a shift from employers hiring fixed-term workers directly – and thereby becoming subject to the Directive – to employers resorting to hiring workers from temporary work agencies, thereby avoiding the Fixed-Term Work Directive.[10]

---

8 One incongruity already revealed concerns the Part-Time Work Directive (Council Directive 97/81/EC of 15 December 1997 concerning the framework agreement on part-time work concluded by UNICE, CEEP and the ETUC, OJ L14/9 of 20 January 1998). In the UK , the relevant Regulations apply to all workers due to the impact of the EU definition of the scope of coverage of equality law (see the Part-time Worker (Prevention of Less Favourable Treatment) Regulations 2000, S.I. 2000, N. 1551, as amended). In contrast, the application in the UK of the Fixed-Term Work Directive (Council Directive 1999/70/EC of 28 June 1999 concerning the framework agreement on fixed-term work concluded by ETUC, UNICE and CEEP, OJ L175/43 of 10 July 1999) is limited to 'employees', not the wider category of 'workers'. See the Fixed-term Employees (Prevention of Less Favourable Treatment) Regulations 2002, S.I. 2002. No. 2034.

9 The so-called 'Christopherson clause', now in Article 137(3) EC.

10 See Vigneau *et al.* (1999).

A similar phenomenon of spillover can operate in national regulation of temporary agency work. Insofar as temporary agency work is attractive to employers by allowing for flexible hiring and firing, reducing the *general* employment protection law against unfair dismissal reduces this competitive advantage of agency workers. Hence the concerns allegedly felt by large temporary work agencies in France when the government proposed to reduce the employment protection against dismissal. Similarly, the adoption of a broader definition of "employee" created anxieties for the UK government which feared that this could have a wider impact on its domestic labour law position.

1.6 Summary and Conclusion

But the consequences of diversity in the case of temporary agency work appeared too great and may have contributed to the current position of a failure to achieve transnational regulation. This may be seen in the comparative success in achieving transnational regulation of part-time and fixed-term work, on which it was possible to achieve greater consensus.

But many other factors led to the current situation, and it is not impossible that changes in these may allow for the emergence of transnational regulation of temporary agency work. Some of these factors are explored in the following sections.

2. What Are the Lessons of the Emergence of Cross-Border Temporary Agency Work in the EU for Labour Regulation in a Transnational Economy?

2.1 Pressures for Transnational Labour Regulation in an Integrated Economy

One of the defining characteristics of the single European Market consists of the free movement of labour and services, freedoms carefully protected by EU law. The emergence of cross-border temporary agency work is the natural consequence of the absence of any, or the existence of only marginal, restrictions on the free movement of workers and services. It is precisely the largely unregulated nature of the European labour market which allows for unregulated cross-border temporary agency work.

In this context, transnational regulation of labour is driven by two considerations. One is the pressure to harmonise conditions of competition among enterprises using temporary agency work in the different Member States, to the ultimate benefit of consumers. The other is the pressure to regulate the operation of temporary work agencies and the conditions of temporary agency workers in the temporary agency work sector, whether this be regulation to protect the working conditions of the latter (workers) or to further facilitate the operations of the former (agencies).

In an increasingly integrated European economy, the emergence of cross-border temporary agency work is to be expected, as are the pressures for its regulation.

2.2 Practical Consequences of Free Movement in an Integrated Economy

The normal pressures for regulation have been exacerbated, however, by two factors. The first was the accession of a large number of new Member States in May 2004. The second was that the accession treaties allowed for the placing by old Member States of limitations on the free movement of workers from the new accession states. This limitation, however, normally did not apply to free movement of services (exceptions being Germany and Austria).

The activities of temporary work agencies qualify as the provision of services. The activities of such agencies in the movement of workers from the new to the old Member States increased the pressures for transnational labour regulation of temporary agency work.

The movement of workers from new to old Member States excited considerable controversy, increasing this pressure. "Polish plumbers" were highlighted as one factor in the French rejection of the Constitutional Treaty in the referendum. The decimation of the German workforce in abattoirs and their replacement by workers from the new accession countries led to protests. The deaths of some Chinese cockle-pickers by drowning led to scrutiny of the use of immigrant workers and produced British legislation seeking to regulate the activities of "gang-master" agencies supplying workers, including those from the new Member States, to the agricultural and food processing sectors.

Not least, the high profile cases of *Laval/Vaxholm*[11] and *Viking*[12] provide evidence of the potential pressures that can lead to transnational labour regulation through legislation or case law. *Laval/Vaxholm*, in particular, raised questions as to the adequacy of the limited transnational regulation that does exist, the Posting of Workers Directive[13] and its implementation in Sweden.[14]

---

11 Case C-341/05, *Laval un Partneri Ltd v Svenska Byggnadsarbetareförbundet, Svenska Byggnadsarbetareförbundet, Avdelning 1, Svenska Elektrikerförbundet.*

12 Case C-438/05, *Viking Line Abp OU Viking Line Eesti v The International Transport Workers' Federation, The Finnish Seamen's Union.*

13 Directive 96/71/EC concerning the posting of workers in the framework of the provision of services. OJ 1996, L18/1.

14 See Ahlberg *et al.* (2006).

In sum, the unregulated movement of workers in an integrated transnational economy creates numerous occasions for public concern, generating pressure for transnational labour regulation.

2.3 Transnational Labour Regulation and National Labour Policy: Pre-emption and Non-regression

The emergence of cross-border temporary agency work and the resultant pressures for transnational labour regulation may be resisted on the grounds that they pre-empt initiatives in national labour policy. Regulation at transnational level may preclude liberalisation (deregulation) at national level, and vice versa. Doctrines of non-regression may make it impossible, once transnational regulation is adopted, to reverse the policy enshrined in it.

The consequence can be either resistance to, or support for, transnational labour regulation. As transnational labour regulation can constrain the ability of Member States to promote national policies, support for transnational labour regulation may depend on whether it is consistent with national policy priorities at present, and/or whether it is perceived as desirable to constrain future national policy choices.

The experience of the attempts at transnational labour regulation of temporary agency work demonstrates this. The Commission's proposed Directives would have required Member States to provide for comparison of working conditions between agency workers and employees of the user undertaking: regulation. But the Directive would also have constrained Member States to scrutinise their legislation with a view to justifying any constraints on temporary agency work, and possibly removing them: liberalisation. The failure of the Commission's proposal to achieve consensus may have been due to the resistance of some Member States to the perceived threat to their future freedom to regulate, and of others to liberalise.

The Nordic Member States provide a specific example. Transnational labour regulation has to take account of the central role of collective bargaining in their national labour laws. The Swedish government indicated that it would block the draft Directive unless it affirmed the autonomy of the social partners to regulate temporary agency work. The *Laval/Vaxholm* case is a concrete illustration of the fears of the Nordic trade unions that their freedom of action might be constrained.

Another example is Germany, where legislation along the lines of the proposed Directive had recently been adopted. The government was unwilling to support the proposed Directive unless and until the experience under its domestic legislation proved to be satisfactory.

2.4 Transnational Labour Regulation as an Instrument of National Labour Policy

The prospect of transnational labour regulation may be instrumentalised to promote particular national labour policies. In the case of temporary agency work, there are national sensitivities to the regulation of transnational temporary agency work: on the one hand, concern over exploitation/*marchandage*, security of employment and immigration; on the other hand, anxiety about social exclusion from the labour market, the monopoly of public employment agencies and the legitimacy of temporary agency businesses.

Various actors concerned, from trade unions through multinational temporary work agencies to governments, may seek to promote or condemn transnational labour regulation to advance their own priorities. One illustration is the way in which the Italian government of Silvio Berlusconi invoked the EU Directive on Fixed-term Work to promote a domestic agenda of liberalisation of the Italian labour market.

2.5 Changing Ideology and Policy in Transnational Labour Regulation

The introduction of new measures of transnational labour regulation implies consistency with earlier measures. This can be problematic when policies or ideological preferences have changed.

In the case of temporary agency work, there was a pre-existing Directive on the Posting of Workers. This laid down specified minimum labour standards to be applied by employers established in one Member State to their workers posted to another Member State. The proposed Services Directive represented an ideological shift by the Commission. It was an attempt to partly change policy to allow these employers to apply to their workers some of the labour standards applicable in the Member State of establishment (the "country of origin" principle).

The effect was to confine the Posting Directive to those workers who fell within its scope, and only with respect to the terms specified. It was thereby changed from a minimum standard applicable to posted workers to a maximum standard: workers falling outside its scope and terms of employment not specified in it were not applicable to workers engaged in providing services.

The perceived difficulties in accommodating the ideology and policy of the Posting Directive to the proposed Services Directive led to the three-year struggle to amend it, and very nearly led to its demise, illustrating the problems of changing policy and ideology in transnational labour regulation.

2.6 Summary and Conclusion

The pressures for transnational labour regulation resulting from the cross-border movement of temporary agency workers posed problems for national labour laws. Member States are faced with the prospect of pre-emption and non-regression, and their choices are conditioned by their policy preferences, present and future. These preferences differ, depending on whether the Member State in question is primarily an "exporter" of agency workers (such as Estonia or Poland) or a state which is on the receiving side, which is the case for old Member States such as Finland and Germany. The temptation of instrumentalisation is always present. Finally, initiatives at transnational level are conditioned by preceding transnational labour regulation, which can be problematic when there are changes of ideology and policy.

3. What are the Lessons of the *Combined* Attempts at Transnational Labour Regulation of Temporary Agency Work through both the European Social Dialogue and the EU Legislative Process?[15]

3.1 The Changing Dynamic of Transnational Labour Law-making in the EU

In the aftermath of the Maastricht Treaty, the dynamic of the early stages of the social dialogue was described as "bargaining in the shadow of the law".[16] This research on temporary agency work refines certain features of that dynamic emerging in the more mature stage of the processes of transnational labour law-making some ten years after Maastricht. In sum, the shadow has become more pronounced, in several respects and in different senses.

First, the social partners have become more experienced in assessing the prospects of legislation should negotiations fail. European employers' organisations remain opposed in principle to regulation. They may calculate that the Commission will not take any initiative, or, as in the case of temporary agency work, enough Member States can be mobilised to prevent any initiative receiving the requisite majority vote for its adoption in the Council of Ministers. Trade unions may be less willing to accept agreements merely for the sake of demonstrating that the social dialogue is capable of producing transnational labour standards, and look

15 It is not proposed here to replicate the valuable conclusions reached by Kerstin Ahlberg in her chapter (Chapter 9) analysing the social dialogue and legislative processes which attempted to regulate temporary agency work.

16 Bercusson (1992, 1996).

to the legislative process which may offer more. The experience of temporary agency work illustrates an outcome, to date, which reveals both these calculations, aptly described by the title of the chapter (Chapter 9) by Kerstin Ahlberg: "A Story of a Failure – But Also of Success", though this might be qualified by "so far".

Secondly, the role of the Commission as a dynamic actor capable of intervention galvanising the social dialogue is not to be taken for granted. The achievement of the Barroso Commission in the area of labour law has been virtually nil, while the preceding years of the twenty-first century managed only to produce extremely modest outcomes.[17] The poverty of the Commission's ambition was evident in its Communication of 9 February 2005 on the Social Agenda 2005–2010.[18] This included only one specific proposal which the Barroso Commission explicitly committed itself to adopting: on transnational collective bargaining.[19] And even this has now been abandoned.[20] The absence of achievement and lack of ambition are evident when compared to the European Commission's

17 The last significant achievement was five years ago, in March 2002 (Council Directive No. 2002/14 establishing a framework for informing and consulting employees in the European Community. OJ 2002, L80/29). Previous developments were directives on discrimination (Directive 2000/78 of 27 November 2000 establishing a general framework for equal treatment in employment and occupation (OJ 2000 L303/16) aims at 'combating discrimination on the ground of religion or belief, disability, age or sexual orientation as regards employment and occupation' (Article 1); Council Directive 2000/43 of 29 June 2000 implementing the principle of equal treatment between persons irrespective of racial or ethnic origin (OJ 2000 L180/22); Council Directive 2002/73/EC (OJ 2002 No. L269/15) amended Council Directive 76/207/EEC of 9 February 1976 on the implementation of the principle of equal treatment for men and women as regards access to employment, vocational training and promotion, and working conditions (OJ 1976, No. L39/40)). There was also consolidation of directives, such as on working time (Directive 2003/88/EC of 4 November 2003 concerning certain aspects of the organisation of working time; OJ L299/9 of 18 November 2003 consolidated Council Directive 93/104/EC of 23 November 1993, OJ L307/18 of 13 December 1993, as amended by Directive 2000/34 of 22 June 2000, OJ L195/41).

18 Communication from the Commission on the Social Agenda, COM(2005) 33 final, Brussels, 9 February 2005.

19 'The Commission plans to adopt a proposal designed to make it possible for the social partners to formalise the nature and results of transnational collective bargaining. The existence of this resource is essential but its use will remain optional and will depend entirely on the will of the social partners'.

20 In a conference organised by the Commission on 27 November 2006, the survey of transnational collective agreements conducted by the Commission was marginalised and the expert study proposing a directive was brusquely buried. Instead it was announced that no regulatory initiative was in prospect and the Commission planned at most another Communication in 2007.

activity in the last decade of the twentieth century. This saw the vast expansion of the EU's labour law and employment policy competences by the Treaties of Maastricht (1991) and Amsterdam (1997). In that ten-year period, the Commission's initiatives produced at least ten significant directives.[21] "Bargaining in the shadow of the law" requires legislative initiatives as a stimulus to bargaining. In the EU law-making process, the power of initiative lies with the Commission. This was manifest during the 1990s. So far, in the twenty-first century incentives for the social partners, particularly employers, to embark on social dialogue in the absence of Commission initiatives are lacking.

Third, the calculus has become more complex as the number of Member States in the Council has increased. The account of the proceedings concerned with the proposed directive on temporary agency work in a Council of 15 Member States reveals the difficulty of reaching consensus and the complexity of the compromises sought, in this case in vain. The prospects for transnational labour law-making through a legislative process in a Council of 27 Member States are even less promising.

Fourth, the composition and engagement of the social partners themselves in the social dialogue has also become more complex. New organisations on the employers' side (UEAPME, CIETT, including powerful multinationals) joined in the negotiations on temporary agency work, leading to different positions being promoted. Decision-making procedures requiring unanimity, as is the case with UNICE's internal procedures, are a further serious obstacle. On the trade union side, past experience led to greater familiarity with the process, but also sensitised national confederations to the issues at stake. Divisions among national confederations and also with European sectoral organisations made adoption of common positions ever more difficult. These problems were exacerbated when divisions among trade union confederations did not always reflect the same divisions among Member States in the Council. Compromises reached within the organisations taking part in the social dialogue, or even in the social dialogue, did not necessarily reflect the same compromises among Member States.

21 On health and safety for temporary and agency workers (1991), mandatory information on employment conditions for employees (1991), protection of pregnant and breastfeeding mothers (1992), working time (1993), European Works Councils (1994), parental leave (1996), part-time work (1997), the burden of proof in cases of sex discrimination (1997), fixed-term work (1999) and substantive amendments to the Directives on collective dismissals (1992) and transfers of undertakings (1998).

Fifth, the European Parliament has increasingly asserted its position as an important player. The Parliament's criticism[22] of the framework agreement on fixed-term work reinforced the reluctance of some national trade union confederations to engage in further social dialogue on temporary agency work. The Parliament's concern that its legislative role in the field of social policy is being usurped is well known.[23] The Parliament's rapporteur, Karin Jöns, was highly critical of the procedure of social dialogue which led to the Fixed-term Work Agreement, describing it as too time-consuming and extremely cumbersome. She concluded that it should not be allowed to become a systematic replacement for the normal legislative procedure. The evidence of the legislative process concerning temporary agency work, however, reveals an even more time-consuming and cumbersome process, with no result after years, never mind months.

It is as yet too early to say whether the original dynamic has been transformed, or merely elaborated, or whether the collective bargaining nature of social dialogue has given way permanently to a more politicised process. On the one hand, the social partners continue to embark on action programmes of social dialogue. But these do not engage the legislative institutions nor lead to legally binding outcomes, at times because of the social partners' own reluctance for such engagement or their preoccupation with autonomy. On the other hand, the legislative institutions remain relatively inactive, with few Commission initiatives and even fewer legislative achievements – a fact which impedes the development of social dialogue since it strips the process of any pressure for positive, concrete outcomes.[24] It is as yet unclear whether the current stalemate, or even paralysis, will be overcome through a revival of the social dialogue and/or revision of legislative processes, or awaits a political stimulus which will achieve either, both or none.

3.2 Constraints on the Scope of Transnational Labour Regulation

Peculiar to the EU system of transnational labour regulation, but especially significant in the processes concerning temporary agency work, was the provision in Article 137(5) of the EC Treaty purporting to exclude pay from the scope of directives adopted under that article. The

---

22 Draft report on the framework agreement on fixed-term work concluded by UNICE, CEEP and ETUC, 12 March 1999, PE 230.208

23 See the discussion in Herzfeld Olsson *et al.* (1998).

24 Cf. the *Report of the High level Group on the Future of Social Policy in an Enlarged European Union*, European Commission, Directorate-General for Employment and Social Affairs, May 2004, p. 75: 'The Commission should continue to play a key role with its right of initiative for new legislation, hereby giving an incentive to social partners to opt for a negotiation route to settle the issues at stake between themselves'.

issue of whether the outcome, either of the social dialogue or the legislative process, could include references to the pay of agency workers was continually raised as an obstacle to agreement. The point is that the process of transnational labour regulation can be inhibited where there is no agreement on the potential scope of regulation.

That the scope is alleged to be the result of legal constraints is incidental. Solutions can be found, as indeed was the case when the particularly damaging effect of the alleged constraint regarding pay was alleviated, albeit late in the day, by the Commission's Legal Service changing its position. But the disruptive effect of lack of consensus on the scope of the proposals was a feature highlighted in the account of both processes, social dialogue and legislative.

The fact that it was not the only disruptive feature was also evident in the dispute over whether use of temporary agency workers as replacements for striking workers was also outside the scope of negotiations, despite the centrality of this issue for the trade union side and the lack of widespread opposition to the principle (of non-replacement) among employers. Again, the lack of consensus on the scope of the proposed measure was expressed through a legalistic point, which acted as a constraint on the progress of transnational labour regulation.

3.3 Competition or Cooperation between Social Dialogue and Legislative Process

The changing dynamic of transnational labour regulation in the EU, as between social dialogue and legislative process, engages the social partners with a number of institutional actors: the Commission, the European Parliament and the Council of Ministers.

The relationship between the Parliament and the social partners is characterised by a degree of competition, at least on the side of the Parliament, jealous of its exclusion from the process of social dialogue. On the other hand, the social partners, at least the trade unions, appear more than willing to cooperate with the Parliament, once the social dialogue is over.

The relationship with the Commission is complex. Apart from its vital role as a potential stimulant by way of taking legislative initiatives, the Commission provides practical support for the social partners and the social dialogue process (premises, interpreters, legal advice, and so on), as well as supplying the experienced chair of the negotiations. If the social dialogue fails to produce an agreement, however, it appears there is some continuity, but also discontinuity. In the case of the social dialogue on temporary agency work, the Commission was able to build on compromises which had been reached, and, indeed, was given the drafts produced by the social partners during negotiations. On the other hand, the Commission official monitoring the social dialogue was not permitted to engage in the subsequent legislative process.

As to the Council, the evidence from the experience of the temporary agency work processes is that there was no apparent contact: once the social dialogue was over, the issue passed to consideration in the Council and the social dialogue was never mentioned in Council. But it was clear that individual Member States were subjected to domestic pressures from their national trade union confederations and employers' organisations.

3.4 Problems of Diversity

The problem of diversity is reflected in the varied positions adopted by national employers' organisations and trade unions in the different Member States. The process of social dialogue does assist in channelling, if not reconciling, these differences through the single spokesperson who represents each side. The contrast is particularly clear with the process in the Council of Ministers, where each Member State speaks and represents itself alone. The problem is acute in COREPER where the ultimate objective is to achieve a solution respecting different member-state practices. The increasing number of Member States makes finding a satisfactory solution all the more problematic.

The problem can be illustrated through the experience of temporary agency work. A key element in the social dialogue, as in the legislative process, was the issue of applying the principle of discrimination, and specifically, the identification of appropriate comparators for temporary agency workers. The problem is much more acute where arrangements for setting wages and conditions of employment are highly individualised than where there are collective arrangements. The former allow for greater diversity and hence offer greater prospects for comparison between individuals, whereas the latter accommodate diversity within collective structures. The differences among Member States on this issue reflected their different traditions of individualisation and collectivism in determining conditions of employment.

3.5 Overload and Spillover

Different processes of transnational labour law-making through social dialogue or legislation have different capacities. The limited infrastructural capacity of the European social dialogue means that it cannot engage with more than one or two issues simultaneously. This not only limits the scope of the social dialogue, but also it can have negative effects insofar as it limits the potential for trade-offs between social dialogues on different issues which might allow for agreements to be reached.

It is arguable that the EU legislative process is much better equipped to deal with multiple issues. But there is the converse risk of negative spillover as problems in one area threaten to contaminate other issues.

The social dialogue on temporary agency work broke down in May 2001. The Commission did not produce its draft directive on temporary agency work until March 2002. The legislative process on temporary agency work appears to have come to a halt in June 2003. In January 2004, the Commission produced its draft directive on the liberalisation of services, which purported to cover services provided by temporary work agencies. This proposed Services Directive excited much controversy. The Services Directive was eventually amended by the European Parliament to exclude temporary work agencies, an amendment reluctantly accepted by the Commission. These developments show how different parts of the Commission pursue different agendas. It is not evident that they were interlinked, but it is hard to ignore the potential for spillover of one agenda into the other.

3.6 Summary and Conclusion

The experience of the combined attempts at transnational labour regulation of temporary agency work at EU level through the social dialogue and legislative processes did not produce an outcome in the form of an agreement or legal measure. But analysis of these processes has yielded a number of important insights into the evolution of transnational labour regulation: a changing dynamic, involving cooperation and competition, problems of constraints, diversity, overload and spillover. Finally, as Kerstin Ahlberg notes in the epilogue to her chapter, transnational processes did have consequences for national regulation of temporary agency work in some Member States.

4. What Did the Process of European Social Dialogue on Temporary Agency Work Reveal about the Efficacy and Democratic Legitimacy of Social Dialogue as a Mechanism of Transnational Labour Regulation?

4.1 Actors, Processes and Outcomes of the Social Dialogue Mechanism of Transnational Labour Regulation

This book describes in detail the process of social dialogue on temporary agency work between the EU social partners.[25] The book focuses on the trade union side of the EU social dialogue because more material was available which illuminated that side of the social dialogue.[26] The analy-

25 An earlier study had provided an outline account of the social dialogue on fixed-term work. See Ahlberg (1999).

26 Kerstin Ahlberg emphasises the problem for researchers of a general lack of accessibility of records of proceedings in the European social dialogue and similarly highlights the greater difficulties of obtaining sources from and communicating with the employers' side.

sis examines the actors, processes and outcomes of the EU intersectoral social dialogue.

The EU social dialogue engages the social partners in the Member States who are affiliated to the EU-level organisations: ETUC, UNICE, UEAPME and CEEP. The relationship between these EU intersectoral organisations and their national affiliates affects crucial aspects of the social dialogue: for example, the decisions to undertake social dialogue on a particular subject, to define the negotiating mandate, to decide whether to approve the agreement reached and to resolve disputes over interpretation of the agreement. In the case of the social dialogue on temporary agency work, the ETUC's wish to enter into negotiations was tempered by the reluctance of some of its affiliates, less than happy with the framework agreement concluded on fixed-term work, who wished to postpone negotiations until the consequences of implementation of the fixed-term agreement could be assessed clearly. Despite this, the ETUC succeeded in convincing these affiliates to allow it to proceed.

The involvement of the social partners in the Member States in the process of EU social dialogue is a function of their ability to participate in and monitor the activities of the negotiators. For example, the flow of information about the progress of negotiations downwards from the negotiators to the national social partners and outwards from them to their affiliates (regional, sectoral, and so on) and the communication of responses and reactions from the national social partners reflects the "internal" dialogue within each of the social partners. The nature and quality of this "internal" dialogue has important consequences for the effectiveness of the social dialogue process, as well as its democratic legitimacy.

Finally, the social partners in the Member States have been allocated a role in the implementation of the outcomes: agreements concluded in the social dialogue and the transposition of resulting directives into national law. The interaction between the social partners at national level and the EU social partners reflects some of the tensions resulting from the different roles played by the social partners in a number of Member States in the transposition into national law of the framework agreements reached through the EU social dialogue.

4.2 The EU "Bargaining Order": Preparing and Conducting Negotiations

The three successful EU social dialogues at intersectoral level which have produced directives provide some basis for establishing an EU "bargaining order": the procedure to be followed by the social partners in conducting the social dialogue. Articles 138–139 of the EC Treaty, which provide the legal basis for the EU social dialogue, are notoriously inadequate as a framework. The absence of an established and structured bargaining order, either in legislation or in an agreement between the social partners themselves, is a serious defect in terms of the legitimacy, transparency and efficacy of the EU social dialogue.

In terms of preparation of the EU social dialogue there are particular points in time which are of maximum concern to affiliates and which may require them to engage more actively: for example, the point of determining the negotiating mandate. The difficulties in determining the negotiating mandate will reflect national differences among the affiliates of the EU intersectoral social partners. Kerstin Ahlberg describes the greater problems in the ETUC agreeing the mandate on temporary agency work as national trade union confederations had different strategies for dealing with this kind of work,[27] while UNICE's position was rendered more complicated by the role of the temporary work agencies employers' confederation, CIETT.[28]

In terms of structuring the social dialogue, the question is how to define the composition and respective roles of the Negotiations and Drafting Groups. The issue is primarily that of the roles of each Group and their interaction. As to their respective roles, the borderline between drafting and negotiating is not always clear. It seems inevitable that there will be a need for a Committee with restricted numbers to undertake some negotiations, which will leave outside the representatives of many affiliates. This makes the reporting-back procedure between a restricted membership Drafting Group and a fully representative Negotiations Group all the more essential.

The ETUC Negotiations Group in the social dialogue on temporary agency work comprised 29 persons. An important point providing continuity of experience was that the spokesperson for the trade union side in both the fixed-term and temporary agency work negotiations was Jean Lapeyre, Deputy General Secretary of the ETUC. In contrast, on the employers' side, the spokesperson in the fixed-term negotiations was Dan McAuley from the Irish employers' confederation; in the temporary agency work negotiations, it was Wilfrid Beirnaert, Chair of UNICE's social affairs committee.

---

27 Thus the French FO and the German IG-Metall both opposed the use of temporary agency work, while trade unions in the UK and Sweden took a more permissive approach. Ahlberg also concludes that one major factor dividing the social partners was whether temporary agency workers with open-ended contracts were covered, and suggests that this was a matter of particular sensitivity to the German trade unions.

28 Ahlberg notes that the ETUC's mandate, finally unanimously adopted on 22 March 2000, was a detailed list comprising two pages, and comments that although there was one formal mandate, the employers seemed to have two separate negotiating agendas.

The Drafting Group on the trade unions' side was similar in both sets of negotiations: two from sectoral federations (European Metalworkers' Federation and UNI-Europa), two from the ETUC, and three from national confederations (in the temporary agency work negotiations, these were from the UK, Spain and the Netherlands). But in the negotiations over temporary agency work, the employers' side included not only UNICE and CEEP, but also representatives from CIETT, the temporary work agencies employers' federation and two observers from UEAPME.

Certain factors may be relevant in constructing a relationship between negotiating and drafting bodies, and between them and the organisations represented on them.

First, in addition to these bodies, there were other ETUC bodies which received regular reports on the negotiations: the ETUC Executive Committee and the ETUC Industrial Relations Committee. Affiliates could keep track of negotiations through these bodies as well as through their representatives on the Negotiations Group.

Secondly, of course, some affiliates were represented on the Drafting Group itself, and this gave them privileged access to developments. While reports went back from this Group to the Negotiations Committee, affiliates whose representatives were on the Drafting Group had some time advantage in consulting their own organisations.

Thirdly there may be scope for horizontal arrangements between groups of national affiliates, which may overcome some of the problems of lack of representatives on the smaller "Executive Committee" of negotiators.

4.3 Internal Constitutional Arrangements of the EU Social Partners

The aspect of the EU bargaining order of concern here is not so much that *between* the social partners, though this is of primary importance.[29] The concern here is with that part of the "bargaining order" which regulates the relationship between the EU social partners and their *affiliates* in the Member States.

The extent to which representatives of the affiliates in the various bodies engaged in negotiations did in practice inform and consult their organisations is crucial. It is not clear whether some affiliates were continuous-

29 Indeed, Ahlberg remarks on the very great differences as regards the behaviour of the employers' side between the negotiations on temporary agency work and those on fixed-term work. Unlike in the latter, in the former negotiations few draft texts were exchanged between the parties and there were no meetings between the drafting groups of the two sides until very late in the negotiations.

ly well-informed and others much less so. Failure to maintain the "internal dialogue" undermines both the effectiveness of negotiators, who are denied information, ideas and proposals coming up from the affiliates, as well as the legitimacy, and indeed the successful ratification of the outcome of negotiations when affiliates are not regularly informed and consulted. The great diversity of organisations of workers in the different Member States and their different traditions of collective bargaining make it difficult to find a common solution to this problem. Yet a solution which can accommodate those traditions is necessary.

4.4 The Sectoral Dimension of the Intersectoral Social Dialogue

Given the weakness or frequent absence of sectoral organisation and initiative on the side of employers at EU level, the engagement of specific EU sectoral organisations (where these exist) in the *intersectoral* dialogue could encourage developments in the EU *sectoral* social dialogue. A striking example of the interaction of intersectoral and sectoral social dialogues at EU level took place in the course of the negotiations over fixed-term work. The sectoral federation, Euro-FIET (now UNI-Europa) agreed with the representative of the employers in the field of temporary agency work (CIETT)[30] to exclude this field from the scope of the negotiations in the intersectoral social dialogue on fixed-term work. A letter addressed to UNICE, CEEP and ETUC, signed by the Director of Euro-FIET and the first vice president of CIETT, dated 3 July 1998, expressed their joint view that it was inappropriate to include temporary work businesses. Significantly, they concluded that it would undermine the progress they were trying to make at the sectoral level.

It was stated, therefore, that any EU-level agreement on fixed-term contracts should exclude triangular agency work relationships. But this exclusion should be accompanied by a commitment to negotiate a specific agreement for this type of relationship at the appropriate EU level. This request was acceded to by the EU intersectoral social partners and temporary agency work was excluded from the scope of the negotiations. The agreement eventually concluded did, however, include the commitment to undertake an EU intersectoral social dialogue on temporary agency work.[31]

Kerstin Ahlberg describes how the intersectoral social dialogue on temporary agency work was stimulated by the activities of CIETT together with UNI-Europa which in 1999 established a sectoral social dia-

30 *Confédération Internationale des Entreprises de Travail Temporaire.*

31 Recital 13: 'Management and labour wished to give particular attention to fixed-term work, while at the same time indicating that it was their intention to consider the need for a similar agreement relating to temporary agency work'.

logue committee. The prospect of the sectoral social partners undertaking to negotiate their own sectoral agreement was problematic for the EU-level intersectoral social partners: for the ETUC, UNI-Europa did not represent temporary agency workers in all sectors; for UNICE, CIETT did not represent the user employers of temporary agency workers. Sectoral initiatives thus provided an incentive for the EU level intersectoral social partners to negotiate on temporary agency work.

On the other hand, Ahlberg describes how the activities of the sectoral organisations could also create problems and exacerbate divisions between and within the social partners involved in the negotiations. She describes how, on 3 July 2000, UNI-Europa and CIETT made a joint declaration expressing strong support for sectoral social dialogue while also stating their support for the ongoing negotiations between ETUC and UNICE/CEEP. The declaration, however, also expressed the view that agency work could play a positive role in the labour market; a statement which created some dissension within the ETUC delegation. At a crucial point in the negotiations on temporary agency work, at a meeting of 9 February 2001, the position of CIETT on some issues differed from that of UNICE and instead CIETT adopted the same viewpoint as the ETUC.

The intersectoral negotiations were ultimately unsuccessful and on 22 March 2001 the ETUC Executive Committee abandoned negotiations and called on the Commission to propose a directive regulating temporary agency work. The Commission finally adopted such a proposal one year later, on 20 March 2002.[32] In between, early in October 2001 the sectoral organisations, UNI-Europa and CIETT, had signed a joint declaration on temporary agency workers in favour of European legislation.[33]

4.5 Bilateral Social Dialogue at National Level as an Aid to Successful EU Social Dialogue

Individual trade union confederations or employers' organisations at national level may pose problems specific to their national context which threaten to block progress in the EU social dialogue.

Contacts between the social partners at national level may attempt to reach compromises where one or more of the national social partners are raising difficulties in the EU negotiations. A dispute could be resolved

32 Proposal for a Directive of the European Parliament and the Council on working conditions for temporary workers, Brussels, 20 March 2002, COM(2002) 149 final, 2002/0072(COD).

33 Immediately afterwards, on 12 October 2001, the EU intersectoral social partners opened negotiations on telework, which this time were successful.

between the national social partners to avoid it contaminating the EU-level negotiations. Ahlberg explains how, in the negotiations on temporary agency work, the British employers' federation, the CBI, once again pushed for the exclusion of pay from the scope of any agreement on temporary agency workers. The employers' side opposed any explicit reference to pay in an agreement, and this persistence raised doubts on the trade union side as to whether the employers were willing or would be able to conclude an agreement.[34]

Ahlberg observes that the EU social dialogue seems to involve disproportionate attention being paid to resolving difficulties with the UK and Ireland. She reports that the standard UNICE solution was to propose to the trade union side that these issues be resolved internally between the social partners in the Member States. This, however, did not suffice in the British context due to the pro-employer attitudes of the British government and the absence of adequate collective bargaining structures at national or sectoral level capable of resolving the difficulties.[35]

4.6 Breaking Deadlocks in Negotiations: The (Temporary) Role of Mini-summits

It is not clear that the EU social dialogue has yet achieved the "normalisation" – the longer term stability – which could ensure that parties' expectations would be that obstacles encountered in negotiations would eventually be overcome. This apparent fragility may offer the temptation to some participants, national affiliates of the EU social partners, to perceive breakdowns in negotiations as more than temporary and "normal" obstacles to be encountered in a mature bargaining process. In particular, the temptation might be to seize the opportunity to wreck the process in its entirety. It may be necessary to develop mechanisms to avoid this temptation and resolve deadlocks.

It seems that a change in the level of negotiations, in the form of "mini-summits" between the leaders of the EU social partners, are used to achieve such breakthroughs. Ahlberg reports on one such unsuccessful attempt which followed the breakdown of negotiations on temporary agency work. On 14 March 2001 Jean Degimbe, the chair of the negotiations, concluded that no agreement was possible. Nonetheless, on

34 On another occasion, Ahlberg reports, an ETUC proposal in a meeting of the drafting groups on 26–28 February 2001 sought explicitly to accommodate a demand from the British employers' confederation regarding derogation by collective agreements.

35 Ahlberg reports the same problem of absence of adequate collective bargaining structures as a factor in the UK government's position on stipulating comparators in the user enterprise for temporary agency workers in the Council negotiations over the proposed Directive.

21 March 2001, UNICE persisted and at a "Social Dialogue mini-summit" in Stockholm, further attempts were made leading to a meeting on 6 April 2001 of the leaders of the EU social partners in the office of the Commissioner for Social Affairs. Further efforts produced some progress, including a proposal by the Commissioner herself on 10 May 2001, but these final attempts were unsuccessful in resolving the deadlock.

In sum, in a mature process of EU social dialogue there should be mechanisms of mediation and conciliation which may successfully break deadlocks and achieve the necessary agreement.[36] Efforts should be made to develop such mechanisms at EU level, and reduce the reliance on interventions from the top level to achieve the necessary breakthrough.

4.7 The Role of the Commission in the EU Social Dialogue

The position of the Commission in the EU social dialogue is extremely delicate. Formally, the person chairing the negotiations and his assistant were paid by the Commission, which also provided logistical and financial support for the meetings of the social partners (for example, paying for interpreters and meeting rooms). But the social partners insisted on the bipartite nature of the social dialogue, autonomous from the Commission. Having said that, the record of documentation of the negotiations reveals something, if only partial, of the dynamic reality behind this formal position.

The potential consequences of Commission intervention were unambiguously revealed in the negotiations on temporary agency work. As described by Ahlberg, at the meeting on 11–12 January 2001 both sides decided to refer to the Commission's Legal Service the question of whether a social dialogue agreement could cover the issue of pay of temporary agency workers, or whether this was excluded by Article 137(5) of the EC Treaty.[37] On 13 February, Jean Degimbe, who was chairing the negotiations, reported that the Commission's Legal Service did not wish to give a written opinion, but orally expressed the view that, in light of Article 137(5), it was not advisable to mention pay in the agreement. He further expressed the Legal Service's view as being that to require agency workers to be paid rates comparable to those in the user company would be to regulate pay contrary to Article 137(5). This intervention had a major negative impact on the substantive position of the trade unions in

---

36 For a study of this issue, see Fernando Valdés Dal-Ré, *Synthesis Report on Conciliation, Mediation and Arbitration in the European Union Countries*, Report for DG Employment and Social Affairs of the European Commission, 2002.

37 'The provisions of this Article shall not apply to pay, the right of association, the right to strike or the right to impose lock-outs'.

the negotiations and Ahlberg opines that this may have had a decisive influence on the outcome of the negotiations. The intervention by the Commission was all the more detrimental in that, as she reports, the Legal Service later reversed its viewpoint and accepted that an agreement on temporary agency work could include pay.[38]

The position of the social partners on the issue of the Commission's role is ambivalent. Considerations, sometimes of a character derived from constitutional traditions in individual Member States, may dictate absolute autonomy of the social partners and their dialogue from any intervention by public authority, at EU level embodied in the Commission.[39] On the other hand, the role of the Commission in the creation and maintenance of the EU social dialogue is undeniable; and, perhaps, unavoidable.

4.8 Summary and Conclusion

The attempt by the European social partners to regulate temporary agency work in the EU failed. But the analysis in this book identifies important issues concerning not only the interactions between the EU social partners, but also the engagement of sectoral federations, and of representatives of the EU social partners' affiliates in the Member States. The relationship between the EU social partners and their national affiliates affects the decisions to undertake the social dialogue on a particular subject, to define the negotiating mandate, to decide whether to approve the agreement reached, and to resolve disputes over interpretation of the agreement. Attention must also be paid to the internal institutional dynamics of the social partners. Experience has also demonstrated the need for mechanisms to break deadlocks and of the importance of the role of the Commission.

---

38 The Commission's initial proposal for a directive on temporary agency work included a provision which made express reference to employment conditions, including pay. Commission of the European Communities, *Proposal for a Directive of the European Parliament and the Council on working conditions for temporary workers*, COM(2002) 149 final, Brussels, 20 March 2002, Article 5. Ahlberg cites the written opinion of the Council's Legal Service of 14 October 2002 which also accepted that the proposed Directive could include pay. Nonetheless, the British and Irish governments continued to contest this.

39 This is reflected in the practice, reported by Ahlberg, that the Commission official acting as secretary to the social dialogue negotiations is never the official in charge of the preparation of a subsequent directive. On the other hand, in the negotiations on temporary agency work, both social partners handed over to the Commission all their draft texts, which gave the Commission considerable insight into their positions.

5. What Does the Adoption of the Services Directive Teach Us about the Balance between Market Forces and the Protection of Labour in Transnational Labour Regulation?

5.1 Achieving a Balance between Economic Freedom and Protection of Workers in Transnational Labour Regulation

The Commission's proposal to liberalise the transnational market in services included the operations of temporary work agencies and temporary agency workers, both part of the free movement of services protected by the law of the EU. Transnational labour regulation balancing the economic freedoms of the agencies with protection of the workers was already reflected in the EU's regulation of the health and safety of temporary workers[40] and certain of their working conditions.[41] The controversy aroused by the Commission's proposal on services, however, revealed that it had failed to achieve a balance in transnational labour regulation between the economic dimension of the internal market (freedom to provide services) and the social dimension (protection of employees). One of the qualities of transnational labour regulation through the social dialogue process is that it is unlikely to ignore this requirement of balance.

5.2 Transnational Labour Regulation as a Political Process

The Commission's proposal was significantly amended by the European Parliament in its passage through the EU's legislative process. The legislative process focused on the "country of origin" principle. This principle aimed to enhance the economic freedom of service providers to engage in cross-border activities. But its application to the workers engaged in the provision of services raised serious questions as to both the protection of labour standards and their effective enforcement.

The implications went beyond the provisions of the Services Directive and were thought to have influenced the negative result in the referendum in France on the proposed Constitutional Treaty. The political passions aroused by the proposed Directive led to intensive lobbying efforts by a variety of interest groups. The European Parliament played a major role in the formulation of the provisions of the Directive, including the deletion of the "country of origin" principle.

Transnational labour regulation was not perceived as peripheral to internal market freedoms, best left to formulation by experts in the

40 Council Directive 91/383 of 25 June 1991 supplementing the measures to encourage improvements in the safety and health of workers with a fixed-duration employment relationship or a temporary employment relationship, OJ 1991 L206/19.

41 Directive 96/71/EC concerning the posting of workers in the framework of the provision of services. OJ 1996, L18/1.

Commission and a decision-making process in a Council lacking in transparency, but rather as a highly political issue requiring wide democratic debate and participation.

5.3 The Relevance of Established International Labour Standards to Transnational Labour Regulation

The Commission's proposed Services Directive disregarded the EU's longstanding commitment to social and labour standards, the *acquis communautaire social*. The European Parliament's refused to follow this path: its amendments to the proposed Directive re-established the basic principles of the *acquis communautaire social*. The primary principle upheld was the reaffirmation of the equal treatment of workers, specifically, authorising the host Member State to apply its labour law rules to employees of service providers from other Member States. Other key amendments included the explicit protection of collective agreements, the acknowledgment of protection of workers as an overriding reason relating to the public interest, and the re-affirmation of the fundamental rights of labour. Transnational labour regulation cannot overlook established international labour standards.

5.4 The Implications of the Services Directive for Transnational Labour Regulation of Temporary Agency Work

The final Services Directive excluded temporary agency work from the scope of application of the Directive. The debates over that measure show how imperative is the need for adoption of a Directive on temporary agency work which achieves a balance between economic and social concerns. As with the Services Directive, transnational labour regulation of temporary agency work should draw on the principles of the *acquis communautaire social*.

The starting point must be that the social protection of workers is not to be subordinated to free movement of services and the interests of service providers. There is a need for specific legal protection of workers having the status of temporary agency workers. A central principle of the *acquis communautaire social* as regards conditions of work is equal treatment. The most effective application of this principle is through collective agreements which avoid the damaging effects of competition among individual workers in the labour market, producing unequal treatment. As stated in the Services Directive: Member States are not to be prevented from applying rules on employment conditions "including those laid down in collective agreements".[42] Protection is to be secured by *nation-*

42 Article 16(3). Article 4(7): 'rules laid down in collective agreements negotiated by the social partners shall not as such be seen as requirements [subject to] within the meaning of this Directive'.

al collective agreements. *Transnational* collective agreements could achieve the same protection specifically as regards the transnational provision of services by temporary work agencies. Finally, the relevant standards should draw on the EU Charter of Fundamental Rights. The Services Directive states: "This directive does not affect the exercise of fundamental rights as recognised in the Member States and by Community law".[43] Regulation of temporary agency work should also respect these fundamental rights.

These starting points can provide the foundation for a specific legal instrument of transnational labour regulation of temporary agency work in the EU.

5.5 Litigation as an Alternative to Transnational Labour Regulation

In the absence of a specific legal measure regulating temporary agency work, the exclusion of temporary agency work from the scope of the Services Directive leaves this task to legal developments in the European Court of Justice. The position under the Services Directive produces uncertainty about the labour standards applicable to transnational temporary agency workers. Inevitably, litigation will follow. Remaining doubts as to the protection of labour standards by the *acquis communautaire social* are already evident in the continuing attempts through litigation in the *Viking* and *Laval/Vaxholm* cases to use the free movement provisions of the Treaty to limit the nationally recognised freedom to take industrial action in the Member States concerned.[44]

5.6 Summary and Conclusion

The contemporaneous debates on the Services Directive and the outstanding proposed Directive on temporary agency work reveal both the need for transnational labour regulation of temporary agency work and the relevant principles of the *acquis communautaire social* which should guide that regulation.

---

43 Article 1(7). That the rights in question are fundamental labour rights is evident in the following text: 'Nor does it affect the right to negotiate, conclude and enforce collective agreements and to take industrial action in accordance with national law and practices which respect Community law'. Recital 15 includes specific reference to the EU Charter.

44 Case C-438/05, *Viking Line Abp OU Viking Line Eesti v. The International Transport Workers' Federation, The Finnish Seamen's Union;* Case C-341/05, *Laval un Partneri Ltd v Svenska Byggnadsarbetareförbundet, Svenska Byggnadsarbetareförbundet, Avdelning 1, Svenska Elektrikerförbundet.* Bercusson (2007).

6. Lessons for the Future of European Labour Law

The Barroso Commission appears to have rediscovered ambition in a Green Paper entitled "Modernising labour law to meet the challenges of the 21st century".[45] An earlier draft of September 2006[46] was entitled "Adapting labour law to ensure flexibility and security for all", echoing the Commission's focus on employment policy, one of the mantras of which had been to balance flexibility and security. The Barroso Commission appears to have lifted its sights from mere labour market reforms of balancing flexibility and security to an approach which looks to "modernising" labour law as a whole.

The Green Paper projects a vision which seeks to transform the nature of labour law itself "to meet the challenges of the 21st century". It takes the view that the original purpose (to offset inequality between employer and employee) and traditional model (secure employment status protected against dismissal) of labour law is no longer appropriate because it operates to the detriment of newcomers and jobseekers. EU labour law is to intervene through legislative and political actions in the conflict between workers ("insiders") and the unemployed and "atypical" workers ("outsiders") by promoting flexibility. Employers become neutral observers of this conflict.

This vision is likely to be contested with the argument that the original purpose and traditional model of labour law remain valid and should be reinforced, not dismantled. Labour law and collective agreements should continue to support the original purpose and reinforce the traditional model. This is not a purely normative position. The economic and legal arguments for EU labour law are well-known ("social policy as a productive factor"), if insufficiently acknowledged.[47] The EU should intervene to secure the efficient functioning of the single European market, which depends on protection of employment security, decent labour standards and the active participation of workers through their collective organisations to ensure their interests are taken account of in economic decision-making at all levels. These are values enshrined in the EU Charter of Fundamental Rights, to which the Commission is ostensibly committed.

The Green Paper poses the question of whether there should be clarification of the responsibilities of various parties within multiple employment relationships (for example, sub-contractors) and, specifically, of the

45 COM(2006) 798 final, Brussels, 22 November 2006.

46 Communication from the Commission, Green Paper, 'Adapting labour law to ensure flexibility and security for all' (n.d.).

47 See, *inter alia*, Majid (2001), Fourage (2003) and Sen (2000).

employment status of temporary agency workers.[48] There was indeed such clarification in the 1991 Directive on health and safety of temporary agency workers.[49] This precedent could be built upon.[50]

But the precedent set by the Barroso Commission's proposal of the Services Directive does not promise that this clarification will reflect the required balance between concerns for market freedoms and the need for protection of workers and social standards. Rather, the future of transnational labour regulation through EU law lies in respect for the *acquis communautaire social* and the EU Charter of Fundamental Rights, to which future Commissions should return.[51]

Bibliography

Ahlberg, K. (1999), "The negotiations on fixed-term work", in C. Vigneau, K. Ahlberg, B. Bercusson and N. Bruun, *Fixed-term Work in the EU: A European Agreement against Discrimination and Abuse,* SALTSA, Stockholm: National Institute for Working Life, pp. 13–38.

Ahlberg, K., N. Bruun and J. Malmberg (2006), "The *Vaxholm* Case from a Swedish and European Perspective", *Transfer: European Review of Labour and Research* 12 (2): 155–66.

Bercusson, B. (1992), "Maastricht: A Fundamental Change in European Labour Law", *Industrial Relations Journal* 23: 177–90.

Bercusson, B. (1996), *European Labour Law*, Law-in-Context Series, London: Butterworths.

Bercusson, B. (ed.) (2006), *European Labour Law and the EU Charter of Fundamental Rights*, Baden-Baden: Nomos.

Bercusson, B. (2007), "The Trade Union Movement and the European Union: Judgment Day", *European Law Journal* 13 (3): 279–308.

Fourage, D. (2003), *Costs of Non-Social Policy: Towards an Economic framework of Quality Social Policies – and the Costs of Not Having Them*, Report for DG Employment and Social Affairs of the European Commission.

Herzfeld Olsson, P., B. Bercusson and N. Bruun (eds.) (1998), *Transnational Trade Union Rights in the European Union*, Workshop Summary, Arbetslivsrapport 36, National Institute for Working Life, Stockholm.

48 In Questions 9 and 10.

49 Council Directive 91/383 of 25 June 1991 supplementing the measures to encourage improvements in the safety and health of workers with a fixed-duration employment relationship or a temporary employment relationship, OJ 1991 L206/19.

50 The responsibility of sub-contractors should be addressed in a number of contexts: public procurement, information and consultation where redundancies or restructuring affect the employees of sub-contractors, and so on.

51 Bercusson (2006).

Majid, N. (2001), "Economic Growth, Social Policy and Decent Work", Employment Paper 2001/19, Geneva: ILO.

Sen, A. (2000), "Work and Rights", 139 *International Labour Review* 119.

Vigneau, C., K. Ahlberg, B. Bercusson, and N. Bruun (1999), *Fixed-term Work in the EU*, SALTSA, Stockholm: National Institute for Working Life.

Appendices

Appendix 1

COM(2002) 149 final

2002/0072(COD)

Proposal for a

DIRECTIVE OF THE EUROPEAN PARLIAMENT AND THE COUNCIL

on Working Conditions for Temporary Workers

THE EUROPEAN PARLIAMENT AND THE COUNCIL OF THE EUROPEAN UNION,

Having regard to the Treaty establishing the European Community and, in particular, Article 137(2) thereof,

Having regard to the proposal from the Commission,[1]

Having regard to the opinion of the Economic and Social Committee,[2]

Having regard to the opinion of the Committee of the Regions,[3]

Acting in accordance with the procedure laid down in Article 251 of the Treaty,[4]

Whereas:

(1) This instrument respects the fundamental rights and complies with the principles recognised by the Charter of Fundamental Rights of the European Union; in particular, it is designed to ensure full compliance with Article 31 of that Charter, which provides that every worker has the right to working conditions which respect his or her health, safety and dignity and to limitation of maximum working hours, to daily and weekly rest periods and to an annual period of paid leave.

(2) Moreover, point 7 of the Community Charter of the Fundamental Social Rights of Workers provides, *inter alia*, that the completion of

1 OJ C of , p. .

2 OJ C of , p. .

3 OJ C of , p. .

4 OJ C of , p. .

the internal market must lead to an improvement in the living and working conditions of workers in the European Community; this process will be achieved by harmonising progress on these conditions, mainly by forms of work other than permanent contracts such as fixed-term contract work, part-time work, temporary work and seasonal work.

(3) The conclusions of the European Council in Lisbon of 23 and 24 March 2000 set the European Union a new strategic target, namely to "become the most competitive and most dynamic knowledge-based economy in the world, capable of sustained economic growth with more and better jobs and greater social cohesion".

(4) In accordance with the European Social Agenda, which, on the basis of the communication from the Commission, was adopted by the European Council in Nice of 7, 8 and 9 December 2000, with the conclusions of the European Council in Stockholm of 23 and 24 March 2000 and with the Council Decision of 19 January 2001 on the 2001 employment guidelines, a satisfactory and flexible work organisation system has to be put in place, with new flexible contracts offering workers a fair degree of job security and enhanced occupational status, which, at the same time, is compatible with the workers' aspirations and undertakings' needs.

(5) The Commission consulted the social partners on the course of action that could be adopted at Community level with regard to flexibility of working hours and job security of workers on 27 September 1995.

(6) After that consultation, the Commission decided that Community action was desirable and consulted the social partners once again with regard to the content of the planned proposal on 9 April 1996.

(7) In the introduction to the framework agreement on fixed-term work concluded on 18 March 1999, the signatories had indicated their intention to consider the need for a similar agreement on temporary work.

(8) The general cross-sector organisations, i.e. the UNICE, CEEP and ETUC, informed the Commission in their joint letter of their desire to implement the procedure provided for by Article 138(4) of the EC Treaty; in a joint letter they asked the Commission for an extension of the deadline by three months; the Commission granted this request by extending the negotiation deadline until 15 March 2001.

(9) On 21 May 2001, the social partners acknowledged that their negotiations on temporary work had not produced any agreement.

(10) There are considerable differences in the legal situation of temporary workers within the Union.

(11) Temporary work should meet undertakings' needs for flexibility and employees' need to reconcile their working and private lives and contribute to job creation and participation and integration in the labour market.

(12) The aim of this directive is to establish a protective framework for temporary workers which also provides temporary agencies operating in the European Community with a consistent and flexible framework which is conducive to their activities, without imposing any administrative, financial or legal constraints which would impede the creation and development of small and medium-sized undertakings.

(13) This Directive shall be implemented in compliance with the Treaty, specifically with regard to freedom to provide services and freedom of establishment and without prejudice to Directive 96/71/EC of the European Parliament and the Council of 16 December 1996[5] concerning the posting of workers in the framework of the provision of services.

(14) Directive 91/383/EEC of 25 June 1991[6] supplementing the measures to encourage improvements in the safety and health at work of workers with a fixed-duration employment relationship or a temporary employment relationship establishes the safety and health provisions applicable to temporary workers.

(15) With respect to basic working and employment conditions, temporary workers should not be treated any less favourably than a "comparable worker", i.e. a worker in the user undertaking in an identical or similar job, taking into account seniority, qualifications and skills.

(16) However, differences in treatment are acceptable if they are objectively and reasonably justified by a legitimate aim under national law.

(17) In the case of workers who have a permanent contract with their temporary agency, and in view of the special protection such a contract offers, provision should be made to permit exemptions from the rules applicable in the user undertaking.

(18) In view of the need to maintain a certain degree of flexibility in the working relationship, provision should be made for the Member States to be able to delegate to the social partners the task of defining basic working and employment conditions tailored to the spe-

5 OJ L 18 of 21.1.1997, p. 1.

6 OJ L 206 of 29.7.1991, p. 19.

cific characteristics of certain types of employment or certain branches of economic activity.

(19) There should be some flexibility in the application of the principle of nondiscrimination in cases of missions effected to accomplish a job which, due to its nature or duration, lasts less than six weeks.

(20) An improvement in the minimum protection for temporary workers occasioned by this Directive will enable any restrictions or prohibitions which may have been imposed on temporary work to be reviewed and, if necessary, lifted if they are no longer justified on grounds of the general interest regarding, in particular the protection of workers.

(21) There must be an effective means of safeguarding temporary workers' rights.

(22) In compliance with the principle of subsidiarity and the principle of proportionality under Article 5 of the Treaty, the aims of the action envisaged above cannot be achieved satisfactorily by the Member States, since the goal is to establish a harmonised Community-level framework of protection for temporary workers; owing to the scale and the impact of the action planned, these objectives can best be met at Community level by introducing minimum requirements applicable throughout the European Community; this directive confines itself to what is required for achieving these objectives,

HAVE ADOPTED THIS DIRECTIVE:

CHAPTER I

GENERAL PROVISIONS

Article 1

Scope

1. This directive applies to the contract of employment or employment relationship between a temporary agency, which is the employer, and the worker, who is posted to a user undertaking to work under its supervision.

2. This directive applies to public and private undertakings engaged in economic activities whether or not they are operating for gain.

3. Member States may, after consulting the social partners, provide that this directive does not apply to employment contracts or relationships concluded under a specific public or publicly supported training, integration or vocational retraining programme.

Article 2

Aim

The purpose of this Directive is:

a) to improve the quality of temporary work by ensuring that the principle of nondiscrimination is applied to temporary workers;

b) to establish a suitable framework for the use of temporary work to contribute to the smooth functioning of the labour and employment market.

Article 3

Definition

1. For the purposes of this directive:

a) "worker" means any person who, in the Member State concerned, is protected as a worker under national employment law;

b) "comparable worker" means a worker in the user undertaking occupying an identical or similar post to that occupied by the worker posted by the temporary agency, account being taken of seniority, qualifications and skills.

c) "posting" means the period during which the temporary worker is placed at the user undertaking;

d) "basic working and employment conditions": working and employment conditions relating to:

i) the duration of working time, rest periods, night work, paid holidays and public holidays;

ii) pay;

iii) work done by pregnant women and nursing mothers, children and young people;

iv) action taken to combat discrimination on the grounds of sex, race or ethnic origin, religion or beliefs, disabilities, age or sexual orientation.

2. This directive shall be without prejudice to national law as regards the definition of contract of employment or employment relationship. However, Member States shall not exclude from the scope of this Directive contracts of employment or employment relationships solely because they concern:

a) part-time workers within the meaning of Council Directive 97/81/EC of 15 December 1997;

b) fixed-term contract workers within the meaning of Council Directive 99/70/EC of 28 June 1999;

c) persons on a posting at a user undertaking.

Article 4

Review of Restriction or Prohibitions

1. Member States, after consulting the social partners in accordance with legislation, collective agreements and national practices, shall review periodically any restrictions or prohibitions on temporary work for certain groups of workers or sectors of economic activity in order to verify whether the specific conditions underlying them still obtain. If they do not, the Member States should discontinue them.

2. The Member States shall notify the Commission of the result of said review. If the restrictions or prohibitions are maintained, the Member States shall inform the Commission why they consider that they are necessary and justified. The restrictions or prohibitions which could be maintained shall be justified on grounds of the general interest regarding, in particular, the protection of workers.

CHAPTER II

EMPLOYMENT AND WORKING CONDITIONS

Article 5

The Principle of Non-discrimination

1. Temporary workers during their posting, shall receive at least as favourable treatment, in terms of basic working and employment conditions, including seniority in the job, as a comparable worker in the user enterprise, unless the difference in treatment is justified by objective reasons. Where appropriate, the *pro rata temporis* principle applies.

2. Member States may provide that an exemption be made to the principle established in paragraph 1 when temporary workers who have a permanent contract of employment with a temporary agency continue to be paid in the time between postings.

3. Member States may give the social partners at the appropriate level the option of concluding collective agreements which derogate from the principle established in paragraph 1 as long as an adequate level of protection is provided for temporary workers.

4 .Without prejudice to the provisions of paragraphs 2 and 3 above, Member States may provide that paragraph 1 shall not apply where a temporary worker works on an assignment or series of assignments with the same user enterprise in a post which, due to its duration or nature, can be accomplished in a period not exceeding six weeks. Member States shall take appropriate measures with a view to preventing misuse in the application of this paragraph.

5. When this directive calls for a comparison to be made with a comparable worker in the user undertaking but no such worker exists, reference

shall be made to the collective agreement applicable in the user undertaking; if no such collective agreement exists, the comparison will be made by reference to the collective agreement applicable to the temporary work agency; if no collective agreement is applicable, the basic working and employment conditions of temporary workers will be determined by national legislation and practices.

6. The implementing procedures for this Article shall be defined by the Member States after consultation of the social partners. The Member States may also entrust the social partners at the appropriate level with the task of defining these procedures for this chapter by means of a negotiated agreement.

Article 6

Access to Permanent Quality Employment

1. Temporary workers shall be informed of any vacant posts in the user undertaking to give them the same opportunity as other workers in that undertaking to find permanent employment.

2. Member States shall take any action required to ensure that any clauses banning or having the effect of preventing the conclusion of a contract of employment or an employment relationship between the user undertaking and the temporary worker after his posting are null and void or may be declared null and void.

3. Temporary agencies shall not charge workers any fees in exchange for arranging for them to be recruited by a user undertaking.

4. Temporary workers shall be given access to the social services of the user undertaking unless there are objective reasons against this.

5. Member States shall take suitable measures or shall promote dialogue between the social partners, in accordance with their national traditions and practices in order to:

- improve temporary workers' access to training in the temporary agencies, even in the periods between their postings, in order to enhance their career development and employability;

- improve temporary workers' access to training for user undertakings' workers.

Article 7

Representation of Temporary Workers

Temporary workers shall count for the purposes of calculating the threshold above which bodies representing workers provided for under national and Community legislation should be formed at the temporary agency.

Member States may provide that, under conditions that they define, these workers count for the purposes of calculating the threshold above which bodies representing workers provided for by national and Community legislation should be formed in the user undertaking.

Article 8

Information of Workers' Representatives

Without prejudice to national and Community provisions which are more stringent and/or more specific on information and consultation, the user undertaking must provide suitable information on the use of temporary workers when providing information on the employment situation in that undertaking to bodies representing the workers set up in accordance with national and Community legislation.

CHAPTER III

FINAL PROVISIONS

Article 9

Minimum Requirements

1. This directive does not prejudice the Member States' right to apply or introduce legislative, regulatory or administrative provisions which are more favourable to workers or to promote or permit collective agreements concluded between the social partners which are more favourable to workers.

2. The implementation of this Directive shall under no circumstances constitute sufficient grounds for justifying a reduction in the general level of protection of workers in the fields covered by this Directive. This shall be without prejudice to the rights of Member States and/or management and labour to lay down, in the light of changing circumstances, different legislative, regulatory or contractual arrangements to those prevailing at the time of the adoption of this Directive, provided always that the minimum requirements laid down in this Directive are adhered to.

Article 10

Penalties

Member States shall lay down rules on sanctions applicable in the event of infringements of national provisions enacted under this directive and shall take all necessary measures to ensure that they are applied. The penalties provided for must be effective proportionate and dissuasive Member States shall notify these provisions to the Commission by the date given in Article 11 at the latest and any subsequent amendment within good time. They shall, in particular, ensure that workers and/or their representatives have adequate means of enforcing the obligations under this directive.

Article 11

Implementation

1. The Member States shall adopt the laws, regulations and administrative provisions necessary to comply with this directive by [two years after adoption] at the latest, or shall ensure that the social partners introduce the necessary provisions by way of an agreement, whereby the Member States must make all the necessary arrangements to enable them to guarantee at any time that the objectives of this directive are being attained. They shall forthwith inform the Commission thereof.

2. When Member States adopt these provisions, they shall contain a reference to this directive or shall be accompanied by such a reference on the occasion of their official publication. The methods of making such reference shall be laid down by the Member States.

Article 12

Review by the Commission

(Five years after adoption of this directive) at the latest, the Commission shall, in consultation with the Member States and social partners at Community level, review application thereof with a view to proposing, where appropriate, the necessary amendments to the Parliament and the Council.

Article 13

Entry into Force

This directive shall enter into force on the twentieth day after its publication in the *Official Journal of the European Communities*.

Article 14

This directive is addressed to the Member States.

Done at Brussels,

For the European Parliament	*For the Council*
The President	*The President*

Appendix 2

COM(2002) 701 final

2002/0072(COD)

Amended Proposal for a

DIRECTIVE OF THE EUROPEAN PARLIAMENT AND THE COUNCIL

on Working Conditions for Temporary Workers

THE EUROPEAN PARLIAMENT AND THE COUNCIL OF THE EUROPEAN UNION,

Having regard to the Treaty establishing the European Community and, in particular,

Article 137(2) thereof,

Having regard to the proposal from the Commission,[4]

Having regard to the opinion of the Economic and Social Committee,[5]

Having regard to the opinion of the Committee of the Regions,[6]

Acting in accordance with the procedure laid down in Article 251 of the Treaty,[7]

Whereas:

(1) This instrument respects the fundamental rights and complies with the principles recognised by the Charter of Fundamental Rights of the European Union; in particular, it is designed to ensure full compliance with Article 31 of that Charter, which provides that every worker has the right to working conditions which respect his or her health, safety and dignity and to restriction of maximum working hours, to daily and weekly rest periods and to an annual period of paid leave.

---

4 OJ C of , p. .

5 OJ C of , p. .

6 OJ C of , p. .

7 OJ C of , p. .

(2) Moreover, point 7 of the Community Charter of the Fundamental Social Rights of Workers provides, *inter alia*, that the completion of the internal market must lead to an improvement in the living and working conditions of workers in the European Community; this process will be achieved by harmonising progress on these conditions, mainly by forms of work other than permanent contracts such as fixed-term contract work, part-time work, temporary work and seasonal work.

(3) The conclusions of the European Council in Lisbon of 23 and 24 March 2000 set the European Union a new strategic target, namely to "become the most competitive and most dynamic knowledge-based economy in the world, capable of sustained economic growth with more and better jobs and greater social cohesion".

(4) In accordance with the European Social Agenda, which, on the basis of the communication from the Commission, was adopted by the European Council in Nice of 7, 8 and 9 December 2000, with the conclusions of the European Council in Stockholm of 23 and 24 March 2000 and with the Council Decision of 19 January 2001 on the 2001 employment guidelines, a satisfactory and flexible work organisation system has to be put in place, *including new statutory flexibility arrangements*, offering workers a fair degree of job security and enhanced occupational status, *and*, at the same time, *reconciling* workers' aspirations and undertakings' needs.

(5) The Commission consulted the social partners on the course of action that could be adopted at Community level with regard to flexibility of working hours and job security of workers on 27 September 1995.

(6) After that consultation, the Commission considered that Community action was desirable and consulted the social partners once again with regard to the content of the planned proposal on 9 April 1996.

(7) In the introduction to the framework agreement on fixed-term work concluded on 18 March 1999, the signatories had indicated their intention to consider the need for a similar agreement on temporary work *and not to include temporary workers in the Directive on fixed-term work.*

(8) The general cross-sector organisations, i.e. the UNICE, CEEP and ETUC, informed the Commission in their joint letter of their desire to implement the procedure provided for by Article 138(4) of the EC Treaty; in a joint letter they asked the Commission for an extension of the deadline by three months; the Commission granted this request by extending the negotiation deadline until 15 March 2001.

(9) On 21 May 2001, the social partners acknowledged that their negotiations on temporary work had not produced any agreement.

(10) There are considerable differences in the legal situation of temporary workers within the Union.

(11) Temporary work should meet undertakings' needs for flexibility and employees' need to reconcile their working and private lives and contribute to job creation and to participation and integration in the labour market.

(12) The aim of this Directive is to establish a protective framework for temporary workers which also provides temporary agencies operating in the European Community with a consistent and flexible framework which is conducive to their activities, without imposing any administrative, financial or legal constraints which would impede the creation and development of small and medium-sized undertakings.

(13) This Directive shall be implemented in compliance with the Treaty, specifically with regard to freedom to provide services and freedom of establishment and without prejudice to Directive 96/71/EC of the European Parliament and the Council of 16 December 1996[8] concerning the posting of workers in the framework of the provision of services.

(14) Directive 91/383/EEC of 25 June 1991[9] supplementing the measures to encourage improvements in the safety and health at work of workers with a fixed-duration employment relationship or a temporary employment relationship establishes the safety and health provisions applicable to temporary workers.

(15) The basic working and employment conditions, *applicable to* temporary workers should *be at least those which would apply to such workers if they were recruited by* the user undertaking *to occupy the same job*.

(16) In the case of workers who have a permanent contract with their temporary agency, and in view of the special protection such a contract offers, provision should be made to permit exemptions from the rules applicable in the user undertaking.

(17) In view of the need to maintain a certain degree of flexibility in the working relationship, provision should be made for the Member States to be able to delegate to the social partners the task of defining basic working and employment conditions tailored to the specific characteristics of certain types of employment or certain branches of economic activity.

---

8 OJ L 18 of 21.1.1997, p. 1.

9 OJ L 206 of 29.7.1991, p. 19.

(18) There should be some flexibility in the application of the principle of nondiscrimination in cases of assignments effected to accomplish a job which, due to its nature or duration, lasts less than six weeks.

(19) An improvement in the minimum protection for temporary workers occasioned by this Directive will enable any restrictions or prohibitions which may have been imposed on temporary work to be reviewed and, if necessary, lifted if they are no longer justified.

They may be justified only on grounds of the general interest regarding, in particular the protection of workers, *the requirements of safety and health at work and the need to ensure that the labour market functions properly and abuses are prevented.*

(20) *The provisions of this Directive on restrictions or prohibitions on temporary work are without prejudice to national legislation or practices prohibiting striking workers being replaced by temporary workers.*

(21) There must be an effective means of safeguarding temporary workers' rights.

(22) In compliance with the principle of subsidiarity and the principle of proportionality under Article 5 of the Treaty, the aims of the action envisaged above cannot be achieved satisfactorily by the Member States, since the goal is to establish a harmonised Community-level framework of protection for temporary workers; owing to the scale and the impact of the action planned, these objectives can best be met at Community level by introducing minimum requirements applicable throughout the European Community *in order to provide the Member States with a common framework to facilitate the integration of European labour markets and cross-border mobility of workers, especially in border regions*; this Directive confines itself to what is required for achieving these objectives,

HAVE ADOPTED THIS DIRECTIVE:

CHAPTER I

GENERAL PROVISIONS

Article 1

Scope

1. This Directive applies to *workers with a* contract of employment or employment relationship *with* a temporary agency, who are posted to user undertakings to work *temporarily* under *their* supervision.

2. This Directive applies to public and private undertakings engaged in economic activities whether or not they are operating for gain, *and which are temporary agencies or user undertakings*.

3. Member States may, after consulting the social partners, provide that this Directive does not apply to employment contracts or relationships concluded under a specific public or publicly supported vocational training, integration or retraining programme.

Article 2

Aim

The purpose of this Directive is:

1. *to ensure the protection of temporary workers and* to improve the quality of temporary work by ensuring that the principle of non-discrimination is applied to temporary workers *and recognising temporary agencies as employers;*

2. to establish a suitable framework for the use of temporary work to contribute to *creating jobs and* the smooth functioning of the labour market.

Article 3

Definition

1. For the purposes of this Directive:

a) "worker" means any person who, in the Member State concerned, is protected as a worker under national employment law;

b) temporary worker: a person with a contract of employment or an employment relationship with a temporary agency with a view to being posted to a user undertaking to work temporarily under its supervision;

c) "posting" means the period during which the temporary worker is placed at the user undertaking *to work temporarily under its supervision*;

d) "temporary agency" means any natural or legal person who, in compliance with national law, concludes contracts of employment or employment relationships with temporary workers in order to post them to user undertakings to work there temporarily under their supervision;

e) "user undertaking" means any natural or legal person for whom and under the supervision of whom a temporary worker works temporarily;

f) "basic working and employment conditions": working and employment conditions *laid down by legislation, regulations, administrative provisions, collective agreements and/or other general provisions* relating to:

i) the duration of working time, *overtime, work breaks*, rest periods, night work, paid holidays and public holidays;

ii) pay.

2. This Directive shall be without prejudice to national law as regards the definition of *pay,* contract of employment or employment relationship *or worker*. Member States shall not exclude from the scope of this Directive *workers*, contracts of employment or employment relationships solely because *they relate to* part-time workers, fixed-term contract workers *or* persons *with a contract of employment or employment relationship with a temporary agency.*

Article 4

Review of restrictions or prohibitions

1. Prohibitions or restrictions on the use of temporary work are justified only on grounds of general interest relating in particular to the protection of temporary workers, the requirements of health and safety at work and the need to ensure that the labour market functions properly and abuses are prevented.

2. The Member States, after consulting the social partners in accordance with national legislation, collective agreements and practices, shall review any restrictions or prohibitions mentioned above in order to verify whether they are justified on the grounds given in paragraph 1. If not, the Member States shall discontinue them. The Member States shall inform the Commission of the results of that review.

3. Paragraphs 1 and 2 are without prejudice to national requirements with regard to registration, licensing, certification, financial guarantees or monitoring of temporary agencies.

CHAPTER II

EMPLOYMENT AND WORKING CONDITIONS

Article 5

The principle of non-discrimination

The basic working and employment conditions of temporary workers shall be, for the duration of their posting at a user undertaking, at least those that would apply if they had been recruited directly by that enterprise to occupy the same job.

When applying the above paragraph, the rules in force in the user undertaking on:

i) protection of pregnant women and nursing mothers and protection of children and young people and

ii) equal treatment for men and women and any action to combat any discrimination based on sex, race or ethnic origin, religion, beliefs, disabilities, age or sexual orientation must be complied with as established by legislation, regulations, administrative provisions, collective agreements and/or any other general provisions.

2. *As regards pay*, Member States may, *after consulting the social partners*, provide that an exemption be made to the principle established in paragraph 1 when temporary workers who have a permanent contract of employment with a temporary agency continue to be paid in the time between postings.

3. Member States may, *after consulting* the social partners at the appropriate level, *give them* the option of *upholding or* concluding collective agreements which derogate from the principle established in paragraph 1 as long as an adequate level of protection is provided for temporary workers.

4. Without prejudice to the provisions of paragraphs 2 and 3 above, Member States may, *with regard to pay*, provide that paragraph 1 shall not apply where a temporary worker works on an assignment or series of assignments with the same user enterprise in a post which, due to its duration or nature, can be accomplished in a period not exceeding six weeks.

Member States shall take appropriate measures with a view to preventing misuse in the application of this paragraph.

5. The implementing procedures for this Article shall be defined by the Member States after consultation of the social partners. The Member States may also entrust the social partners at the appropriate level with the task of defining these procedures for this chapter by means of a negotiated agreement, *in accordance with national practices*.

Article 6

Access to Permanent Quality Employment

1. Temporary workers shall be informed of any vacant posts in the user undertaking to give them the same opportunity as other workers in that undertaking to find permanent employment. *Such information may be provided by a general announcement in a suitable place in the undertaking for which and under whose supervision temporary workers are engaged.*

2. Member States shall take any action required to ensure that any clauses prohibiting or having the effect of preventing the conclusion of a contract of employment or an employment relationship between the user undertaking and the temporary worker after his posting are null and void or may be declared null and void. *This paragraph is without prejudice to provisions*

under which temporary agencies receive a reasonable level of recompense for services rendered to user undertakings for posting, recruitment and training of temporary workers.

3. Temporary agencies shall not charge workers any fees, *especially* in exchange for arranging for them to be recruited by a user undertaking, *or for concluding a contract of employment or an employment relationship with a user undertaking after carrying out a posting in that undertaking.*

4. Temporary workers shall be given access to the *amenities or collective services* of the user undertaking *especially canteen, child care and transport services under the same conditions as workers employed directly by the undertaking*, unless there are objective reasons against this.

5. Member States shall take suitable measures or shall promote dialogue between the social partners, in accordance with their national traditions and practices in order to:

– improve temporary workers' access to training in the temporary agencies, even in the periods between their postings, in order to enhance their career development and employability;

– improve temporary workers' access to training for user undertakings' workers.

Article 7

Representation of Temporary Workers

Temporary workers shall count, *under conditions established by the Member States*, for the purposes of calculating the threshold above which bodies representing workers provided for under Community *and national law and collective agreements* are to be formed at the temporary agency.

Member States may provide that, under conditions that they define, these workers count for the purposes of calculating the threshold above which bodies representing workers provided for by Community *and national law and collective agreements* are to be formed in the user undertaking, *in the same way as if they were workers employed directly for the same period of time by the user undertaking.*

Article 8

Information of Workers' Representatives

Without prejudice to national and Community provisions on information and consultation which are more stringent and/or more specific, the user undertaking must provide suitable information on the use of temporary workers when providing information on the employment situation in that undertaking to bodies representing the workers set up in accordance with national and Community legislation.

CHAPTER III

FINAL PROVISIONS

Article 9

Minimum Requirements

1. This Directive does not prejudice the Member States' right to apply or introduce legislative, regulatory or administrative provisions which are more favourable to workers or to promote or permit collective agreements concluded between the social partners which are more favourable to workers.

2. The implementation of this Directive shall under no circumstances constitute sufficient grounds for justifying a reduction in the general level of protection of workers in the fields covered by this Directive. This shall be without prejudice to the rights of Member States and/or management and labour to lay down, in the light of changing circumstances, different legislative, regulatory or contractual arrangements to those prevailing at the time of the adoption of this Directive, provided always that the minimum requirements laid down in this Directive are adhered to.

Article 10

Penalties

Member States shall lay down rules on penalties applicable in the event of infringements of national provisions enacted under this Directive and shall take all necessary measures to ensure that they are applied. The penalties provided for must be effective, proportionate and dissuasive. Member States shall notify these provisions to the Commission by the date given in Article 11 at the latest and any subsequent amendment within good time. They shall, in particular, ensure that workers and/or their representatives have adequate means of enforcing the obligations under this Directive.

Article 11

Implementation

1. The Member States shall adopt the laws, regulations and administrative provisions necessary to comply with this Directive by [two years after adoption] at the latest, or shall ensure that the social partners introduce the necessary provisions by way of an agreement, whereby the Member States must

make all the necessary arrangements to enable them to guarantee at any time that the objectives of this Directive are being attained. They shall forthwith inform the Commission thereof.

2. When Member States adopt these provisions, they shall contain a reference to this Directive or shall be accompanied by such a reference on the occasion of their official publication. The methods of making such reference shall be laid down by the Member States.

Article 12

Review by the Commission

(Five years after adoption of this Directive) at the latest, the Commission shall, in consultation with the Member States and social partners at Community level, review application thereof with a view to proposing, where appropriate, the necessary amendments to the Parliament and the Council.

Article 13

Entry into Force

This Directive shall enter into force on the twentieth day after its publication in the *Official Journal of the European Communities*.

Article 14

This Directive is addressed to the Member States.

Done at Brussels,

For the European Parliament	*For the Council*
The President	*The President*

Biographies

KERSTIN AHLBERG is a researcher at the Institute for Social Private Law, Department of Law, Stockholm University. From 1996 to 2007 she worked at the Swedish National Institute for Working Life (*Arbetslivsinstitutet*) as a researcher and editor. From 2003 she was the Head of the Institute's Department of Labour Law, Labour Market and Citizenship and a member of the Institute's management committee. In 2002 she was designated *Juris Doctor honoris causa* at Stockholm University. Her research has focussed mainly on EU labour law and on industrial relations at national and EU level. She is the editor of the Nordic newsletter *EU & arbetsrätt* (EU & Labour Law) and the web portal *Forum for Labour Law Research.*

BRIAN BERCUSSON is Professor of European Social and Labour Law at King's College, University of London. From 1997 to 2006 he was Guest Professor at the Swedish National Institute for Working Life (*Arbetslivsinstitutet*) in Stockholm. In 2002 he was Herman Phleger Visiting Professor of Law at Stanford Law School. Since 2003 he has taught on the Law and Economic Globalisation programme at the *Institut d'Etudes Politiques* (*Sciences Po'*) in Paris. He is Director of the European Law Unit of Thompsons, Solicitors, London, and coordinates the Research Group on Transnational Trade Union Rights for the European Trade Union Institute (ETUI) in Brussels. He is the author of *European Labour Law* (1996, 2nd ed. forthcoming, 2008, Cambridge University Press).

NIKLAS BRUUN is Professor of Private Law at the University of Helsinki. From 1986 to 2006 he was first Professor in Business Law and later Professor in EU Labour Law at the Swedish School of Economics and Business Administration (Hanken), Helsinki. From 1993 to 2007 he was linked in different positions to the Swedish National Institute for Working Life (*Arbetslivsinstitutet*) as an Academic Supervisor for EU Labour Law research. In 2000 he was designated *Juris Doctor honoris causa* at Stockholm University. He is a Member of the ILO Freedom of Association Committee. He is the author or joint author of several books on EC labour law and on Nordic labour law, and has had many expert commissions from the Finnish and Swedish governments, the ILO and the EU.

HARIS KOUNTOUROS read Law with European Legal Studies at the University of Southampton, UK, and the Catholic University of Leuven, Belgium, and completed his PhD at King's College, University of London. He has taught European Law at King's College and legal theory at London Metropolitan University. Since September 2006 he has been working as an official at the European Parliament and is currently the Head of Sector for parliamentary assistance allowance at the Parliament's DG Finance. He is also a member of the European Labour Law Network, as the expert for Cyprus. His research interests include the qualitative aspects of employment, work and globalisation, collective labour law, atypical work, human rights and discrimination. He writes in his personal capacity.

CHRISTOPHE VIGNEAU, PhD from the European University Institute (Florence), is Senior Lecturer in Law at the University of Paris I Panthéon Sorbonne. He is the author of various publications on labour law, European social law and comparative labour law.

LOREDANA ZAPPALÀ, PhD in European Labour Law, is Senior Lecturer at the Faculty of Political Sciences of the University of Catania. Her research activity has been devoted mainly to the study of EU labour law, with particular attention to issues related to flexibility and atypical work. She is a member of the teaching board of the PhD Programme in European Labour Law run by the University of Catania and founding member of the Massimo D'Antona Research Centre for the Study of European Labour Law.

"Work & Society"

The series "Work & Society" analyses the development of employment and social policies, as well as the strategies of the different social actors, both at national and European levels. It puts forward a multi-disciplinary approach – political, sociological, economic, legal and historical – in a bid for dialogue and complementarity.

The series is not confined to the social field *stricto sensu*, but also aims to illustrate the indirect social impacts of economic and monetary policies. It endeavours to clarify social developments, from a comparative and a historical perspective, thus portraying the process of convergence and divergence in the diverse national societal contexts. The manner in which European integration impacts on employment and social policies constitutes the backbone of the analyses.

Series Editor: Philippe POCHET, Director of the Observatoire Social Européen (Brussels) and Digest Editor of the Journal of European Social Policy

Recent Titles

No.60 – *Transnational Labour Regulation. A Case Study of Temporary Agency Work*, Kerstin AHLBERG, Brian BERCUSSON, Niklas BRUUN, Haris KOUNTOUROS, Christophe VIGNEAU & Loredana ZAPPALÀ, 2008, 376 p., ISBN 978-90-5201-417-3

No.59 – *Changing Liaisons. The Dynamics of Social Partnership in Twentieth Century West-European Democracies*, Karel DAVIDS, Greta DEVOS & Patrick PASTURE (eds.), 2007, 268 p., ISBN 978-90-5201-365-7.

No.58 – *Work and Social Inequalities in Health in Europe*, Ingvar LUNDBERG, Tomas HEMMINGSSON & Christer HOGSTEDT (eds.), SALTSA, 2007, 538 p., ISBN 978-90-5201-372-5.

No. 57 – *European Solidarities*, Lars MAGNUSSON & Bo STRÅTH (eds.), 2007, 355 p., ISBN 978-90-5201-363-3.

No. 56 – *Industrial Relations in the Small Scale Entreprises*, Christian DUFOUR, Adelheid HEGE, Sofia MURHEM, Wolfgang RUDOLPH, Wolfram WASSERMANN (eds.), SALTSA, 2007, ISBN 978-90-5201-360-2.

No. 55 – *The European Sectoral Social Dialogue. Actors, Developments and Challenges*, Anne DUFRESNE, Christophe DEGRYSE and Philippe POCHET (eds.), SALTSA/Observatoire social européen, 2006, 342 p., ISBN 978-90-5201-052-6.

No. 54 – *Reshaping Welfare States and Activation Regimes in Europe*, Amparo SERRANO PASCUAL & Lars MAGNUSSON (eds.), SALTSA, 2007, 319 p., ISBN 978-90-5201-048-9.

No. 53 – *Shaping Pay in Europe. A Stakeholder Approach*, Conny Herbert ANTONI, Xavier BAETEN, Ben J.M. EMANS, Mari KIRA (eds.), SALTSA, 2006, 287 p., ISBN 978-90-5201-037-3.

No. 52 – *Les relations sociales dans les petites entreprises. Une comparaison France, Suède, Allemagne*, Christian DUFOUR, Adelheid HEGE, Sofia MURHEM, Wolfgang RUDOLPH & Wolfram WASSERMANN, 2006, 243 p., ISBN 978-90-5201-323-7.

No. 51 – *Politiques sociales. Enjeux méthodologiques et épistémologiques des comparaisons internationales / Social Policies. Epistemological and Methodological Issues in Cross-National Comparison*, Jean-Claude BARBIER & Marie-Thérèse LETABLIER (eds.), 2005, 2nd printing 2006, 295 p., ISBN 978-90-5201-294-0.

No. 50 – *The Ethics of Workplace Privacy*, Sven Ove HANSSON & Elin PALM (eds.), SALTSA, 2005, 186 p., ISBN 978-90-5201-293-3.

No. 49 – *The Open Method of Co-ordination in Action. The European Employment and Social Inclusion Strategies*, Jonathan ZEITLIN & Philippe POCHET (eds.), with Lars MAGNUSSON, SALTSA/Observatoire social européen, 2005, 2nd printing 2005, 511 p., ISBN 978-90-5201-280-3.

No. 48 – *Le Moment Delors. Les syndicats au cœur de l'Europe sociale*, Claude DIDRY & Arnaud MIAS, 2005, 2nd printing 2005, 349 p., ISBN 978-90-5201-274-2.

No. 47 – *A European Social Citizenship? Preconditions for Future Policies from a Historical Perspective*, Lars MAGNUSSON & Bo STRÅTH (eds.), SALTSA, 2004, 361 p., ISBN 978-90-5201-269-8.

No. 46 – *Restructuring Representation. The Merger Process and Trade Union Structural Development in Ten Countries*, Jeremy WADDINGTON (ed.), 2004, 414 p., ISBN 978-90-5201-253-7.

No. 45 – *Labour and Employment Regulation in Europe*, Jens LIND, Herman KNUDSEN & Henning JØRGENSEN (eds.), SALTSA, 2004, 408 p., ISBN 978-90-5201-246-9.

No. 44 – *L'État social actif. Vers un changement de paradigme?*, Pascale VIELLE, Philippe POCHET & Isabelle CASSIERS (dir.), 2005, 2e tirage 2006, ISBN 978-90-5201-227-8.

C. DUFOUR, A. HEGE, S. MURHEM, W. RUDOLPH & W. WASSERMANN

Industrial Relations in Small Companies
A Comparison: France, Sweden and Germany

Reference is often made to small companies, but little is known about them, especially regarding industrial relations. How can small companies be defined? Is their small size a sufficient feature for them to be considered the same? If they are different from each other, what makes them so? Is the distinction between them and other companies – big ones – relevant? In what way is life organised in such units, where employer and employees are in very close contact with each other? In order to answer these questions, the authors of this innovative book carried out surveys together in France, Sweden and Germany. They met employers, employees, union members and industrial relations specialists. Comparisons of these three national cases show that small companies do have common features that transcend frontiers. They do, however, also have national characteristics. They, therefore, warrant being analysed and understood in something other than merely negative terms. It thus appears that small companies are not so far off resembling big ones...

Christian Dufour, sociologist, is deputy director of IRES (Institute for Economic and Social Research, France) and a specialist in French and international industrial relations.

Adelheid Hege, sociologist, is a researcher at IRES (France) and specialises in international comparative industrial relations.

Sofia Murhem, economist and historian, was a researcher at the National Institute for Working Life (Arbetslivsinstitutet, Uppsala, Sweden)

Wolfgang Rudolph is a researcher at the Office for Social Research (Büro für Sozialforschung, Kassel, Germany). His main areas of research concern the development of works councils, employee representation in small companies and regional development.

Wolfram Wassermann, sociologist, is a researcher at the Office for Social Research (Büro für Sozialforschung, Kassel, Germany). His research concerns codetermination, the sociology of small companies and the trade unions.

Brussels, P.I.E. Peter Lang, 978-90-5201-360-2, 2007

SFR 47.00 / €* 32.00 / €** 32.90 / € 29,90 / £ 20.90 / US-$ 35.95
* includes VAT - only valid for Germany
** includes VAT - only valid for Austria

Amparo SERRANO PASCUAL & Lars MAGNUSSON (eds.)

Reshaping Welfare States and Activation Regimes in Europe

The activation-based intervention paradigm is being adopted by several European countries resulting in major reforms to the social welfare system. The spread of the activation paradigm has had major repercussions, not only for welfare interventions aimed at combating unemployment, but also for the political regulation of the social question and citizenship. Citizenship is being redefined in contractual terms and greater emphasis is being placed on its economic aspects. Nevertheless, a wide range of policies are labelled with recourse to this interpretative framework and a pluralistic approach to implementation could serve just as well to empower as to weaken workers'/citizens' position in society.

This book analyses the extent of these changes from a cross-cultural perspective. Institutional settings as well as prevailing work values and social representation of social exclusion (activation regimes) have a key role in defining the instruments to be used in national activation strategies to regulate the behaviour of job seekers. In this book, a discussion about the range of social welfare model reforms throughout Europe and a typology of activation regimes is proposed.

Amparo Serrano Pascual is Lecturer and Researcher at the Complutense University in Madrid (Faculty of Political Sciences and Sociology). She has published and edited several books and articles on the concept of activation and employability, comparative labour market policies, the European Employment Strategy, the European social model, the regulatory nature of the EU institution and gender mainstreaming.

Lars Magnusson is Vice-rector of Uppsala University and Professor and Chair in Economic History at the same university. He is the Chairman of SALTSA and has published a number of works dealing with the political economy of Europe, the social dimension of Europe and the European Employment Strategy. He is a regular visitor at the European University Institute in Florence.

Brussels, P.I.E. Peter Lang, 978-90-5201-048-9, 2007

SFR 51.00 / € * 35.20 / €** 36.20 / € 32.90 / £ 23.00 / US-$ 38.95
* includes VAT - only valid for Germany
** includes VAT - only valid for Austria

C. H. ANTONI, X. BAETEN, B. J.M. EMANS & M. KIRA (eds.)

Shaping Pay in Europe
A Stakeholder Approach

"Shaping Pay in Europe: A Stakeholder Approach" focuses on pay systems applied in the European Un-ion. Giving due attention to the institutional setting of the European pay systems, the book discusses how European companies may approach pay as an integral part of their operational and strategic framework. Pay is an important topic for several stakeholders on the labour market. The book discusses the perspec-tives of various stakeholders – employees, employers, trade unions, and employer associations – on the issue of pay. Secondary analysis of earlier statistical studies and new empirical material on European pay systems is also presented in the book.

The book also aims at contributing to a better understanding of pay systems. If one wants to understand the various pay systems of a company, which pay elements and pay characteristics should one focus on? Which are the essential pay characteristics shaping an individual's pay and how could these characteristics be studied or audited? The book provides answers to both questions by presenting a practical, yet sophisti-cated model of essential pay characteristics.

Conny Herbert Antoni is the professor for Work and Organizational Psychology at the University of Trier. His research interests include reward and performance management, socio-technical system design and organ-izational development.

Xavier Baeten is a manager at Vlerick Leuven Gent Management School, and responsible for the school's activities on reward management.

Ben J.M. Emans is an associate professor in HRM and Organizational Behaviour at the faculty of Man-agement and Organization of the University of Groningen. His research interests and publications are all in the field of organizational behaviour.

Mari Kira has worked as a European Commission Marie Curie Fellow at University of Kassel, Germany. Her research interests include sustainability in work organizations and reward system development.

Brussels, P.I.E. Peter Lang, 978-90-5201-037-3, 2007

SFR 46.00 / €* 31.60 / €** 32.50 / € 29.50 / £ 20.70 / US-$ 34.95
* includes VAT - only valid for Germany
** includes VAT - only valid for Austria